Lecture Notes in Computer Science

Edited by G. Goos, J. Hartmanis, and J. van Leeuw

T0250847

Springer
Berlin
Heidelberg
New York
Barcelona
Hong Kong
London
Milan
Paris
Tokyo

Dragan Bošnački   Stefan Leue (Eds.)

Model Checking Software

9th International SPIN Workshop
Grenoble, France, April 11-13, 2002
Proceedings

 Springer

Series Editors

Gerhard Goos, Karlsruhe University, Germany
Juris Hartmanis, Cornell University, NY, USA
Jan van Leeuwen, Utrecht University, The Netherlands

Volume Editors

Dragan Bošnački
Eindhoven University of Technology
Faculty of Mathematics and Computer Science
P.O. Box 513, 5600 MB Eindhoven, The Netherlands
E-mail: dragan@win.tue.nl

Stefan Leue
Albert-Ludwigs-University Freiburg
Institute for Computer Science
Georges-Koehler-Allee Geb. 051, 79199 Freiburg, Germany
E-mail: leue@uni-freiburg.de

Cataloging-in-Publication Data applied for

Die Deutsche Bibliothek - CIP-Einheitsaufnahme

Model checking software : proceedings / 9th International SPIN
Workshop, Grenoble, France, April 11 - 13, 2002. Dragan Bošnački ;
Stefan Leue (ed.). - Berlin ; Heidelberg ; New York ; Barcelona ;
Hong Kong ; London ; Milan ; Paris ; Tokyo : Springer, 2002
   (Lecture notes in computer science ; Vol. 2318)
   ISBN 3-540-43477-1

CR Subject Classification (1998): F.3, D.2.4, D.3.1

ISSN 0302-9743
ISBN 3-540-43477-1 Springer-Verlag Berlin Heidelberg New York

Springer-Verlag Berlin Heidelberg New York
a member of BertelsmannSpringer Science+Business Media GmbH

http://www.springer.de

© Springer-Verlag Berlin Heidelberg 2002
Printed in Germany

Typesetting: Camera-ready by author, data conversion by Olgun Computergrafik
Printed on acid-free paper   SPIN 10846644   06/3142   5 4 3 2 1 0

Preface

The SPIN workshop series brings together researchers and practitioners interested in explicit state model checking technology as it is applied to the verification of software systems.

Since 1995, when the SPIN workshop series was instigated, SPIN workshops have been held on an annual basis at Montréal (1995), New Brunswick (1996), Enschede (1997), Paris (1998), Trento (1999), Toulouse (1999), Stanford (2000), and Toronto (2001). While the first SPIN workshop was a stand-alone event, later workshops have been organized as more or less closely affiliated events with larger conferences, in particular with CAV (1996), TACAS (1997), FORTE/PSTV (1998), FLOC (1999), World Congress on Formal Methods (1999), FMOODS (2000), and ICSE (2001). This year, SPIN 2002 was held as a satellite event of ETAPS 2002, the European Joint Conferences on Theory and Practice of Software. The co-location of SPIN workshops with conferences has proven to be very successful and has helped to disseminate SPIN model checking technology to wider audiences. Since 1999, the proceedings of the SPIN workshops have appeared in Springer-Verlag's "Lecture Notes in Computer Science" series.

The history of successful SPIN workshops is evidence for the maturing of model checking technology, not only in the hardware domain, but increasingly also in the software area. While in earlier years algorithms and tool development around the SPIN model checker[1] were the focus of this workshop series, the scope has recently widened to include more general approaches to software model checking. Current research in this area concentrates not so much on completely verifying system models, but rather on analyzing source code in order to discover software faults. The state space sizes that this analysis has to cope with require building adequate abstractions as well as algorithmic optimizations, which is reflected in a number of papers presented at SPIN 2002.

Out of the 20 research papers submitted, 10 were selected by the program committee. Every paper received three reviews. The reviewing and acceptance decision making for a submitted research paper for which one of the editors of this volume was a co-author was handled by a sub-committee chaired by Moshe Vardi. A further 3 out of the 20 submitted papers were accepted as extended abstracts in the "work in progress" category which was introduced to give emerging research ideas an opportunity for presentation. One submitted research paper was accepted as a tool demonstration. All three submitted tool presentations were accepted in that category. One tutorial was submitted, and it was also accepted in the tutorial category.

In addition to the selected technical program, SPIN 2002 featured two invited presentations. Edmund M. Clarke (Carnegie-Mellon University), one of the founding fathers of model checking technology, presented work on the use of SAT

---

[1] Freely available on the web from
http://netlib.bell-labs.com/netlib/spin/whatispin.html.

solvers in the context of counterexample guided abstraction refinement. Patrick Cousot (ENS Paris), who pioneered research on abstract interpretation, talked about theory and practice of abstract interpretation. For the first time a SPIN workshop offered an invited beginners' tutorial aimed at teaching participants a) how to write models, and b) how to write models that can be efficiently analyzed by the SPIN model checker. This tutorial was given by Theo Ruys (University of Twente) and was open to all ETAPS 2002 participants.

Since overcoming barriers between academia and industry is essential to the advancement of model checking science and technology, industrial usage reports were invited for presentation, as in previous years, and included as extended abstracts into this proceedings volume. Cindy Eisner (IBM) and Doron Peled (University of Texas) presented a comparison of the use of symbolic and explicit model checking techniques in an industrial application environment. Per Bjesse (Prover Technology) discussed perspectives for and limitations of the industrial use of SAT-based model checking techniques. Finally, Yves-Marie Quemener (France Telecom) illustrated the use of model checking technology in the generation of test cases for XML-based telecommunications equipment.

Acknowledgements. The volume editors wish to thank all members of the program committee as well as the external reviewers for their tremendous effort which led to the selection of this year's program. We furthermore wish to thank ETAPS 2002 for inviting us to hold SPIN 2002 as a satellite event. Our particular appreciation goes to Susanne Graf, who acted as our liaison to ETAPS 2002, for accommodating the needs of SPIN 2002. Finally, we wish to thank METAFrame Technologies GmbH for allowing us to use their Conference Online Service system free of charge.

April 2002   Dragan Bošnački
                                                                                             Stefan Leue

Organization

SPIN 2002 was held in cooperation with ACM SIGPLAN as a satellite event of ETAPS 2002, the European Joint Conferences on Theory and Practice of Software, which was organized by the Laboratoire Verimag, Grenoble, France.

Organizing Committee

Program Chair: Stefan Leue (Albert-Ludwigs-University Freiburg, D)
Organizing Chair: Dragan Bošnački (Eindhoven University of Technology, NL)

Advisory Committee

Gerard Holzmann (Bell Labs, USA, chair)
Amir Pnueli (Weizmann, IL)

Steering Committee

Matt Dwyer (Kansas State, USA)
Stefan Leue (Freiburg, D)
Moshe Vardi (Rice, USA, chair)
Pierre Wolper (Liège, B)

Program Committee

Dragan Bošnački (Eindhoven, NL, organization chair)
Ed Brinksma (Twente, NL)
Marsha Chechik (Toronto, CA)
Dennis Dams (Bell Labs, USA and Eindhoven, NL)
Rob Gerth (Intel, USA)
Susanne Graf (Verimag, F)
John Hatcliff (Kansas State, USA)
Klaus Havelund (NASA Ames, USA)
Gerard Holzmann (Bell Labs, USA)
Bengt Jonsson (Uppsala, S)
Stefan Leue (Freiburg, D, chair)
Doron Peled (Austin, USA)
Sriram Rajamani (Microsoft Research, USA)
Riccardo Sisto (Torino, I)
Moshe Vardi (Rice, USA)
Willem Visser (NASA Ames, USA)
Pierre Wolper (Liège, B)

Referees

Victor Bos	Leszek Holenderski	Corina Mitrohin
Stefan Edelkamp	Angelika Mader	Theo Ruys

Table of Contents

Work in Progress

Invited Industrial Presentations

Model Checking Tools

SAT-Based Counterexample Guided Abstraction Refinement

Edmund M. Clarke

Department of Computer Science
Carnegie Mellon University

(This is joint research with Anubhav Gupta and Ofer Strichman)

Abstract. We describe new techniques for model checking in the counterexample guided abstraction / refinement framework. The abstraction phase 'hides' the logic of various variables, hence considering them as inputs. This type of abstraction may lead to 'spurious' counterexamples, i.e. traces that cannot be simulated on the original (concrete) machine. We check whether a counterexample is real or spurious with a SAT Checker. We then use a combination of Integer Linear Programming (ILP) and machine learning techniques for refining the abstraction based on the counterexample. The process is repeated until either a real counterexample is found or the property is verified. We have implemented these techniques on top of the model checker NuSMV and the SAT solver Chaff. Experimental results prove the viability of these new techniques.

D. Bošnački and S. Leue (Eds.): SPIN 2002, LNCS 2318, p. 1, 2002.
© Springer-Verlag Berlin Heidelberg 2002

Abstract Interpretation: Theory and Practice

Patrick Cousot

École normale supérieure
Département d'informatique
45 rue d'Ulm
75230 Paris cedex 05, France
Patrick.Cousot@ens.fr
http://www.di.ens.fr/~cousot/

Our objective in this talk is to give an intuitive account of abstract interpretation theory [1,2,3,4,5] and to present and discuss its main applications [6].

Abstract interpretation theory formalizes the conservative approximation of the semantics of hardware or software computer systems. The *semantics* provides a formal model describing all possible behaviors of a computer system in interaction with any possible environment. By *approximation* we mean the observation of the semantics at some level of abstraction, ignoring irrelevant details. *Conservative* means that the approximation can never lead to an erroneous conclusion.

Abstract interpretation theory provides *thinking tools* since the idea of abstraction by conservative approximation is central to reasoning (in particular on computer systems) and *mechanical tools* since the idea of an effectively computable approximation leads to a systematic and constructive formal design methodology of automatic semantics-based program manipulation algorithms and tools (e.g. [7]).

Semantics have been studied in the framework of abstract interpretation [8,9] and compared according to their relative precision. A number of semantics including among others small-step, big-step, termination and nontermination semantics, Plotkin's natural, Smyth's demoniac, Hoare's angelic relational and corresponding denotational semantics, Dijkstra's weakest precondition and weakest liberal precondition predicate transformers and Hoare's partial and total axiomatic semantics have all been derived by successive abstractions starting from an operational maximal trace semantics of a transition system. This results in a hierarchy of semantics providing a complete account of the structure and relative precision of most well-known semantics of programming languages [10].

Program transformation (such as online and offline partial evaluation, program monitoring (e.g. for security policy enforcement or scheduling), etc.) is an abstract interpretation [11] where the program syntactic transformation is an effective approximation of a corresponding undecidable transformation of the program semantics. The correctness of this program transformation is expressed as an observational equivalence of the subject and transformed semantics at some level of abstraction.

Typing, that is formal type systems and type inference algorithms, is an approximation of the denotational semantics of higher-order functional programs

D. Bošnački and S. Leue (Eds.): SPIN 2002, LNCS 2318, pp. 2–5, 2002.

[12]. The abstraction is powerful enough to show statically that "typable programs cannot go wrong" in that the denotational semantics of these programs cannot raise at run-time those errors excluded by typing. This point of view leads to a hierarchy of type systems, which is part of the lattice of abstract interpretations of the untyped lambda-calculus. This hierarchy includes classical Milner/Mycroft and Damas/Milner polymorphic type schemes, Church/Curry monotypes and Hindley principal typing algorithm as well as new à la Church/Curry polytype systems.

Model-checking classical linear-time and branching-time state-based algorithms are sound and complete abstract interpretations of the trace-based semantics of transition systems [13]. Surprisingly, for the $\widehat{\mu}$-calculus, a novel general temporal specification language featuring a natural and rich time-symmetric trace-based semantics, model-checking turned out to be incomplete, even for finite systems [13]. Moreover, any model-checking algorithm for the $\widehat{\mu}$-calculus abstracting away from sets of traces will be necessarily incomplete [14].

Static program analysis is the first and most prevalent application of abstract interpretation [1,3,4]. By effective approximation of the fixpoint semantics of programs through abstraction [3,4] and convergence acceleration [3,15], a program analyzer will produce maybe incomplete but always sound information about the run-time behavior of programs. Abstract interpretation provides a general theory behind all program analyzers, which only differ in their choice of considered programming languages (e.g. imperative [16,17], parallel [18,19], functional [20], logic [21], etc), program properties (among many others, run-time errors [16,22], precision [23], security [24,25], fair liveness [26], probabilistic termination [27], etc) and their abstractions. Finally, we will discuss the various possible designs of program analyzers, from general-purpose to application-specific ones.

References

1. Cousot, P.: Méthodes itératives de construction et d'approximation de points fixes d'opérateurs monotones sur un treillis, analyse sémantique de programmes. Thèse d'État ès sciences mathématiques, Université scientifique et médicale de Grenoble, Grenoble (1978)
2. Cousot, P.: Semantic foundations of program analysis. In Muchnick, S., Jones, N., eds.: Program Flow Analysis: Theory and Applications. Prentice-Hall (1981) 303–342
3. Cousot, P., Cousot, R.: Abstract interpretation: a unified lattice model for static analysis of programs by construction or approximation of fixpoints. In: 4th POPL, Los Angeles, ACM Press (1977) 238–252
4. Cousot, P., Cousot, R.: Systematic design of program analysis frameworks. In: 6th POPL, San Antonio, ACM Press (1979) 269–282
5. Cousot, P., Cousot, R.: Abstract interpretation frameworks. J. Logic and Comp. **2** (1992) 511–547
6. Cousot, P.: Abstract interpretation based formal methods and future challenges, invited paper. In Wilhelm, R., ed.: « Informatics — 10 Years Back, 10 Years Ahead ». Volume 2000 of LNCS. Springer-Verlag (2000) 138–156

7. Cousot, P.: Calculational design of semantics and static analyzers by abstract interpretation. NATO Int. Summer School 1998 on Calculational System Design. Marktoberdorf. Organized by F.L. Bauer, M. Broy, E.W. Dijkstra, D. Gries and C.A.R. Hoare. (1998)
8. Cousot, P.: Constructive design of a hierarchy of semantics of a transition system by abstract interpretation. ENTCS **6** (1997) http://www.elsevier.nl/locate/entcs/volume6.html, 25 pages.
9. Cousot, P., Cousot, R.: Inductive definitions, semantics and abstract interpretation. In: 19th POPL, Albuquerque, ACM Press (1992) 83–94
10. Cousot, P.: Constructive design of a hierarchy of semantics of a transition system by abstract interpretation. Theoret. Comput. Sci. (To appear (Preliminary version in [8]))
11. Cousot, P., Cousot, R.: Systematic design of program transformation frameworks by abstract interpretation. In: 29th POPL, Portland, ACM Press (2002) 178–190
12. Cousot, P.: Types as abstract interpretations, invited paper. In: 24th POPL, Paris, ACM Press (1997) 316–331
13. Cousot, P., Cousot, R.: Temporal abstract interpretation. In: 27th POPL, Boston, ACM Press (2000) 12–25
14. Ranzato, F.: On the completeness of model checking. In Sands, D., ed.: Proc. 10th ESOP '2001. Genova, 2–6 Apr. 2001, LNCS 2028, Springer-Verlag (2001) 137–154
15. Cousot, P., Cousot, R.: Comparing the Galois connection and widening/narrowing approaches to abstract interpretation, invited paper. In Bruynooghe, M., Wirsing, M., eds.: Proc. 4th Int. Symp. PLILP '92. Leuven, 26–28 Aug. 1992, LNCS 631, Springer-Verlag (1992) 269–295
16. Cousot, P., Cousot, R.: Static determination of dynamic properties of programs. In: Proc. 2nd Int. Symp. on Programming, Dunod (1976) 106–130
17. Cousot, P., Cousot, R.: Static determination of dynamic properties of recursive procedures. In Neuhold, E., ed.: IFIP Conf. on Formal Description of Programming Concepts, St-Andrews, Canada, North-Holland (1977) 237–277
18. Cousot, P., Cousot, R.: Semantic analysis of communicating sequential processes. In de Bakker, J., van Leeuwen, J., eds.: 7th ICALP. LNCS 85, Springer-Verlag (1980) 119–133
19. Cousot, P., Cousot, R.: Invariance proof methods and analysis techniques for parallel programs. In Biermann, A., Guiho, G., Kodratoff, Y., eds.: Automatic Program Construction Techniques. Macmillan (1984) 243–271
20. Cousot, P., Cousot, R.: Higher-order abstract interpretation (and application to comportment analysis generalizing strictness, termination, projection and PER analysis of functional languages), invited paper. In: Proc. 1994 ICCL, Toulouse, IEEE Comp. Soc. Press (1994) 95–112
21. Cousot, P., Cousot, R.: Abstract interpretation and application to logic programs. J. Logic Programming **13** (1992) 103–179 (The editor of J. Logic Programming has mistakenly published the unreadable galley proof. For a correct version of this paper, see http://www.di.ens.fr/~cousot.).
22. Miné, A.: A new numerical abstract domain based on difference-bound matrices. In Danvy, Filinski, A., eds.: Proc. 2nd Symp. PADO '2001. Århus, 21–23 May 2001, LNCS 2053, Springer-Verlag (2001) 155–172
23. Goubault, É.rtel, M., Putot, S.: Asserting the precision of floating-point computations: a simple abstract interpreter. In: Proc. 11th ESOP '02. Grenoble, Springer-Verlag (2002)

24. Blanchet, B.: An efficient cryptographic protocol verifier based on prolog rules. In: 14th IEEE Computer Security Foundations Workshop (CSFW-14)pe Breton, Canada, IEEE Comp. Soc. Press (2001) 82–96

25. Feret, J.: Abstract interpretation-based static analysis of mobile ambients. In Cousot, P., ed.: Proc. 8th Int. Symp. SAS '01. Paris, LNCS 2126, Springer-Verlag (2001) 413–431

26. Mauborgne, L.: Tree schemata and fair termination. In Palsberg, J., ed.: Proc. 7th Int. Symp. SAS '2000. Santa Barbara, LNCS 1824. Springer-Verlag (29 June – 1 Jul. 2000) 302–321

27. Monniaux, D.: An abstract analysis of the probabilistic termination of programs. In Cousot, P., ed.: Proc. 8th Int. Symp. SAS '01. Paris, LNCS 2126, Springer-Verlag (2001) 111–127

SPIN Tutorial:
How to Become a SPIN Doctor
(Extended Abstract)

Theo C. Ruys

Faculty of Computer Science, University of Twente,
P.O. Box 217, 7500 AE Enschede, The Netherlands
http://www.cs.utwente.nl/~ruys/

Abstract. SPIN is a model checker for the verification of software systems. SPIN uses a high level language called PROMELA to specify systems descriptions. The goal of this tutorial is to introduce novice users to both PROMELA and SPIN. The tutorial itself is divided into two parts. The BASIC SPIN part is targeted towards novice users of SPIN. The ADVANCED SPIN part of the tutorial could also be of considerable interest to intermediate SPIN users.

1 Introduction

SPIN [2,3] is a model checker for the verification of software systems. During the last decade, SPIN has been successfully applied to trace logical design errors in distributed systems, such as operating systems, data communications protocols, switching systems, concurrent algorithms, railway signaling protocols, etc. [7]. SPIN checks the logical consistency of a specification; it reports on deadlocks, unspecified receptions, flags incompleteness, race conditions, and unwarranted assumptions about the relative speeds of processes [2]. SPIN is considered to be one of the most powerful and advanced model checkers (freely) available today. SPIN is widely distributed and has a large user base.

SPIN Beginner's Tutorial. SPIN uses a high level language called PROMELA (PROcess MEta LAnguage) to specify systems descriptions. The purpose of this tutorial at the SPIN 2002 Workshop is to introduce novice users to both PROMELA and SPIN. The first part of the tutorial (BASIC SPIN) gives an introduction to PROMELA and presents an overview of the validation and verification features of SPIN. The material will be illustrated by several demo's using XSPIN, the graphical user interface to SPIN. The second part of the tutorial (ADVANCED SPIN) discusses guidelines to construct efficient PROMELA models and shows how to use SPIN in the most effective way. Topics to be discussed include: SPIN's optimisation algorithms, directives and options to tune verification runs with SPIN, guidelines for effecitve PROMELA modelling, using SPIN as a debugger, validation management, etc.

D. Bošnački and S. Leue (Eds.): SPIN 2002, LNCS 2318, pp. 6–13, 2002.

Although the "SPIN Beginner's Tutorial" at the SPIN 2002 Workshop will be targeted towards novice users of SPIN, this 'extended abstract' focuses more on some advanced SPIN topics. The reason for not including 'beginner's material' is twofold. First of all, an abstract is clearly too short to present a thorough introduction to SPIN and PROMELA. But more importantly, there is already a wealth of excellent introductory material available on SPIN; either online or in print (see below).

The organisation of this extended abstract is as follows. To guide the beginning SPIN user through all the available SPIN material, Section 2 provides some pointers to SPIN resources. Section 2 also presents a general procedure that can be followed when verifying a property with XSPIN. Section 3 presents several guidelines with respect to the effective use of PROMELA and SPIN. Some of these guidelines may be too concise to be fully understood. Most of the topics in this extended abstract, however, are discussed in much greater depth in the author's PhD Thesis [10].

2   Basic SPIN

SPIN Material. As said, this paper is not meant as a tutorial for PROMELA or SPIN. Users not yet familiar with the basic operations of SPIN have to turn to other sources of introductory information on SPIN. The usual first piece of advice for beginning users is as always: RTFM – *Read The Fine Manual*. And this time, the documentation is really fine. Apart from the book on the first version of SPIN by Gerard Holzmann [3], the recent versions of SPIN come with extensive online documentation in accessible .html format on both the tool and the PROMELA language. For beginning users of SPIN, the following documents are highly recommended:

- *(online)* The Basic SPIN Manual [11] is a general introduction to the language PROMELA and the tool SPIN. This document only discusses the basic use of SPIN. It does not discuss extensions to the language that have been introduced in the later versions of SPIN, i.e. 2.x and 3.x, which are documented elsewhere [15].

- *(online)* The document Guidelines for Verification with XSPIN [12] explains how to use SPIN using the graphical interface XSPIN, which runs independently from SPIN itself and helps by generating the proper SPIN commands based on menu selections.

- And albeit slightly older, [4] is still a good tutorial to get started with SPIN. Naturally, the newer language and tool additions are not covered, but the core of the system – which has not changed over the years – is nicely introduced.

After browsing these documents, one is advised to plunge into the comprehensive set of examples and exercises:

- SPIN Verification Examples and Exercises – a sample set of exercises with SPIN [13].

General procedure to verify a (general) property ϕ on a PROMELA model M using the model checker SPIN:

1. *Sanity check.* Perform some interactive and random simulation runs on the model M and the property ϕ either using XSPIN or SPIN.
2. *Partial check.* Use SPIN's bitstate hashing mode to quickly sweep over the state space. SPIN's bitstate hashing mode is fast and if there are some silly mistakes in the model, chances are high, that SPIN will find them quickly. This 'partial check' is especially useful if the model M is big and it is estimated that the verification will take considerable time.
3. *Exhaustive check.* Run an exhaustive check on the model M and the property ϕ. If the exhaustive verification fails because there is not enough memory to hold the complete state space, there are several ways to proceed:
   - *Compression.* Try one of SPIN's memory compression options, to reduce the size of the state space.
     - The compile-time option -DCOLLAPSE collapses state vectors sizes by up to 80% to 90% [6].
     - The compile-time option -DMA=N makes **pan** use a minimized DFA encoding [8] for the state space assuming a maximum of N bytes in the state vector. This option is very effective, but will also increase the running time of the verification run considerably.

     Both options can be combined.
   - *Optimisations.* Make sure that the model is optimised in terms of the number of states and the size of the state vector. Follow the guidelines in Section 3 to optimise the model M as aggressively as possible.
   - *Abstractions.* If the memory compression options do not work (or are not really an option due the implications on the time of the verification run), one should try to make the model M smaller by making *abstractions* of the model. Go back to step 1 and try to verify the abstracted model.
   - *Bitstate hashing:* If the other methods do not work to get M verified, one might use SPIN's bitstate hashing or hash compaction verification modes to *partially* verify the model.

Fig. 1. Verification of a property ϕ for a PROMELA model M using the model checker SPIN.

The investment into the exercises will be well spent in the sense that one will get a good feeling of the systems and PROMELA models that can be analysed with SPIN.

For the intermediate to advanced user, the online documentation contains reference information on all language constructs [14] and a concise language reference by Rob Gerth [1]. The SPIN community is quite active in testimony whereof the (at least) yearly SPIN Workshops, which are being organised since 1995. The proceedings of these workshops – which are publicly available online via the SPIN home-page [2] – contain a wealth of information on, among others:

- discussions on new and significant algorithms within SPIN;
- contributions and proposals to improve or extend SPIN;
- reports on (successful) industrial applications with SPIN;
- proven best practices when applying SPIN.

Validation Procedure. XSPIN is a so-called *Integrated Validation Environment* (IVE) on top of SPIN; it allows the user to edit, simulate and verify PROMELA models. Most users start using SPIN through XSPIN. For casual use and small to moderate verification projects, XSPIN suffices. And even for the more advanced user of SPIN, XSPIN is very convenient as it releases the user of remembering all options and directives to tune the verification runs with SPIN: most of these options can be set via dialog boxes within XSPIN.

Although XSPIN is user-friendly and straightforward to use, most beginning SPIN users do not know where to start to effectively apply XSPIN (or SPIN) to check a property. Fig. 1 presents a validation procedure to verify a model M against a property ϕ using XSPIN. Step 1. and 2. of Fig. 1 require some user guidance and inspection but are generally quite fast. Step 3. may take much longer but after pressing the Run button does not need any additional user input.

3   Advanced SPIN

In this section we discuss some more advanced topics with respect to application of SPIN. We focus on the effective use of the modelling language PROMELA. In the tutorial at the SPIN 2002 Workshop other more pragmatic issues will be discussed as well.

Extreme Modelling. Now that model checking tools in general and SPIN in particular are becoming more widespread in use [5], these tools are starting to be applied by people that only want to press the button and that do not know precisely what is 'under the hood' of such verification tools. Press-the-button verification is only feasible for small to medium-sized applications. Industrial-size applications need aggressive use of the modelling language, the properties to be checked and the verification tool itself. There is generally a big difference in efficiency in the models developed by a 'casual' user and the models developed by an 'expert' user. Moreover, the 'expert' user knows how to exploit the directives and options of the model checker to optimise the verification runs. Efficient use of model checking tools seems to require an 'assembler programming' approach to model building: use all tricks of the model checker to minimise the state space of the model and make the verification process as efficient as possible. The 'expert' verification engineer resembles the seasoned programmer, who not only has a deep knowledge and understanding of data structures and algorithms but also knows the options and directives to tune the programming tools that he or she is using.

From XSPIN*'s* **Help**, **Reducing Complexity** *dialog box:*
When a verification cannot be completed because of computational complexity;
here are some strategies that can be applied to combat this problem.

0. *Slicing.* Run the **Slicing Algorithm** (in the **Run Menu**) to find potential redundancy in your model for the stated properties.
1. *Abstraction.* Try to make the model more general, more abstract. Remember
   that you are constructing a verification model and not an implementation.
   SPIN's strength is in proving properties of *interactions* in a distributed system (the implicit assumptions that processes make about each other) – its
   strength is *not* in proving things about local *computations*, data dependencies, etc.
2. *Redundancy.* Remove everything that is not directly related to the property
   you are trying to prove: redundant computations, redundant data. *Avoid
   counters*; avoid incrementing variables that are used for only book-keeping
   purposes. The **Syntax Check** in the **Run Menu** option will warn about the
   gravest offenses.
3. *Channels.* Asynchronous channels are a significant source of complexity
   in verification. Use a synchronous (rendez-vous) channel where possible.
   Reduce the number of slots in asynchronous channels to a minimum (use
   2, or 3 slots to get started).
4. *Intermediate processes.* Look for processes that merely transfer messages.
   Consider if you can remove processes that only copy incoming messages
   from one channel into another, by letting the sender generate the final message right away. If the intermediate process makes choices (e.g. to delete or
   duplicate, etc.), let the sender make that choice, rather than the intermediate process.
5. *Local computations.* Combine local computations into `atomic` or `d_step`
   sequences.
6. *Temporary data.* Avoid leaving scratch data around in variables. You can
   reduce the number of states by, for instance, resetting local variables that
   are used inside `atomic` sequences to zero at the end of those sequences; so
   that the scratch values aren't visible outside the sequence. Alternatively:
   introduce some extra global 'hidden' variables for these purposes (see the
   WhatsNew.html document [15]). Use the predefined variable "_" as a write-
   only scratch variable wherever possible.
7. *Combine behaviour.* If possible to do so: combine the behaviour of two processes into a single one. Generalise behaviour; focus on coordination aspects
   (i.e. the interfaces between processes), rather than the local computation
   inside processes.
8. *Exploit PO.* Try to exploit the partial order reduction strategies. Use the `xr`
   and `xs` assertions (see **WhatsNew.html** [15]); avoid sharing channels between
   multiple receivers or multiple senders. Avoid merging independent data-
   streams into a single shared channel.

Fig. 2. The **Reducing Complexity** guidelines of the XSPIN 3.4.x **Help**.

Guidelines to construct PROMELA models for efficient verification with SPIN:

- The macro processor `m4` is more powerful than `cpp` and can be used to generalise PROMELA models.
- Beware of infinite loops in the presence of `atomic` and `d_step` clauses.
- A non-deterministic random construct should be constructed using an `if`-clause.
- Do not use an array of `bits` in Promela; use a (self-defined) `bitvector` instead.
- Variables whose values are always smaller than `16` should be declared as `unsigned` variables.
- User defined types can be efficiently implemented in PROMELA using (`inline`) macros and `d_step` constructs.
- Lossy channels can best be modelled by letting the sending process 'lose' messages or by a 'stealing daemon' process.
- A multicast or broadcast application is best modelled on top of a multicast or broadcast *service*.
- Use *local* variables for variables that are only used within a single process. If a local variable is to be used in a `never` claim, one should define it as a `local` *global* variable.
- PROMELA processes that may terminate should not be created last in a PROMELA model, unless you want the terminating processes to be replaced by new processes.
- Do not use an unguarded monitor process with an `assert` statement to check for invariance if the original model contains a `timeout` statement.
- Changing the layout of the state vector can have (positive) effects on the effectiveness of SPIN's bitstate hashing mode.
- When checking an invariant property with SPIN, use a monitor process with a guarded `assert` statement.

Fig. 3. Summary of the PROMELA and SPIN 'recipes' presented in [9,10].

Fortunately, it is not necessary to become an 'expert' verification engineer to use SPIN *effectively*. Several pragmatic guidelines and rules of thumb have been identified over the last few years which can be applied by novice and intermediate users to develop verification-effective PROMELA models (see below).

Optimisation Order. With model checking tools there is – just as with programming – a trade-off between time and space requirements. For the model checking process, however, the space requirements are much more important than the time requirements. With respect to effective model checking with SPIN, the following optimisation order should be adopted:

1. *Number of states.* Because of the state space explosion, it is crucial to reduce the number of states as much as possible. So reduction of the number of states is the first consideration.

2. *State vector size.* The minimization of the size of the state vector (i.e. the amount of memory which is needed to encode a single state) is the next concern.
3. *Size of search stack.* Our next priority lies with the minimisation of SPIN's depth-first search stack of states.
4. *Verification time.* Only in the last case, reduction of the verification time should be taken into account.

SPIN has several optimisation algorithms to make verification runs more effective, for instance: partial order reduction, minimised automaton encoding of states, state vector compression and bitstate hashing. SPIN supports several command-line options and directives to tune these optimisation algorithms. Not surprisingly, many of these options are related to the trade-off between space and time requirements. Within XSPIN, these options and directives can be accessed and modified via: Run → Set Verification Parameters → Set Advanced Options. These options and directives are concisely explained in XSPIN's Help.

Reducing Complexity. In Fig. 1 we mentioned that one should *optimise* the PROMELA model to make the verification with SPIN feasible. Users that are new to SPIN, however, might not know what is meant by an 'optimised' PROMELA model.

The best advice to reduce the complexity of a PROMELA model stems from the help system of the XSPIN program itself. Under Help, Reducing Complexity, Gerard Holzmann has listed several rules of thumb that should be applied first to reduce the complexity of the PROMELA model under verification. For reference, we have included this list of guidelines in Fig. 2. The SPIN user who already lives by all these rules-of-thumb, is on the right track.

Additional Guidelines. For his PhD Thesis [10], the author has investigated several 'expert' techniques to optimise both the modelling and verification process when using SPIN. These techniques are mostly concerned with the minimisation of the number of states or the reduction of the state vector. The proposed techniques are verified and checked using numerous controlled experiments with SPIN itself. Fig. 3 summarises most lessons learned from [9,10]. In the tutorial at the SPIN 2002 Workshop a few of these guidelines will be discussed in greater depth.

4   Conclusions

SPIN is considered to be one of the most powerful and advanced model checkers (freely) available today. When provided with a model M and a property ϕ to be verified, *in principle*, SPIN comes up with a result fully automatically. Problems arise when the state space of the PROMELA model is too large to be checked exhaustively. Although users of SPIN do not have to know what is happening 'under-the-hood' of SPIN, one should obey certain 'rules-of-thumb' to reduce the complexity of PROMELA models as much as possible. SPIN users should be aware of these guidelines when constructing their verification models.

Acknowledgements

Gerard Holzmann, the SPIN master, is thanked for his approval to reprint the Reducing Complexity guidelines of XSPIN in this paper.

References

1. R. Gerth. Concise Promela Reference. *Accessible from [2]*.
2. G. J. Holzmann. SPIN homepage: http://netlib.bell-labs.com/netlib/spin/.
3. G. J. Holzmann. *Design and Validation of Computer Protocols*. Prentice Hall, Englewood Cliffs, New Jersey, USA, 1991.
4. G. J. Holzmann. Tutorial: Design and Validation of Protocols. *Computer Networks and ISDN Systems*, 25(9):981–1017, 1993.
5. G. J. Holzmann. SPIN Model Checking - Reliable Design of Concurrent Software. *Dr. Dobb's Journal*, pages 92–97, October 1997.
6. G. J. Holzmann. State Compression in SPIN: Recursive Indexing and Compression Training Runs. In *Proceedings of SPIN97, the Third International Workshop on SPIN*, University of Twente, Enschede, The Netherlands, April 1997. Also available from URL: http://netlib.bell-labs.com/netlib/spin/ws97/gerard.ps.Z.
7. G. J. Holzmann. The Model Checker SPIN. *IEEE Transactions on Software Engineering*, 23(5):279–295, May 1997.
8. G. J. Holzmann and A. Puri. A Minimized Automaton Representation of Reachable States. *Software Tools for Technology Transfer (STTT)*, 3(1), 1999.
9. T. C. Ruys. Low-Fat Recipes for SPIN. In K. Havelund, J. Penix, and W. Visser, editors, *SPIN Model Checking and Software Verification, Proceedings of the 7th International SPIN Workshop (SPIN'2000)*, volume 1885, pages 287–321, Stanford, California, USA, August 2000.
10. T. C. Ruys. *Towards Effective Model Checking*. PhD thesis, University of Twente, Enschede, The Netherlands, March 2001. *Available from the author's homepage*.
11. SPIN Online Documentation. Basic SPIN Manual. *Accessible from [2]*.
12. SPIN Online Documentation. Guidelines for Verification with XSPIN – SPIN Verifier's Roadmap: using XSPIN. *Accessible from [2]*.
13. SPIN Online Documentation. SPIN Verification Examples and Exercises. *Accessible from [2]*.
14. SPIN Online Documentation. SPIN Version 3.3: Language Reference – Man-Pages and Semantics Definition. *Accessible from [2]*.
15. SPIN Online Documentation. What's New in SPIN Versions 2.0 and 3.0 – Summary of changes since Version 1.0. *Accessible from [2]*.

Abstraction in Software Model Checking:
Principles and Practice
(Tutorial Overview and Bibliography)

Dennis Dams

Bell Labs, Lucent Technologies, 600 Mountain Ave, Murray Hill, NJ 07974, USA
dennis@research.bell-labs.com

Abstract. This paper provides a brief description, including a bibliography, of
the SPIN2002 tutorial on abstraction in model checking of software.

1 Introduction

The tutorial assumes familiarity with the principles of model checking ([CGP99]),
which is an approach to the formal verification of temporal correctness properties of
finite state systems. The starting point of a model checker is a verification model: a
formal system description, called *abstract system* henceforth, having a state space that is
small enough to render model checking feasible. The goal is to establish correctness of
the original system being modelled. When a (more detailed) formal description is also
available for this *concrete system*, one can try and formalize the relation between these
systems, possibly with the aim of offering automated support for the abstraction process.
In the context of model checking, the term *abstraction* refers to methodology, theory,
techniques, and tools that deal with the relation between formalized system descriptions
at different levels of detail.

Abstraction methodologies are concerned with the *process* of abstraction: Given a
concrete system and a property to be checked, how to get to a suitable abstract system?
This process typically involves a form of trial-and-error, and depends on rules-of-thumb
and ingenuity. Abstraction theory focuses on formalizing the relation between the semantic models of concrete and abstract systems. A prime requirement of such a relation
is that it ensures *preservation* of correctness properties: A property checked to be true for
the abstract system should also hold for the concrete system being modelled. By abstraction techniques we mean the methods that can be employed to construct abstract systems
from concrete ones. These range from slicing and variable hiding to more general, less
algorithmic approaches like program transformation based on abstract interpretation,
which may require human interaction. There exist several software tools that implement
such abstraction techniques. At its front end such a tool offers what is essentially a programming language in which a system description may be entered. The core of the tool
consists of a collection of components that implement techniques, sometimes several alternative ones, for abstraction. Also, methodological guidelines may be provided aiding
in the selection of a sequence of abstraction steps. At the back end, a verification model
is then produced in a form that is accepted by a model checker.

D. Bošnački and S. Leue (Eds.): SPIN 2002, LNCS 2318, pp. 14–21, 2002.

As abstraction is a very broad field, we cannot discuss all relevant approaches. Techniques that can be viewed as instances of abstraction but that will not be further touched upon here include data-independence, (de)compositionality, parameterization, partial order reduction, real time verification, and symmetry techniques. The focus will be mostly on model checking of software source code – as a consequence BBD-based approaches to abstraction will receive less attention.

Much of the tutorial is based on [Dam96].

2 Methodology

There is relatively little research into the methodological aspects of combining model checking and abstraction. Generally, the process follows the cycle that occurs in all approaches to software validation. For the case of model checking the steps are summarized in [CGP99], p. 4: modeling, specification, verification. If the last of these steps fails, then inspection of the counterexample will indicate an error in the system, in the model, or in the specification, leading to a repetition of the steps.

For an approach that combines model checking with formal abstraction, an instance of this cycle is commonly proposed. In this setting, the model can be viewed as the result of applying an abstraction to the concrete system, and thus the triple (system, model, specification) may be replaced by (system, abstraction, specification). A negative answer produced by running a model checker on this may indicate an error in any of the three ingredients. The term *false negative* refers to the case that the abstraction is too coarse – inspection of the counterexample may then suggest a way to refine it.

More or less explicit descriptions of methodologies are found in [BH99, BR01, DHJ$^+$01, Hol01, HS02, LBBO01, WC99], often embedded in reports on case studies, or in descriptions of verification tools by which they are supported. A paper discussing methodological issues in formal methods at a more general level is [Hei98].

3 Theory

Because of its strong roots in the formal methods community, there is a large body of theory on abstraction. Here we focus on papers that provide the common theoretical underpinnings. Papers that provide the foundations for specific techniques and tools may be found through references given in the sections below.

State-transition systems are commonly used as the formal semantics on both the concrete and abstract sides. Results on property-preserving relations between these draw on the theory of formal languages and automata ([HU79]), in particular on results about homomorphisms and language inclusion ([Gin68]), minimization and partition refinement ([BFH$^+$92, GV90, Hop71, KS90, PT87]), and on extensions of automata to infinite words ([Buc60]). The topic of comparative semantics has also been extensively studied in the context of process algebra ([BW90]), see e.g. [DN87, vG90]. In particular the notion of *bisimulation* ([Par81]), weaker equivalences and pre-orders related to it ([GW89, Mil71, Mil80]), and their connection to modal and temporal logic ([ASB$^+$94, BCG88, BFG$^+$91, BR83, Cho95, DNV90, GKP92, GS84, HM80, Kur94, Sti89, vBvES94]) are relevant.

The partition refinement algorithms mentioned above may be used in a *quotient construction* that produces a minimal transition system that is equivalent to the original system under some notion of behavioural (bisimulation-like) equivalence. The starting point for model checking under abstraction is usually a more drastically reduced system which is related to the concrete system through a behavioural pre-order like simulation ([CGL94]). The satisfaction of (temporal) logic formulas over these abstract systems is usually non-standard: properties may evaluate to "unknown" as a result of abstracting away certain information. A similar notion of incomplete information is common in the related area of program analysis and Abstract Interpretation ([CC77, NNH99]). Reasoning with it in terms of modal and temporal logic, in the context of model checking, is a topic that is receiving considerable attention: [BG99, CDE+01, DGG00a, HJS01]. An overview of many-valued modal logics is given in [Fit91, Fit92].

In a general framework for abstracting transition systems that accommodates for the preservation of universal as well as existential temporal properties, not only the evaluation of atomic propositions in states, but also the treatment of transitions between states becomes non-standard. Notions of abstract transition systems that feature two different, dual transition relations are presented in [CIY94, DGG94, GHJ01, Kel95], and the approach in [LGS+95] uses two separate transition systems – intuitively, one representing an over- and the other an under-approximation. *Modal transition systems* ([LT88]) also combine two transition relations ("may" and "must") but there they are not strictly dual.

An orthogonal duality is formed by the distinction between *invariance* and *progress* properties. Although both are preserved in most of the frameworks mentioned above, abstraction tends to introduce more false counterexamples to progress than to safety properties. In terms of Floyd-Hoare style correctness proofs, abstractions tend to be more like *invariants* than *ranking functions*. This problem is addressed in [BLS00, CS01, DGG00b].

The question whether a finite abstraction that is suitable for model checking any given temporal property always exists, is answered positively in [KPV99].

4   Techniques/Algorithms

Abstraction techniques are the methods or algorithms that can be employed to construct abstract systems from concrete ones. One approach consist in having the user choose *abstract interpretations*, given a concrete system and a property to be verified. These are replacements of data types with smaller-sized types that only reflect certain aspects of the original values; operations on these types will then have to be lifted correspondingly. Such abstracted data types may already exists, e.g. in the form of a library, or they may be newly constructed ([DHJ+01, dMGM99]). In the latter case, *safety* of the abstractions may have to be proven ([SBLS99]).

More ambitious are the attempts to automatically derive suitable abstractions, e.g. [ASSSV94, BLO98, CU98, DGG93, GS97, NK00, RS99]. The technique proposed in [GS97] is now known as *predicate abstraction* and has inspired many case studies, tools, and approaches to abstraction refinement, see e.g. [AKN02, BHPV00, BMMR01, BPR, CGJ+00, DDP99, GQ01].

On the other hand there are several techniques that are less general but fully automatic, like slicing ([HDZ00]), variable hiding ([BH99, DHH02]), and localization reduction ([Kur94]).

5 Tools

Some tools that combine model checking with abstraction and the URLs at which they can be found are:

α**Spin**: http://polaris.lcc.uma.es/~gisum/fmse/tools/
Bandera: http://www.cis.ksu.edu/santos/bandera/
SLAM: http://www.research.microsoft.com/projects/slam/
FeaVer: http://cm.bell-labs.com/cm/cs/what/feaver/
InVeSt: http://www-verimag.imag.fr/~async/INVEST/
JPF: http://ase.arc.nasa.gov/visser/jpf/
STeP: http://www-step.stanford.edu/

References

AKN02.   Nina Amla, Robert P. Kurshan, and Kedar S. Namjoshi. AutoAbs: Syntax-directed program abstraction, 2002. Submitted.

ASB$^+$94.   Adnan Aziz, Vigyan Singhal, Felice Balarin, Robert K. Brayton, and Alberto L. Sangiovanni-Vincentelli. Equivalences for fair Kripke structures. In Serge Abiteboul and Eli Shamir, editors, *Automata, Languages and Programming*, number 820 in LNCS, pages 364–375, Springer-Verlag, Berlin, 1994.

ASSSV94.   Adnan Aziz, Thomas R. Shiple, Vigyan Singhal, and Alberto L. Sangiovanni-Vincentelli. Formula-dependent equivalence for compositional CTL model checking. In David L. Dill, editor, *Computer Aided Verification*, number 818 in LNCS, pages 324–337, Springer-Verlag, Berlin, 1994.

BCG88.   M.C. Browne, E.M. Clarke, and O. Grumberg. Characterizing finite Kripke structures in propositional temporal logic. *Journal of Theoretical Computer Science*, 59:115–131, 1988.

BFG$^+$91.   A. Bouajjani, J.C. Fernandez, S. Graf, C. Rodriguez, and J. Sifakis. Safety for branching time semantics. In J. Leach Albert, B. Monien, and M. Rodríguez Artalejo, editors, *Automata, Languages and Programming*, number 510 in LNCS, pages 76–92, Springer-Verlag, New York, 1991.

BFH$^+$92.   A. Bouajjani, J.-C. Fernandez, N. Halbwachs, P. Raymond, and C. Ratel. Minimal state graph generation. *Science of Computer Programming*, 18:247–269, 1992.

BG99.   Glenn Bruns and Patrice Godefroid. Model checking partial state spaces with 3-valued temporal logics. In Halbwachs and Peled [HP99], pages 274–287.

BH99.   Ramesh Bharadwaj and Constance L. Heitmeyer. Model checking complete requirements specifications using abstraction. *Automated Software Engineering: An International Journal*, 6(1):37–68, January 1999.

BHPV00.   G. Brat, K. Havelund, S. Park, and W. Visser. Model checking programs. In *IEEE International Conference on Automated Software Engineering (ASE)*, 2000.

BLO98.   Saddek Bensalem, Yassine Lakhnech, and Sam Owre. Computing abstractions of infinite state systems compositionally and automatically. In Hu and Vardi [HV98], pages 319–331.

BLS00.   Kai Baukus, Yassine Lakhnech, and Karsten Stahl. Verifying universal properties
            of parameterized networks. In M. Joseph, editor, *Proceedings of the Sixth Interna-
            tional Symposium on Formal Techniques in Real-Time and Fault-Tolerant Systems,
            FTRTFT2000*, number 1926 in LNCS, pages 291–303, Springer, Berlin, 2000.

BMMR01.   Thomas Ball, Rupak Majumdar, Todd Millstein, and Sriram K. Rajamani. Automatic
            predicate abstraction of C programs. *SIGPLAN Notices*, 36(5):203–213, 2001.

BPR.   Thomas Ball, Andreas Podelski, and Sriram K. Rajamani. Relative completeness of
            abstraction refinement for software model checking. To appear in TACAS 2002.

BR83.   Stephen D. Brookes and William C. Rounds. Behavioural equivalence relations
            induced by programming logics. In J. Diaz, editor, *Automata, Languages and Pro-
            gramming*, number 154 in LNCS, pages 97–108, Springer-Verlag, Berlin, 1983.

BR01.   Thomas Ball and Sriram K. Rajamani. Automatically validating temporal safety
            properties of interfaces. In Matthew Dwyer, editor, *Model Checking Software*, num-
            ber 2057 in LNCS, pages 103–122, Springer, Berlin, 2001.

Buc60.   J. Buchi. Weak second-order arithmetic and finite automata. *Zeitschrift fur Mathe-
            matische Logik und Grundlagen der Mathematik*, 6:66–92, 1960.

BW90.   J.C.M. Baeten and W.P. Weijland. *Process Algebra*. Number 18 in Cambridge Tracts
            in Theoretical Computer Science. Cambridge University Press, Cambridge, 1990.

CC77.   P. Cousot and R. Cousot. Abstract interpretation: A unified lattice model for static
            analysis of programs by construction or approximation of fixpoints. In *Proc. 4th
            ACM Symp. on Principles of Programming Languages*, pages 238–252, Los Angeles,
            California, 1977.

CDE⁺01.   Marsha Chechik, Benet Devereux, Steve Easterbrook, Albert Y. C. Lai, and Victor
            Petrovykh. Efficient multiple-valued model-checking using lattice representations.
            In K. G. Larsen and M. Nielsen, editors, *International Conference on Concurrency
            Theory*, number 2154 in LNCS, pages 441–455, Springer, Berlin, 2001.

CGJ⁺00.   Edmund M. Clarke, Orna Grumberg, Somesh Jha, Yuan Lu, and Helmut Veith.
            Counterexample-guided abstraction refinement. In Emerson and Sistla [ES00], pages
            154–169.

CGL94.   E.M. Clarke, O. Grumberg, and D.E. Long. Model checking and abstraction. *ACM
            Transactions on Programming Languages and Systems*, 16(5):1512–1542, Septem-
            ber 1994.

CGP99.   Edmund M. Clarke, Orna Grumberg, and Doron A. Peled. *Model Checking*. The
            MIT Press, Cambridge, Mass., 1999.

Cho95.   Ching-Tsun Chou. A simple treatment of property preservation via simulation.
            Technical Report 950014, Comp. Sc. Dept., University of California at Los Angeles,
            March 1995.

CIY94.   R. Cleaveland, S. P. Iyer, and D. Yankelevich. Abstractions for preserving all CTL*
            formulae. Technical Report 94-03, Dept. of Comp. Sc., North Carolina State Uni-
            versity, Raleigh, NC 27695, April 1994.

CS01.   Michael Colon and Henny Sipma. Synthesis of linear ranking functions. In Margaria
            and Yi [MY01], pages 67–81.

CU98.   Michael Colon and Tomas E. Uribe. Generating finite-state abstractions of reactive
            systems using decision procedures. In Hu and Vardi [HV98], pages 293–304.

Dam96.   Dennis René Dams. *Abstract Interpretation and Partition Refinement for Model
            Checking*. PhD thesis, Eindhoven University of Technology, P.O. Box 513, 5600 MB
            Eindhoven, The Netherlands, July 1996.

DDP99.   Satyaki Das, David L. Dill, and Seungjoon Park. Experience with predicate abstrac-
            tion. In Halbwachs and Peled [HP99], pages 160–171.

DGG93.   Dennis Dams, Rob Gerth, and Orna Grumberg. Generation of reduced models
            for checking fragments of CTL. In Costas Courcoubetis, editor, *Computer Aided
            Verification*, number 697 in LNCS, pages 479–490, Springer-Verlag, Berlin, 1993.

DGG94.   Dennis Dams, Orna Grumberg, and Rob Gerth. Abstract interpretation of reactive
            systems: Abstractions preserving $\forall CTL^*$, $\exists CTL^*$ and CTL^*. In E.-R. Olderog,
            editor, *Proceedings of the IFIP WG2.1/WG2.2/WG2.3 Working Conference on Pro-
            gramming Concepts, Methods and Calculi (PROCOMET)*, IFIP Transactions, Am-
            sterdam, June 1994. North-Holland/Elsevier.

DGG00a.   Dennis Dams, Rob Gerth, and Orna Grumberg. Fair model checking of abstrac-
            tions (extended abstract). In Michael Leuschel, Andreas Podelski, C.R. Ramakrish-
            nan, and Ulrich Ultes-Nitsche, editors, *Proceedings of the Workshop on Verification
            and Computational Logic (VCL'2000)*, number DSSE-TR-2000-6, University of
            Southampton, July 2000.

DGG00b.   Dennis Dams, Rob Gerth, and Orna Grumberg. A heuristic for the automatic genera-
            tion of ranking functions. In Ganesh Gopalakrishnan, editor, *Workshop on Advances
            in Verification (WAVe'00)*, pages 1–8, School of Computing, university of Utah, July
            2000.

DGLM99.   Dennis Dams, Rob Gerth, Stefan Leue, and Mieke Massink, editors. *Theoretical
            and Practical Aspects of SPIN Model Checking*, number 1680 in LNCS, Springer,
            Berlin, 1999.

DHH02.   Dennis Dams, William Hesse, and Gerard Holzmann. Abstracting C with abC, 2002.
            Submitted.

DHJ$^+$01. Matthew Dwyer, John Hatcliff, Roby Joehanes, Shawn Laubach, Corina Pasareanu,
            Robby, Willem Visser, and Hongjun Zheng. Tool-supported program abstraction
            for finite-state verification. In *Proceedings of the 23rd International Conference
            on Software Engineering*, Toronto, Canada, May 12-19 2001. ICSE 2001, IEEE
            Computer Society.

dMGM99.   Maria del Mar Gallardo and Pedro Merino. A framework for automatic construction
            of abstract promela models. In Dams et al. [DGLM99], pages 184–199.

DN87.   Rocco De Nicola. Extensional equivalences for transition systems. *Acta Informatica*,
            24:211–237, 1987.

DNV90.   Rocco De Nicola and Frits Vaandrager. Three logics for branching bisimulation. In
            1990 IEEE Fifth Annual Symposium on Logic in Computer Science, pages 118–129,
            Los Alamitos, CA, 1990. IEEE Computer Society Press.

ES00.   E. Allen Emerson and A. Prasad Sistla, editors. *Computer Aided Verification*, number
            1855 in LNCS, Springer, Berlin, 2000.

Fit91.   Melvin Fitting. Many-valued modal logics. *Fundamenta Informaticae*, 15(3–
            4):335–3, 1991.

Fit92.   Melvin C. Fitting. Many-valued modal logics II. In A. Nerode and M. Taitslin,
            editors, *Proc. LFCS'92*, number 620 in LNCS. Springer-Verlag, 1992.

GHJ01.   Patrice Godefroid, Michael Huth, and Radha Jagadeesan. Abstraction-based model
            checking using modal transition systems. In K. G. Larsen and M. Nielsen, editors,
            International Conference on Concurrency Theory, number 2154 in LNCS, pages
            426–440, Springer, Berlin, 2001.

Gin68.   A. Ginzburg. *Algebraic Theory of Automata*. ACM Monograph Series. Academic
            Press, New York/London, 1968.

GKP92.   Ursula Goltz, Ruurd Kuiper, and Wojciech Penczek. Propositional temporal logics
            and equivalences. In W.R. Cleaveland, editor, *CONCUR '92*, number 630 in LNCS,
            pages 222–236, Springer-Verlag, Berlin, 1992.

GQ01.   R. Giacobazzi and E. Quintarelli. Incompleteness, counterexamples and refinements in abstract model-checking. In P. Cousot, editor, *Proc. of The 8th International Static Analysis Symposium, SAS'01*, volume 2126 of *Lecture Notes in Computer Science*, pages 356–373. Springer-Verlag, 2001.

GS84.   S. Graf and J. Sifakis. A modal characterization of observational congruence on finite terms of CCS. In Jan Paredaens, editor, *Proc. of the Eleventh International Colloquium on Automata Languages and Programming (ICALP)*, number 172 in LNCS, pages 222–234, Springer-Verlag, Berlin, 1984.

GS97.   S. Graf and H. Saidi. Construction of abstract state graphs with PVS. In Orna Grumberg, editor, *Computer Aided Verification*, number 1254 in LNCS, pages 72–83, Springer, Berlin, 1997.

GV90.   Jan Friso Groote and Frits Vaandrager. An efficient algorithm for branching bisimulation and stuttering equivalence. In M. S. Paterson, editor, *Automata, Languages and Programming*, number 443 in LNCS, pages 626–638, Springer-Verlag, New York, 1990.

GW89.   R. J. van Glabbeek and W. P. Weijland. Branching time and abstraction in bisimulation semantics (extended abstract). In G. X. Ritter, editor, *Information Processing 89*, pages 613–618, Amsterdam, 1989. North-Holland.

HDZ00.   John Hatcliff, Matthew B. Dwyer, and Hongjun Zheng. Slicing software for model construction. *Higher-Order and Symbolic Computation*, 13(4):315–353, 2000.

Hei98.   Constance L. Heitmeyer. On the need for practical formal methods. In A.P. Ravn and H. Rischel, editors, *Formal Techniques in Real-Time and Fault-Tolerant Systems*, number 1486 in LNCS, pages 18–26, Springer, Berlin, 1998.

HJS01.   Michael Huth, Radha Jagadeesan, and David A. Schmidt. Modal transition systems: A foundation for three-valued program analysis. In D. Sands, editor, *Programming Languages and Systems*, number 2028 in LNCS, pages 155–169, Springer, Berlin, 2001.

HM80.   Matthew Hennessy and Robin Milner. On observing nondeterminism and concurrency. In J.W. de Bakker and J. van Leeuwen, editors, *Proc. of the Seventh International Colloquium on Automata Languages and Programming (ICALP)*, number 85 in LNCS, pages 299–309, Springer-Verlag, Berlin, 1980.

Hol01.   G.J. Holzmann. From code to models. In *Proc. 2nd Int. Conf. on Applications of Concurrency to System Design*, pages 3–10, Newcastle upon Tyne, U.K., June 2001.

Hop71.   John Hopcroft. An $n \log n$ algorithm for minimizing states in a finite automaton. In Zvi Kohavi and Azaria Paz, editors, *Theory of Machines and Computations*, pages 189–196, Academic Press, New York, 1971.

HP99.   Nicolas Halbwachs and Doron Peled, editors. *Computer Aided Verification*, number 1633 in LNCS, Springer, Berlin, 1999.

HS02.   G.J. Holzmann and Margaret H. Smith. An automated verification method for distributed systems software based on model extraction. *IEEE Trans. on Software Engineering*, 28(4), April 2002.

HU79.   John E. Hopcroft and Jeffrey D. Ullman. *Introduction to Automata Theory, Languages, and Computation*. Addison-Wesley, Reading, Massachusetts, 1979.

HV98.   Alan J. Hu and Moshe Y. Vardi, editors. *Computer Aided Verification*, number 1427 in LNCS, Springer, Berlin, 1998.

Kel95.   Peter Kelb. *Abstraktionstechniken für automatische Verifikationsmethoden*. PhD thesis, Carl von Ossietzky University of Oldenburg, Germany, December 1995.

KPV99.   Y. Kesten, A. Pnueli, and M. Vardi. Verification by augmented abstraction: The automata-theoretic view. In *Proceedings of the Annual Conference of the European Association for Computer Science Logic (CSL-99)*, LNCS, pages 307–321, Springer, Berlin, 1999.

KS90.   P.C. Kanellakis and S.A. Smolka. CCS expressions, finite state processes, and three problems of equivalence. *Information and Computation*, 86:43–68, 1990.

Kur94.   R. Kurshan. *Computer-aided Verification of Coordinating Processes: The Automata-Theoretic Approach*. Princeton University Press, 1994.

LBBO01.   Y. Lakhnech, S. Bensalem, S. Berezin, and S. Owre. Incremental verification by abstraction. In Margaria and Yi [MY01], pages 98–112.

LGS+95.   C. Loiseaux, S. Graf, J. Sifakis, A. Bouajjani, and S. Bensalem. Property preserving abstractions for the verification of concurrent systems. *Formal Methods in System Design*, 6:11–44, January 1995.

LT88.   Kim G. Larsen and Bent Thomsen. A modal process logic. In *1988 IEEE Symposium on Logic in Computer Science*, pages 203–210, Computer Society Press, Washington, 1988.

Mil71.   R. Milner. An algebraic definition of simulation between programs. In *Second International Joint Conference on Artificial Intelligence*, pages 481–489, British Computer Society, London, 1971.

Mil80.   R. Milner. *A Calculus of Communicating Systems*. Number 92 in LNCS. Springer-Verlag, Berlin, 1980.

MY01.   Tiziana Margaria and Wang Yi, editors. *Tools and Algorithms for the Construction and Analysis of Systems*, number 2031 in LNCS, Springer, Berlin, 2001.

NK00.   Kedar S. Namjoshi and Robert P. Kurshan. Syntactic program transformations for automatic abstraction. In Emerson and Sistla [ES00], pages 435–449.

NNH99.   Flemming Nielson, Hanne Riis Nielson, and Chris Hankin. *Principles of Program Analysis*. Springer, Berlin, 1999.

Par81.   D. Park. Concurrency and automata on infinite sequences. In Peter Deussen, editor, *Theoretical Computer Science*, number 104 in LNCS, pages 167–183, Springer-Verlag, Berlin, 1981.

PT87.   Robert Paige and Robert E. Tarjan. Three partition refinement algorithms. *SIAM Journal of Computation*, 16(6):973–989, 1987.

RS99.   Vlad Rusu and Eli Singerman. On proving safety properties by integrating static analysis, theorem proving and abstraction. In W. Rance Cleaveland, editor, *Tools and Algorithms for the Construction and Analysis of Systems (TACAS '99)*, number 1579 in LNCS, pages 178–192, Springer, Berlin, 1999.

SBLS99.   K. Stahl, K. Baukus, Y. Lakhnech, and M. Steffen. Divide, abstract, and model-check. In Dams et al. [DGLM99].

Sti89.   Colin Stirling. Comparing linear and branching time temporal logics. In B. Banieqbal, H. Barringer, and A. Pnueli, editors, *Temporal Logic in Specification*, number 398 in LNCS, pages 1–20, Springer-Verlag, Berlin, 1989.

vBvES94.   Johan van Benthem, Jan van Eijck, and Vera Stebletsova. Modal logic, transition systems and processes. *Journal of Logic and Computation*, 4(5):811–855, 1994.

vG90.   R.J. van Glabbeek. *Comparative Concurrency Semantics and Refinement of Actions*. PhD thesis, Free University of Amsterdam/Center for Math. and Comp. Sc., Amsterdam, 1990.

WC99.   Andre Wong and Marsha Chechik. Formal modeling in a commercial setting: A case study. In *FM'99 - Formal Methods*, number 1708 in LNCS, pages 590–607, Springer, Berlin, 1999.

Symmetry Reduction Criteria
for Software Model Checking*

Radu Iosif

Computer and Information Sciences Department,
318 Nichols Hall, Kansas State University
Manhattan, KS 66502, USA
iosif@cis.ksu.edu

Abstract. Symmetry reduction techniques exploit symmetries that occur during the execution of a system, in order to minimize its state space
for efficient verification of temporal logic properties. This paper presents
a framework for concisely defining and evaluating two symmetry reductions currently used in software model checking, involving heap objects
and, respectively, processes. An on-the-fly state space exploration algorithm combining both techniques is also presented. Second, the relation
between symmetry and partial order reductions is investigated, showing
how one's strengths can be used to compensate for the other's weaknesses. The symmetry reductions presented here were implemented in
the dSPIN model checking tool. We performed a number of experiments
that show significant progress in reducing the cost of finite state software
verification.

1 Introduction

The increasing complexity in the design of concurrent software artifacts demands
new validation techniques. Model checking [4] is a widespread technique for
automated verification of concurrent systems that has been recently applied to
the verification of software. Unfortunately, the use of model checking tools [13]
is often limited by the size of the physical memory, due to the state explosion
problem. In order to deal with this problem, various reduction techniques have
been proposed in the literature. Among those, symmetry reductions [3], [8] and
partial-order reductions [10], [22] have gained substantial credibility over the past
decade. Both techniques are automatic and can be applied on-the-fly, during
model checking. The reduction achieved can be significant, in the best cases
exponential in the size of the state space.

Symmetry reductions exploit the structure of states in order to identify symmetries that occur during verification. The intuition behind these strategies is

* This work was supported in part by NSF under grant CCR-9703094, by the U.S.
Army Research Laboratory and the U.S. Army Research Office under agreement
number DAAD190110564, and from the Formal Verification of Integrated Modular Avionics Software cooperative agreement, NCC-1-399, sponsored by Honeywell
Technology Center and NASA Langley Research Center.

D. Bošnački and S. Leue (Eds.): SPIN 2002, LNCS 2318, pp. 22–41, 2002.

that the order in which state components (processes, objects) are stored in a state does not influence the future behavior of the system. That is, the successors of two symmetric states are also symmetric. Many criteria have been proposed to decide whether two states are symmetric on-the-fly, without any information about the future states. They usually exploit the ordering of processes [6], communication channels and the structure of temporal logic formulas used to express correctness requirements [8]. Ideally, the reduced state space will have only one state representing each symmetry equivalence class. Unfortunately, detecting all symmetries usually requires very expensive computations, that may make such reductions impractical.

Partial order reductions exploit the commutativity of concurrent transitions, which result in the same state when executed in different orders. The decision whether two transitions are independent, so that they can be safely swapped, is usually made using compile-time static analysis. In practice, this information is a conservative approximation of the real run-time independence. As in the case of symmetry reductions, using more information about the system helps detecting more independence, however it is computationally more expensive. It has been shown [7] that symmetry and partial order reductions are orthogonal strategies and can be used in combination to achieve better verification results.

The main contribution of this paper is applying both techniques to a particular class of software, namely dynamic programs, for which the number of state components (processes, objects) is continuously modified as a result of their ongoing execution. This concept can be used to formalize the semantics of most high-level object-oriented programs, such as the ones written in Java or C++. We show how existing reduction techniques can be specialized to exploit the dynamic nature of software systems in order to achieve more effective verification results.

The present paper is, to some extent, the continuation of our work reported in [19]. There we presented a canonical symmetry reduction that applies only to the heap of the program. Here we combine the heap symmetry reductions with more traditional approaches, such as process symmetries [6]. We first define a framework that allows us to express both reductions formally and compare their efficiency, in terms of canonical properties. Then we describe an explicit-state exploration algorithm that combines heap with process symmetry reduction on-the-fly. Finally, we investigate further optimizations by relating heap symmetries with partial order reductions. Preservation of temporal logic properties is discussed throughout the paper. A prototype implementation of the ideas described in this paper has been done in dSPIN [17], an extension of SPIN [13], especially designed for software model checking. We performed a number of experiments on two non-trivial test cases in order to obtain a practical assessment of our ideas.

1.1 Related Work

Among the first to use symmetries in model checking were Clarke, Filkorn and Jha [3], Emerson and Sistla [8] and Ip and Dill [20]. These approaches consider systems composed of a fixed number of active components (processors) [3], variables of a special symmetry-preserving data type (scalarset) [20] as well as symmetries of specifications [8]. Using sorting permutation to reduce the complexity of representatives computations has been addressed by the work of Bosnacki and Dams [6]. The problem of exploiting heap symmetries in software model checking has been informally addressed by Visser and Lerda in [21]. To our knowledge, they are the only other group that have addressed heap symmetries to date. Their approach looks attractive due to its simplicity, but no formal evidence of its canonical properties has yet been provided by the authors.

2   Preliminaries

In this section we present some background notions regarding symmetry. The classical framework [3], [8] starts from the basic notion of *group of automorphisms* in order to define symmetry as an equivalence between states. Since automorphisms preserve graph structure, it can be shown that the symmetry induced by a group of automorphisms is a bisimulation in the sense of Milner [12]. It is therefore possible to define a quotient structure in which each state is a (representative of a) symmetry equivalence class. Model checking the reduced structure preserves all properties that can be expressed using temporal logics [4].

Unfortunately, applying this framework directly to software model checking faces the difficulty of giving the automorphisms appropriate semantic definitions. Indeed, when considering a program in which the number of state components (such as objects or threads) may experience an unbounded growth along an execution path, one cannot consider only one group of permutations as the group of system automorphisms. Instead, we consider a (possibly infinite) family of such groups and chose one at each step, by keeping track of the number of components in every state.

Let G_n denote the set of all permutations on the set $\{1, \ldots, n\}$. It is easy to see that G_n forms a group with function composition, inverse and the identity mapping as neutral element. Formally, we represent program executions by an (augmented) Kripke structure $K = (S, R, L, \mathcal{N})$ over a set of atomic propositions $\mathcal{P}$ and a set of actions Σ, where:

- S is a set of states,
- $R \subseteq S \times \Sigma \times S$ is a transition relation,
- $L : S \to 2^{\mathcal{P}}$ is a function that labels states with sets of atomic propositions,
- $\mathcal{N}$ is a family of functions $\eta_\tau : S \to \mathbf{IN}$, where $\eta_\tau(s)$ is the number of components of type τ occurring in state s.

In cases where the last ($\mathcal{N}$) component is irrelevant for the discussion, we may omit it. A transition $(s, \alpha, t) \in R$ is also denoted by $s \xrightarrow{\alpha} t$. We consider that permutations on numbers induce permutations on states. Let $\pi \in G_n$ be a permutation. We denote by $\pi_\tau(s)$ the application of π only to the components of type τ in s, given that $\eta_\tau(s) = n$. More precisely, let $S_{\tau,n} = \{s \in S \mid \eta_\tau(s) = $

n} be the set of all states whose number of τ-components is n. Any bijection $\pi_\tau : S_{\tau,n} \to S_{\tau,n}$ is a state permutation. In Section 3 we formally express π_τ in function of π for two types of state components: heap-allocated objects and processes.

Definition 1. *Let $K = (S, R, L, \mathcal{N})$ be a structure. For some component type τ, a binary relation $\equiv_\tau \subseteq S \times S$ is a τ-symmetry iff, for all $s \equiv_\tau t$, the following hold:*

- $L(s) = L(t)$,
- $\eta_{\tau x}(s) = \eta_x(t)$, for all $\eta_x \in \mathcal{N}$,
- $\pi_\tau(s) = t$ for some $\pi \in G_{\eta_\tau(s)}$.

Using basic group theory, it can be proved that $\equiv_\tau$ is an equivalence relation. The equivalence class, also known as the *orbit*, of a state s is denoted by $[s]_\tau$. Throughout this paper we omit τ whenever it is implicit or irrelevant to the discussion. The *quotient* structure w.r.t. a τ-symmetry is defined as follows:

Definition 2. *Given a structure $K = (S, R, L, \mathcal{N})$ and a symmetry relation $\equiv_\tau$ on S, the quotient structure for K w.r.t to $\equiv_\tau$ is $K_{/\equiv_\tau} = (S_\tau, R_\tau, L_\tau, \mathcal{N}_\tau)$, where:*

- $S_\tau = \{[s]_\tau \mid s \in S\}$,
- $R_\tau = \{([s]_\tau, \alpha, [t]_\tau) \mid (s, \alpha, t) \in R\}$,
- $L_\tau([s]_\tau) = L(s)$, for all $s \in S$,
- $\eta_x([s]_\tau) = \eta_x(s)$, for all $\eta_x \in \mathcal{N}$

The states of a quotient structure are equivalence classes of states from the original structure and a transition occurs between two equivalence classes whenever a transition (labeled with the same action) occurs between states from the original structure. It is clear, from the first two points of Definition (1), that L_τ and $\mathcal{N}_\tau$ are well defined for the quotient structure. Since the set S_τ is a (possibly non-trivial) partition of S, it is potentially more efficient to model check a temporal logic formula on $K_{/\equiv_\tau}$ instead of K, provided that they represent equivalent computations. We use here the notion of bisimulation in the sense of Milner [12] strengthened with equivalence w.r.t to the set of atomic propositions $\mathcal{P}$:

Definition 3. *Let $K_1 = (S_1, R_1, L_1)$ and $K_2 = (S_2, R_2, L_2)$ be Kripke structures over the set of actions Σ. A binary relation $\approx \subseteq S_1 \times S_2$ is a bisimulation iff, for all $s_1 \approx s_2$ and $\alpha \in \Sigma$, all the following hold:*

- $L_1(s_1) = L_2(s_2)$,
- $\forall\, t_1 \in S_1\;.\;(s_1, \alpha, t_1) \in R_1 \;\Rightarrow\; \exists\, t_2 \in S_2\;.\;(s_2, \alpha, t_2) \in R_2$ and $t_1 \approx t_2$,
- $\forall\, t_2 \in S_2\;.\;(s_2, \alpha, t_2) \in R_2 \;\Rightarrow\; \exists\, t_1 \in S_1\;.\;(s_1, \alpha, t_1) \in R_1$ and $t_1 \approx t_2$.

If $\approx$ is total on S_1 and S_2 we say that K_1 and K_2 are bisimilar, and denote this by $K_1 \approx K_2$. It is known fact that bisimilar states cannot be distinguished by formulas of mu-calculus or any of its sub-logics, such as computation-tree logic (CTL) or linear-time temporal logic (LTL) [4].

Using the symmetry framework in explicit-state model checking requires computation of representatives for each equivalence class. Unfortunately, finding the general solution to this problem is known to be as hard as proving graph isomorphism, for which no polynomial-time solution is known to exist [3]. Solutions proposed in the literature either deal with incomplete equivalence classes for which the orbit problem has polynomial solution [3] (i.e., the *bounded orbit problem*), or use heuristic strategies [6], [19].

Definition 4. *Given a structure $K = (S, R, L)$ and a symmetry relation $\equiv_\tau$, a function $h : S \to S$ is said to be a canonical representative for $\equiv_\tau$ iff, for all $s, s' \in S$ both the following hold:*

- $s \equiv_\tau h(s)$, *and,*
- $s \equiv_\tau s' \iff h(s) = h(s')$.

Throughout this paper we use sorting heuristics, as the ones described in [6], [19]. Below we introduce a formal definition that captures the idea of such strategies.

Definition 5. *Let $K = (S, R, L, \mathcal{N})$ be a structure and $\xi : S \times \mathbb{N} \times \mathbb{N} \to \{true, false\}$ be a partial boolean mapping. Given a state s and component type τ, a permutation $\pi^\xi \in G_{\eta_\tau}$ is said to be sorting for s iff for all $0 \le i, j < \eta_\tau(s)$, $\pi^\xi(i) < \pi^\xi(j) \iff \xi(s, i, j) = true$.*

In the following, we refer to the ξ function as to the *sorting criterion*. The reason why ξ is allowed to be partial is a rather technical formality: we are not interested in the values $\xi(s, i, j)$ where i or j is greater than $\eta_\tau(s)$. The intuition behind sorting criteria and sorting permutations are better explained with an example. Let $v : \{1, \ldots, n\} \to \mathbb{N}$ be a (finite) vector whose elements are natural numbers. Obviously, the vector is sorted when, for all $1 \le i < j \le n$ we have $v(i) \le v(j)\ (= \xi(v, i, j))$. Otherwise, for some $k < l$ the condition $\xi(v, k, l)$ is not met. In this case, a permutation $\pi \in G_n$ exists such that the new vector $v \circ \pi$ is sorted. Then we say that π is sorting for v w.r.t to the ξ criterion.

The heuristics used in this paper follow the same pattern. Given a state s and a sorting criterion ξ we compute a sorting permutation π^ξ for s w.r.t. ξ. The representative of the symmetry equivalence class $[s]_\tau$ will be $h(s) = \pi^\xi_\tau(s)$. Necessary and sufficient conditions for the representative function to be canonical in the sense of Definition (4) are given by the following theorem. Due to space limitations, all proofs are omitted from this paper.

Theorem 1. *Let $K = (S, R, L, \mathcal{N})$ be a structure, $\equiv_\tau\ \subseteq\ S \times S$ be a symmetry relation and ξ be a sorting criterion. Then the sorting permutations induced by ξ are canonical representatives for $\equiv_\tau$ iff, for each state $s \in S$ and $0 \le i, j < \eta_\tau(s)$, $i \ne j$, both the following hold:*

- ξ *remains invariant under permutations of s, i.e, $\forall \pi \in G_{\eta_\tau(s)}$, $\xi(s, i, j) = \xi(\pi_\tau(s), \pi(i), \pi(i))$ and,*
- ξ *induces a strict total order on the set $\{0, \ldots, \eta_\tau(s) - 1\}$ i.e., $\xi(s, i, j) \vee \xi(s, j, i) = true$ and $\neg\xi(s, i, j) \vee \neg\xi(s, j, i) = true$.*

The above result leverages the difficult task of proving strategies canonical. It will be applied in Section 3 in order to compare two techniques, involving the detection of state symmetries induced by permutations of heap objects and processes. It will be also shown that the reduction strategy involving heap objects is canonical, while the one involving processes is not.

3   Semantic Definitions of State Symmetries

In this section we are concerned with defining state symmetries i.e., symmetries that can be discovered by inspecting the structure of the state. We present a (partial) semantic definition of programs that modify the number of state components (objects, processes) as part of their execution. This class of programs is also referred to in the literature as *dynamic* programs [17]. For space reasons, we are not going to enter here all the details of language definition. For more details, the interested reader is referred to [16]. Instead, in the following we define program configurations and give small-step operational semantic rules only for some of the allocator statements.

$$Store = Variable \longmapsto Location \qquad Process = ProcCnt \times Store$$
$$Heap = Location \longmapsto Store \qquad ProcPool = ProcId \longmapsto Process$$
$$StateHeap = Heap \times Location \qquad StateProc = ProcPool \times ProcId$$

Fig. 1. Semantic domains

3.1   Domains and Rules

Consider the semantic domains in Figure 1. The definition of *Store* is the classical one: a partial mapping between variables and values. For simplicity reasons we assume that all variables will take memory reference values from the set *Location*. A *Heap* consists of a partial mapping between memory locations and stores. We may refer to the stores in the range of a heap as to *objects*. The second component of a *StateHeap* is a location used to describe the implementation of object allocator statements; it holds the last allocated location. A *Process* is a pair consisting of a program counter and a store for local variables. Processes are referred to by means of *ProcId* values, and the *ProcPool* domain represents a collection of active processes. Similarly, the second component of a *StateProc* represents the last allocated *ProcId*. We conclude our description of the semantic domains with the following assumptions:

1. there exists a strict total ordering $\prec_v \subseteq Variable \times Variable$.
2. there exists a strict total ordering $\prec_i \subseteq ProcId_\top \times ProcId_\top$, where $ProcId_\top = ProcId \cup \{\top\}$ and $\top$ is less than every element of $ProcId$.

3. there exists a strict total ordering $\prec_c \subseteq ProcCnt \times ProcCnt$ and a function $next : ProcCnt \to ProcCnt$ such that $next(c)$ always returns the next element w.r.t. to $\prec_c$ i.e, the program location of the next statement within the process; computations are assumed to be infinite; the least element in the order is denoted by $init$.

4. there exists a strict total ordering on $Location$ and a function $new : Location \to Location$ such that $new(l)$ always returns the next location in that ordering; the least element is denoted by $null$; the set $Location$ is assumed to be infinite and countable.

With the above definitions and assumptions, we consider a program configuration (state) to be an element of the $State$ set, defined as follows:

$$\sigma \in State = Store \times StateHeap \times StateProc$$

Intuitively, the first component of the triple σ is a store that holds global variables, the second is a heap referencing all existing objects, and the third is the thread pool referencing all active threads in σ.

Figure 2 presents structural rules that define the small-step semantics of object allocator statements. These rules are needed mostly for the discussion in Section 5. For some $j \in ProcId$, the notation $\sigma \vdash_j \text{ast} \Longrightarrow \sigma'$ expresses the fact that the process referred to by j in state σ, executing the statement given by the abstract syntax tree ast changes the program state into σ'.

$$\frac{\begin{array}{c} \sigma = (s, (h, l), (p, i)), \quad s(x) \neq \bot, \quad p(j) = (c, s') \\ c' = next(c), \quad l' = new(l), \quad o = \lambda v.null \end{array}}{\sigma \vdash_j \text{x} = \text{new()} \Longrightarrow ([x \to l']s, ([l' \to o]h, l'), ([j \to (c', s')]p, i))} \quad (NEW1)$$

$$\frac{\begin{array}{c} \sigma = (s, (h, l), (p, i)), \quad p(j) = (c, s'), \quad s'(x) \neq \bot, \quad c' = next(c) \\ l' = new(l), \quad s'' = [x \to l']s', o = \lambda v.null, \end{array}}{\sigma \vdash_j \text{x} = \text{new()} \Longrightarrow (s, ([l' \to o]h, l'), ([j \to (c', s'')]p, i))} \quad (NEW2)$$

Fig. 2. Allocator Rules

The first rule (NEW1) describes the state changes that occur due to an object allocation where the left hand side of the statement is a global variable ($s(x) \neq \bot$). Analogous, the second rule (NEW2) describes the state changes caused by a heap allocation where the left hand side is a local variable. All rules reflect also the implicit change of control within the current process. It is to be noticed that the allocation strategies exploit the order on the set of memory locations. Namely, the next available element, as returned by the new function, is used for allocation of fresh components. Such allocation strategies are commonly used in real-life implementation of dynamic programming languages. For the purposes of this paper, we will refer to these techniques as to *next-free allocation* strategies.

We are now able to complete the formal definition of state symmetries by defining the meaning of a permutation π applied to the heap and process components of a state $\sigma = (s, (h, l), (p, i))$. Formally, since the set *Location* in Figure 1 has been considered countable, we have $Location = \{l_0, l_1, \ldots, \}$ and by $\pi(l_x)$ we actually denote $l_{\pi(x)}$. A similar notation is used for the application of permutations to the elements of the set *ProcId* below.

$$\pi_{heap}(\sigma) = (\pi_{heap}(s), (\pi_{heap}(h), l), (\pi_{heap}(p), i)) \tag{1}$$

$$\pi_{heap}(s) = \lambda v.\pi(s(v)) \tag{2}$$

$$\pi_{heap}(h) = \lambda l v.\pi(h(\pi^{-1}(l), v)) \tag{3}$$

$$\pi_{heap}(p) = \lambda i(\lambda cs.(c, \pi_{heap}(s)))p(i) \tag{4}$$

$$\pi_{proc}(\sigma) = (s, (h, l), (\pi_{proc}(p), i)) \tag{5}$$

$$\pi_{proc}(p) = \lambda i.p(\pi^{-1}(i)) \tag{6}$$

Informally, the equations (1 - 4) say that, applying a permutation to a state, will permute all locations that are values of reference variables in the global store, local stores within processes, and in each heap object. The objects in the heap are also permuted, by the inverse permutation, in order to consistently reflect this change. Permuting processes (5 - 6) is easier, since we consider that processes are not referenced by variables, in our simple language.

3.2 Heap and Process Sorting Criteria

The other issue that remains to be dealt with in order to use heap and process symmetries in practical software model checking, is the complexity of computing the representatives of symmetry equivalence classes. As mentioned before, in Section 2, we rely on sorting heuristics in order to improve the performance of our reduction algorithm. In the remainder of this section, we will briefly explain the ideas behind such heuristics using sorting criteria, as introduced by Definition (5). Sorting heap objects is discussed in more detail in [19], while specific information regarding sorting processes can be found in [6].

Since the heap is not a linear structure, finding a canonical order can be done via topological sorting. However, a topological order is usually partial. Normally, a total order can be derived from a partial one by linearization and in our case we achieve that assuming a strict total order on variables ($\prec_v$) and process identifiers ($\prec_i$). In practice, it is often the case that a strict total order on the set of variables can be found at compile-time, and one might consider for instance alphabetical order, declaration order, etc. This automatically induces the required order on the set of sequences of variables prefixed by a process identifier. There is need for a process identifier as prefix in order to distinguish between local variables. Identical processes will contain multiple copies of the same local variable and they can only be ordered using unique process identifiers. Record fields can be distinguished from global or local variables by prefixing them with the name of the record, as it is done in most object-oriented compilers.

Intuitively, when sorting a heap structure, we take into account, for each object, reachability information that is, the chains of variables including global, local or field variables, that reach every object. Formally, let $Variable^*$ denote the set of sequences of variables and let $\prec_v^*$ be the lexicographical order induced by $\prec_v$ on sequences. Also, let $\prec^*$ be a strict total order on the set $Chain = ProcId_\top \times Variable^*$ naturally induced by both the order on $ProcId_\top$ ($\prec_i$) and $\prec_v^*$. As a convention, we use the literals i, j to denote process identifiers, v, u to denote sequences and x, y to denote variables. The notation min^* denotes the greatest lower bound with respect to $\prec^*$ and $\langle v, u \rangle$ is sequence concatenation. The $\bot$ symbol denotes undefinedness of partial mappings. Consider the following partial mappings:

$$reach \; : \; State \times Chain \to Location$$

$$reach(\sigma, v) = \begin{cases} s(x) & v = \langle \top, x \rangle \\ s'(x) & p(i) = (c, s') \wedge v = \langle i, x \rangle \\ h(reach(\sigma, u), x) & reach(\sigma, u) \neq \bot \wedge v = \langle u, x \rangle \\ \bot & otherwise \end{cases}$$

$$trace \; : \; State \times Location \to Chain$$

$$trace(\sigma, l) = \begin{cases} min^*\{v \mid reach(\sigma, v) = l\} & \exists u \in Chain \; . \; reach(\sigma, u) = l \\ \bot & otherwise \end{cases}$$

The sorting criterion for heap objects is denoted by ξ_{heap} and is defined as follows:

$$\xi_{heap}(\sigma, m, n) = (trace(\sigma, l_m) \prec^* trace(\sigma, l_n)) \tag{7}$$

In order to asses the performance of this sorting criterion, we will show that it actually can be the base for a canonical reduction strategy.

Lemma 1. For all $\pi \in G_{\eta_{heap}(\sigma)}, l \in Location,\ trace(\sigma, l) = trace(\pi_{heap}(\sigma), \pi(l))$.

The first condition of Theorem 1 holds as a consequence of Lemma 1. The second condition holds due to the fact that $\prec^*$ was assumed to be a strict total order on the set $Chain$ and that each chain uniquely identifies a reachable object location (one variable cannot point to two different objects, from the definitions of $Store$ and $Heap$). Consequently, the strategy based on heap objects is canonical, yielding optimal reductions.

The heuristics proposed in [6] use the idea of sorting processes. One such strategy, called *pc-sorted*, uses the values of the program counters in the sorting criterion. Let $c' \preceq_c c''$ stand for $c' \prec_c c'' \vee c' = c''$. Formally, we denote by ξ_{proc} the following predicate:

$$\sigma = (s, (h, l), (p, i))$$
$$\xi_{proc}(s, m, n) = (p(m) = (c', s') \wedge p(n) = (c'', s'') \wedge c' \preceq_c c'') \tag{8}$$

It is easy to see that the first condition of Theorem 1 is met by ξ_{proc}, while the second one is not aways met. Indeed, it can be often the case that two identical processes are at the same location, that is, the values of their program counters are equal. This situation violates the second requirement of Theorem 1, therefore the reduction strategy induced by ξ_{proc} is not necessarily canonical.

4   Combining Heap and Process Symmetries

The main contribution of this section is the presentation of a reduced state space search algorithm that combines the heap and process symmetry reduction strategies defined in Section 3 on-the-fly. For heap symmetries, we briefly describe the algorithm used to compute canonical sorting permutations.

Assuming the existence of a representative function rep, Figure 3 shows the basic depth first search algorithm [15] with symmetry reductions. The correctness of the algorithm in Figure 3 is ensured by the fact that for each s, we have $s \equiv rep(s)$ by Definition (4). In case $rep(s)$ is already in the state space when the search reaches s, all its outgoing transitions have been already explored by DFS and since all transitions originating in s are bisimilar to the ones originating in $rep(s)$, the search algorithm can safely backtrack. The extension of the correctness argument to the cycle detection algorithm [5], which is the base of the automata-theoretic approach [5] in SPIN, was reported in [2].

```
DFS(s)
if error(s) then report error fi
add(rep(s), Statespace)
for each successor t of s do
        if rep(t) not in Statespace then DFS(t) fi
od
end DFS
```

Fig. 3. Symmetry Reduced Depth First Search

In the following, we discuss the effective computation of $rep(s)$. Intuitively, the algorithm used to implement rep can be decomposed into two distinct phases. First we generate a sorting permutation π for s; the result of rep will be the application of this permutation to the family τ of components in s, i.e., $\pi_\tau(s)$. The rules for applying a permutation to heap objects and processes in s are the ones given by equations (1 - 6) in Section 3.

For heap objects, the algorithm used to compute sorting permutations is presented in Figure 4. Let us remember the fact that a total strict order $\prec_v$ on the set of variables is assumed to exist. We consider a function $ordered$: $Stores \rightarrow Variables^*$ that returns, for a given store, the $\prec_v$-ordered sequence of variables that are defined in that store.

The correctness of the algorithm in Figure 4 has been discussed in great detail in [19]. In this case, correctness implies that the generated permutation π_{heap} always meets the sorting criterion ξ_{heap}, defined in Section 3. Informally, it can be noticed that, every (reachable) object stored at location l in state σ, will

Input: configuration $\sigma = (s, (h, l), (p, i))$
Output: sorting permutation $\pi_{heap} \in G_{\eta_{heap}}(\sigma)$

```
SORT(store)                          begin main
for next v from ordered(store) do    k = 0; π_heap = λx. ⊥
    l_i = store(v)                   SORT(s)
    if l_i not marked do             for each 0 ≤ i ≤ η_proc(σ) do
        mark l_i                     (*) (c, s') = p(i)
        π_heap = [i → k]π_heap            SORT(s')
        k = k + 1                    od
        SORT(h(l_i))                 end main
    od
od
end SORT
```

Fig. 4. Generation of Sorting Permutations for Heap Objects

be eventually reached by a call to the SORT procedure. The complexity of the sorting permutation algorithm for heap objects is $O(\eta_{heap}(\sigma))$, since SORT visits every object and every field connecting two objects only once. Let us notice that in this case, the maximum number of outgoing edges from an object is bounded by a compile-time constant which is the maximum number of variables declared in the program.

The problem of computing sorting permutations for processes reduces to the vector sorting problem, which can be solved by existing algorithms in time $O(\eta_{proc}(\sigma) \log(\eta_{proc}(\sigma)))$. As a remark, the process ordering strategies presented in [6] do not explicitly separate sorting permutation computation and application, but rather compute representatives in one step. Here we need to keep that distinction in order to describe the composition of the two reduction strategies. The following discussion will present the combined strategy.

The idea of combining the two reduction techniques originates from the observation that the application of two permutations ρ and π to heap objects and processes respectively, as defined by equations (1 - 6), operate independently on different types of components. Therefore their composition could be easily defined, i.e., $\rho_{heap}(\pi_{proc}(\sigma))$. It is clear from the equations (1 - 6), that the composition is commutative, in the following sense: $\rho_{heap}(\pi_{proc}(\sigma)) = \pi_{proc}(\rho_{heap}(\sigma))$. However, using this straightforward composition to define the representative function rep for the algorithm in Figure 3 faces the following problem: if ρ has been computed in σ using the sorting criterion ξ_{heap}, it might be the case that ρ is no longer sorting, according to ξ_{heap}, for $\pi_{proc}(\sigma)$. Analogously, computing ρ in $\pi_{proc}(\sigma)$ might not satisfy ξ_{heap} for σ. As a result, applying the heap permutations computed according to ξ_{heap} (by the algorithm in Figure 4) does not give the canonical representatives for heap symmetric states. The reason lies within the definition of ξ_{heap} (Section 3), since a chain that reaches a location may be prefixed with a process identifier, and therefore the minimal chain $trace(\sigma, l)$ may depend on the order of processes. In other words, permuting processes may affect the canonical property of the heap symmetry reduction. In order to overcome this difficulty, we need to record information that allows us to establish a fixed order on processes during the state space search. The following definition captures the formal meaning of the combined symmetry:

Definition 6. *Let $K = (S, R, L, \mathcal{N})$ be a structure, with $\mathcal{N} = \{\eta_{heap}, \eta_{proc}\}$. Two states σ, σ' are said to be fully symmetrical, denoted by $\sigma \equiv_{full} \sigma'$ iff the following hold:*

- $L(\sigma) = L(\sigma')$,
- $\eta_{heap}(\sigma) = \eta_{heap}(\sigma')$ and $\eta_{proc}(\sigma) = \eta_{proc}(\sigma')$,
- $\zeta_{heap}(\pi_{proc}(\sigma)) = \sigma'$ for some $\zeta \in G_{\eta_{heap}}(\sigma)$ and $\pi \in G_{\eta_{proc}}(\sigma)$.

We will proceed under the simplifying assumption that all processes are created (statically) in the initial state of the program[1]. We consider two functions $sort_{heap} : S \times G \to G$ and $sort_{proc} : S \to G$ that generate sorting permutations according to the ξ_{heap} and ξ_{proc} sorting criteria, respectively. Let us notice that $sort_{heap}$ now takes into account a process permutation in order to produce a canonical heap permutation. The state space search algorithm with combined reductions is presented in Figure 5.

```
RDFS(s, π)
if error(s) then report error fi
add(s, Statespace)
for each successor t of s do
      π' = sort_proc(t)
(#)ρ = sort_heap(t, π)
      t' = ρ_heap(π'_proc(t))
      if t' not in Statespace then RDFS(t', π' ∘ π)
od
end RDFS
```

Fig. 5. Depth First Search Combining Heap and Process Symmetry

Informally, the search algorithm in Figure 5 keeps track of the process permutation resulting from the cumulative composition of all process permutations computed along every path within the quotient structure. Formally, let $\Pi(w, k) = \pi_0 \circ \pi_1 \circ \ldots \circ \pi_{k-1}$ where $w = s_0, s_1, \ldots, s_{k-1}$ and $\pi_i = sort_{proc}(s_i)$. Intuitively, $\Pi(w, k)$ gives the information needed to restore, in each state, the initial order of processes. It is easy to show that, in a (recursive) call to RDFS in Figure 5 such that w is sequence of states passed as first parameter, $\Pi(w, |w|)$ represents the permutation passed as second parameter.

The implementation of the $sort_{heap}$ function uses a modified version of the heap sorting algorithm in Figure 4, in which the line marked by (*) has been changed into:

---

[1] The extension of the algorithm to handle the dynamic creation of processes is considered as future work.

$$(*) \ \ (c, s') = p(\pi^{-1}(i))$$

Here by π we denote the second argument in the invocation of $sort_{heap}$, as in the line marked with (#) in Figure 5. The idea is to use the inverse permutation in order to restore the original order of processes and maintain the canonical properties of the algorithm in Figure 4.

The following result gives sufficient conditions under which our combined algorithm still performs a canonical heap reduction. Let Id_n denote the identity permutation (neutral element) of G_n.

Lemma 2. Let $\sigma = (s, (h, l), (p, i))$ and $\sigma' = (s', (h', l), (p', i))$ be two states such that $\sigma \equiv_{full} \sigma'$.

1. Let $\pi \in G_{\eta_{proc}(\sigma)}$ be a process permutation such that $p' = \pi_{proc}(p)$. Let $\zeta = sort_{heap}(\sigma, Id_{\eta_{proc}}(\sigma))$ and $\zeta' = sort_{heap}(\sigma', \pi)$ be two heap permutations computed by the algorithm in Figure 4 with the (*) modification. Then $\zeta_{heap}(\pi_{proc}(\sigma)) = \zeta'_{heap}(\sigma')$.
2. Let $w = \sigma_0, \sigma_1, \ldots, \sigma_k = \sigma$ and $w' = \sigma_0, \sigma'_1, \ldots, \sigma'_l = \sigma'$ be two paths. Let $\zeta = sort_{heap}(\sigma, \Pi(w, k))$ and $\zeta' = sort_{heap}(\sigma', \Pi(w', l))$ be two heap permutations computed by the algorithm in Figure 4 with the (*) modification. Then $\zeta(\sigma) \equiv_{proc} \zeta'(\sigma')$.

Informally, Lemma 2 shows that using the algorithm in Figure 5 and computing heap permutations using the modified version of the algorithm in Figure 4 still preserves the properties of the original heap symmetry reduction, without process symmetry.

5   Symmetry versus Partial Order Reductions

In this section we investigate the relation between symmetry and partial order reductions applied to the model checking of dynamic programs that execute allocation statements. The previous work of Godefroid [11] also uses partial order information to detect symmetries between states, however it focuses mostly on flat programs, by defining permutations of actions and inferring that symmetric states are reached from the initial state by transition-symmetric paths. Our approach exploits the nature of dynamic programs that make use of the next-free allocation policy for which a semantics has been provided in Section 3. The notion of independence is extended via symmetry to define *symmetric independence*. It can be shown that paths differing only by a permutation of adjacent symmetric independent actions lead to symmetric states. In practice, this corresponds to the very common situation in which various interleavings of threads that perform heap allocations generate heap symmetric states. By conservatively exploiting this observation, when using partial order reductions in combination with symmetry reductions we can achieve better results when dynamic models of behavior are considered.

For the rest of this section, let $K = (S, R, L)$ be a Kripke structure over the set of actions Σ. An action α is said to be *enabled* in state s if there exists a state t such that $s \xrightarrow{\alpha} t$ in R. By $enabled_K(s)$ we denote the set of all actions enabled in s, according to the structure K. We can now introduce the concept of independent actions.

Definition 7. *A symmetric irreflexive relation $I \in \Sigma \times \Sigma$ is said to be an independence relation for K iff for all $(\alpha, \beta) \in I$ and for each $s \in S$ such that $\alpha, \beta \in enabled_K(s)$, we have:*

- *if $s \xrightarrow{\alpha} t$ then $\beta \in enabled_K(t)$*
- *if for some $s', s'' \in S$, $s \xrightarrow{\alpha} s' \xrightarrow{\beta} t$ and $s \xrightarrow{\beta} s'' \xrightarrow{\alpha} t'$, then $t = t'$.*

All partial order reduction algorithms [10], [22], [14] exploit (conservative under-approximations) of action independence. In practice, it has been shown that larger independence relations yield better partial order reductions. The contribution of this work to improving partial order reductions is based on defining and exploiting a weaker notion than the one from Definition 7.

Definition 8. *Given a symmetry relation $\equiv$ on S, a symmetric irreflexive relation $I_S \in \Sigma \times \Sigma$ is said to be a symmetric independence relation for K iff for all $(\alpha, \beta) \in I_S$ and for each $s \in S$ such that $\alpha, \beta \in enabled_K(s)$, we have:*

- *if $s \xrightarrow{\alpha} t$ then $\beta \in enabled_K(t)$*
- *if for some $s', s'' \in S$, $s \xrightarrow{\alpha} s' \xrightarrow{\beta} t$ and $s \xrightarrow{\beta} s'' \xrightarrow{\alpha} t'$, then $t \equiv t'$.*

The only change with respect to the Definition (7) is that, in I_S, two transitions are allowed to commute modulo symmetry. An independence relation is trivially a symmetric independence. Let us notice however that I_S can be much larger than I, since the number of states in a symmetry equivalence class can be exponential in the number of state components e.g., objects, processes. Dually, one can refer to the notion of *dependence*, which is defined as $D = \Sigma \times \Sigma \setminus I$. Similarly, we can define the notion of *symmetric dependence* as $D_S = \Sigma \times \Sigma \setminus I_S$. We can now formally relate the two notions of independence.

Lemma 3. *Given a symmetry relation $\equiv \subseteq S \times S$, I is a symmetric independence for K iff I is an independence for $K_{/\equiv}$.*

A second point of our discussion concerns visibility of actions. An action α is said to be *invisible* with respect to a set of atomic propositions $P \subseteq \mathcal{P}$ iff, for all $s, t \in S$ such that $s \xrightarrow{\alpha} t$ it is the case that $L(s) \cap P = L(t) \cap P$. Given the quotient structure $K_{/\equiv} = (S', R', L')$, by Definition (2) we have that $L(s) = L'([s])$ for each $s \in S$, therefore an action is invisible in K iff it is invisible in $K_{/\equiv}$.

The correctness result of this section is based on the main result of [7]: performing partial order reduction on an already built quotient structure yields the same structure as using an on-the-fly algorithm that combines both partial order and symmetry reduction. Figure 6 (a) shows a classical state space exploration algorithm with partial order reductions on the already built quotient structure $K_{/\equiv} = (S', R', L')$, while Figure 6 (b) depicts the changes done to the

```
DFS([s])                                DFS(s)
add([s], Statespace)                    add(rep(s), Statespace)
push([s], Stack)                        push(rep(s), Stack)
for each l in ample_a([s]) do           for each l in ample_b(s) do
    let [t] such that [s] -l-> [t]          let t such that s -l-> t
    if [t] ∉ Statespace DFS([t]) fi         if rep(t) ∉ Statespace DFS(t) fi
od                                      od
pop(Stack)                              pop(Stack)
end DFS                                 end DFS
        (a)                                     (b)
```

Fig. 6. Depth First Search with Partial Order and Symmetry Reductions

algorithm in order to use both partial order and symmetry reduction on-the-fly. Assume that $rep : S \to S$ is a canonical representative function (see Definition 4). We consider two functions $ample_a : S' \to \Sigma$ and $ample_b : S \to \Sigma$ that return, for a state s, a subset of the set of enabled actions in s for the quotient and original structures respectively, i.e., $ample_a(s) \subseteq enabled_{K/\equiv}(s)$ and $ample_b(s) \subseteq enabled_K(s)$. In order for the reduction to be sound[2], $ample_a$ must satisfy the following requirements [4], for each state s:

C0-a $ample_a([s]) \neq \emptyset \iff enabled_{K/\equiv}([s]) \neq \emptyset$

C1-a on every path that starts with $[s]$ in $K_{/\equiv}$, an action that is *dependent* on some action in $ample_a([s])$ cannot be taken before an action from $ample_a([s])$ is taken.

C2-a if $ample_a([s]) \subset enabled_{K/\equiv}([s])$ then every $\alpha \in ample_a([s])$ is invisible.

C3-a if $ample_a([s]) \subset enabled_{K/\equiv}([s])$ then for every $\alpha \in ample_a([s])$ such that $[s] \xrightarrow{\alpha} [t]$, then $[t] \notin Stack$ holds.

In order to define the $ample_b$ function (used by the algorithm in Figure 6 (b)), we change conditions [C0-a] and [C2-a] into [C0-b], [C2-b] by syntactically replacing $ample_a$ with $ample_b$, $[s]$ with s and $K_{/\equiv}$ with K. Since K and $K_{/\equiv}$ are bisimilar, conditions [C0-a] and [C0-b] are actually equivalent. From the previous discussion concerning visibility of actions, we can conclude that also [C2-a] and [C2-b] are equivalent. The rules [C1-b] and [C3-b] are as follows:

C1-b on every path that starts with s in K, an action that is *symmetric dependent* on some action in $ample_b(s)$ cannot be taken before an action from $ample_b(s)$ is taken.

C3-b if $ample_b(s) \subset enabled_K(s)$ then for every $\alpha \in ample_b(s)$ such that $s \xrightarrow{\alpha} t$, then $rep(t) \notin Stack$ holds.

A consequence of Lemma (3) is that conditions [C1-a] and [C1-b] are equivalent. Equivalence of [C3-a] and [C3-b] can be shown as an invariant of the lockstep

---

[2] Property preservation for partial order reductions uses the notion of *stuttering path equivalence*, a weaker notion than bisimulation. For more details, the interested reader is referred to [22]

execution of the algorithms in Figure 6. The proof of the following theorem can be done between the lines of Theorem 19 in [7].

Theorem 2. *The state space explored by the algorithm (a) running on the quotient structure $K_{/\equiv}$ is isomorphic to the one explored by the algorithm (b) running on the original structure K.*

According to [22], partial order reduction preserves all formulas of the LTL_X (next-free LTL) logic. An algorithm for partial order reduction that preserves properties expressible in CTL^*_X can be found in [9]. As a consequence of this and Theorem 2, combining partial order with symmetry reductions will preserve all properties written as next-free temporal logic formulas.

Having discussed the correctness of our partial order reduction that uses directly symmetric independence, we need to identify actions (program statements) that are (globally) symmetric independent without inspecting the program executions described by K or the reduced structure $K_{/\equiv}$. The operational semantics defined in Section 3 comes into place now. In particular, we are interested by the rules (NEW1) and (NEW2) that define object allocator actions. It can be noticed that the first-free allocation policy used by both (NEW1) and (NEW2) actions is sufficient to obtain the second point of Definition (8). non-deterministic choices in our language. In the following, let a and b denote two distinct program variables.

Lemma 4. *Let $\sigma = (s, (h, l_k), (p, i))$ be a state and $\alpha = [\mathtt{a} = \mathtt{new}]$, $\beta = [\mathtt{b} = \mathtt{new}]$ be two actions whose semantics are described by either one of the rules (NEW1) or (NEW2). If $\sigma', \sigma'', \theta'$ and θ'' are states such that $\sigma \xrightarrow{\alpha} \sigma' \xrightarrow{\beta} \theta'$ and $\sigma \xrightarrow{\beta} \sigma'' \xrightarrow{\alpha} \theta''$, then $\theta' \equiv_{heap} \theta''$.*

In order to meet the first requirement of Definition (8), one can take the classical [14] approach of defining *safe* actions. A safe action belonging to a process $p(i)$ is globally independent from all actions belonging to other processes $p(j)$ $(i \neq j)$ and invisible with respect to the set of atomic propositions that occur in a property expressible as a temporal logic formula. Both requirements are met by actions x = new where x is a local variable, in cases where the property refers only to global variables. Otherwise, static analysis can be used to compute a conservative over-approximation of the set of aliases in the program and consequently, conservatively under-approximate the set of safe actions enabled in a state.

To conclude, we have shown how the concept of symmetry can be used to extend the notion of independence used by partial order reductions. Identifying symmetric independent actions can be done by a syntactic analysis of the program and using them in the model checking algorithm may result in a better partial order reduction. As a remark, none of the two reduction techniques considered in this paper can fully replace the other. Since it uses a conservative under-estimation of the symmetric independence relation, partial order reduction might not always detect all symmetric states caused by different interleavings of allocators. Symmetry reduction is therefore needed in order to deal with these cases. On the other hand, it has been shown that partial order reduction that uses symmetric independence is equivalent to performing classical partial order reduction on an already built quotient structure, the result being a subset of the quotient structure that preserves meaningful properties. In cases where all symmetrical states are generated by interleavings of safe allocator actions, partial order reductions alone can actually outperform symmetry reductions.

6   Implementation and Experience

The heap symmetry and partial order reductions with symmetric independence have been implemented in the dSPIN model checker [17]. We performed experiments involving two test cases: the first one is a model of an ordered list shared between multiple updater threads, and the second models an interlocking protocol used for controlling concurrent access to a shared B-tree structure. Both models are verified for absence of deadlocks, as we performed these tests mainly to assess the effectiveness of our reduction techniques.

dSPIN is an automata theoretic explicit-state model checker designed for the verification of software. It provides a number of novel features on top of standard SPIN's [13] state space reduction algorithms, e.g., partial-order reduction and state compression. The input language of dSPIN is a dialect of the PROMELA language [13] offering, C-like constructs for allocating and referencing dynamic data structures. On-the-fly garbage collection is also supported [18]. The presence of garbage collector algorithms in dSPIN made the implementation of heap symmetry reductions particularly easy. The algorithm used to compute sorting permutations is in fact an instrumented *mark and sweep* garbage collector. The explicit representation of states allowed the embedding of such capabilities directly into the model checker's core. This served to bridge the semantic gap between high-level object oriented languages, such as Java or C++, and formal description languages that use abstract representations of systems, such as finite-state automata.

The first test case represents a dynamic list ordered by node keys. The list is updated by two processes that use node locks to synchronize: an inserter that adds given keys into the list, and an extractor that removes nodes with given keys from the list. The example scales in the maximum length of the list (L).

The second example is an interlocking protocol that ensures the consistency of a B-tree* data structure accessed concurrently by a variable number of replicated updater processes. Various mutual exclusion protocols for accessing concurrent B-tree* structures are described in [1] and our example has been inspired by this work. The example scales in the number of updater processes (N), B-tree order (K) and maximum depth of the structure (D).

Symmetries arise in both examples because different interleavings of the updater processes cause different allocation orderings of nodes with the same data. The results of our experiments are shown in Table 1. The table shows the number of states generated by the model checker with standard partial order reduction only (-), with partial order based on symmetric independence only (SI), with

Table 1. Experimental Results

i. Ordered List Example

L	SI+SR	SR	SI	-
8	296159	296159	766297	766297
9	727714	727714	2.29669e+06	2.29669e+06
10	1.75287e+06	1.75287e+06	4.62012e+06	4.62012e+06

ii. B-Tree* Example

N, K, D	SI+SR	SR	SI	-
2, 2, 3	1259	6816	1259	94105
2, 4, 3	3027	18773	3027	766842
2, 4, 4	32998	142371	out of memory	out of memory

symmetry reductions only (SR) and with combined partial order and symmetry reductions (SI+SR).

In the first example (Ordered List) partial order reductions using symmetric independence do not contribute to the overall reduction of the state space. The reason is that the allocator statements in this model handle only global variables, being therefore labeled as "unsafe" by the dSPIN transition table constructor. On the contrary, in first two instances of the second example (Btree*) partial order reductions using symmetric independence manage to detect all heap symmetries arising as result of interleaving allocators, therefore symmetry reductions do not contribute any further to the overall reduction. The results show that combining partial order with symmetry reductions can outperform each reduction technique applied in isolation.

7   Conclusions

In this work, we have tackled issues related to the application of model checking techniques to software verification. Programs written in high-level programming languages have a more dynamic nature than hardware and network protocols. The size of a program state is no longer constant, as new components are added along executions. We have formalized this matter by means of semantic definitions of program states and actions. This semantics allows definition of various symmetry criteria for programs. We gave such criteria formal definitions, and described algorithms for on-the-fly symmetry reductions in automata theoretic model checking. In particular, we have discussed the combination of two orthogonal symmetry reductions, related to heap objects and processes. We have also shown how our heap symmetry reduction technique relates with partial order reductions. The emphasis is on how to adapt existing state space reduction techniques to software model checking. The ideas in this paper have been implemented in a software model checker that extends SPIN with dynamic features. Using this prototype implementation, a number of experiments have been performed. Preliminary results are encouraging, making us optimistic about the role symmetry and partial order reductions can play in enhancing model checking techniques for software.

Acknowledgments

The author wishes to thank Dennis Dams, Dragan Bosnacki and Willem Visser, for interesting discussions and suggestions, Matthew Dwyer and John Hatcliff for valuable corrections of the previous versions of this paper, and the anonymous referees for comments leading to the discovery of an erroneous claim in the submission draft.

References

1. R. Bayer and M. Schkolnick: Concurrency of Operations on B-Trees. Acta Informatica, Vol. 9 (1977) 1–21
2. Dragan Bosnacki: Enhancing State Space Reduction Techniques for Model Checking. PhD Thesis, Technical University of Eindhoven (2001)
3. Edmund M. Clarke, Somesh Jha, Reinhard Enders and Thomas Filkorn: Exploiting Symmetry In Temporal Logic Model Checking. Formal Methods in System Design, Vol.9, No. 1/2 (1996) 77–104
4. Edmund M. Clarke, Orna Grumberg and Doron Peled: Model Checking. MIT Press (2001)
5. Constantin Courcoubetis, Moshe Y. Vardi, Pierre Wolper and Mihalis Yannakakis: Memory-Efficient Algorithms for the Verification of Temporal Properties. Formal Methods in System Design, Vol. 1, No 2/3 (1992) 275–288
6. Dennis Dams, Dragan Bosnacki and Leszek Holenderski: A Heuristic for Symmetry Reductions with Scalarsets. Proc. Formal Methods Europe (2001) 518–533
7. E. Emerson, S. Jha and D. Peled: Combining Partial Order and Symmetry Reductions. Proc. Tools and Algorithms for Construction and Analysis of Systems, Lecture Notes in Computer Science, Vol. 1217 (1997) 19–34
8. E. Emerson and A. P. Sistla: Symmetry and Model Checking. Formal Methods in System Design, Vol.9, No. 1/2 (1996) 105–131
9. R. Gerth, R. Kuiper, D. Peled and W. Penczek: A Partial Order Approach to Branching Time Logic Model Checking. Proc. 3rd Israel Symposium on Theory on Computing and Systems (1995) 130–139
10. P. Godefroid: Partial-Order Methods for the Verification of Concurrent Systems. Lecture Notes in Computer Science Vol. 1032 (1996)
11. P. Godefroid: Exploiting Symmetry when Model-Checking Software. Proc. Formal Methods for Protocol Engineering and Distributed Systems (FORTE/PSTV) (1999) 257–275
12. M. Hennessy and R. Milner: Algebraic Laws for Nondeterminism and Concurrency. Journal of the ACM Vol. 32 (1985) 137–161
13. G.J. Holzmann: The SPIN Model Checker. IEEE Trans. on Software Engineering Vol. 23 (1997) 279–295
14. G. J. Holzmann and D. Peled: An Improvement in Formal Verification. Formal Description Techniques, Chapman & Hall, (1994) 197–211
15. G. Holzmann, D. Peled and M. Yannakakis: On Nested Depth First Search. Proc. 2nd SPIN Workshop (1996)

16. R. Iosif: Symmetric Model Checking for Object-Based Programs. Technical Report KSU CIS TR 2001-5 (2001)
17. R. Iosif and R. Sisto: dSPIN: A Dynamic Extension of SPIN. Proc. 6th SPIN Workshop, Lecture Notes in Computer Science Vol. 1680 (1999) 261–276
18. R. Iosif and R. Sisto: Using Garbage Collection in Model Checking. Proc. 7th SPIN Workshop, Lecture Notes in Computer Science Vol. 1885 (2000) 20–33
19. R. Iosif: Exploiting Heap Symmetries in Explicit-State Model Checking of Software. Proc. 16th IEEE Conference on Automated Software Engineering (2001) 254 – 261
20. C. Ip and D. Dill: Better Verification Through Symmetry. Formal Methods in System Design, Vol.9, No. 1/2 (1996) 41–75
21. F. Lerda and W. Visser: Addressing Dynamic Issues of Program Model Checking. Proc. 8th SPIN Workshop, Lecture Notes in Computer Science Vol. 2057 (2001) 80–102
22. D. Peled: All from One, One from All: on Model Checking using representatives. Proc. 5th Conference on Computer Aided Verification, Lecture Notes in Computer Science Vol. 697 (1993) 409–423

Bytecode Model Checking:
An Experimental Analysis[*]

David Basin[1], Stefan Friedrich[1],
Marek Gawkowski[1], and Joachim Posegga[2]

[1] Institut für Informatik,
Universität Freiburg, Germany
[2] SAP AG, Corporate Research,
Karlsruhe, Germany

Abstract. Java bytecode verification is traditionally performed by a polynomial time dataflow algorithm. We investigate an alternative based on reducing bytecode verification to model checking. Despite an exponential worst case time complexity, model checking type-correct bytecode is polynomial in practice when carried out using an explicit state, on-the-fly model checker like SPIN. We investigate this theoretically and experimentally and explain the practical advantages of this alternative.

1 Introduction

Java is a popular programming language that is well suited for building distributed applications where users can download code that they can locally execute. To combat the security risks associated with mobile code, Sun has developed a security model for Java and a central role is played by bytecode verification [7,18], which ensures that no malicious code is executed by a Java Virtual Machine (JVM). Bytecode verification takes place when loading a Java class file and the process verifies that the loaded bytecode program has certain properties that the interpreter's security builds upon. By checking these properties statically before execution, the JVM can safely omit the corresponding runtime checks.

In this paper we show how model checking can be used to check type safety properties (which is the essential, and non-trivial, part of bytecode verification) of Java class files. We have built a system for this task, shown in Figure 1. The system takes as input a Java class file as well as a specification of an abstraction of the Java virtual machine. From these, the system produces an intermediate representation consisting of a transition system (for the abstracted machine) and a specification of safety properties formalizing conditions sufficient for bytecode type safety. Afterwards, these descriptions are translated into the input language of public domain model checkers, currently the SPIN [4] and SMV [5] systems.

[*] The research presented in this paper was partially funded by T-Systems Nova GmbH in the ByCoMoChe project.

D. Bošnački and S. Leue (Eds.): SPIN 2002, LNCS 2318, pp. 42–59, 2002.
© Springer-Verlag Berlin Heidelberg 2002

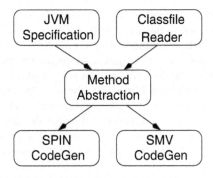

Fig. 1. Overall System Architecture

Motivation and Contributions

There are three reasons why we focused on this problem. First, we were interested in using formal methods to improve the security of the entire verification and execution process. In formalizing the Java Virtual Machine and its abstraction, we show how to explicitly model bytecode verification in a precise language that makes explicit the exact nature of the bytecode verification problem. This goes far beyond the Java documentation [7], which gives only a semi-formal description of bytecode verification and leaves numerous aspects of both the bytecode verifier and the Java Virtual Machine either ambiguous or underspecified. Moreover, by basing a bytecode verifier directly on a general model checker, our approach reduces the chance of errors arising during an implementation of specialized dataflow algorithms. It is noteworthy in this regard that, as Stärk and Schmid point out [16], there are legal Java programs whose compiled bytecode is type correct but are not accepted by Sun's bytecode verifier. The classes of programs that they define (based on calling subroutines in different contexts) are unproblematic for our approach.

Second, we were interested in determining whether this approach is practical and scales to realistic examples. The answer is not obvious. In contrast to conventional bytecode verification, which is based on dataflow analysis and has polynomial time complexity, using a model checker for this task has a time complexity that is exponential in the worst case. We show that for type correct bytecode, model checking can yield results comparable to dataflow procedures. The reason for this is that despite the exponential number of states, for correct code, only polynomially many are reachable (see Section 3 for the exact analysis). Our experiments validate that the use of SPIN, which constructs the state space incrementally, on-the-fly, produces results in agreement with these bounds. This is in contrast to symbolic BDD-based model checking approaches like SMV that must represent the entire state space and therefore turn out to be impractical for this kind of problem. For incorrect bytecode, both explicit state and symbolic methods may fail to terminate (or exhaust memory). This is not an issue in practice; when too many resources are used, one may either time out (giving a conservative answer) or use an alternative approach (e.g., property simplification, as described in Section 3.3) to detect an error.

Our result suggests the usefulness of bytecode verification by model checking, especially in domains where time and space requirements are less important than correctness and possible extensibility. One such application is Java for smart cards (JavaCard). The JavaCard is a highly secure smart card platform with a simplified JVM. Due to memory limitations, bytecode verification must be performed off-card (where correct code can then be digitally signed by the verifier), instead of by the run-time environment. Our original motivation for this work was to investigate whether model checking could be used as an alternative in this domain, a question we can now answer positively.

There is a final, independent reason why we think this is an interesting problem: there is an unlimited supply of scalable, real life examples. The Java distribution, for example, comes with thousands of class files that we could use for testing our system. Indeed, for this reason, we would like to suggest bytecode verification as a problem domain to be generally used to test and compare different model checkers. Our system is freely available for such benchmarking purposes.

Related Work

The widespread use of Java and the lack of formal treatment originally given in [7] have motivated considerable research. A number of different approaches have been proposed for type checking bytecode and [6] contains an excellent overview of the area. Most of this work is theoretically oriented and is concerned with formalizing the JVM [2] and defining related type systems [3,12,13,17]. There has also been considerable work on formally proving the soundness of various approaches or verifying sufficient conditions for bytecode verifiers to be correct [2,8,10,11].

In the recent years there has been a convergence of ideas in static analysis and model checking: different kinds of program analysis can be performed by fixed-point computations and these computations can either be carried out by specialized algorithms or by general purpose model checkers [14,15]. Whereas static analysis techniques have a longstanding history, the application of model checking to static analysis problems is more recent. The idea of using model checking for bytecode verification was originally suggested by Posegga and Vogt [9]. They carried out a few small examples by hand to suggest how, in principle, this approach could work for a subset of the JVM. Our work represents the first large scale effort to apply model checking to this problem and to study its practical significance.

Organization

The remainder of this paper is organized as follows. In Section 2 we explain the reduction of bytecode verification to model checking. Afterwards, in Section 3 we present experimental results and an analysis. We draw conclusions in Section 4.

```
class Test {                        Method int fac(int)
                                  >> max_stack=4, max_locals=2 <<
int fac (int i) {                     0 iload_1
   if ( i == 0 )                      1 ifne 4
      return 1;                       2 iconst_1
   else                               3 ireturn
      return i*fac(i-1);              4 iload_1
   }                                  5 aload_0
}                                     6 iload_1
                                      7 iconst_1
                                      8 isub
                                      9 invokevirtual <Test.fac(int):int>
                                     10 imul
                                     11 ireturn
```

Fig. 2. Java code and Bytecode of method fac

2   Abstracting Classfiles to Model Checking Problems

2.1   Background

In this section we briefly explain the bytecode verification problem and describe
the main elements of our approach.

Bytecode and the JVM. Java programs are compiled to bytecode instructions
that are interpreted by the JVM (see Figure 2 for a small example). The result
of compilation, a classfile, contains a symbol table (called the constant pool)
describing the fields of the class and a list of the methods of the class. The
JVM supports object orientation and there are specific bytecode instructions
for generating and accessing the objects of a class. The overall architecture is
that of a stack machine: the JVM possesses an operand stack, which is used for
the evaluation of expressions. For instance, an imul instruction multiplies the
topmost two elements of the operand stack, discards those elements from the
stack, and pushes the result of the multiplication back on the operand stack.
In addition to the stack, the JVM also uses an array of registers to store local
variables.

Most JVM instructions are typed. For instance, the getfield $C.f.\tau$ instruction, which accesses the field f of type τ in class C, requires that the operand
stack contains a reference to an object of class C (and not, for instance, an integer, which would correspond to an attempt to forge a reference). The operand
stack and the registers (local variables) however are not typed.

Bytecode Verification. To guarantee the secure operation of the JVM, one must
show that each method is well-typed, i.e., that one can assign a state type to
each point in the program. The state type specifies what kind of values the
operand stack and the local variables may contain at the given program point.
For example, the state type $(0, \mathsf{Empty}, loc[0 \mapsto \mathsf{REF}(Test), 1 \mapsto \mathsf{INT}])$ associates

to the program point 0 those states with an empty operand stack whose first local variable contains an object of class *Test* and whose second local variable contains an integer. Given this notion of a well-typing, one can show that the execution of a well-typed method will never lead to a bad state of the JVM, that is, a state where the instructions operate on inappropriate data. This allows the JVM to execute more efficiently by eliminating runtime type checks.

Conventional Bytecode Verification. Conventional bytecode verification works by abstracting a method to a state transition system and then computing a type of the method by dataflow analysis. The bytecode verifier checks, on-the-fly, that the computed type is a well-typing, i.e. satisfies the conditions for the correct execution of the instructions.

Type construction is carried out by computing the supremum of the state types of all possible execution paths. This requires the unique existence of such a supremum, which is however, in the presence of multiple inheritance (interfaces), not the case. There are several solutions to address this problem, including considering sets of types instead of single types or checking correct implementation of interfaces at runtime (as done by SUN's bytecode verifier).

Conventional bytecode verification is further complicated by the existence of subroutines, which are used to compile the `finally` part of a Java `try-catch-finally` construct. The complication is due to the fact that one can call (`jsr`) and return from (`ret`) subroutines from different program points where the calling contexts (the stack and the register values not used by the subroutine) of different execution paths can be incompatible. This results in non-trivial complications; solutions include structural restrictions on bytecode (Sun's approach) and polyvariant dataflow analysis [6]. It is an open question which solution is best. The polyvariant approach seems more elegant but has a time complexity that is exponential in the depth of subroutine nesting.

Model Checking Approach. In our approach we also abstract a method to a state transition system. However, instead of performing a dataflow analysis, we formalize the correctness properties as predicates of the states of the abstract transition system and use an off-the-shelf model checker like SPIN or SMV to check that these properties are satisfied. The model checker then either reports the correctness of the method, or it provides a counter example in form of an execution trace that leads to a failure.

This approach is simpler than conventional bytecode verification, as the requirements for the correctness can be clearly and comprehensibly formalized in an easy to understand language, which helps to avoid errors in the formalization. Moreover, with our approach, multiple inheritance is not problematic since the formalization of the correctness properties requires only that the types are ordered.

Note further that the problems alluded to above concerning subroutines do not arise in our approach since model checkers consider all possible runs of the system; they are, in the words of [6, p281], "the ultimate polyvariant analysis".

However, the cost is a time complexity exponential in the depth of subroutine nesting. We investigate this problem and its implications in Section 3.2.

2.2 Abstraction/Transition System

We abstract a method M to a finite state transition system (Q, q_0, Δ). The set $Q \subseteq \mathbb{N} \times (\mathcal{T} \text{ stack}) \times (\mathcal{T} \text{ array})$ of states contains triples that consist of the program counter, the operand stack, and the array of local variables of the method M. The set $\mathcal{T}$ of types contains the primitive types and the reference types of the JVM (NULL represents the polymorphic type of the null reference) and the program addresses that can be targets of ret instructions. We add an element UNDEF to represent uninitialized values.

$$prim = \{\text{INT}, \text{FLOAT}, \text{LDOUBLE}, \text{HDOUBLE}, \text{LLONG}, \text{HLONG}\}$$
$$ref = \{\text{REF}(cn) \mid cn \in classnames\} \cup \{\text{NULL}\}$$
$$adr = \{\text{ADR}(i) \mid i \in \mathbb{N}\}$$
$$\mathcal{T} = \{\text{UNDEF}\} \cup prim \cup ref \cup adr$$

Since only a finite subset of $\mathcal{T}$ occurs in a particular transition system, we can compute this subset by inspecting the signature and the method body. The signature of a method, which has the form

$$S = (M, result\_type, [arg\_type_1, \ldots, arg\_type_n])$$

specifies the method's name, its argument types and its result type. The method body is given as a list ins of bytecode instructions. The various instructions in the method body also introduce new types, e.g.,

$$\begin{aligned}
\text{types\_of\_ins(imul)} &= \{\text{INT}\} \\
\text{types\_of\_ins(new } C) &= \{C\} \\
\text{types\_of\_ins(getfield } C.f.\tau) &= \{C, \tau\}
\end{aligned}$$
$$\vdots$$

Thus the set T of types occurring in a method that belongs to class C is

$$T = \{\text{REF}(C), result\_type, arg\_type_1, \ldots, arg\_type_n\} \cup \bigcup_{p \in \{0, \ldots, |ins|-1\}} \text{types\_of\_ins}(ins_p).$$

We compute the initial state q_0 of the transition system for a method M with signature S that belongs to a class C as follows: Execution starts at program counter 0 with an empty operand stack, the this reference, and the actual parameters, which are passed through the first $n+1$ local variables. The remaining local variables $loc[n+1], \ldots, loc[maxloc]$ are initially undefined ($maxloc$ is specified in the classfile), i.e.,

$$q_0 = (0, \text{Empty}, loc), \text{ where } \begin{cases} loc[0] = \text{REF}(C) \\ loc[1] = arg\_type_1, \ldots, loc[n] = arg\_type_n \\ loc[n+1] = \text{UNDEF}, \ldots, loc[maxloc] = \text{UNDEF}. \end{cases}$$

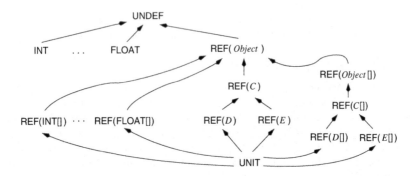

Fig. 3. Subtyping relation $\sqsubseteq_\Gamma$

The transition relation of the abstract method is defined by the instructions of the method. We give here a few representative examples, which show how the program counter pc, the operand stack $opst$, and the local variables loc are modified:

$$
\begin{array}{ll}
\texttt{istore } n & (pc, opst, loc) \mapsto \{(pc+1, opst, loc[n \mapsto \mathsf{top}(opst)])\} \\
\texttt{iload } n & (pc, opst, loc) \mapsto \{(pc+1, loc[n].opst, loc)\} \\
\texttt{imul} & (pc, opst, loc) \mapsto \{(pc+1, \mathsf{INT}.\mathsf{pop}(\mathsf{pop}(opst)), loc)\} \\
\texttt{new } C & (pc, opst, loc) \mapsto \{(pc+1, \mathsf{REF}(C).opst, loc)\} \\
\texttt{getfield } C.f.\tau & (pc, opst, loc) \mapsto \{(pc+1, \tau.\mathsf{pop}(opst), loc)\} \\
\texttt{ifeq } \mathit{offset} & (pc, opst, loc) \mapsto \{(pc+1, \mathsf{pop}(opst), loc), \\
& \qquad\qquad\qquad\quad (pc+\mathit{offset}, \mathsf{pop}(opst), loc)\} \\
\texttt{jsr } \mathit{offset} & (pc, opst, loc) \mapsto \{(pc+\mathit{offset}, \mathsf{ADR}(pc+1).opst, loc)\} \\
\texttt{ret } n & (pc, opst, loc) \mapsto \{(\mathsf{retaddr}(loc[n]), opst, loc)\}
\end{array}
$$

2.3 Type Safety Properties

We formalize correctness properties as predicates on the states of the abstract transition system. These properties must hold globally for all possible runs of the system and this motivates our use of a temporal specification formalism. Two different kinds of properties are required.

First, the operand stack must not overflow. The operand stack is only used to evaluate expressions and hence the maximal stack-height $maxstack$ can be computed in advance. This value is given as a method attribute in the classfile of the method. We can formulate the corresponding condition as $\mathsf{size}(opst) \leq maxstack$.

Second, each instruction must always operate on data of the appropriate type. Note that due to object orientation, for some instructions different types of data are acceptable as determined by the subtyping relation $\sqsubseteq_\Gamma$, which depends on the program Γ. Figure 3 shows the subtyping relation $\sqsubseteq_\Gamma$ for a program Γ consisting of three classes C, D, and E. In the specification of the JVM, the well-typing conditions can be formalized in a straightforward, declarative way. We give here a few representative examples:

$$
\begin{array}{ll}
\texttt{aload}\ n & \mapsto loc[n] \in \mathit{ref} \cap T \\
\texttt{iload}\ n & \mapsto loc[n] = \mathsf{INT} \\
\texttt{imul} & \mapsto (\mathsf{top}(\mathit{opst}) = \mathsf{INT}) \wedge (\mathsf{top}(\mathsf{pop}(\mathit{opst})) = \mathsf{INT}) \\
\texttt{getfield}\ C.f.\tau & \mapsto \mathsf{top}(\mathit{opst}) \sqsubseteq_\Gamma \mathsf{REF}(C) \\
\texttt{putfield}\ C.f.\tau & \mapsto \mathsf{top}(\mathsf{pop}(\mathit{opst})) \sqsubseteq_\Gamma \mathsf{REF}(C) \wedge \mathsf{top}(\mathit{opst}) \sqsubseteq_\Gamma \tau
\end{array}
$$

For a given program Γ, the relation $\sqsubseteq_\Gamma$ is finite and thus the conditions can be unfolded and automatically checked. The condition for the $\texttt{getfield}\ C.f.\tau$ instruction, for instance, would be unfolded to

$$
\begin{aligned}
\mathsf{local\_cond}(\texttt{getfield}\ C.f.\tau) \ \equiv\ & \mathsf{top}(\mathit{opst}) = \mathsf{REF}(C) \vee \mathsf{top}(\mathit{opst}) = \mathsf{REF}(D) \vee \\
& \mathsf{top}(\mathit{opst}) = \mathsf{REF}(E) \vee \mathsf{top}(\mathit{opst}) = \mathsf{UNIT}.
\end{aligned}
$$

The overall correctness property for a method is the conjunction of the global property for the stack height and the local property for each program point.

$$
(\mathsf{size}(\mathit{opst}) \leq \mathit{maxstack}) \wedge \bigwedge_{p \in \{0,\ldots,|\mathit{ins}|-1\}} (\mathit{pc} = p \Rightarrow \mathsf{local\_cond}(\mathit{ins}_p))
$$

2.4   Backends for SPIN and SMV

We have implemented two different backends: one for SPIN and one for SMV. The basic idea in both is the same. From our intermediate representation we produce a transition system in the input language of the model checker and a property specification. The property specification states globally invariant correctness properties, i.e., properties that must hold at every program point. In LTL this corresponds to checking $\Box\varphi$ for a state property φ and in CTL this corresponds to checking $\mathsf{AG}(\varphi)$.

We briefly describe here the SPIN backend (SMV is similar in most respects). The formalization of the transition system in SPIN's input language PROMELA is straightforward. The types of the transition system, i.e. the elements of the set T, are represented as integers. The stack and the array of local variables are modeled as arrays of integers. As an example, Figure 4 shows the abstract transition system for the *fac* bytecode presented in Section 1. The data required to model this method are the address labels $\{\mathsf{ADR}(0),\ldots,\mathsf{ADR}(11)\}$ and the types $\{\mathsf{UNDEF},\mathsf{INT},\mathsf{UNIT},\mathsf{REF}(\mathit{Test})\}$. They are represented (in this order) by the numbers 0 through 15. Initially the operand stack is empty, the local variable $loc[0]$ contains the *this* reference $\mathsf{REF}(\mathit{Test})$ and the local variable $loc[1]$ contains the INT argument of the method. Each transition modeling an instruction is carried out as an atomic step. A branching instruction, which produces two possible successor states, is modeled using a nondeterministic if-statement.

Note that in SPIN the invariant φ can be expressed in different ways, e.g., as an observer process or using a never-claim. We have chosen the former: The observer process runs in parallel to the abstract state transition system

```
init { atomic { loc[0]=15; loc[1]=13; opst_ptr=0; pc=0 };
       run assertions (); run transitions () }

proctype transitions( ) {
  do
  :: pc==0 -> atomic { opst[opst_ptr]=loc[1]; opst_ptr=opst_ptr+1; pc=1 };
  :: pc==1 -> if
                :: atomic { opst_ptr=opst_ptr-1; pc=2 };
                :: atomic { opst_ptr=opst_ptr-1; pc=4 }
              fi;
  :: pc==2  -> atomic { opst[opst_ptr]=13;      opst_ptr=opst_ptr+1; pc=3 };
  :: pc==3  -> atomic { break };
  :: pc==4  -> atomic { opst[opst_ptr]=loc[1]; opst_ptr=opst_ptr+1; pc=5 };
  :: pc==5  -> atomic { opst[opst_ptr]=loc[0]; opst_ptr=opst_ptr+1; pc=6 };
  :: pc==6  -> atomic { opst[opst_ptr]=loc[1]; opst_ptr=opst_ptr+1; pc=7 };
  :: pc==7  -> atomic { opst[opst_ptr]=13;      opst_ptr=opst_ptr+1; pc=8 };
  :: pc==8  -> atomic { opst[opst_ptr-2]=13;    opst_ptr=opst_ptr-1; pc=9 };
  :: pc==9  -> atomic { opst[opst_ptr-2]=13;    opst_ptr=opst_ptr-1; pc=10 };
  :: pc==10 -> atomic { opst[opst_ptr-2]=13;    opst_ptr=opst_ptr-1; pc=11 };
  :: pc==11 -> atomic { break }
  od
}
```

Fig. 4. Abstract transition system for the *fac* bytecode in SPIN

and it contains an assertion statement that states the correctness property that must hold at each state. This approach is simple and has the practical advantage that temporal formulas need not be translated separately to automata. Figure 5 shows the correctness properties for our sample bytecode. For example, for the invokevirtual<Test.fac(int):int> instruction at $pc = 9$, we require that the topmost element of the operand stack is an INT (i.e. opst[opst_ptr-1]==13) and the next element is a reference to an instance of the class *Test* (i.e. opst[opst_ptr-2]==15).

We will not provide here a formal proof of the correctness of the translation. However, the basis is given in the work of [11] where they specify sufficient conditions for Java bytecode verifiers to be correct. The main idea is that a method is well-typed when it can be assigned a type (composed of state types, described in Section 2.1) and the existence of such a well-typing guarantees that method execution proceeds without type errors (stack overflow or improper arguments to instructions). It is possible to show that when a method is successfully model checked in our setting then such a well-typing exists.

3   Experimental Results and Analysis

We have carried out two different kinds of experiments to investigate the applicability and scalability of using model checking for bytecode verification. First, to test the practical applicability of this approach, we model checked all the methods associated with a large Java library, namely all methods of the java.lang package. Second, to better understand how the complexity of bytecode checking

```
proctype assertions() {
  assert (opst_ptr<=4 &&
          (pc!=0  || loc[1]==13) &&
          (pc!=1  || opst[opst_ptr-1]==13) &&
          (pc!=3  || opst[opst_ptr-1]==13) &&
          (pc!=4  || loc[1]==13) &&
          (pc!=5  || loc[0]==14 || loc[0]==15) &&
          (pc!=6  || loc[1]==13) &&
          (pc!=8  || opst[opst_ptr-2]==13 && opst[opst_ptr-1]==13) &&
          (pc!=9  || opst[opst_ptr-1]==13 && opst[opst_ptr-2]==15) &&
          (pc!=10 || opst[opst_ptr-2]==13 && opst[opst_ptr-1]==13) &&
          (pc!=11 || opst[opst_ptr-1]==13) )
}
```

Fig. 5. Correctness properties for *fac*

depends on parameters such as method length, nesting of subroutines, or number of variables and the types involved, we carried out systematic "stress tests" where we varied each parameter individually, while leaving the others fixed.

3.1 Practical Applicability

To test the applicability of our approach to the verification of real bytecode, we tested it on all the methods of the java.lang package. This package contains 109 classes with 841 methods. These methods are representative for Java bytecode as they contain all the instructions of the JVM. Moreover, they vary considerably in their complexity in terms of the different parameters mentioned above. Also representative is their size. Most Java methods in practice are modestly sized. In this package, only 32 methods contain more than 100 instructions. As Figure 6 indicates, SPIN checks almost all of these methods in negligible time[1]. Only the largest five, which each contain more than 600 instructions, require more than half a second. This is sufficient for the most applications and in particular is more than adequate for off-line verification (e.g., smart cards) and for applications with on-line verification, such as web applets, where methods are generally quite small. The picture for SMV is completely different; even small methods with less than 100 instructions can require more than two minutes to verify and, for 29 methods, SMV ran out of memory. This suggests that, for this problem domain, explicit state on-the-fly methods are superior to symbolic methods. Our systematic tests shed light on some of the reasons for this.

3.2 Systematic Tests

We carried out four different "stress tests" to isolate and investigate the influence of various parameters on the complexity of the model checking problem. In particular, we investigated the effects of individually varying the following:

---

[1] In all experiments, times are measured in seconds. All timings are performed on an 800-Megahertz Pentium III PC with 256 MB memory.

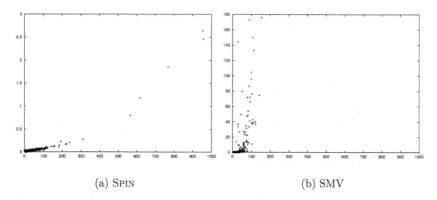

(a) SPIN   (b) SMV

Fig. 6. Verification times depending on the number of instructions in a method

```
                static int z;

                public static int m_n (int x) {
            ⎧    z = z + x;
            ⎪     ⋮
  n times  ⎨
            ⎪    z = z + x;
            ⎩    return z; }
```

Fig. 7. Schema of methods to test dependency of complexity on code length

1. The length of the method, i.e. the number of instructions,
2. the number of local variables,
3. the depth of the class hierarchy, i.e. the number of types that are used to model a method, and
4. the depth of the nesting of subroutines.

The methods checked were automatically produced by generating and compiling appropriate Java programs as explained below.

Method Length. We investigated the influence of a method's length by generating methods that consist of a single expression repeated n times, for $n \in \{1, \ldots, 100\}$. Figure 7 shows the form of these methods. The corresponding bytecode uses only one local variable x and one class variable z. The method is declared in a static class that is a direct subclass of Object; thus the class hierarchy has depth one. The repeated line of code, z = z + x, is translated to a sequence of four bytecode instructions.

As Figure 8 shows, SPIN runtimes scale roughly quadratically with the size of the method and the associated constant factors are small enough to allow practical large scale verification. In contrast, SMV has acceptable verification times until a threshold of around 200 instructions, and then scales quite poorly. It may

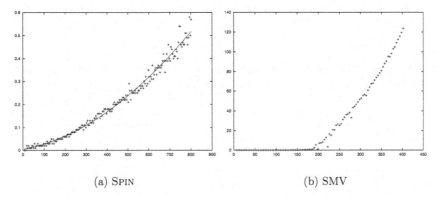

(a) SPIN   (b) SMV

Fig. 8. Verification time depending on the number of instructions

be possible to delay this threshold by tuning different system specific parameters (e.g., the size of hash tables). However, the symbolic representation of the entire state space in SMV can lead to memory problems, even with good variable orderings, and results in runtimes orders of magnitude larger than SPIN's. Perhaps surprisingly, these problems appear in even such a simple test.

Number of Variables. In this test, we varied the number of local variables, which also constitute the arguments of the method. To insure that all variables are used, the method body simply cyclically permutes the contents of the variables. This is done in such a way that the number of assignments, and thus the number of instructions, is the same in each method.

Figure 10 displays the results. For SPIN, the number of variables has little effect on the explicit state-space exploration: the time consumed grows very slowly as a function of the number of variables[2]. The slight variations are caused by the time required to initialize the transition system (that is, SPIN's `init` routine, which assigns to each variable its initial value), which is linear in the number of variables. Apart from this, the time required is constant as only a constant set of states (one for each program point, cf. Section 3.3) is reachable. In contrast, SMV's time complexity grows rapidly in the number of variables and quickly becomes impractical with more than 20 variables. This is not too surprising since SMV must represent and manipulate the complete transition system. Symbolic representation using BDDs provides some help here: As suggested by Figure 11 (logarithmic scale for the y-axis), the growth is subexponential since BDDs can compress the representation somewhat. Still, this is, in general, the major bottleneck with symbolic model checking, and it is a substantial problem in this particular domain.

---

[2] Due to limited timing accuracy, this slow growth manifests itself in Figure 10 in a subtle way. Namely, almost all times lie between 0.06 and 0.08 seconds, but the concentration at 0.07 and 0.08 is higher as more variables are added.

```
void m_1(int v0)       void m_2(int v0, int v1)    void m_3(int v0, int v1, int v2)
{ v0 = v0;             { v0 = v1;                   { v0 = v1;
  v0 = v0;               v1 = v0;                     v1 = v2;
  v0 = v0; }             v0 = v1; }                   v2 = v0; }
```

Fig. 9. Schema of methods to test dependency of complexity on the number of local variables

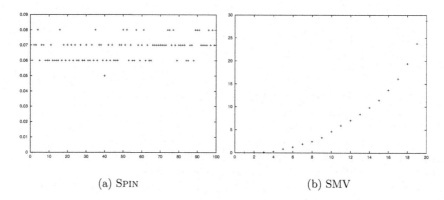

(a) SPIN   (b) SMV

Fig. 10. Verification time versus number of local variables

Class Hierarchy Depth. For this test we generated a linear hierarchy of 100 classes, $C_1, \ldots, C_{100}$, such that C_{i+1} is a direct subclass of C_i. An additional class contains 100 methods, $m_1, \ldots m_{100}$, to be checked. Each of these method takes 100 arguments. The arguments all have the same type in the first method. The second method has arguments of two different types and, in the general case, the ith method's arguments are of i different types. For each method, the method body consists of a single assignment statement. Since these assignments are all identical, the abstract transition system is the same for every method. However, the state space grows as more types are present; moreover, the properties to be checked also become more complex. In the case of SPIN, the depth of the class hierarchy has no effect on the verification time as the set of reachable states does not change as more types are added (the variation of 0.01 seconds is due to inaccurate timing).

In the case of SMV, the verification time grows linearly with the number of different types. Examining the graph, we can identify four different groups of methods, where the ith group contains methods using 2^i to $2^{i+1} - 1$ different class types. The reason for this grouping is that for the ith group SMV requires $i + 2$ bits to represent these types and it appears that a small additional amount of time (corresponding to the small gap between the groups) is required to manipulate the larger BDDs. Note that the 100 local variables used do not blow up the state space as only c_1 is actually used; that is, in this example the BDDs achieve an exponential compression of the state space.

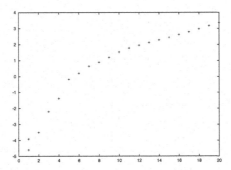

Fig. 11. Verification time versus number of local variables for SMV(logarithmic scale)

```
public void m_1    (C_1 c_1, C_1 c_2,  ..., C_1    c_100) {c_1.field = 0;}
public void m_2    (C_1 c_1, C_2 c_2,  ..., C_1    c_100) {c_1.field = 0;}
                                   :
public void m_100 (C_1 c_1, C_2 c_2,  ..., C_100 c_100) {c_1.field = 0;}
```

Fig. 12. Schema of methods for testing dependency of complexity of depth of class hierarchy

Depth of Subroutine Nesting. Our last test considered methods that contain nested subroutines where the depth of the nesting is increased in each method. As explained in Section 2.2, verifying subroutines is one of the more delicate issues in bytecode verification. The fact that verifying subroutines by model checking is much simpler than verifying them conventionally comes at the price of exponential time consumption! Both SPIN and SMV do not cope well with checking nested subroutines, as Figure 15 illustrates. Since subroutines are polymorphic in the local variables that are not used in the subroutine, the reachable state space in this case is exponential in the depth of subroutine nesting. BDDs do not have any significant impact on this explosion.

3.3   Analysis

In the following we compare the complexity of conventional bytecode verification with model checking. Let *ins* be the number of program points, T the number of types, *maxloc* the number of local variables, and *maxstack* the maximal stack height. For conventional bytecode verification, the size of the state space is

$$ins \cdot \left(2^T\right)^{maxloc+maxstack},$$

as each program point is (due to multiple inheritance) associated with a set of types for the local variables and stack positions. Despite the size of this search

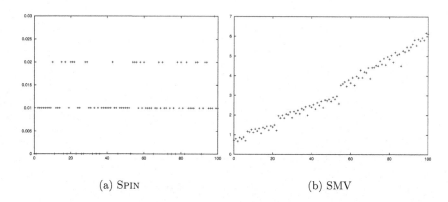

(a) SPIN   (b) SMV

Fig. 13. Verification time versus depth of class hierarchy

```
public void m_1() {              public void m_2() {
  int x = 0;                       int x = 0;

  x++;   // repeated 52 times      x++;   // repeated 39 times
  try {throw new Exception();}     try {throw new Exception();}
  catch (Exception e) {}           catch (Exception e) {}
  finally {} }                     finally{
                                     try{throw new Exception();}
                                     catch (Exception e) {}
                                     finally{} } }
```

Fig. 14. Sample method for testing complexity of subroutine nesting

space, in conventional bytecode verification, only linearly many states ever need to be explored. In particular, the method type that associates a state type with every program point is computed by iterating an abstract interpretation of the method. The algorithm starts with a method type that associates the bottom type to each program point. In each iteration, the state types belonging to different execution paths are merged by taking their supremum. This yields a new state type for each program point that is larger or equal (under the subtyping order) than that of the previous iteration. This process terminates when a fixed point is reached or an error is found. Structural restrictions placed on bytecode (e.g. no two subroutines can be terminated by the same return instruction) guarantee that the number of iterations required is linear in the number of program points. Since no iteration can decrease the types associated with any program position, a fixed point must be reached in $O(ins \cdot T \cdot (maxloc + maxstack))$ iterations.

In the case of model checking, the state space is also exponential. However, as program points are associated with types, instead of sets of types, the size is

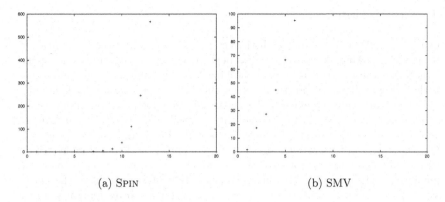

(a) SPIN   (b) SMV

Fig. 15. Verification time versus depth of the subroutine nesting

$$ins \cdot T^{maxloc+maxstack}.$$

The complexity of model checking itself depends on the algorithm used. Symbolic methods manipulate a representation of the entire state space and, as we have seen, can require exponential resources to do so. However, assuming that the nesting of subroutines has some fixed upper bound (in practice the nesting is almost never greater than two), in correct methods only $O(ins)$ of these states are reachable since there is only one state type possible for each program point.

This tractability result only holds for type-correct bytecode. For incorrect bytecode there can indeed be exponentially many reachable states since any type can be associated with any local variable or stack position at each program point. Preliminary experiments with incorrect bytecode confirm that checking it is considerably more resource intensive than checking correct bytecode. For even small methods consisting of less than 100 instructions, both SPIN and SMV are incapable of finding errors; typically SPIN fails to terminate and SMV runs out of memory. This is not a problem in practice; when too many resources are used, one may either time out (giving a conservative answer) or use an alternative approach to detect an error.

For detecting errors in incorrect code we have found the following "property simplification" approach useful. Instead of checking the correctness properties for all instructions simultaneously (e.g., the large conjunct in Figure 5), the properties checked are split (divide-and-conquer) into subproperties, which are individually checked in separate model checking runs. In the extreme case, we can individually check the safety of each transition from each possible program point (e.g., perform a model checking run for each conjunct in Figure 5). This trades off space for time, reducing the size of the overall transition system for each run, which is the product of the transition system modeling the method and the transition system representing the properties. This approach has proved adequate for finding type flaws in our tests. Bounded model checking [1] is an interesting possible alternative, as normally the paths to errors are fairly small.

4   Conclusion

Our investigation is the first, realistic, large scale study of bytecode verification by model checking. Moreover, to the best of our knowledge, it is one of the larger case studies in using model checking for static analysis. Our conclusion is that, despite being theoretically intractable in the worst case, model checking is in fact practically viable. The key insight is that for practical applications, validating *correct* code is important; this is feasible since only linearly many states are accessible (provided subroutine nesting is limited, as it is in practice). Our tests confirm that explicit state, on-the-fly model checkers like SPIN can be successfully employed for these kinds of problems; this is in contrast to symbolic model checkers like SMV that must manipulate representations of the entire state space. However, it is open, and an area for further investigation whether alternative encodings of the transition system and the correctness requirements could result in competitive performance.

The system we have implemented can model check full JVM bytecode, i.e., it models all 200 instructions of the JVM. Currently, the only feature missing is code to model object initialization. This has been implemented, but it is not yet completely tested and remains as future work. This issue is rather subtle as explained in [3,6]. In addition, as future work we would also like to investigate the question of how such a general framework can be used to go beyond model checking type safety properties and validate other kinds of security properties of bytecode.

References

1. A. Biere, A. Cimatti, E. Clarke, and Y. Zhu. Symbolic model checking without BDDs. In *TACAS'99*, volume 1579 of *LNCS*, Amsterdam, the Netherlands, 1999. Springer-Verlag.
2. R. Cohen. The defensive java virtual machine specification. Technical report, Computational Logic Inc., 1997.
3. S. N. Freund and J. C. Mitchell. The type system for object initialization in the Java bytecode language. *ACM Transactions on Programming Languages and Systems*, 21(6):1196–1250, Nov. 1999.
4. G. J. Holzmann. The Spin model checker. *IEEE Transactions on Software Engineering*, 23(5):279–295, May 1997.
5. K. McMillan. *Symbolic Model Checking: An Approach to the State Explosion Problem*. PhD thesis, School of Computer Science, Carnegie Mellon University, Pittsburgh, PA, May 1992. CMU-CS-92-131.
6. X. Leroy. Java bytecode verification: An overview. In *Computer Aided Verification, 13th International Conference*, volume 2001 of *LNCS*, pages 265–285, Paris, France, July 2001. Springer-Verlag.
7. T. Lindholm and F. Yellin. *The Java Virtual Machine Specification*. Number 1102 in The Java Series. Addison-Wesley, Reading, MA, USA, Jan. 1997.
8. T. Nipkow. Verified bytecode verifiers. In *Foundations of Software Science and Computation Structures (FOSSACS 2001)*, volume 2030 of *LNCS*, pages 347–363. Springer-Verlag, 2001.

9. J. Posegga and H. Vogt. Byte code verification for Java smart cards based on model checking. In *Proceedings of the Fifth ESORICS*, volume 1485 of *LNCS*, pages 175–190, Louvain-la-Neuve, Belgium, Sept. 1998. Springer-Verlag.

10. C. Pusch. Formalizing the Java Virtual Machine in Isabelle/HOL. Technical Report TUM-I9816, Institut für Informatik, Technische Universiät München, 1998.

11. C. Pusch. Proving the soundness of a Java bytecode verifier specification in Isabelle/HOL. In *Tools and Algorithms for the Construction and Analysis of Systems (TACAS'99)*, volume 1579 of *LNCS*, pages 89–103, Amsterdam, the Netherlands, 1999. Springer-Verlag.

12. Z. Qian. A formal specification of Java virtual machine instructions for objects, methods and subroutines. In *Formal Syntax and Semantics of Java*, volume 1523 of *LNCS*, pages 271–311. Springer-Verlag, 1999.

13. Z. Qian. Standard fixpoint iteration for Java bytecode verification. *ACM Transactions on Programming Languages and Systems*, 22(4):638–672, 2000.

14. D. Schmidt. Data flow analysis is model checking of abstract interpretations. In *Conference record of POPL '98*, pages 38–48, San Diego, 1998. ACM Press.

15. D. Schmidt and B. Steffen. Program analysis as model checking of abstract interpretations. In *Proceedings of Static Analysis Symposium (SAS'98)*, volume 1503 of *LNCS*, pages 351–380, Pisa, Italy, September 1998. Springer-Verlag.

16. R. F. Stärk and J. Schmid. Java bytecode verification is not possible. In *Formal Methods and Tools for Computer Science, Eurocast*. Universidad de Las Palmas de Gran Canaria, 2001. Extended Abstract.

17. R. Stata and M. Abadi. A type system for Java bytecode subroutines. *ACM Transactions on Programming Languages and Systems*, 21(1):90–137, Jan. 1999.

18. F. Yellin. Low level security in Java. In *World Wide Web Journal: The Fourth International WWW Conference Proceedings*, pages 369–380, Cambridge, MA, 1995. O'Reilly.

The Influence of Software Module Systems on Modular Verification

Harry C. Li[2], Kathi Fisler[1], and Shriram Krishnamurthi[2]

[1] Department of Computer Science, Worcester Polytechnic Institute
[2] Computer Science Department, Brown University

Abstract. The effectiveness of modular model checking for hardware makes it tempting to apply these techniques to software. Existing modular techniques have been driven by the parallel-composition semantics of hardware. New architectures for software, however, combine sequential and parallel composition. These new, *feature-oriented*, architectures mandate developing new methodologies. They repay the effort by yielding better modular verification techniques.

This paper demonstrates the impact of feature-oriented architectures on modular model checking. We have implemented an explicit-state model checker and applied it to a real software system to validate our prior, theoretical work on feature-oriented verification. Our study highlights three results. First, it confirms that the state-space overhead arising from our methodology is minimal. Second, it demonstrates that feature-oriented architectures reduce the need for the property decompositions that often plague modular verification. Third, it reveals that, independent of our methodology, feature-oriented designs inherently control state-space explosion.

1 Introduction

Recent advances and successes in the computer-aided verification of hardware fuel the desire to effectively apply these ideas to software. Such work aims to develop models and analyses that simplify early detection of software design errors without disrupting the design flow. Early detection requires that techniques for *verifying* software be closely intertwined with the techniques and tools for *designing* and *producing* software. Verification techniques and development techniques must therefore evolve together if verification is to be viable for substantial software systems.

The hardware model-checking community has long demonstrated that the bond between design and verification can go beyond necessity to symbiosis: in particular, that decomposing designs according to their modular structure can reduce an intractable verification problem into a collection of tractable ones. The results of the tractable verifications can be combined into results on the otherwise-intractable overall design. The general idea of modular verification applies to software as well, but with a technical twist: *modules in software design are evolving towards a model that violates the assumptions underlying existing modular verification techniques.*

D. Bošnački and S. Leue (Eds.): SPIN 2002, LNCS 2318, pp. 60–78, 2002.

Traditional modules encapsulate participants (or *actors*) and contain the code that the actor needs to implement the features (operations/services) of the system. Modern software modules encapsulate *features* rather than actors. These *feature-oriented designs* realign the module boundaries so that all of the code pertaining to a single operation lies in the same module; the modules therefore *cross-cut* actors. Researchers have proposed feature-oriented modules under many names (*refinements* [7], *units* [18], *aspects* [29], *collaborations* [33], *hyper-slices* [35], and others); some have spoken of feature-oriented programming [37] or feature engineering [40] in more general terms. Ongoing research on feature-oriented modules shows that they simplify key software engineering problems such as configurability, maintainability, and evolution [4,18].

Since features often operate exclusively from one another, feature-oriented modules do not compose in parallel. Instead, their composition model employs a certain combination of parallel and sequential composition. Existing modular verification techniques assume either purely parallel or purely sequential composition; accordingly, none of them apply to feature-oriented designs. In previous work, we proposed a methodology for modular verification of feature-oriented designs [20]. The existence of this methodology, however, does not address the more crucial practical question: do feature-oriented modules simplify or facilitate verification in practice?

This paper argues that feature-oriented modules are better suited for modular verification than traditional module systems. We present a case study on verifying a substantial feature-oriented software design with our new modular verification methodology. We base our claims about the superiority of feature-oriented modules for verification on the following observations:

- They simplify the problem of decomposition in verification because such modules naturally align with properties. This reduces, and often even eliminates, the current need for property decomposition in modular verification.
- They provide a felicitous framework for composing results of modular verifications into results on whole systems, while avoiding some of the circularity difficulties inherent in classical modular verification work.
- Their design discipline appears to even inherently control state-space explosion.

Section 2 motivates and illustrates feature-oriented modules by describing the software system that we use in the case study. Section 3 summarizes our methodology for feature-oriented modular verification. Section 4 presents our case study using this methodology to verify the design described in Section 2. Section 5 discusses related work, and Section 6 offers concluding remarks and outlines future work.

2   FSATS: An Example of Feature-Oriented Design

FSATS is a simulator for command-and-control missions. Missions involve a hierarchy of (military) personnel; each person in the hierarchy commands a set of weapons. In a simulated mission, certain personnel identify potential targets and initiate a communication protocol to determine who (if anyone) will attack the target. This decision is based on a series of factors including the nature and location of the target, as well as the availability of weapons at each point of the hierarchy. Once a person accepts responsibility for a mission, he commands his weapons to attack the target.

One of the main challenges a programmer experiences in implementing FSATS is that the personnel and weapons hierarchies need to be sufficiently flexible to simulate a variety of military scenarios. This requires several kinds of customizations:

- Certain terrains preclude certain classes of weapons; the weapons controlled by each person must change according to the terrain under simulation.
- Different branches of the military employ different personnel hierarchies; each person's superiors in the hierarchy must therefore be flexible.
- Different situations may require personnel to respond differently to the same nature and location of target; thus the algorithm for deciding whether someone can accept a mission requires flexibility, sometimes on-the-fly.

Constructing separate simulators from scratch for each potential scenario is infeasible. FSATS implementations therefore need to be customizable along all of these lines with minimal reconfiguration effort. Linking is acceptable when building a new simulator, but modification to existing code is not. Batory, Johnson, MacDonald, and von Heeder [5] designed and implemented FSATS using feature-oriented modules to endow it with these capabilities. This implementation uses Batory's JTS system [6], a Java front-end developed to support feature-oriented modules. This section uses their decisions and observations to motivate (Section 2.1) and define (Section 2.2) feature-oriented design.

2.1   Feature-Oriented Designs

FSATS consists of personnel and weapons (collectively called the *actors*) and missions for firing on targets (the *features* or operations that the actors cooperate to implement). For each actor/mission pair such that the actor participates in the mission, FSATS contains code fragment(s) implementing the actor's role in the mission. The architecture organizes these code fragments into cohesive constructs, such as classes and modules. Viewing the actor/mission pairs as a grid, two organizations jump to mind (Figure 1): modules can align with actors/columns (actor-oriented modules), or modules can align with missions/rows (feature-oriented modules). The figure shows the code fragments as state machines, which is how the FSATS design expresses its mission protocols. The extraction of FSATS to our state machine models therefore required no special or intensive effort.

To motivate the appeal of feature-oriented modules, consider the problem of adding or removing missions from a simulator. For a given set of target conditions, several actors are involved in deciding which mission to execute. Altering

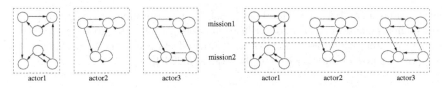

Fig. 1. Two modularizations of FSATS: actor-oriented (left) and feature-oriented (right); the dashed boxes delimit module boundaries in each figure

missions under actor-oriented modules therefore requires modifying the modules for each actor involved in the mission. As the code corresponding to a single mission may not be cleanly isolated in the original code (since multiple missions may involve similar decision-making processes), this editing operation is potentially expensive (not to mention error prone). With feature-oriented modules, in contrast, each module encapsulates code for a mission centered around a particular weapon under a certain set of conditions. To remove a weapon from the system, a programmer can simply re-compose the system without the missions (modules) that use a weapon; the original implementor performed the necessary decomposition, so no editing of code is required.

Feature-oriented modules have been called *collaborations*, since a module encapsulates the code through which the actors collaborate to perform an operation. We adopt the term *collaboration* in the rest of this paper. In FSATS, each actor/mission code fragment is a class. A collaboration is therefore an ordered tuple of classes, one per actor. Collaboration composition connects the classes for each actor via object-oriented inheritance. The resulting (single) class contains all of the code needed to implement each mission for that (single) actor.

FSATS's requirement of flexible personnel hierarchies mandates that classes within collaborations have parameterized super-classes. For example, assume that battalion leaders report to brigade leaders in one simulator and to division command in another. These simulators require different collaborations for their core communications protocols. A designer implementing a mission involving battalions does not know which communication collaboration to use; that decision happens at system-composition time[1]. The designer therefore cannot fix the super-classes of the classes in his collaboration; he can, however, impose constraints on them through interfaces. Classes with parameterized super-classes are called *mixins* [10,22,38,42].

Collaborations comprised of mixins provide the flexibility needed to implement FSATS. Different FSATS simulators are built by selecting weapons and communications collaborations and composing them to form a complete simulator. As described here, collaborations obey the characteristics of components [22], such as separate compilation, multiple instantiability and external linkage. A brief sampling of other successful designs in this domain includes

---

[1] In other words, collaborations are composed through *client-controlled* or *third-party* linking.

protocol layers and database modules [7,8,41], a programming environment [17], test-bench generators [25] and verification tools [21,39]. The growing application of collaboration-based architectures also reflects in the increased language support for programming with collaborations [6,22,34].

2.2   A Formal Model of FSATS

Having motivated the overall architecture of FSATS, we now describe a more formal model of collaborations, their interfaces, and their compositions that we use in our verification methodology. In FSATS, two pieces of code implement a particular actor's role in a mission. The first is a state machine fragment that specifies a mission-specific communication protocol. The second is a set of rules that govern whether an actor is equipped to accept a particular mission (based on his weapons' status and capacity). Our case study verifies properties of the communication protocol, not of the weapons selection rules. We therefore adopt a simpler view of FSATS in which each collaboration consists of a tuple of state machine fragments and an interface for composing collaborations; each state machine fragment extends an existing (base) state machine by adding nodes, edges, and/or paths between states in the base machine.

Each base or composed design specifies interfaces, in terms of states, at which clients may attach extensions (i.e additional collaborations). We define interfaces formally below. In our experience, new features generally attach to the base design at common or predictable points; the set of interfaces is therefore small. This is important, as the interface states will indicate information that we must gather about a design in order to perform compositional verification of collaborations; a large number of interfaces might require too much overhead in our methodology.

The following formal definition from our earlier paper [20] makes our model of collaboration-based designs precise. The definitions match the intuition in the figures, so a casual reader may wish to skip the formal definition.

Definition 1 A *state machine* is a tuple $\langle S, \Sigma, \Delta, s_0, R, L \rangle$, where S is a set of states, Σ is the input alphabet, Δ is the output alphabet, $s_0 \in S$ is the initial state, $R \subseteq S \times PL(\Sigma) \times S$ is the transition relation (where $PL(\Sigma)$ denotes the set of propositional logic expressions over Σ), and $L : S \rightarrow 2^{\Delta}$ indicates which output symbols are true in each state.

Definition 2 A *base system* is a tuple $\langle M_1, \ldots, M_k \rangle$ of state machines and a set of *interfaces*. We denote the elements of machine M_i as $\langle S_{Mi}, \Sigma_{Mi}, \Delta_{Mi}, s_{0_{Mi}}, R_{Mi}, L_{Mi} \rangle$. An interface contains a sequence of pairs of states

$$\langle \langle exit_1, reentry_1 \rangle, \ldots, \langle exit_k, reentry_k \rangle \rangle.$$

Each $exit_i$ and $reentry_i$ is a state in machine M_i. State $exit_i$ is a state from which control can enter an extension machine, and $reentry_i$ is a state from which control returns to the base system. Interfaces also contain a set of properties and other information which are derived from the base system during verification; we describe these properties in detail in later sections.

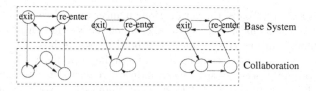

Fig. 2. Collaborations, interfaces, and composition

Definition 3 An *extension* is a tuple $\langle E_1, \ldots, E_n \rangle$ of state machines. Each E_i must induce a connected graph, must have a single initial state with in-degree zero, and must have a single state with out-degree zero. For each E_i, we refer to the initial state as in_i and the state with out-degree zero as out_i. States in_i and out_i serve as placeholders for the states to which the collaboration will connect when composed with a base system. Neither of these states is in the domain of the labeling function L_i.

Given a base system B, one of its interfaces I, and an extension E, we can form a new system by connecting the machines in E to those in B through the states in I, as shown in Figure 2. For the purposes of this paper, we assume that B and E contain the same number of state machines. This restriction is easily relaxed; the relaxed form allows actors to not participate in each new feature, or to allow new actors as required by new features. We also assume that the states in the constituent machines of base systems and extensions are distinct.

Definition 4 Composing base system $B = \langle M_1, \ldots, M_k \rangle$ and extension collaboration $E = \langle E_1, \ldots, E_k \rangle$ via an interface $I = \langle \langle exit_1, reentry_1 \rangle, \ldots, \langle exit_k, reentry_k \rangle \rangle$ yields a tuple $\langle C_1, \ldots, C_k \rangle$ of state machines. Each $C_i = \langle S_{Ci}, \Sigma_{Ci}, \Delta_{Ci}, s_{0_{Ci}}, R_{Ci}, L_{Ci} \rangle$ is defined from $M_i = \langle S_{Mi}, \Sigma_{Mi}, \Delta_{Mi}, s_{0_{Mi}}, R_{Mi}, L_{Mi} \rangle$ and its corresponding extension $E_i = \langle S_{Ei}, \Sigma_{Ei}, \Delta_{Ei}, s_{0_{Ei}}, R_{Ei}, L_{Ei} \rangle$ as follows: $S_{Ci} = S_{Mi} \cup S_{Ei} - \{in_i, out_i\}$; $s_{0_{Ci}} = s_{0_{Mi}}$; R_{Ci} is formed by replacing all references to in_i and out_i in R_{Ei} with $exit_i$ and $reentry_i$, respectively, and unioning it with R_{Mi}. All other components are the union of the corresponding pieces from M_i and E_i. We will refer to the cross-product of $C_1, \ldots, C_k$ as the *global composed state machine*.

Definition 4 allows composed designs to serve as subsequent base systems by creating additional interfaces as necessary. This supports the notion of compound components that is fundamental in most definitions of component-based systems.

3   Modular Verification of Collaborative Designs

Modular verification succeeds when the designer can isolate portions of a design that are relevant to properties. Assume we wish to verify a property that all actors participate in executing. An actor-oriented architecture naturally decomposes into individual actor modules. The property, however, typically relates to a *feature*, not an actor. Thus, the verification engineer must *decompose the property to align with the modular structure*. Experience shows that this task can be extremely difficult in practice because it is hard to isolate how one particular actor (or small set of actors) contributes to satisfying a property. Furthermore, actor-based property decompositions can induce circularity in the assumptions of behavior between modules [13]. Despite techniques for avoiding circularity problems [3,24], decomposition remains challenging in practice.

In contrast, collaboration-based designs often avoid both property decomposition and circularity problems because the modules naturally decompose around features. If the property concerns a feature, collaborations isolate the relevant portion of the system by design. Ideally, we should thus be able to verify a property of a feature by analyzing the relevant collaborations in isolation from the rest of the system. Our methodology provides a mechanism for doing this.

What about properties that concern actors rather than features? Wouldn't an actor-oriented architecture be more suitable for proving those properties? Collaborations actually support both actor-oriented and feature-oriented decompositions. A full design is composed from a set of collaborations, which are tuples of mixins. If a property concerns the behavior of a single actor across multiple features, a verification tool can extract the actor's mixins from the collaborations, compose them via inheritance, and verify the property against the result. In short, collaborations can be composed either vertically or horizontally (as shown in Figure 1) as needed. Designing systems to support both actor- and feature-oriented composition does, however, force designers to break actors down into feature-sized pieces. The variety of systems that designers have built using collaborations suggests that programmers are willing to do this work in exchange for the benefits associated with collaboration-based designs.

A Methodology for Verifying Collaborations Modularly

This section summarizes our methodology for verifying properties against individual collaborations using CTL model checking; the full formal details appear in a separate paper [20]. The methodology currently supports the following activities:

1. Proving a CTL property of individual or compositions of collaborations.
2. Deriving *preservation constraints* on the interface states of a collaboration that are sufficient to preserve each property after composition.
3. Proving that a collaboration satisfies the preservation constraints of another collaboration (or existing system). We establish preservation by analyzing only the extension, not the composition of the two collaborations.

The main challenge in the methodology lies in the first activity. In order to model check a property against a collaboration, we need a single state machine for the global cross-product of the machine fragments in that collaboration. We discuss the issues in constructing this cross product below. The second activity involves recording some information during the CTL model checking process.

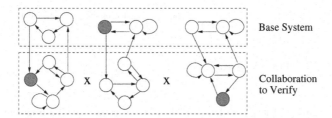

Fig. 3. Constructing collaboration cross-products to enable model checking. The shaded states represent a reachable state in the overall system; this cross-collaboration state arises during the transition from one feature to another.

The third involves mostly routine CTL model checking, with an initial seeding of labels on certain states of a design. We use CTL rather than LTL because the CTL semantics supports the state labelings that we need for our methodology; adapting our methodology to LTL is an open problem.

Let us examine the task of constructing the cross-product of the state machine fragments in a collaboration. Figure 3 illustrates the situation: we wish to verify the lower collaboration in isolation from the upper one. Since actors operate in parallel within a collaboration, we must therefore construct the cross product of the state machine fragments in the lower collaboration (as the x's between the fragments in the lower collaboration indicate). Cross-product constructions begin with a set of initial (cross-product) states. What, though, are the initial states of the lower collaboration? Only the base system contains the initial states for the final, fully composed design. For other collaborations, only their "in" states (in the interface) give any indication of how to start running the collaboration.

It is tempting to assume that all actors will enter the collaboration for a feature at the same time: that is, to assume that the tuple of "exit" states from the interface is reachable. Unfortunately, practice violates this simplistic assumption. In FSATS, the person accepting a mission enters the collaboration for that mission and sends a message to that effect along the chain of command. As other people receive the message, they too enter the collaboration. While it is true that once one actor enters the collaboration the others will (eventually) follow, they do not enter the collaboration all at once. Figure 3 illustrates this situation through the shaded states; two actors have entered the collaboration, while the middle actor has not yet made that transition. Detecting the initial states of the collaboration to verify is therefore non-trivial. Furthermore, the shaded states also illustrate that some reachable cross-product states span collaborations. Such states are reachable only during the transition from one collaboration (feature) to another.

In FSATS, all mission collaborations (all collaborations other than the base system) attach to the base system. We have presented a formal algorithm that exploits this organization to identify the cross-collaboration states; our methodology uses these states to drive the cross-product construction for the collab-

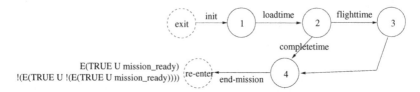

Fig. 4. A example of the methodology. The depicted state machine fragment is the FSATS state machine for the mortar actor in the mortar mission. The dashed states are placeholders for the interface states to which the mortar collaboration attaches. The formulas next to the "re-enter" state are the seeded labels; these labels were copied from the mortar actor base machine (not depicted). CTL model checking determines labels on the "exit" state based on the seeded labels.

oration [20]. The construction includes the cross-collaboration states with the collaboration cross-product, which guarantees that our methodology visits all reachable cross-product states; details appear in our earlier work [20]. This process may add a few states to the state machine fragments in each collaboration; we explore the impact of these extra states experimentally in Section 4. Once we identify the initial states, we use a standard cross-product construction to obtain a single state machine suitable for model checking the collaboration.

Having computed the cross-product for a collaboration, we use the standard CTL model checking algorithm [12] to verify properties. Proving that composition preserves the property is the next challenge. This is where collaboration-based verification diverges from standard approaches to modular verification. Under parallel composition, modular verification techniques assume that composition does not add new behaviors to a module. This is a reasonable assumption since the states of two modules interact only through a cross-product construction. In contrast, composing collaborations adds transitions, and thus behaviors, to states in a given module. These extensions are a natural and important part of collaborative designs. This characteristic, however, inhibits the use of modular verification techniques based on parallel composition.

Fortunately, the limited communication between collaborations—which occurs only at the interface states between the collaborations—reduces modular verification to a form of sequential verification. We use Laster and Grumberg's algorithm [32] for compositional model checking under sequential composition for this step. Briefly, when model checking a property against a collaboration, we record the labels that the CTL model checking algorithm assigns to the interface states. When we attach a new collaboration to those states, we check that the new collaboration will not invalidate any of those labels. We perform this step by attaching two dummy states to the new collaboration (one each for exit and re-entry), seeding the dummy re-entry state with the saved interface labels, and using the CTL model checking algorithm to derive labels on the dummy exit state (see Figure 4). If the derived labels are consistent with the recorded labels, the composition will preserve the property of the original collaboration.

With the exception of seeding states with properties, our methodology uses standard CTL model checking algorithms. The contribution of our methodology lies in techniques for computing cross-products of collaborations and in identifying necessary constraints on collaboration interactions to guarantee that our approach is sound with respect to a conventional actor-oriented modularization. We base soundness on the claim that our method would explore the same set of global states as in an actor-oriented, parallel composition of the state-machine fragments. In other words, the state spaces obtained by the two modularizations shown in Figure 1 are equivalent. Our prior work [20] presents the additional constraints needed to achieve soundness; intuitively, these constraints require forms of synchronization between actors at feature boundaries[2].

4   Results on FSATS

Our FSATS case study was designed with several goals in mind:

- To validate our modular verification methodology on a significant software example. FSATS suits this role well: a full FSATS system contains at least 14 actors participating in at least 15 different mission types. The case study reported in this paper used 3 representative mission types over 14 actors.
- To determine the levels of state-space reduction we can achieve through feature-oriented modular decomposition.
- To determine the overhead due to our verification methodology.
- To explore whether feature-oriented modules provide decompositions that naturally align with properties.

This case study employed a base system containing the core communications protocol and three missions: one in which the battalion fires a mortar, one in which a platoon attacks with an artillery unit, and one in which the division commander fires a set of rocket launchers. The mortar and artillery missions embody simple protocols and yield small state machines. The rocket launcher protocol is more complicated because launchers must scurry out of hiding places in order to fire, then return to hiding places to reload during an attack. The coordination of launchers across hiding places gives rise to a protocol similar to *cache coherence*: the division officer must know where the rockets are at all times, and no two rockets can hide in the same spot at the same time.

We chose these three layers for several reasons. First, the mortar and artillery layers share some common design variables, so there is potential for property clashes when these modules are composed. Second, only a portion of the command hierarchy participates in deciding whether to use mortar or artillery, so we have the potential to eliminate unnecessary participants, as we would do in a standard parallel decomposition. Finally, the rocket launcher collaboration is substantially larger than the other two; ignoring this collaboration when reasoning about either of the other two collaborations should noticeably moderate the resources required during verification.

---

[2] These constraints are, incidentally, also necessary for modular testing.

4.1   A Model Checker Supporting the Methodology

Although our methodology centers around the standard CTL model checking algorithm, existing CTL model checkers do not support it well. These checkers embody a closed-world assumption, in which all variables involved in the model are generated within the model. This assumption is invalid in collaborative modular verification. When we verify that composition does not invalidate existing properties of collaborations, we must seed states with non-trivial CTL formulas that would be true in that state after composition. Existing model checkers do not permit this seeding; they instead require all formula labels to be derived during model checking. We could augment the model to accomplish seeding—by adding an automaton sufficient to generate the desired labels—but this change is both drastic and painstaking to perform manually; it also artificially increases the size of the model.

We have implemented a prototype custom model checker that allows seeding of states with arbitrary CTL formulas. If no states are seeded, the model checker behaves as a conventional CTL checker. If states are seeded, then model checking results are valid under the assumption that the seeded formulas hold in their corresponding states. The rest of the methodology discharges this assumption.

Our checker also confirms that models satisfy the constraints that our methodology requires for soundness. These constraints involve checking reachability of certain specific states that we identify based on the interfaces between collaborations. It also confirms that collaborations do not deadlock; this is important for the correctness of our methodology (otherwise the sequential composition does not result in a continuously running system). We have written the prototype in PLT Scheme [17].

4.2   Experiments on the Impact on State-Space Size

Our first experiment assumes that a property is primarily characteristic of one collaboration. We want to verify that property against that collaboration alone for two reasons. First, until we have established that the collaboration correctly implements the property, it isn't worth verifying the property against other collaborations. Second, as independent developers, we may not even know the other collaborations at development time; only the final system integrator will know all the collaborations.

Figures 5-a and 5-b depict two approaches to constructing a state space for this verification. The collaborative design of 5-a allows us to consider just the collaboration of interest. The system in 5-b results from cross-producting actor-oriented machines; each actor-oriented machine results from connecting the base and extension machines via transitions as specified in the interface. For our experiment, we obtained these latter machines by manually linking the machine fragments across collaborations, as we discuss in Section 3. The table below presents this comparison[3].

---

[3] These sizes do not include the environment models that may be needed for model checking.

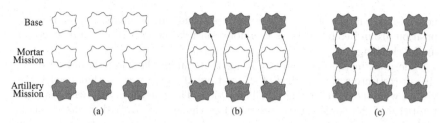

Fig. 5. State-spaces contrasted in our experiments. Each shape represents a state-machine fragment implementing a particular mission (rows) for a particular actor (columns). The shaded shapes indicate which fragments are included in each comparison. If a comparison includes multiple fragments for an actor (as in experiments (b) and (c)), those fragments are linked together prior to constructing the cross product of the individual actors; the arrows between the fragments illustrate these links.

Mission	States in Collaboration Cross-Product (Fig. 5-a)	States in Collab+Base Cross-Product (Fig. 5-b)
Mortar	23	84
Artillery	63	104
Rockets	4,994	14,783

A realistic system consists of numerous missions, not just one. Therefore, a more thorough assessment of state spaces would study the machine sizes that result from composing multiple missions. We contrast two verification tasks. The first verifies properties against the cross-product of an actor-oriented decomposition. This may be given by the programmer; in FSATS, we construct the actors by combining their machine fragments from multiple collaborations (Figure 5-c). The second verifies properties against each of the collaborations separately, in the manner described in section 3. The first two columns of the following table present information on the actor-oriented systems; the third column contrasts this against the sum of the sizes of each collaboration cross-product (because the verifications are performed independently).

Missions (Plus Base)	States in Whole System (Fig. 5-c)	Transitions	(Sum of) States in Individual Collabs
Mortar, Artillery	176	243	23 + 63
Mortar, Rockets	45,773	97,865	23 + 4994
Mortar, Artillery, Rockets	90,260	185,158	23 + 63 + 4994

These data underscore that verifying properties of multiple missions results in additive state-space growth with collaboration-based verification; the growth with no modular verification is potentially multiplicative.

The results in these two tables clearly establish that feature-oriented decomposition can result in substantial state-space reductions. As we would expect, the savings grow more impressive as we add missions to the simulator, because new missions do not affect the state spaces of individual collaborations. Decomposition around collaborations therefore controls the growth of state spaces in model checking.

The data in the first table indicate that our methodology is indeed effective in restricting the number of states from the base system that need to be visited while model checking a collaboration. The following table contrasts the total size of the base system (restricted to the actors involved in the mission) with the number of base system states needed to drive the construction of the collaboration cross-product:

Mission	States in Base Cross-Product	States from Base To Drive Collaboration
Mortar	11	1
Artillery	35	2
Rockets	44	2

In the course of our experiments, we discovered that the choice of interface states can affect our methodology's overhead. In our first model, the Mortar weapon had an almost trivial state machine in the base layer: one state for starting a mission and another for ending a mission. These two states were the interface states to which we attached collaborations involving mortars. The mission starting state was also the initial state for the mortar in the base system. Having the same state be both the initial state of an actor (in the base) and the interface "exit" state caused the number of overhead states to bloat artificially to include the entire base system cross product; this had 11 states in the case of the Mortar mission actors. After introducing a separate state to use as the interface state, the overhead dropped to 1 state, which was what we expected.

Our experiments yielded another surprising result. Based on the sizes of the state machines for the individual actors (between 5 and 100 states per mission for each of 14 actors), we expected the number of cross-product states in each simulator to grow dramatically as we added missions. While we did observe noticeable growth, particularly after adding the rocket mission, the growth was not strictly multiplicative. We later realized that *the synchronization between actors needed to properly implement collaborations naturally limits state explosion, even under standard parallel composition* (since the requirements limit the number of global states involving states from multiple collaborations). This characteristic of collaborations is orthogonal to our methodology, and instead reflects a general benefit of feature-oriented architectures.

To validate this claim, we removed some of the synchronization between actors at collaboration boundaries and recomposed the simulators. Removing the synchronization allows one actor to start a new mission upon completion of an old one, without negotiating with the other actors. This led to a noticeable increase in state-space size in most cases. While Base+Mortar+Artillery did not change in size, the unsynchronized Base+Rocket simulator, which had 14,783 states with synchronization, grew to 534,448 states. We were unable to finish computing the unsynchronized size for the simulator for some configurations, though

Base+Mortar+Rocket grew to over 394,000 states, and Base+Mortar+Artillery+Rocket exceeded 375,000 states before exhausting available memory.

4.3 Modular Verification Experience

Applying existing modular verification techniques can be difficult in practice due to the need to decompose properties while avoiding circular arguments. We therefore wanted to gauge whether our methodology helped or hindered the verification process. This section discusses our observations from using our model checker to verify several properties of FSATS. We do not discuss the actual properties or running times and memory usage. The properties are standard CTL invariants and eventualities. We omit the resource usage data for two reasons. First, we are using explicit-state model checking, so state-space size is a reasonable predictor of performance (unlike with BDDs). Second, our current tool is a proof-of-concept prototype for our algorithms so we expect the resource usage would be artificially high.

Assume a user wants to verify a property about the mortar mission, such as "once started, the mortar eventually fires all rounds". The user provides our model checker with three pieces of information: the base machines for the FSATS actors, the collaboration implementing the mission, and the property to verify. Our tool automatically constructs the cross-product of the collaboration (using information from the base machines), checks whether the collaboration satisfies needed synchronization restrictions, and calls the model checker. Error traces, if any, are of the usual flavor and are expressed relative to the collaboration cross-product. The property and the constraints needed to confirm that it holds after composition are stored with the collaboration. When a user composes a new collaboration onto a system, our tool automatically confirms that existing properties of the collaboration and system are preserved.

In short, a user's interaction with this system is similar to that with a conventional model checker, with the exception of indicating which collaboration each property should be proven against. There is no need to decompose the system or the property. The tool manages all of the assumptions required for modular verification (this entails deriving labels during earlier model checking runs). There is no danger of introducing circularity, because the user does not need to introduce any information; all of the decomposition information comes directly from the design architecture.

Our tool's automated checks for synchronization requirements (mostly various reachability checks) also helped us detect some design errors. For example, the re-entry interface states must be reachable within a collaboration. Our early model of FSATS had some errors that violated this restriction. None of the properties we tried to check would have detected the problem. Thus, our methodology does provide some simple sanity checks on designs that can help locate real errors in system models.

5   Related Work

Several verification techniques use design information to restrict the state space to the portion relevant to a given property. *Cone-of-influence reductions* [31] use dependence analyses between variables to eliminate portions of the state space. These analyses retain portions of the state space needed to reach the relevant portion of the design from the initial states; our method eliminates most of the states traversed from the initial states to the point of entry to a collaboration. Cone-of-influence reductions are also less effective if multiple parts of the design involve the same variables. Multiple FSATS layers refer to shared variables that also occur in the properties we wish to verify; all of these layers would be explored under a cone-of-influence reduction.

Variants of code layering have been used in both software engineering and verification contexts. The term "layered architecture", however, generally assumes that each layer refines a more abstract layer already in the system. Such assumptions correspond to abstraction or refinement layers in verification, in which one layer is shown to subsume the behavior of another [31]. This work is orthogonal to ours, which does not require any abstraction relationship between collaborations. Techniques that combine these two forms of layering is a subject for further research.

Several researchers have described modular verification techniques based on parallel composition [19,23,30,36]. Some preliminary research [2,14,32] considers modular model checking under sequential composition, which is closer to the model used in software. Laster and Grumberg's approach [32] handles designs with only one state machine; it also lacks a design framework, such as collaboration-based design, to drive the decomposition of the design. Subsequent work obtains this decomposition from hierarchical state machines [2] or State-Charts [14], but still considers designs with only one state machine. Our work, in contrast, includes *multiple state machines per collaboration*, which greatly complicates the verification problem. Alur and Yannakakis cite the problem of sequential verification over multiple state machines as open for future work [2]. Alur *et al.* [1] discuss analysis techniques for sequential refinements within modules that are composed in parallel; their work, unlike ours, does not support *coordination* between sequential refinements across modules. None of these works compares the state space sizes in their techniques against those of traditional model checking.

Work on pre- and post-condition verification in theorem proving is another form of modular reasoning under sequential composition. Such work views code at the level of individual, stand-alone functions and instructions, rather than at the level of coordination between multiple actors in a system.

Feature-oriented specifications are common within the community working on the *feature-interaction problem*. Work in this area looks at feature-based specification languages [27], and seeks techniques to detect undesirable interactions between features [9,11]. In some ways, our work has similar goals. Keck and Kuehn provide an extensive survey of the feature interaction problem and approaches to solving it, including several verification-based approaches [28]. To the best of our knowledge, none of these works are specifically considering modular formal verification strategies for features that span multiple actors.

One could view our work as a preliminary verification methodology for a restricted form of aspect-oriented programming [29]. Aspects in their full generality lack a suitable verification methodology; current efforts are still geared at providing a formal semantics of aspect-oriented programming [44]. We believe more restricted models of features than full aspects are necessary to support modular verification strategies.

6   Conclusions and Future Work

Modular verification is an attractive approach to managing state explosion. Modules, by design, delineate somewhat independent portions of a system. In theory, we should be able to exploit this independence to decompose intractable verification problems into tractable ones about each module (or small groups of modules). Experience shows that modular verification is extremely difficult to use in practice. The main challenge lies in *property decomposition*: the need to decompose a property of a system into sub-properties of its modules. Traditional modules reflect *physical* independence (different devices on a chip, for instance) rather than *behavioral* independence. Since properties concern behavior, conventional modular structures are misaligned with properties and make modular decomposition difficult.

Collaborations are modules that encapsulate code involved in the same operation in a system. They have received increasing attention in software engineering because their separation of behavior simplifies software evolution, configuration, and maintenance. This paper explores the effect of these designs on modular model checking, especially on state space sizes and on the need for property decomposition.

We present a case study of applying a new model checker we have developed to a real command-and-control simulator called FSATS. The results are extremely positive. Collaborations dramatically reduced the size of the state space to be explored during model checking, while requiring no property decomposition. Furthermore, we observed that the programming discipline of collaborations requires certain synchronizations that naturally control state-space growth. The ease of modular verification in this framework, combined with the measured reductions in state space sizes, suggest that collaborations provide more useful modularizations for verification than conventional modules do. While we needed to develop a custom model checker for this work, the differences between our checker and standard ones are conceptually simple; we therefore believe one could integrate our approach into existing CTL checkers with a little re-engineering.

Section 3 explained that we use CTL rather than LTL in our work. CTL is more amenable to our state-labeling method because CTL algorithms traverse and label individual states. LTL algorithms, in contrast, reduce to cycle detection on automata and do not consider state labelings. This difference arises from the semantics of the two languages; CTL is state-oriented while LTL is path-oriented. The numerous advantages of LTL over CTL [43], however, make an LTL-based version of our methodology attractive. Extending our work to handle LTL remains an open problem that we hope to address in the near future.

We plan to continue our study along several lines. First, we need to confirm our hypothesis that collaboration-based decomposition achieves greater reductions than cone-of-influence analysis. Second, we need to extend our current methodology to support data-intensive designs, instead of just control-intensive ones. FSATS will continue to be an interesting example for this effort, as it involves a combination of a control-intensive communications protocol between personnel and data-intensive decisions within the protocol. Third, our current methodology assumes that collaborations specify control-flow via state machines. We would like to extend existing work on deriving state machines from source code [15,16,26] to extract collaboration-oriented models. A related question asks whether our collaboration-based organization is too restrictive; it may be possible to extract collaboration-like behavior from code that is composed in parallel, perhaps by examining synchronization points.

Acknowledgment

The authors thank Don Batory for access to and assistance with the FSATS source and for many fruitful discussions on feature-oriented design. This work was supported by NSF grant ESI-0010064.

References

1. R. Alur, R. Grosu, and M. McDougall. Efficient reachability analysis of hierarchic reactive machines. In *International Conference on Computer-Aided Verification*, volume 1855 of *Lecture Notes in Computer Science*, pages 280–295. Springer-Verlag, 2000.
2. R. Alur and M. Yannakakis. Model checking of hierarchical state machines. In *Symposium on the Foundations of Software Engineering*, pages 175–188, 1998.
3. N. Amla, E. A. Emerson, K. S. Namjoshi, and R. Trefler. Assume-guarantee based compositional reasoning for synchronous timing diagrams. In *Conference on Tools and Algorithms for the Construction and Analysis of Systems*, 2001.
4. D. Batory, C. Johnson, B. MacDonald, and D. von Heeder. Achieving extensibility through product-lines and domain-specific languages: A case study. In *International Conference on Software Reuse*, June 2000.
5. D. Batory, C. Johnson, B. MacDonald, and D. von Heeder. FSATS: An extensible C4I simulator for army fire support. In *Workshop on Product Lines for Command-and-Control Ground Systems at the First International Software Product Line Conference (SPLC1)*, August 2000.
6. D. Batory, B. Lofaso, and Y. Smaragdakis. JTS: Tools for implementing domain-specific languages. In *International Conference on Software Reuse*, June 1998.
7. D. Batory and S. O'Malley. The design and implementation of hierarchical software systems with reusable components. *ACM Transactions on Software Engineering and Methodology*, 1(4):355–398, Oct. 1992.

8. E. Biagioni, R. Harper, P. Lee, and B. G. Milnes. Signatures for a network protocol stack: A systems application of Standard ML. In *ACM Symposium on Lisp and Functional Programming*, 1994.
9. J. Blom, R. Bol, and L. Kempe. Automatic detection of feature interactions in temporal logic. Technical Report DoCS 95/61, Department of Computer Systems, Uppsala University, 1995.
10. G. Bracha. *The Programming Language Jigsaw: Mixins, Modularity and Multiple Inheritance.* PhD thesis, University of Utah, Mar. 1992.
11. K. Braithwaite and J. Atlee. Towards automated detection of feature interactions. In *Feature Interactions in Telecommunications Systems*, pages 36–59. IOS Press, 1994.
12. E. Clarke, E. Emerson, and A. Sistla. Automatic verification of finite-state concurrent systems using temporal logic specifications. *ACM Transactions on Programming Languages and Systems*, 8(2):244–263, 1986.
13. E. Clarke, O. Grumberg, and D. Peled. *Model Checking.* MIT Press, 2000.
14. E. M. Clarke and W. Heinle. Modular translation of Statecharts to SMV. Technical Report CMU-CS-00-XXX, Carnegie Mellon University School of Computer Science, August 2000.
15. J. C. Corbett, M. B. Dwyer, J. Hatcliff, S. Laubach, C. S. Pasareanu, Robby, and H. Zheng. Bandera : Extracting finite-state models from java source code. In *International Conference on Software Engineering*, 2000.
16. M. B. Dwyer and L. A. Clarke. Flow analysis for verifying specifications of concurrent and distributed software. Technical Report UM-CS-1999-052, University of Massachusetts, Computer Science Department, August 1999.
17. R. B. Findler, J. Clements, C. Flanagan, M. Flatt, S. Krishnamurthi, P. Steckler, and M. Felleisen. DrScheme: A programming environment for Scheme. *Journal of Functional Programming*, 2001. To appear.
18. R. B. Findler and M. Flatt. Modular object-oriented programming with units and mixins. In *ACM SIGPLAN International Conference on Functional Programming*, pages 94–104, 1998.
19. B. Finkbeiner, Z. Manna, and H. Sipma. Deductive verification of modular systems. In *Compositionality: The Significant Difference*, volume 1536 of *Lecture Notes in Computer Science*, pages 239–275. Springer-Verlag, 1998.
20. K. Fisler and S. Krishnamurthi. Modular verification of collaboration-based software designs. In *Symposium on the Foundations of Software Engineering*, Sept. 2001.
21. K. Fisler, S. Krishnamurthi, and K. E. Gray. Implementing extensible theorem provers. In *International Conference on Theorem Proving in Higher-Order Logic: Emerging Trends*, Research Report, INRIA Sophia Antipolis, September 1999.
22. M. Flatt, S. Krishnamurthi, and M. Felleisen. Classes and mixins. In *ACM SIGPLAN-SIGACT Symposium on Principles of Programming Languages*, pages 171–183, January 1998.
23. O. Grumberg and D. Long. Model checking and modular verification. In *International Conference on Concurrency Theory*, volume 527 of *Lecture Notes in Computer Science*. Springer-Verlag, 1991.
24. T. A. Henzinger, S. Qadeer, and S. K. Rajamani. Decomposing refinement proofs using assume-guarantee reasoning. In *IEEE International Conference on Computer-Aided Design*, pages 245–252, 2000.
25. Y. Hollander, M. Morley, and A. Noy. The e language: A fresh separation of concerns. In *Proceedings of TOOLS Europe*, Mar. 2001.

26. P. Inverardi, A. Wolf, and D. Yankelevich. Static checking of system behaviors using derived component assumptions. *ACM Transactions on Software Engineering and Methodology*, 9(3):239–272, July 2000.

27. M. Jackson and P. Zave. Distributed feature composition: A virtual architecture for telecommunications services. *IEEE Transactions on Software Engineering*, 24(10):831–847, Oct. 1998.

28. D. O. Keck and P. J. Kuehn. The feature and service interaction problem in telecommunications systems: A survey. *IEEE Transactions on Software Engineering*, 24(10):779–796, Oct. 1998.

29. G. Kiczales, J. Lamping, A. Mendhekar, C. Maeda, C. V. Lopes, J.-M. Loingtier, and J. Irwin. Aspect-oriented programming. In *European Conference on Object-Oriented Programming*, June 1997.

30. O. Kupferman and M. Y. Vardi. Modular model checking. In *Compositionality: The Significant Difference*, volume 1536 of *Lecture Notes in Computer Science*. Springer-Verlag, 1998.

31. R. P. Kurshan. *Computer-Aided Verification of Coordinating Processes: The Automata-Theoretic Approach*. Princeton University Press, 1994.

32. K. Laster and O. Grumberg. Modular model checking of software. In *Conference on Tools and Algorithms for the Construction and Analysis of Systems*, 1998.

33. K. Lieberherr, D. Lorenz, and M. Mezini. Programming with aspectual components. Technical Report NU-CCS-99-01, College of Computer Science, Northeastern University, Mar. 1999.

34. S. McDirmid, M. Flatt, and W. Hsieh. Jiazzi: New age components for old fashioned java. In *Conference on Object-Oriented Programming, Systems, Languages, and Applications*, 2001.

35. H. Ossher and P. Tarr. Multi-dimensional separation of concerns in hyperspace. Technical Report RC 21452(96717), IBM, Apr. 1999.

36. C. S. Pasareanu, M. B. Dwyer, and M. Huth. Assume-guarantee model checking of software: A comparative case study. In *Theoretical and Practical Aspects of SPIN Model Checking*, volume 1680 of *Lecture Notes in Computer Science*. Springer-Verlag, 1999.

37. C. Prehofer. Feature-oriented programming: A fresh look at objects. In *European Conference on Object-Oriented Programming*, number 1241 in Lecture Notes in Computer Science. Springer-Verlag, 1997.

38. Y. Smaragdakis and D. Batory. Implementing layered designs and mixin layers. In *European Conference on Object-Oriented Programming*, pages 550–570, July 1998.

39. K. Stirewalt and L. Dillon. A component-based approach to building formal-analysis tools. In *International Conference on Software Engineering*, 2001.

40. C. R. Turner, A. Fuggetta, L. Lavazza, and A. L. Wolf. A conceptual basis for feature engineering. *Journal of Systems and Software*, 49(1):3–15, Dec. 1999.

41. R. van Renesse, K. Birman, M. Hayden, A. Vaysburd, and D. Karr. Building adaptive systems using Ensemble. Technical Report 97-1638, Department of Computer Science, Cornell University, July 1997.

42. M. VanHilst and D. Notkin. Using role components to implement collaboration-based designs. In *ACM SIGPLAN Conference on Object-Oriented Programming Systems, Languages & Applications*, 1996.

43. M. Y. Vardi. Branching vs. linear time: Final showdown. Available at http://www.cs.rice.edu/ vardi/papers/index.html, 2001.

44. M. Wand, G. Kiczales, and C. Dutchyn. A semantics for advice and dynamic join points on aspect-oriented programming. In *Proceedings of the 9th Workshop on Foundations of Object-Oriented Languages (FOOL)*, 2002.

Extending the Translation from SDL to Promela

Armelle Prigent[1], Franck Cassez[2], Philippe Dhaussy[1], and Olivier Roux[2]

[1] ENSIETA, Brest, France <firstname.name>@ensieta.fr
[2] IRCCyN, Nantes, France <firstname.name>@irccyn.ec-nantes.fr

Abstract. This paper tackles the problem of model-checking SDL programs that use the **save** operator. Previous work on model-checking SDL programs with SPIN consisted in translating SDL into IF (using `sdl2if`) and finally IF to Promela (`if2pml`). However, the **save** operator of SDL is not handled by the (final) translator `if2pml`. We propose an extension of the `if2pml` tool that translates IF into Promela programs with **save** operators. We also add an abstraction method on buffer messages to `if2pml` allowing the user to gather some buffer messages into one abstract value. We use our extended version of `if2pml` to validate an Unmanned Underwater Vehicle (UUV) subsystem specified with SDL.

Keywords: SDL formalism, save operator, model-checking, data abstraction

1 Introduction

SDL for Industrial Applications. The developments of embedded reactive systems are subject to a tight integration of the formal methodologies into the existing software development cycle in order to increase design quality. Our research group is involved in the design of advanced robotics control systems, and we have recently developed pieces of software for an Unmanned Underwater Vehicle (UUV). In this project, as well as for various industrial requirements, we had to specify the system with the SDL formalism, normalized by ITU[1], recommendation Z.100 [ITU94b]. The software has many critical parts involving (ad hoc) communication protocols we have developed, hence the need for a formal verification of safety requirements.

SDL and Formal Verification with SPIN. The SDL VERILOG [VER99] and TELELOGIC [TEL98] tools allow the user to check for a restricted subset of properties like deadlocks, infinite loops or exceeded queue lengths. In many cases such safety requirements are not sufficient to ensure good software quality and the need for expressing more subtle properties (e.g. using temporal logics) arises. In order to check temporal properties on SDL specifications, Bosnaki & al. [BDHS00] have proposed to translate SDL specifications into Promela programs that can be model-checked with SPIN [Hol97]. The method consists in (1) translating an SDL program into the intermediate format IF (via `sdl2if` [BFG+99]); (2) the IF program is then translated into Promela (using `if2pml` presented in [BDHS00]).

---

[1] International Telecommunication Union

D. Bošnački and S. Leue (Eds.): SPIN 2002, LNCS 2318, pp. 79–94, 2002.
© Springer-Verlag Berlin Heidelberg 2002

Our Contribution. In the development of the UUV system, we make extensive use of the SDL save operator. Although this operator exists in the IF language the translation of the IF save operator into Promela with the if2pml tool has not yet been implemented. We then had to extend the if2pml tool to handle this operator. One of the impediments we encountered in the development and model-checking of our UUV software was of course the state-explosion problem. This problem was amplified because the translation of the save operator duplicates buffers and so brings about an exponential growth in the number of states of the system. To tackle this problem we once again extended the if2pml tool with a *message abstraction* capability so that some messages could be gathered and abstracted away following the method proposed by Clarke & al. in [CGL92].

Outline of the Paper. The paper is organized as follows: section 2, deals with the implementation of the translation of the save operator into if2pml to produce Promela programs. Section 3 is devoted to the presentation of message abstraction via Clarke's abstraction algorithm and its implementation in an extended version of if2pml. Finally, the applications of the above techniques are presented on the UUV system in section 4 and we conclude in section 5.

2   Translating SDL Events Savings into Promela

2.1   SDL Programs

An SDL program consists of a set of processes described in graphical language. Each process has an *input FIFO queue* in which events to be processed are stored. A process can output events to other input queues. The informal semantics of a single step of an SDL process[2] is roughly:

1. process an event from the input queue;
2. output events,
3. go to step 1.

The communication between processes is asynchronous. One of the features of SDL processes is the capability of *storing* events in order to process them later. This capability is very similar to the one used in the Electre reactive language [CR95] where the semantic model is a FIFFO (First In First Fireable Out) automaton [SFRC99]. In SDL programs, some of the events of the input queue cannot be processed in particular states and so are stored for later processing. This feature is explicitly implemented with the SDL save operator. An event in a queue is actually a complex structure which contains the SDL identifier of the events (its name), (the list of SDL data values carried by the event) and the Pid of the sender: in the following we will deal only with the event and the Pid value attached to it (e.g. *c(sender)* for event *c* that was sent by process *sender*).

---

[2] see [ITU94a] for a formal definition.

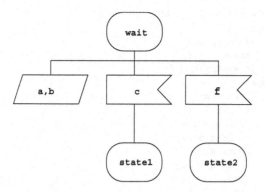

Fig. 1. Sample part of an SDL process using saved events

2.2   The save Operator

A **save** operator specifies a set of events that cannot be processed in a particular state and are to be kept in the input queue for later processing. Figure 1 gives an example of the use of the (SDL graphical) **save** operator. When the process is in state *wait* only events c, f can be processed, whereas a, b must be left in the input queue, and d, e are neither saved nor processed and thus are discarded[3]. Based on [ITU94b], the formal semantics for the processing of events for one process P is the following:

- let $\mathcal{B}_s$ be the set of saved events when process P is in state s, $\mathcal{T}_s$ be the set of events that can be processed in state s, $\widetilde{\mathcal{T}}_s$ the set of events that are discarded in state s; then $\mathcal{B}_s \cup \mathcal{T}_s \cup \widetilde{\mathcal{T}}_s = \mathcal{E}$ is a partition of the set of all input events of P;
- let $\varphi \in \mathcal{E}^*$ be the current input queue when process P is in state s,
- then
  - either $\varphi = w.e.w'$ with $e \in \mathcal{T}_s$, $w \in (\mathcal{B}_s \cup \widetilde{\mathcal{T}}_s)^*$, $w' \in \mathcal{E}^*$. From state s, P will reach a new state s' and the new queue is[4] $\varphi' = w_{|\mathcal{B}_s}.w'$.
  - or $\varphi \in (\mathcal{B}_s \cup \widetilde{\mathcal{T}}_s)^*$. in this case no event can be processed and the queue is left unchanged: $\varphi' = \varphi$. This agrees with the semantics of discarded events given in [BDHS00] (which is different from the one in [ITU94b]).

To sum up, P will process the first (the oldest) *non saved* event of its input queue if it can be taken into account in state s. All the preceeding discarded events are removed from the queue.

For instance, if $\mathcal{E} = \{a, b, c, d, e\}$, in state *wait* of Figure 1 we have $\mathcal{B}_s = \{a, b\}$, $\mathcal{T}_s = \{c, f\}$ and $\widetilde{\mathcal{T}}_s = \{d, e\}$. If the input queue is *abcd*, c will be processed and

---

[3] actually, d(or e) will be discarded if it is before the first processable event in the queue.

[4] for $\Sigma' \subseteq \Sigma$ and $w \in \Sigma^*$, we denote by $w_{|\Sigma'}$ the word obtained from w by removing all the letters not belonging to Σ'.

```
process proc_i0 :buffer q_proc_i0;
  var
    sender : pid;
    parent : pid;
    offspring : pid;
  state
    start :init;
    wait
      discard d,e
        in q_proc_i0;
      save a,b
        in q_proc_i0;
      end;
    state1;
    state2;
  transition
    from start to wait;
    from wait
        input c(sender) from q_proc_i0 to state1;
    from wait
        input f(sender) from q_proc_i0 to state2;
    from state1 to wait;
    from state2 to wait;
```

Fig. 2. The translated IF code for the SDL state *wait*

the new input queue is *abd*. Now if the input queue is *abdc*, *c* is processed and *d* removed leading to *ab*. If the queue is *abddcfd*, a single step will lead to *abfd*.

2.3   Translation of SDL save into IF save

An SDL process P is translated into an IF process proc_P by the sdl2if program presented in [BFG+99]. In this translation, an input buffer q_proc_P is associated to proc_P. Figure 2 gives the IF code of the sample part of the process depicted on Figure 1. The translation of the IF process into Promela does not yet take into account the saved events.

Nevertheless, the semantics of the **save** operator exists in the IF language. The dynamic semantics of IF programs [BGG+99] that gives the meaning of the **save** IF construct is essentially the same as the one given in section 2.2. The translation of an SDL program composed of n processes is an IF program composed of the n IF translations of the processes.

The crucial points when implementing this semantics in Promela is that it implies a recursive processing of the input queue until an event that can be processed is found. This type of search and dequeing anywhere in the queue cannot be translated directly using Promela primitives.

2.4 Translation of IF save into Promela

A naive way of translating the processing of a queue φ in state s into Promela that preserves the semantics of the **save** operator would be:

- let $\mathcal{B}_s$ be the set of saved events in s, $\widetilde{\mathcal{T}}_s$ the set of discarded events and $\mathcal{T}_s$ the set of processable events,
- process φ as follows:
  1. if $\exists e \in \varphi \wedge e \in \mathcal{T}_s$ then
     (a) add a fresh end token $\perp$ at the end of the queue φ,
     (b) do:
         dequeue e' from φ and if $e' \in \mathcal{B}_s$ enqueue e' in φ
         until $\varphi = e.w$ with $e \in \mathcal{T}_s$;
     (c) remove e from φ and change the state of the process P according to the e-transition;
     (d) dequeue e' from φ and enqueue e' while $e' \neq \perp$;
     (e) dequeue $\perp$.
  2. otherwise do nothing.

It is quite obvious that for a buffer of length n every processing needs at most $2(n+1)$ steps of dequeuing + inqueuing. In practice, this algorithm requires a free slot to enqueue $\perp$. This means that if we want to store at most n events, we take an actual buffer of length $n + 1$. Moreover, before any enqueuing we have to add a test in the Promela program on the length of the buffer.

We present a solution that uses a temporary queue but avoids testing buffer length at each enqueuing. Suppose the queue is of the form $\phi = w.e.w'$ with $e \in \mathcal{T}_s$, $w \in (\mathcal{B}_s \cup \widetilde{\mathcal{T}}_s)^*$, $w' \in \mathcal{E}^*$ (with $\mathcal{B}_s, \mathcal{T}_s, \widetilde{\mathcal{T}}_s$ defined in section 2.2).

The algorithm using an intermediate queue φ' involves the following sequence:

1. do:
   dequeue e' from φ and if $e' \in \mathcal{B}_s$ enqueue e' in φ'
   until $\varphi = e.w$ with $e \in \mathcal{T}_s$;
2. process e: remove e from φ and change the state of the process P according to the e-transition;
3. do :
   dequeue e' from φ and enqueue e' in φ'
   until $\varphi = \epsilon$ (ϵ is the empty word);

In the end φ' contains the new updated queue. We illustrate our algorithm in Figure 3.

Let **wait** be the SDL state mentioned in Figure 1. The processing of events c or f is considered with two configurations (I) and (II). The left-hand buffer is the input buffer of the process (φ) and the right-hand one the temporary buffer φ'. From step 1, we enqueue saved events leading to step 2. In step 2, the first event of φ is a non-saved event and is processed. Step 3 consists in enqueuing each event in φ' until φ is empty. In the last step, each event temporarily stored

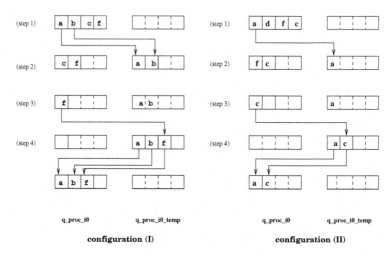

Fig. 3. Example of a processing of the input buffer

in φ' is appended to φ ($[\varphi := \varphi']$). This step respects the initial event order in buffer φ. The translation of the IF program of Figure 2 into a Promela program is given in Figure 4. The proc process manages two buffers: the initial one q_proc_i0 corresponds to φ and the temporary buffer q_proc_i0_tmp is φ'. They are declared with the same size as the initial SDL buffer. The first test (step 1) is to verify that one of the expected events (c or f) is in the buffer (q_proc_i0??[c]|| q_proc_i0??[f]). The saved events preceding c or f in the buffer are then stored in the temporary buffer (step 2) (q_proc_i0_tmp!a and q_proc_i0_tmp!b). Discarded events are consumed and removed from the queue. When c or f is encountered (q_proc_i0?c or q_proc_i0?f), a first loop is executed. This one consists in appending all events still in the initial buffer to the temporary buffer. When q_proc_i0 is empty, the last step is to move q_proc_i0_tmp into this buffer. Each event is appended to the buffer until the temporary buffer q_proc_i0_tmp is empty. When the new queue is ready in buffer q_proc_i0, the actions associated with the processed event are taken and the new state is reached.

Our extended version of the if2pml translator implements this algorithm and the Promela code of Figure 4 is an example of its output.
The implementation of the **save** primitive requires a new temporary queue for each input queue. Then the number of states of the resulting Promela program is multiplied in the worst case by the number of states of the FIFO queues.

Of course, this does not rule out situations where the queue is full and one has to make sure that the length of the queue is large enough to handle all pending events.

The systems we are developing make require a lot of buffers and the state blow-up is particularly high when considering the number of events in a buffer. Let B be a buffer with p places in which k event values can be stored. This buffer

```
wait:
atomic{
if
::(q_proc_i0??[c]|| q_proc_i0??[f])->
    do
    :: q_proc_i0?b(sender)->q_proc_i0_temp!b(sender);
    :: q_proc_i0?a(sender)-> q_proc_i0_temp!a(sender);
    :: q_proc_i0?e,_->
    :: q_proc_i0?d,_->
    :: q_proc_i0?c->
            do   /* for x=a,b,c,d,e,f */
            :: q_proc_i0?x -> q_proc_i0_temp!x(sender);
            :: empty(q_proc_i0)-> break;
            od;
            do   /* for x=a,b,c,d,e,f */
            :: q_proc_i0_temp?x(sender)-> q_proc_i0!x(sender);
            :: empty(q_proc_i0_temp)-> break;
            od;
            goto state1;
    :: q_proc_i0?f->
            do   /* for x=a,b,c,d,e,f */
            :: q_proc_i0?x -> q_proc_i0_temp!x(sender);
            :: empty(q_proc_i0)-> break;
            od;
            do   /* for x=a,b,c,d,e,f */
            :: q_proc_i0_temp?x -> q_proc_i0!x(sender);
            :: empty(q_proc_i0_temp)-> break;
            od;
            goto state2;
    od;
fi; }
```

Fig. 4. Promela code obtained from the SDL program of Figure 1

has $\sum_{n=0}^{n=p} k^n$ possible values. So, a 3-place buffer with 4 different events has 85 possible values.

For a buffer of length n every processing needs at most $2(n+1)$ steps of dequeuing + inqueuing. For space complexity, we use another intermediate buffer φ'. As $|\varphi'| = |\varphi| = n$, we need more space than the naive algorithm presented at the beginning of the section.

To overcome this problem we give in the next section an implementation of an abstraction method on buffer messages.

3 Message Buffer Abstraction

3.1 Abstract Interpretation

Abstract interpretation [CC77] consists in building an abstract model $\widehat{M}$ of a system from a concrete one M preserving some relations between the two models.

The aim is to reduce the state space of the system so that some properties of the system are preserved from the abstract to the concrete model.

Usually the abstract system constructed has more behaviours than the initial program, and the *preservation result* [CGL92] states that properties quantifying over all paths of the abstract system are preserved whereas existentially quantified properties are not.

For instance the preserving result applies to a subset of the branching time logic CTL^* in which only the path quantifier $\forall$ is allowed: this subset is usually referred to as $\forall CTL^*$. As a consequence it can also be applied to LTL properties as they quantify over all paths[5]. Of course the formula on the abstract model has to be expressed in terms of abstract data: let $\widehat{\phi}$ denote the abstract property obtained from the concrete property ϕ[6]. Then, for a formula $\phi \in \forall CTL^*$, if $\widehat{M} \models \widehat{\phi}$ then $M \models \phi$.

3.2   Data Abstraction

The abstraction algorithm consists in interpreting the concrete program to obtain directly the abstract version of the system. The initial model is a labelled transition system. This abstraction can be applied to IF programs during the translation into Promela. Indeed, each IF process is associated with a labelled transition system. The benefit of this method is that the abstract model is constructed directly from the initial program. This is particularly interesting for infinite or large systems.

In the sequel, we use Clarke's algorithm [CGL92] to build an abstract model of the system where some buffer messages are abstracted away. We apply this technique to the IF program obtained from a SDL program which is the concrete model, to build an abstract Promela version of the program.

3.3   Buffer Abstraction on IF Program

In the abstraction algorithm we use, the abstraction mapping deals with the buffer contents.

Let $\mathcal{E}$ represent the possible events that can be stored in a buffer B of the system. $\mathcal{E}^*$ is then the set of possible values of the buffer. We denote $\mathcal{E}^A$ the set of abstract events $\left(\left(\mathcal{E}^A\right)^*\right.$ is then the set of abstract contents of the buffers.) The abstraction mapping $h : \mathcal{E} \to \mathcal{E}^A$ associates to each event $e_1, e_2, \ldots, e_n \in \mathcal{E}$ an abstract value in $\mathcal{E}^A$. We denote $h(e) = e^A$.

Together with the abstraction mapping, we have to define *abstract primitives* on buffers. The abstract operators on buffers are defined straightforwardly from the concrete ones by:

$$
\begin{aligned}
h(input(sig)) &= input(sig^A) \\
h(output(sig)) &= output(sig^A) \\
h(save(sig)) &= save(sig^A)
\end{aligned}
$$

[5] as LTL is a subset of $\forall CTL^*$.
[6] $\widehat{\phi}$ depends on the abstraction mapping chosen to build $\widehat{M}$.

The translation from IF to Promela is computed compositionally. Indeed, for a composition $(P_1|\cdots|P_n)$ of n IF processes we will have

$$(P_1|\cdots|P_n)^A = (P_1^A|\cdots|P_n^A)$$

where P^A denotes the abstract process obtained from P. The abstract interpretation then consists in constructing an abstraction for each IF process in the system and composing the abstracted processes.

Practically, the abstract interpretation of the system is done during the translation of the IF system into the corresponding Promela program (if2pml).

3.4   Application

To illustrate this method, we apply the buffer abstraction on the state wait described in Figure 1. The buffer abstraction mapping gathers events a and b under the label SIG_ABST. Formally, using the relation h, we write : $h(b) = h(a) = $ SIG_ABST and $h(x) = x$ for the other events. The abstracted version in Promela of the IF program of Figure 4 is shown Figure 5.

In state wait, the events a, b have been abstracted into SIG_ABST. This abstraction reduces the number of save in the transition relation and then the number of possible transitions in the system.

3.5   An Extension of if2pml to Automatically Abstract Buffers

We have implemented the buffer abstraction for SDL programs via the the translation into IF. We have extended the translator if2pml developed by [BDHS00] with the abstraction feature. Our implementation uses a file describing the abstract mapping. For the example given in Figure 5, this file (fic.grp) contains the following line: SIG_ABST : a,b; meaning that a and b are abstracted into the same event SIG_ABST. For any other events, abstraction is the identity mapping. It may be possible to have more than one abstract signal. Then using the command line if2pml -a fic.grp prog.if produces the given abstracted Promela code.

4   Case Study: Verification of the Obstacle Avoidance System of the UUV

4.1   Obstacle Avoidance System

The UUV information system is based on a distributed architecture that is comprised of several subsystems. One is the Obstacle Avoidance System (OAS). The principle of this system we are developing is to manage in an integrated way a digital terrain model estimation method, a 3D stabilized and mechanically steered front looking sonar, and computational methods devoted to safe trajectories computation. It consists of four subsystems (inside the dashed box in Figure 6):

```
wait:
atomic{
if
::(q_proc_i0??[c]|| q_proc_i0??[f])->
   do
   :: q_proc_i0?SIG_ABST(sender) ->
                            q_proc_i0_temp!SIG_ABST(sender);
   :: q_proc_i0?e,_->
   :: q_proc_i0?d,_->
   :: q_proc_i0?c->
        do
        :: q_proc_i0?SIG_ABST(sender) ->
                            q_proc_i0_temp!SIG_ABST(sender);
        /* for x=c,d,e,f */
        :: q_proc_i0?x(sender)-> q_proc_i0_temp!x(sender)
        :: empty(q_proc_i0)-> break;
        od;
        do
        :: q_proc_i0_temp?SIG_ABST(sender) ->
                            q_proc_i0!SIG_ABST(sender);
        /* for x=c,d,e,f */
        :: q_proc_i0_temp?x(sender)-> q_proc_i0!x(sender)
        :: empty(q_proc_i0_temp)-> break;
        od;
        goto state1;
   :: q_proc_i0?f->
        do
        :: q_proc_i0?SIG_ABST(sender) ->
                            q_proc_i0_temp!SIG_ABST(sender);
        /* for x=c,d,e,f */
        :: q_proc_i0?x(sender)-> q_proc_i0_temp!x(sender)
        :: empty(q_proc_i0)-> break;
        od;
        do
        :: q_proc_i0_temp?SIG_ABST(sender)->
                            q_proc_i0!SIG_ABST(sender);
        /* for x=c,d,e,f */
        :: q_proc_i0_temp?x(sender)-> q_proc_i0!x(sender)
        :: empty(q_proc_i0_temp)-> break;
        od;
        goto state2;
   od;
fi; }
```

Fig. 5. Abstracted Promela code

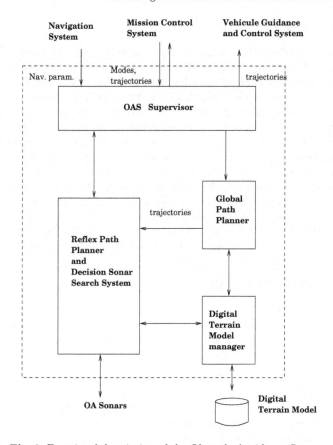

Fig. 6. Functional description of the Obstacle Avoidance System.

1. The digital terrain manager (DTM), which estimates the partially known terrain by using an occupancy grid representation and updating process,
2. the global planner (GP) to generate way points guiding the UUV towards a given target whilst avoiding terrain obstacles,
3. the reflex planner (RP) to check that the trajectories planned by the GP are safe, even in the presence of a disturbance, in the sense that they do not lead to collision,
4. the OAS Supervisor which manages the communication with environmental subsystems.

Communication between the OAS system and the other UUV systems is based on an Ethernet network and a CAN bus coupled to actuators and sensors. The internal OAS process communication mechanism is implemented with the VxWorks message queues primitives.

4.2 SDL Model

The Obstacle Avoidance System has the three following operation modes: *Rerouting*, *Terrain following* and *Security*. When necessary, the supervisor is alerted by Mission Control (event changeMode) that a mode change is required. Periodically the Navigation System sends navigation data, Mission Control sends a target set to be reached and the current target number (nav, consign, wayPoint and noWp) to the supervisor process. The latter will be in charge of redistributing it to other processes. The trajectory request comes from Control System with event simuTimeout. The trajectory is computed by the process concerned with the current operation mode (*Rerouting* or *Terrain following* or *Security*). The verification with the model-checker SPIN requires the the system to be closed, and we have defined an environment process model in SDL. This particular process is in charge of simulating interactions between the OAS SDL model and the Navigation System, Control System, Sonar and Mission Control System. Figure 7 presents the SDL system and events exchanges between these processes.

4.3 Verification of the OAS

Properties of the OAS. Using the tools described in section 2 and 3 we can check for various properties (and for those in $\forall CTL^*$ we can use the abstraction presented previously) of the OAS system. The properties we want to check are the following:

— *"the system does not get stuck in one of the operation modes"*; this means that the operation mode is alternatively changed during the execution of the system. The mode could be *terrain following* (terfolMode), *rerouting* (reroutMode), or *security* (securMode). This property can be expressed in LTL by (but it is not in $\forall CTL^*$):

$$\neg\Diamond\Box\text{terfolMode} \land \neg\Diamond\Box\text{reroutMode} \land \neg\Diamond\Box\text{securMode} \qquad (1)$$

— *"The supervisor and sonarManager processes must run under the same execution mode"*. e.g when the supervisor process is in a terrain following mode, the sonar manager process is in a terrain following mode too. The corresponding $\forall CTL^*$ property is:

$$\Box(\text{terfolMode} \land \text{SonManTerfolMode}) \qquad (2)$$

— *"The trajectory is computed by the process concerned with the current operation mode"*. e.g. in *rerouting* mode, the trajectory has to be computed by process rerout. The trajectory is computed by a process when it receives event nav1. We then define trajRerout to be equivalent to process rerout receives event nav1: q_rerouting_i0?[nav1]. The $\forall CTL^*$ property to be checked is:

$$\forall\Box\neg(\text{terfolMode} \land \text{trajRerout}) \qquad (3)$$

Table 1. Reduction of the number of states and transitions

	# states	# trans.	% states ratio	% trans. ratio
$h_0 = Id$	95 633	505 341	-	-
h_1	86 225	403 077	10 %	9 %
h_2	67 951	369 035	40 %	36 %

- *"In a rerouting or security operation mode the* sonar manager *does not send data to the* model *process"*, i.e. in $\forall CTL^*$:

$$\forall \Box \neg((\texttt{reroutMode} \vee \texttt{securMode}) \wedge \texttt{sentDataModel}) \qquad (4)$$

All these properties involve a number of events in many buffers and the SDL description of the OAS system makes extensive use of **save** operators. We have used our extended version of `if2pml` to check for properties (2)–(3)–(4). Property (1) was checked on the concrete system as abstraction is not safe for this property which does not belong to the $\forall CTL^*$ subset of CTL^*.

Results. Table 1 presents the different reduction percentages obtained on the OAS system for different abstraction mappings h_1 and h_2. h_1 groups 4 events into one, h_2 makes two groups of 4 events for each one. $h_0 = Id$ is the identity mapping giving the number of states and transitions of the concrete system. The ratio columns corresponds respectively to $1 - \dfrac{\#\ states\ of\ abstract}{\#\ states\ of\ concrete}$ and $1 - \dfrac{\#\ trans.\ of\ abstract}{\#\ trans.\ of\ concrete}$.

Property (1) is true on the concrete model and property (3) is true on the abstracted models. Property (2) is violated on our abstraction. Indeed, the **supervisor** can receive a trajectory computed by the **terfol** process whereas *rerouting* mode is activated. As the relation between the abstracted and the concrete model is a simulation, the property violation detected in the abstract system does not allow us to affirm the violation in the concrete model. Nevertheless, the MSC[7] of the incorrect behaviour produced by SPIN has been analyzed and input to the SDL concrete system. This incorrect behaviour has been reproduced in the concrete SDL system with a simulation. We then checked that the property is really violated in the concrete SDL model. This incorrect behaviour has been detected and fixed in our OAS model.

5   Conclusion and Future Work

In this paper we have extended the tool `if2pml` with the two following features:

- translation of the **save** operator into Promela;
- implementation of an abstraction mapping on buffers' messages.

---

[7] Message Sequence Charts

These techniques turn out to be useful when proving SDL programs that use the save operator. The designer can explicitly group messages into one abstract message. The reduction obtained in the number of states and transitions of the system we want to check are rather significant, and reach 40%. We have successfully applied our extended version of if2pml on the development of an Unmanned Underwater Vehicle for which safety properties were checked.

As an incorrect behaviour had been detected on the abstract system with SPIN for property (2), we had to verify that this incorrect behaviour really existed on the concrete initial SDL system. Such a verification could be automated using the SPIN MSC counter example to produce automatically the corresponding SDL MSC which could be played on the concrete SDL model.

References

BDHS00. Dragan Bosnacki, Dennis Dams, Lesek Holenderski, and Natalia Sidorova. Model checking sdl with spin. In Susanne Graf and Michael Schwartzbach, editors, *Tools and Algorithms for the Construction and Analysis of Systems,*, number 1785, pages 363–377, Berlin, 2000. LNCS, Springer.

BFG$^+$99. M. Bozga, J.C. Fernandez, L. Ghirvu, S. Graf, J.P. Krimm, L. Mounier, and J. Sifakis. If: An Intermediate Representation for SDL and its Applications. In *Proceedings of SDL-FORUM'99, Montreal, Canada*, June 1999.

BGG$^+$99. M. Bozga, L. Ghirvu, S. Graf, L. Mounier, and J. Sifakis. The Intermediate Representation IF: Syntax and semantics. Technical report, Vérimag, Grenoble, 1999.

CC77. P. Cousot and R. Cousot. Abstract interpretation: A unified lattice model for static analysis of programs by cons truction or approximation of fixpoints. In ACM Press, editor, *Proceedings of the 4th Annual Symposium on Principles of Programming Languages,*, 1977.

CGL92. E. Clarke, O. Grumberg, and D. Long. Model checking and abstraction. In *Proceedings of the 19th ACM symposium on principles of programming languages*, ACM press, New-York, 1992.

CR95. Franck Cassez and Olivier Roux. Compilation of the ELECTRE reactive language into finite transition systems. *Theoretical Computer Science*, 146(1–2):109–143, July 1995.

Hol97. G.J. Holzmann. The model checker spin. In *IEEE Trans. on Software Engineering*, volume 23, May 1997.

ITU94a. ITU-T International Telecommunication Union. *Annex F.3 to Recommendation Z.100, Specification and Description Language (SDL) – SDL Formal Definition: Dynamic Semantics.* 1994.

ITU94b. ITU-T International Telecommunication Union. *Recommendation Z.100, Specification and Description Language (SDL).* 1994.

SFRC99. G. Sutre, A. Finkel, O. Roux, and F. Cassez. Effective recognizability and model checking of reactive fiffo automata. In *Proc. 7th Int. Conf. Algebraic Methodology and Software Technology (AMAST'98), Amazonia, Brazil, Jan. 1999*, volume 1548 of *Lecture Notes in Computer Science*, pages 106–123. Springer, 1999.

TEL98. TELELOGIC. *TAU/SDT 3.3.* TELELOGIC, June 1998.

VER99. VERILOG. *ObjectGEODE 4.0.* CS VERILOG, March 1999.

A   SDL Model of OAS

A.1   SDL System

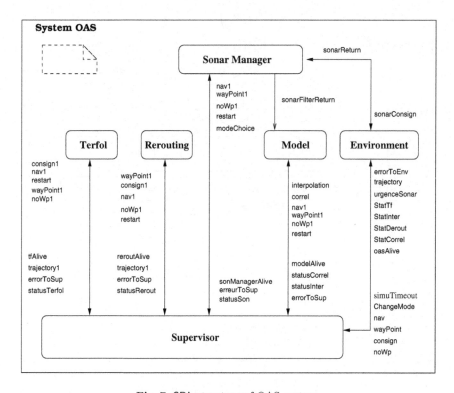

Fig. 7. SDL structure of OAS system

94   Armelle Prigent et al.

A.2 SDL Environment Process

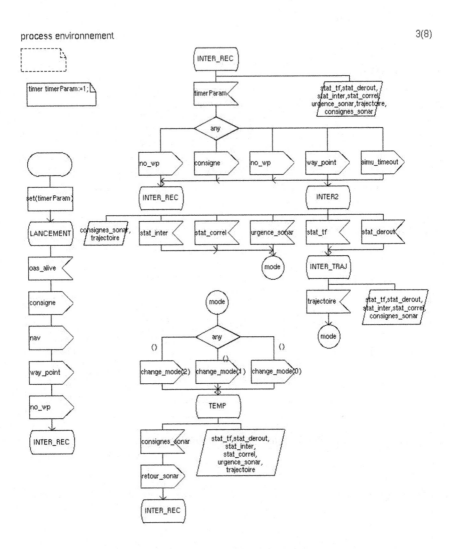

Fig. 8. SDL environment process (partially)

Model Checking Knowledge and Time

Wiebe van der Hoek[1,2] and Michael Wooldridge[2]

[1] Universiteit Utrecht
Institute of Information and Computing Sciences
3584 CH Utrecht, The Netherlands
wiebe@cs.uu.nl
[2] Department of Computer Science
University of Liverpool
Liverpool L69 7ZF, U.K.
M.Wooldridge@csc.liv.ac.uk

Abstract. Model checking as an approach to the automatic verification of finite state systems has focussed predominantly on system specifications expressed in temporal logic. In the distributed systems community, *logics of knowledge* (epistemic logics) have been advocated for expressing desirable properties of protocols and systems. A range of logics combining temporal and epistemic components have been developed for this purpose. However, the model checking problem for temporal logics of knowledge has received (comparatively) little attention. In this paper, we address ourselves to this problem. Following a brief survey of the relevant issues and literature, we introduce a temporal logic of knowledge (Halpern and Vardi's logic CKL_n). We then develop an approach to CKL_n model checking that combines ideas from the *interpreted systems* semantics for knowledge with the *logic of local propositions* developed by Engelhardt et al. With our approach, local propositions provide a means to reduce CKL_n model checking to linear temporal logic model checking. After introducing and exploring the ideas underpinning our approach, we present a case study (the bit transmission problem) in which SPIN was used to establish temporal epistemic properties of a system implemented in PROMELA.

1 Introduction

Since the mid 1980s, *modal logics of knowledge* have been increasingly deployed in the formal specification of distributed systems, where they are used to make precise the concept of what a process knows [6,18]. Temporal logics of knowledge – temporal logics enriched by modal knowledge operators – have also been widely used for reasoning about distributed systems [9,25].

Model checking as an approach to the automatic verification of finite state systems has focussed predominantly on system specifications expressed in temporal logic – linear temporal logic in the case of SPIN [13,14] and FORSPEC [24], branching temporal logic in the case of SMV [17] and its relatives. However, the model checking problem for *temporal logics of knowledge* has received comparatively little attention. While Halpern and Vardi proposed the use of model

D. Bošnački and S. Leue (Eds.): SPIN 2002, LNCS 2318, pp. 95–111, 2002.
© Springer-Verlag Berlin Heidelberg 2002

checking as an alternative to deduction for logics of knowledge as long ago as 1991, their proposal focussed on logics with no temporal component [10]. Ron van der Meyden studied the complexity of the model checking problem for a particular class of (essentially infinite state) systems of knowledge and time, and showed that the problem was complex (PSPACE-complete in the best case, undecidable in the worst) for this class [22].

In this paper, we address ourselves to the problem of model checking as an approach to showing that finite state systems satisfy specifications expressed in logics that combine temporal and knowledge components.

The remainder of this paper is organised as follows. In section 1.1, we shortly elaborate on modal logics of knowledge – readers familiar with the epistemic logic literature may wish to skip this section. In Section 2, we introduce a temporal logic of knowledge (Halpern and Vardi's logic CKL_n [9]). We then develop an approach to CKL_n model checking that combines ideas from the *interpreted systems* semantics for knowledge [6] with the *logic of local propositions* developed by Engelhardt et al [5]. In our approach, CKL_n model checking can be reduced to linear temporal logic model checking. After introducing and exploring the ideas underpinning the approach, we present a case study – the bit transmission problem – in which SPIN was used to establish temporal epistemic properties of a PROMELA system: the alternating bit protocol. We conclude with some comments on issues for future research.

1.1   Background

Model checking techniques originated – and are most widely understood – as a technique for automatically verifying that finite state systems satisfy formal specifications [2]. These formal specifications are most commonly expressed either as formulae of the branching time temporal logic CTL (in the case of the SMV model checker and its relatives [17,2]) or as formulae of Linear Temporal Logic (in the case of SPIN [13,14] and FORSPEC [24]). Comparatively little attention has been given in the model checking community to *epistemic logic*: the modal logic of knowledge. Epistemic modal logics are widely recognised as having originated in the work of Jaakko Hintikka, a philosopher who in the early 1960s showed how certain modal logics could be used to formally capture some intuitions about the nature of knowledge [12]. In the 1980s, it was recognised that epistemic logics have an important role to play in the theory of distributed systems. In particular, it was demonstrated that epistemic logics can be used to formally express the desired behaviour of protocols. For example, when specifying a communication protocol, it is quite natural to wish to represent requirements such as "if process i knows that process j has received packet m, then i should send packet $m+1$". Using epistemic logic, such requirements can be expressed both formally and naturally.

One of the key reasons why modal logics of knowledge have achieved such prominence was the discovery by Halpern and colleagues in the mid 1980s that S5 epistemic logics could be given a natural interpretation in terms of the states of processes – commonly called *agents* – in a distributed system. The model that has received the most widespread interest is known as the *interpreted systems* model [6].

In addition to interest in the use of epistemic logics in the specification of communicating systems, there has recently been interest in the use of knowledge logics for directly programming systems [6,7]. A *knowledge-based program* has the general form:

$$
\begin{aligned}
&\textsf{case of}\\
&\quad \textsf{if } K_i\varphi_1 \textsf{ do } a_1\\
&\quad \cdots\\
&\quad \textsf{if } K_i\varphi_n \textsf{ do } a_n\\
&\textsf{end case}
\end{aligned}
$$

The intuitive interpretation of such a program is that of a collection of rules; the left-hand side of each rule represents a condition, expressed in epistemic logic, of what an agent knows. If the condition is satisfied, then the corresponding action (program statement) is executed. Along with other researchers, (e.g., [5]), we take the view that such programs are best understood as specifications for systems – knowledge-based programs are not in a form that can be directly executed. There have been some studies on the computational complexity of automatically synthesising executable programs from knowledge-based programs [20,21].

Despite the level of interest in using logics of knowledge for specifying communicating systems, there has been comparatively little work on *model checking* for such logics. In 1991 – somewhat prior to the current growth in interest in model checking – Halpern and Vardi proposed the use of model checking as an alternative to deduction for modal logics of knowledge [10]. They showed that the model checking problem for multi-agent S5 logics of knowledge was tractable, and speculated that the approach might have wider applications in this community; but to the best of our knowledge (no pun intended), no further work on this topic was reported. While the computational complexity of the satisfiability and validity problems for temporal logics of knowledge has been studied exhaustively by Halpern and Vardi [9], no such similar studies appear to have been carried out with respect to model checking. The closest work with which we are familiar is that of Vardi [23], who investigated the problem of when a concrete program could be said to implement a knowledge-based program. He showed that in the general case – where the knowledge-based program could contain knowledge tests with temporal modalities – the complexity of the problem coincided with that of the model checking problem for Linear Temporal Logic, i.e., it is PSPACE-complete (see, e.g., [4]).

Also closely related is the work of van der Meyden, who investigated the model checking problem for a small class of temporal knowledge logics: those in which agents are assumed to have *perfect recall* [22]. He established that the model checking problem for this class varies from PSPACE-complete in the "best" case to undecidable in the worst. However, van der Meyden did not investigate "practical" model checking for knowledge and time. Rao and Georgeff investigated the model checking problem for a range of logics combining temporal (CTL) and modal components, although their study was rather abstract – they did not implement any of the techniques they developed, and did not consider S5 logics of knowledge [19]. Finally, Benerecetti and Giunchiglia developed techniques for similar temporal modal logics, but these logics had an unusual (non-Kripke) semantics [1].

2   A Temporal Logic of Knowledge

We are concerned with modelling systems composed of multiple agents, each of which is an independently operating process. Let $Ag = \{1, \ldots, n\}$ denote the set of agents. We assume each agent $i \in Ag$ can be in any of a set L_i of local states. An agent's local state contains all the information required to completely characterise the state of the agent: the value of each of its local variables, together with the value of its program counter. In particular, the *information* available to an agent is determined by its local state. The state of a system at any moment can thus be characterised by a tuple $\langle l_1, \ldots, l_n \rangle$, where $l_i \in L_i$ is the local state of agent i at this moment. We let $G \subseteq L_1 \times \cdots \times L_n$ denote the *reachable global states* of the system (i.e., the set of states that a system may possibly enter during a legal computation sequence). (Notice that we have not explicitly introduced *environments*, although it is quite common to do so in the literature [6]: for simplicity, we assume that an environment can be modelled as an agent in the system.)

A *run* is a function

$$r : I\!N \to G$$

which associates with every natural number $u \in I\!N$ a global state $r(u)$. The idea is that a run represents one possible computation of a system: in general, a system may have a number of possible runs, and so we say a *system* is a set of runs; we use $\mathcal{R}$ to denote a system. A run together with a time point is a *point*: a point (r, u) defines a global state $r(u)$. We denote the i'th component of the tuple $r(u)$ by $r_i(u)$. Thus $r_i(u)$ is the local state of agent i in run r at "time" u.

Following conventional practice, we associate with every agent $i \in Ag$ an equivalence relation $\sim_i$ over the set of points [6, p.111]:

$$(r, u) \sim_i (r', v) \qquad \text{iff} \qquad r_i(u) = r'_i(v).$$

If $(r, u) \sim_i (r', v)$, then we say that (r, u) is indistinguishable from (r', v) from the point of view of i, or, alternatively, that i carries exactly the same information in (r, u) as in (r', v).

We use the relation $\sim_i$ to give a semantics to the knowledge modalities in CKL_n. To give a semantics to the "common knowledge" modality C_Γ, we introduce two further relations, $\sim_\Gamma^E$ and $\sim_\Gamma^C$. Given a set $\Gamma \subseteq Ag$ of agents, we define the relation $\sim_\Gamma^E$ as $\sim_\Gamma^E \triangleq \bigcup_{i \in \Gamma} \sim_i$ and we define the relation $\sim_\Gamma^C$ as the transitive closure of $\sim_\Gamma^E$.

A *model* or *interpreted system* for CKL_n is a pair $\mathcal{I} = \langle \mathcal{R}, \pi \rangle$, where $\mathcal{R}$ is a system and

$$\pi : \mathcal{R} \times I\!N \to 2^\Phi$$

is a valuation function, which gives the set of primitive propositions true at each point in $\mathcal{R}$ [6, pp.110–111].

Notice that we model a system as a set of infinite runs, which may at first sight appear to be at odds with the notion of the finite state systems that model checking is generally applied to. In fact, there is no contradiction. Given a Kripke structure $\langle G, R \subseteq G \times G, G_0 \subseteq G, \pi \rangle$ for a CTL-like logic (where R is a total "next time" relation and G_0 are initial states), we can obtain an interpreted system by "unwinding" the relation R starting from initial states G_0 to obtain a set of infinite runs.

Syntactically, CKL_n is propositional temporal logic augmented by an indexed set of modal operators K_i, one for each agent $i \in Ag$, and common knowledge operators C_Γ, where $\Gamma \subseteq Ag$. The formula $K_i\varphi$ is read as "agent i knows φ"; the formula $C_\Gamma\varphi$ means "it is common knowledge in Γ that φ".

Formulae are constructed from a set $\Phi = \{p, q, r, \ldots\}$ of *primitive propositions*. The language contains the standard propositional connectives $\neg$ (not), $\vee$ (or), $\wedge$ (and), $\rightarrow$ (implies) and $\leftrightarrow$ (if, and only if). For the temporal dimension we take the usual set of future-time connectives $\bigcirc$ (*next*), $\Diamond$ (*sometime* or *eventually*), $\square$ (*always*), $\mathcal{U}$ (*until*) and $\mathcal{W}$ (*unless* or *weak until*).

The set $wff(CKL_n)$ of well-formed formulae of CKL_n is defined by the following grammar:

$$
\begin{array}{lll}
\langle wff \rangle ::= & \textbf{true} & \text{/* logical constant for truth */} \\
& |\ \text{any element of } \Phi & \text{/* primitive propositions */} \\
& |\ \neg\langle wff \rangle & \text{/* negation */} \\
& |\ \langle wff \rangle \vee \langle wff \rangle & \text{/* disjunction */} \\
& |\ \bigcirc\langle wff \rangle & \text{/* next */} \\
& |\ \langle wff \rangle\,\mathcal{U}\,\langle wff \rangle & \text{/* until */} \\
& |\ K_i\langle wff \rangle & \text{/* } (i \in Ag) \text{ agent } i \text{ knows */} \\
& |\ C_\Gamma\langle wff \rangle & \text{/* } (\Gamma \subseteq Ag) \text{ it is common knowledge in } \Gamma \text{ that */}
\end{array}
$$

The semantics of CKL_n are given via the satisfaction relation "$\models_{CKL_n}$", which holds between pairs of the form $\langle \mathcal{I}, (r, u) \rangle$, (where $\mathcal{I}$ is an interpreted system and (r, u) is a point in $\mathcal{I}$), and formulae of CKL_n. We read $\langle I, (r, u) \rangle \models_{CKL_n} \varphi$ as "φ is satisfied (equivalently, is true) at point (r, u) in $\mathcal{I}$". The rules defining $\models_{CKL_n}$ are given in Figure 1.

Semantic rules are only given for the temporal connectives $\bigcirc$ and $\mathcal{U}$: the remaining temporal connectives are introduced as abbreviations, as follows.

$$\Diamond\varphi \hat{=} \textbf{true}\,\mathcal{U}\,\varphi$$
$$\square\varphi \hat{=} \neg\Diamond\neg\varphi$$
$$\varphi\,\mathcal{W}\,\psi \hat{=} \varphi\,\mathcal{U}\,\psi \vee \square\varphi$$

The remaining propositional connectives ($\wedge, \rightarrow, \leftrightarrow$) are also assumed to be defined in terms of $\vee$ and $\neg$.

Notice that CKL_n is an expressive language. In particular, using the language it is possible to express the fact that a statement is true in all states of an interpreted system that can play a part in the interpretation of a formula. To

$$
\begin{aligned}
&\langle \mathcal{I},(r,u)\rangle \models_{CKL_n} \textbf{true} \\
&\langle \mathcal{I},(r,u)\rangle \models_{CKL_n} p && \text{iff } p \in \pi(r,u) && \text{(where } p \in \Phi) \\
&\langle \mathcal{I},(r,u)\rangle \models_{CKL_n} \neg\varphi && \text{iff } \langle \mathcal{I},(r,u)\rangle \not\models_{CKL_n} \varphi \\
&\langle \mathcal{I},(r,u)\rangle \models_{CKL_n} \varphi \vee \psi && \text{iff } \langle \mathcal{I},(r,u)\rangle \models_{CKL_n} \varphi \text{ or } \langle \mathcal{I},(r,u)\rangle \models_{CKL_n} \psi \\
&\langle \mathcal{I},(r,u)\rangle \models_{CKL_n} K_i\varphi && \text{iff for all } (r',v) \text{ in } \mathcal{I}, \text{ if } (r,u) \sim_i (r',v) \text{ then } \langle \mathcal{I},(r',v)\rangle \models_{CKL_n} \varphi \\
&\langle \mathcal{I},(r,u)\rangle \models_{CKL_n} C_\Gamma\varphi && \text{iff for all } (r',v) \text{ in } \mathcal{I}, \text{ if } (r,u) \sim_\Gamma^C (r',v) \text{ then } \langle \mathcal{I},(r',v)\rangle \models_{CKL_n} \varphi \\
&\langle \mathcal{I},(r,u)\rangle \models_{CKL_n} \bigcirc\varphi && \text{iff } \langle \mathcal{I},(r,u+1)\rangle \models_{CKL_n} \varphi \\
&\langle \mathcal{I},(r,u)\rangle \models_{CKL_n} \varphi \mathcal{U} \psi && \text{iff } \exists v \in I\!N \text{ s.t. } (u \leq v) \text{ and } \langle \mathcal{I},(r,v)\rangle \models_{CKL_n} \psi \\
& && \text{and } \forall w \in \{u,\ldots,v-1\}, \text{ we have } \langle \mathcal{I},(r,w)\rangle \models_{CKL_n} \varphi
\end{aligned}
$$

Fig. 1. Semantics of CKL_n

see how this is done, we define a *universal modality* $\Box^*$ operator, which is defined as the maximal solution to the following fixed point formula:

$$\Box^*\varphi \leftrightarrow \Box(\varphi \wedge C_{Ag} \Box^*\varphi).$$

To illustrate the properties of $\Box^*$, we define a *reachability relation*. First, we say point (r',v) is *directly* reachable from (r,u) (written $(r,u) \rightsquigarrow (r',v)$) iff:

- $r = r'$ and $v \geq u$ or
- $(r,u) \sim_i (r',v)$ for some agent $i \in Ag$.

We then define the reachability relation $\rightsquigarrow^*$ as the transitive closure of $\rightsquigarrow$. Now:

Proposition 1 ([3]). *Let $\mathcal{I}$ be an interpreted system and (r,u) and (r',v) be points in $\mathcal{I}$ such that $\langle \mathcal{I},(r,u)\rangle \models_{CKL_n} \Box^*\varphi$ and $(r,u) \rightsquigarrow^* (r',v)$. Then $\langle \mathcal{I},(r',v)\rangle \models_{CKL_n} \varphi$.*

Linear Temporal Logic and Propositional Logic

Now consider the language and logic obtained from CKL_n by omitting knowledge and common knowledge modalities: we get *Linear Temporal Logic* (LTL) (see, e.g., [15,16]). Formula of LTL are interpreted with respect to points in interpreted systems, as with CKL_n, but note that the interpretation of an LTL formula will depend *only* on the run within which it is interpreted. The truth or falsity of an LTL formula φ when interpreted on a point (r,u) in $\mathcal{I}$ will depend only on the run r, and will not be dependent on other runs in $\mathcal{I}$. This is not the case for knowledge modalities, as these can express properties of other runs. We write $\langle \mathcal{I},(r,u)\rangle \models_{\text{LTL}} \varphi$ to indicate that LTL formula φ is satisfied at point (r,u) in $\mathcal{I}$: thus "$\models_{\text{LTL}}$" serves as the LTL satisfaction relation. We refer to the subset of LTL obtained by not permitting temporal logic connectives as propositional logic.

Knowledge, Common Knowledge, and Local Propositions

We now introduce the notion of a *local* proposition [5]. Local propositions play an important role in our reduction of CKL_n model checking to LTL model checking.

If i is an agent, then an i-local proposition is a formula of propositional logic whose interpretation is the same in each of the points in each equivalence class induced by the $\sim_i$ relation. Formally, a propositional logic formula φ is said to be i-local iff:

for all points $(r, u), (r', v)$ in $\mathcal{I}$,
if $(r, u) \sim_i (r', v)$, then $\langle \mathcal{I}, (r, u) \rangle \models_{CKL_n} \varphi$ iff $\langle \mathcal{I}, (r', v) \rangle \models_{CKL_n} \varphi$

To further understand the idea of an i-local proposition, assume – without loss of too much generality – that the local state of any agent i is a tuple of local variables $\langle b_{i_1}, \ldots, b_{i_k} \rangle$ each of which has the value 0 or 1 at any given time. (Of course, this is *exactly* what the state of any conventional computer process actually is.) The indexed set $\Phi_i = \{b_{i_1}, \ldots, b_{i_k}\} \subseteq \Phi$ of primitive propositions is assumed to form part of the vocabulary of the CKL_n language: $\Phi = \bigcup_{i \in Ag} \Phi_i$. Note that the Φ_i's need not be mutually disjoint – it is possible that variables are *shared* between agents, if the same variable appears in the state of more than one agent (although this requires an addition semantic constraint, described below).

We assume the obvious interpretation of local variables: $b_{i_j} \in \pi(r, u)$ iff the bit b_{i_j} has the value 1 in the state $r_i(u)$. If a variable b is shared between agents i and j, then we require that the variable has the same value inside both agents in any given system state: this requirement ensures that the valuation function π can give a unique, well-defined value to shared variables. It is straightforward to show the following:

Proposition 2. *If φ is a formula of propositional logic containing only variables over Φ_i, then φ is i-local.*

Proof. Immediate from the fact that $(r, u) \sim_i (r', v)$ iff $r_i(u) = r'_i(v)$.

The idea of such local propositions is that they relate the semantic definition of knowledge as given in Figure 1 with a syntactic one: let g be a global state verifying the i-local proposition φ_g. Then we have $\langle \mathcal{I}, (r, u) \rangle \models_{KL_n} K_i \psi$ iff for all (r', v) in $\mathcal{I}$, if $\langle \mathcal{I}, (r', v) \rangle \models_{KL_n} \varphi_g$ then $\langle \mathcal{I}, (r', v) \rangle \models_{KL_n} \psi$.

We can extend the notion of a local proposition to sets of agents. Given a set $\Gamma \subseteq Ag$ of agents and a propositional formula φ, we say that φ is Γ-*local* iff φ is i-local for all $i \in \Gamma$. We can prove an immediate analogue of Proposition 2:

Proposition 3. *If φ is a formula of propositional logic containing only variables that are shared by the agents in Γ, then φ is Γ-local.*

Proof. We need to show that if φ depends only on Γ-shared variables, then if $(r, u) \sim_\Gamma^C (r', v)$ then $\langle \mathcal{I}, (r, u) \rangle \models_{CKL_n} \varphi$ iff $\langle \mathcal{I}, (r', v) \rangle \models_{CKL_n} \varphi$. Assume $(r, u) \sim_\Gamma^C (r', v)$. Then there is a sequence of points $(r_1, u_1), (r_2, u_2), \ldots, (r_k, u_k)$ such that $(r, u) = (r_1, u_1)$, $(r', v) = (r_k, u_k)$, and for all $1 \leq l < k$, we have $(r_l, u_l) \sim_i (r_{l+1}, u_{l+1})$ for some agent $i \in \Gamma$. Now if $(r_l, u_l) \sim_i (r_{l+1}, u_{l+1})$ then by definition the local state of i in must the same in (r_l, u_l) and (r_{l+1}, u_{l+1}), and in particular, any Γ-shared variables must have the same values in (r_l, u_l) as (r_{l+1}, u_{l+1}). So any formula depending on these values will have the same interpretation in (r_l, u_l) and (r_{l+1}, u_{l+1}). Thus $\langle \mathcal{I}, (r, u) \rangle \models_{CKL_n} \varphi$ iff $\langle \mathcal{I}, (r', v) \rangle \models_{CKL_n} \varphi$.

In addition, we can show:

Proposition 4. *Let $\mathcal{I}$ be an interpreted system, let (r, u) and (r', v) be points in $\mathcal{I}$, and let φ be a Γ-local proposition. Then if $(r, u) \sim_{\Gamma}^{C} (r', v)$ then $\langle \mathcal{I}, (r, u) \rangle \models_{CKL_n} \varphi$ iff $\langle \mathcal{I}, (r', v) \rangle \models_{CKL_n} \varphi$.*

Proof. Assume $(r, u) \sim_{\Gamma}^{C} (r', v)$. Then as before, there exists a sequence of points $(r_1, u_1), (r_2, u_2), \ldots, (r_k, u_k)$ such that $(r, u) = (r_1, u_1)$, $(r', v) = (r_k, u_k)$, and for all $1 \leq l < k$, we have $(r_l, u_l) \sim_i (r_{l+1}, u_{l+1})$ for some agent $i \in \Gamma$. As φ is Γ-local, it is i-local for all $i \in \Gamma$. Hence by the definition of i-local, $\langle \mathcal{I}, (r_l, u_l) \rangle \models_{CKL_n} \varphi$ iff $\langle \mathcal{I}, (r_{l+1}, u_{l+1}) \rangle \models_{CKL_n} \varphi$. Hence $\langle \mathcal{I}, (r, u) \rangle \models_{CKL_n} \varphi$ iff $\langle \mathcal{I}, (r', v) \rangle \models_{CKL_n} \varphi$.

3 CKL_n Model Checking through LTL Model Checking

The *model checking* problem for CKL_n is as follows. Given an interpreted system $\mathcal{I} = \langle \mathcal{R}, \pi \rangle$, together with a formula φ of CKL_n, return the set of points at which φ is satisfied in $\mathcal{I}$, i.e., the set

$$\{(r, u) \mid r \in \mathcal{R}, u \in I\!N, \text{ and } \langle \mathcal{I}, (r, u) \rangle \models_{CKL_n} \varphi\}.$$

This problem is too abstract for most practical model checking problems (invariant properties will be true in every state of the system – there is clearly no way a practical model checker would be able to enumerate this set!). For this reason, we are generally concerned with a slightly simpler version of this problem. Hereafter, when we refer to the model checking problem for CKL_n, we mean the problem of determining whether, given an interpreted system $\mathcal{I} = \langle \mathcal{R}, \pi \rangle$ and a formula φ, the formula φ is true in the initial state of every run in $\mathcal{R}$, i.e., whether or not

$$\forall r \in \mathcal{R} \text{ we have } \langle \mathcal{I}, (r, 0) \rangle \models_{CKL_n} \varphi.$$

We say that $\mathcal{I}$ realises φ if it satisfies this property. Given an interpreted system $\mathcal{I}$ and CKL_n formula φ, we write $mc_{CKL_n}(\mathcal{I}, \varphi)$ to stand for the fact that $\mathcal{I}$ realises φ, i.e.,

$$mc_{CKL_n}(\langle \mathcal{R}, \pi \rangle, \varphi) \quad \text{iff} \quad \forall r \in \mathcal{R} \text{ we have } \langle \langle \mathcal{R}, \pi \rangle, (r, 0) \rangle \models_{CKL_n} \varphi.$$

The Main Idea

At present, we do not have a model checker for CKL_n (although there is no reason in principle why one should not be implemented). What we *do* have available, however, is a model checker for Linear Temporal Logic (LTL), for example in the form of SPIN [13,14]. SPIN takes as input a system, (described using the PROMELA language), and a formula of propositional LTL: it then checks whether or not this formula is satisfied in the first state of every run of the system. If it is not – if there is a run that fails to satisfy the formula – then it reports this run as a counter example. The model checking problem that SPIN solves is thus as follows. For any system $\mathcal{I} = \langle \mathcal{R}, \pi \rangle$ and formula φ of LTL, it determines whether or not:

$$\forall r \in \mathcal{R} \text{ we have } \langle \mathcal{I}, (r, 0) \rangle \models_{\text{LTL}} \varphi.$$

If φ is an LTL formula and $\mathcal{I}$ is a system, then we write $mc_{\text{LTL}}(\mathcal{I}, \varphi)$ to indicate that $\mathcal{I}$ realises φ:

$$mc_{\text{LTL}}(\langle \mathcal{R}, \pi \rangle, \varphi) \quad \text{iff} \quad \forall r \in \mathcal{R} \text{ we have } \langle \langle \mathcal{R}, \pi \rangle, (r, 0) \rangle \models_{\text{LTL}} \varphi.$$

We now turn to one of the main ideas underpinning this article: we show how CKL_n model checking can be reduced to LTL model checking. Our approach takes inspiration from work on the Logic of Local Propositions (LLP) [5]. LLP is a modal logic with a single universal modality, Nec, and which allows quantification over propositions. A formula $\text{Nec } \varphi$ of LLP means that φ is true in all states. LLP has a collection of quantifiers $\forall_i, \exists_i,$ (where i is an agent), which allow quantification over propositions that are *local* to an agent. The intuition is that a proposition is local to an agent i if i is able to determine its truth using only locally available information – information available in its state. The key insight of [5] is that by using these quantifiers, one can define knowledge modalities. For example:

$$K_i \varphi \hat{=} \exists_i q[q \wedge \text{Nec}(q \rightarrow \varphi)] \tag{1}$$

Thus an agent i knows φ iff there is a proposition q local to i such that q is true, and whenever q is true, φ is also true. In [5], it is proved that this definition of knowledge corresponds to the conventional one, given in terms of Kripke structures and accessible worlds [6].

We now show how we can make use of these ideas when considering the model checking problem for CKL_n. Suppose we want to determine whether or not the property $\Diamond K_i p$ is true of some system $\mathcal{I}$. That is, we want to determine whether or not

$$mc_{CKL_n}(\mathcal{I}, \Diamond K_i p)$$

Now (1) suggests the following approach to this problem. In order to show this, all we have to do is find some proposition ψ that is local to i (i.e., ψ is a predicate over i's state), such that

$$mc_{\text{LTL}}(\mathcal{I}, \Diamond \psi \wedge \Box(\psi \rightarrow p))$$

Notice that the formula to be model checked has two components. The first ($\Diamond \psi$) corresponds in structure to the original input formula (with knowledge modalities replaced by propositions). The second component ($\Box(\psi \rightarrow p)$) represents a constraint (an invariant) that must hold.

Thus we have reduced a CKL_n model checking problem to an LTL model checking problem – and since we have LTL model checking tools available – SPIN – this suggests that we can – at least partially – automate the process of model checking CKL_n.

The Formal Details

We now present the formal details of our reduction approach. To begin with, we will consider just how model checking a statement of the form $K_i\varphi$ can be reduced to LTL model checking. We define a function lp_i, which takes as argument an interpreted system, and an LTL formula φ, and returns a local proposition that globally implies φ:

$$lp_i(\mathcal{I},(r,u),\varphi) \; \hat{=} \; \begin{cases} \psi & \psi \text{ is an } i\text{-local proposition such that} \\ & mc_{\text{LTL}}(\mathcal{I},\; \Box(\psi \to \varphi)) \\ & \text{and } \langle \mathcal{I},(r,u)\rangle \models_{\text{LTL}} \psi \\ \textbf{false} & \text{if no such formula exists.} \end{cases}$$

If $lp_i(\mathcal{I},(r,u),\varphi) = \psi$, then we say that ψ serves as an i-local proposition for φ in (r,u). (As an aside, note that the lp_i function is very similar in spirit to the "sound local predicate" function S_i of Engelhardt et al [5].) We can now show the following.

Proposition 5. *Let $\mathcal{I}$ be an interpreted system, let (r,u) be a point in $\mathcal{I}$, and let φ be an LTL formula such that $lp_i(\mathcal{I},(r,u),\varphi) = \psi$. Then:*

$$\langle \mathcal{I},(r,u)\rangle \models_{CKL_n} K_i\varphi \qquad \textit{iff} \qquad \langle \mathcal{I},(r,u)\rangle \models_{\text{LTL}} \psi$$

Proof. (Left to right.) Immediate from the definition of lp_i. (Right to left.) We need to show that $\langle \mathcal{I},(r,u)\rangle \models_{\text{LTL}} \psi$ implies $\langle \mathcal{I},(r,u)\rangle \models_{CKL_n} K_i\varphi$. From the definition of lp_i, we know that $\langle \mathcal{I},(r,u)\rangle \models_{\text{LTL}} \psi$ and in addition, that $mc_{\text{LTL}}(\mathcal{I},\; \Box(\psi \to \varphi))$. Since $mc_{\text{LTL}}(\mathcal{I},\; \Box(\psi \to \psi))$, then for all points (r',v) in $\mathcal{I}$, we have $\langle \mathcal{I},(r',v)\rangle \models \psi \to \varphi$, and in particular, $\langle \mathcal{I},(r'',w)\rangle \models_{\text{LTL}} \psi \to \varphi$ for all (r'',w) such that $(r,u) \sim_i (r'',w)$. Since ψ is i-local, then if $\langle \mathcal{I},(r,u)\rangle \models_{\text{LTL}} \psi$ then $\langle \mathcal{I},(r'',w)\rangle \models_{\text{LTL}} \psi$ for all (r'',w) such that $(r,u) \sim_i (r'',w)$, and thus $\langle \mathcal{I},(r'',w)\rangle \models_{\text{LTL}} \varphi$ for all (r'',w) such that $(r,u) \sim_i (r'',w)$ and so $\langle \mathcal{I},(r,u)\rangle \models_{CKL_n} K_i\varphi$.

In the same way, we can extend the function lp_i to sets of agents. If $\Gamma \subseteq Ag$, then we can define lp_Γ as:

$$lp_\Gamma(\mathcal{I},\varphi) \; \hat{=} \; \begin{cases} \psi & \psi \text{ is an } \Gamma\text{-local proposition such that} \\ & mc_{\text{LTL}}(\mathcal{I},\; \Box(\psi \to \varphi)) \\ & \text{and } \langle \mathcal{I},(r,u)\rangle \models_{\text{LTL}} \psi \\ \textbf{false} & \text{if no such formula exists.} \end{cases}$$

The following result can now be proved.

Proposition 6. *Let $\mathcal{I}$ be an interpreted system, let (r,u) be a point in $\mathcal{I}$, and let φ be an LTL formula such that $lp_\Gamma(\mathcal{I},(r,u),\varphi) = \psi$. Then:*

$$\langle \mathcal{I},(r,u)\rangle \models_{CKL_n} C_\Gamma\varphi \qquad \textit{iff} \qquad \langle \mathcal{I},(r,u)\rangle \models_{\text{LTL}} \psi$$

Proof. As Proposition 5, making use of Proposition 4.

Finally, suppose we have some LTL formula φ such that $mc_{\mathrm{LTL}}(\mathcal{I}, \Box\varphi)$. In this case φ is an invariant of system $\mathcal{I}$ – it is true in all the states of $\mathcal{I}$ that are reachable through some possible computation. From this we can immediately conclude the following.

Proposition 7. *Let $\mathcal{I}$ be an interpreted system, and let φ be an LTL formula such that $mc_{\mathrm{LTL}}(\mathcal{I}, \Box\varphi)$. Then for any point (r, u) in $\mathcal{I}$, we have $\langle\mathcal{I}, (r, u)\rangle$ $\models_{CKL_n} \Box^*\varphi$.*

We now have a route to model checking (a subset of) CKL_n formulae by using only LTL model checking: When faced with the problem of determining whether $\langle\mathcal{I}, (r, u)\rangle \models_{CKL_n} K_i\varphi$, we can attempt to find a ψ such that $lp_i(\mathcal{I}, (r, u), \varphi) = \psi$, and check that $\langle\mathcal{I}, (r, u)\rangle \models_{\mathrm{LTL}} \psi$. Notice that finding the i-local proposition ψ will itself require solving the LTL model checking problem $mc_{\mathrm{LTL}}(\mathcal{I}, \Box(\psi \to \varphi))$.

Notice that the approach can deal with nested knowledge operators. We will see an example of this in the following section.

4 A Case Study: The Bit Transmission Problem

We now present a case study, in the form of the *bit transmission problem*. We adapt our discussion of this problem from [18, pp.39–44]. The bit transmission protocol was first studied in the context of epistemic logic by Halpern and Zuck [11]. The basic idea is that there are two agents, a sender and a receiver, who can communicate with one another through an unreliable communication medium. This medium may delete messages, but if a message does arrive at the recipient, then the message is correct. (It is also assumed that the environment satisfies a kind of fairness property, namely that if a message is sent infinitely often, then it eventually arrives.) The sender has a sequence of bits $x_0, x_1, \ldots, x_k$ that it desires to communicate to the receiver; when the receiver receives the bits, it prints them out. The goal is to derive a protocol that satisfies the safety requirement that the receiver never prints incorrect bits, and the liveness requirement that every bit will eventually be printed by the receiver.

The obvious solution to this problem involves sending acknowledgment messages, to indicate when a message was received. Halpern and Zuck's key insight was to recognise that an acknowledgment message in fact carries information about the knowledge state of the sender of the message. This motivated the development of the following knowledge-based protocol. After obtaining the first bit, the sender transmits it to the receiver. However, it cannot stop at this point, because for all it knows, the message may have been deleted by the environment. It thus continues to transmit the bit *until it knows the bit has been received*. At this point, the receiver knows the value of the bit that was transmitted, and the sender knows that the receiver knows the value of the bit – but the receiver does not know whether or not its acknowledgment was received. So the sender repeatedly sends a second acknowledgment, until it receives back a third acknowledgment from the receiver; when it receives this acknowledgment, it starts

```
scount is a natural number variable
rcount is a natural number variable
Sender
      scount := 0
      while true do
            read x_scount
            send x_scount until K_S K_R(x_scount)
            send "K_S K_R(x_scount)" until K_S K_R K_S K_R(x_scount)
            scount := scount + 1
      end-while
end-Sender
Receiver
      when K_R(x_0) set rcount := 0
      while true do
            write x_rcount
            send "K_R(x_rcount)" until K_R K_S K_R(x_rcount)
            send "K_R K_S K_R(x_rcount)" until K_R(x_rcount+1)
            rcount := rcount + 1
      end-while
end-Receiver
```

Fig. 2. The bit transmission protocol.

to transmit the next bit. When the receiver receives this bit, this indicates that its final (third) acknowledgment was received.

A pseudo-code version of the protocol is presented in Figure 2 (from [18, pp.39–44]). Note that we write x_i as a shorthand for "the value of bit x_i". Thus $K_R(x_i)$ means that the receiver (R) knows the value of bit x_i.

To demonstrate our ideas in a concrete setting, consider the PROMELA code given in Figure 3, where, for simplicity, we assume that message delivery is guaranteed. In a more complicated version, we may add deletion errors by having a process that can "steal" messages, but the knowledge properties at the specific points in the program – the labels, see below – would be the same.

Code is given for the sender and receiver agents and main variable declarations. The initialisation code is unremarkable, with one subtle exception. Suppose we were to initialise the Send[] array with the bits to be transmitted using a straightforward assignment statement. Then this array would remain fixed throughout every execution of the program – *and the values of the bits in this array would therefore be common knowledge to all agents in the system.* To get around this problem, we exploit SPIN's non-deterministic execution mechanism. We have a macro INITIAL(V), where V is a variable name, which assigns a "random" (sic) bit to V.

```
#define INITIAL(V) \
  if                \
  :: 1 -> V = 0;   \
  :: 1 -> V = 1;   \
  fi
```

```
#define ACK    10     /* K_R(x_i) */
#define ACK2   11     /* K_S K_R(x_i) */
#define ACK3   12     /* K_R K_S K_R(x_i) */
chan S = [10] of {int}; /* outward from sender */
chan R = [10] of {int}; /* outward from receiver */
int Send[11];          /* message sent */
int Recv[11];          /* message received */
int s_count = 0;       /* sender bit count */
int r_count = 0;       /* receiver bit count */
proctype SENDER() {
    S0: do
        :: (s_count < 10) ->
        S1: printf("sender sends bit %d", s_count);
        S2: S!Send[s_count];
        S3: R?ACK;
        S4: S!ACK2;
        S5: R?ACK3;
        S6: s_count++;
        :: (s_count == 10) ->
        S7: break
        od
}
proctype RECEIVER() {
    R0: do
        :: (r_count < 10) ->
        R1: S?Recv[r_count];
        R2: printf("receiver receives bit %d", r_count);
        R3: R!ACK;
        R4: S?ACK2;
        R5: R!ACK3;
        R6: r_count++;
        :: (r_count == 10) ->
        R7: break
        od
}
```

Fig. 3. The bit transmission protocol in PROMELA (message delivery is guaranteed).

This macro is used to initialise both the Send[] and Recv[] arrays in the init process, ensuring that the values in these arrays may initially have different values in different computations. The goal of the protocol is that eventually, the values in the Recv[] array will have the same values that were initially in the Send[] array.

The general form of properties we prove is as follows:

$$at_i(\ell) \rightarrow K_i \varphi \tag{2}$$

where ℓ is a *program label*, and the unary predicate $at_i(\ell)$ means that the program counter of agent i is at the instruction labelled by ℓ. The use of the $at_i(\ldots)$ predicate in this way is common practice when reasoning about programs using temporal logic (see, e.g., [8, pp.70–71]). We use SPIN's remote reference mechanism (P[X]@L) to define $at_i(\ldots)$ predicates.

The first property we prove is that whenever the receiver is at state R_3, (and so is about to send the acknowledgment), that it knows the value of the bit it has received.

$$\Box(at_R(R_3) \rightarrow K_R(Recv[r\_count] = Send[s\_count])) \qquad (3)$$

To deal with this, we must first find an R-local proposition for

$$Recv[r\_count] = Send[s\_count] \qquad (4)$$

to serve as the output of the function lp_R. But notice that (4) is itself R-local, and so this statement will itself do. We proceed to generate a SPIN LTL claim for (3) as follows. We define propositions p0 and p1 to represent the CKL_n propositions $at_R(R_3)$ and (4) respectively.

```
#define p0 (RECEIVER[2]@R3)
#define p1 (Recv[r_count] == Send[s_count])
```

Finally, the property to be checked is written as the SPIN LTL formula:

```
!<>(p0 && !p1)
```

(We negate the claim to be verified, so that it can be used in a **never** claim, in the conventional manner for SPIN LTL claims.)

Next, we show the corresponding property for **SENDER**: when **SENDER** is at label **S3**, (i.e., about to send an **ACK2** message), then it knows that the receiver knows the value of the bit that was most recently sent.

$$\Box(at_S(S_4) \rightarrow K_S K_R(Recv[r\_count] = Send[s\_count])) \qquad (5)$$

Notice that this is a nested knowledge formula. To deal with it, we must first find an R-local proposition for $Recv[r\_count] = Send[s\_count]$, as before. But, again, this proposition is itself R-local. This reduces the problem of checking (5) to that of checking:

$$\Box(at_S(S_4) \rightarrow K_S(Recv[r\_count] = Send[s\_count]))$$

So we must find an S-local proposition for (4) – but as this statement is S-local as well as R-local, then we can further reduce (5) to the following.

$$\Box(at_S(S_4) \rightarrow Recv[r\_count] = Send[s\_count])$$

Given the following macro

```
#define p2 (SENDER[1]@S4)
```

this property is easily represented and checked as the following SPIN LTL formula:

`!<>(p2&&!p1)`

In exactly the same way, we can check the following property:

$$\Box(at_R(R_5) \rightarrow K_R K_S K_R(Recv[r\_count] = Send[s\_count]))) \qquad (6)$$

Finally, we give an example of proving the *absence* of knowledge. Let's suppose that agent R is at label R_0. Then in this case, the bits in the `Recv[]` array will have their initially assigned (essentially random) values. It may be that the bits are "correct", in the sense that they match those in `Send[]` but this is not necessarily the case:

$$\Box(at_R(R_0) \rightarrow \neg K_R(Recv[r\_count] = Send[s\_count]))$$

Now this formula will be *invalid* in a system if there is a single run of the system that satisfies the following property

$$\Diamond(at_R(R_0) \wedge Recv[r\_count] \neq Send[s\_count])$$

This property can be directly encoded and checked using SPIN.

5 Concluding Remarks

Model checking as an approach to automatic verification has focussed almost exclusively on specifications expressed in temporal logic. Little attention has been given to temporal epistemic logics, although such logics have proven to be very useful and widely advocated in the specification of protocols [6]. In this paper, we have considered the model checking problem for such logics. We have introduced Halpern and Vardi's well-known temporal epistemic logic CKL_n, and demonstrated how, using ideas from the *interpreted systems* paradigm and the *logic of local propositions*, it is possible to reduce CKL_n model checking to LTL model checking. We then gave a case study – the bit transmission problem – which was implemented in PROMELA, and showed how desirable temporal epistemic properties of this system could be proved using SPIN. Engelhardt et al suggested that local propositions might be used in a similar manner for implementing knowledge-based programs [5].

The main limitation of our approach is that, while it makes extensive use of model checking, the verification process still requires input from a human verifier (to obtain the local propositions used when reducing the CKL_n specification to LTL). A "direct" implementation of CKL_n model checking – perhaps as an extension or refinement to SPIN – would thus be desirable. However, there are some obstacles to building such a system: unlike pure LTL formulae, CKL_n formulae can express properties of *multiple runs*. For the moment, therefore, we believe our approach has something to offer which is theoretically well-founded and practically valuable to the verifier who desires to check epistemic temporal properties of systems. And, given the extent of interest in epistemic logic and its applications in the specification of communicating systems [6], we believe that our approach is potentially very valuable indeed.

The first step for future work is to further investigate the theoretical foundations of our work, and in particular to discover the extent to which the approach is applicable. We also plan to extend our ideas here to other knowledge programs, and also like to determine classes of programs for which the local propositions that are needed can be easily determined. Using model checking to verify that programs implement knowledge-based programs is another obvious application. Also, the role and use of these local propositions, especially in contexts different from distributed systems, is, to the best of our knowledge, still not explored.

Acknowledgments

This work was supported by the UK EPSRC (project GR/R27518 – "Verifiable Languages and Protocols for Multiagent Systems"), and by the European Commission's IST programme (project IST-1999-10948 – "Sustainable Lifecycles for Information Ecosystems"). We would like to thank Alessio Lomuscio and Ron van der Meyden, who both gave detailed helpful comments on a preliminary draft of this paper.

References

1. M. Benerecetti, F. Giunchiglia, and L. Serafini. A model checking algorithm for multiagent systems. In J. P. Müller, M. P. Singh, and A. S. Rao, editors, *Intelligent Agents V (LNAI Volume 1555)*. Springer-Verlag: Berlin, Germany, 1999.
2. E. M. Clarke, O. Grumberg, and D. A. Peled. *Model Checking*. The MIT Press: Cambridge, MA, 2000.
3. C. Dixon, M. Fisher, and M. Wooldridge. Resolution for temporal logics of knowledge. *Journal of Logic and Computation*, 8(3):345–372, 1998.
4. E. A. Emerson. Temporal and modal logic. In J. van Leeuwen, editor, *Handbook of Theoretical Computer Science Volume B: Formal Models and Semantics*, pages 996–1072. Elsevier Science Publishers B.V.: Amsterdam, The Netherlands, 1990.
5. K. Engelhardt, R. van der Meyden, and Y. Moses. Knowledge and the logic of local propositions. In *Proceedings of the 1998 Conference on Theoretical Aspects of Reasoning about Knowledge (TARK98)*, pages 29–41, Evanston, IL, July 1998.
6. R. Fagin, J. Y. Halpern, Y. Moses, and M. Y. Vardi. *Reasoning About Knowledge*. The MIT Press: Cambridge, MA, 1995.
7. R. Fagin, J. Y. Halpern, Y. Moses, and M. Y. Vardi. Knowledge-based programs. *Distributed Computing*, 10(4):199–225, 1997.
8. R. Goldblatt. *Logics of Time and Computation (CSLI Lecture Notes Number 7)*. Center for the Study of Language and Information, Ventura Hall, Stanford, CA 94305, 1987. (Distributed by Chicago University Press).
9. J. Y. Halpern and M. Y. Vardi. The complexity of reasoning about knowledge and time. I. Lower bounds. *Journal of Computer and System Sciences*, 38:195–237, 1989.

10. J. Y. Halpern and M. Y. Vardi. Model checking versus theorem proving: A manifesto. In V. Lifschitz, editor, *AI and Mathematical Theory of Computation - Papers in Honor of John McCarthy*, pages 151–176. The Academic Press: London, England, 1991.

11. J. Y. Halpern and L. D. Zuck. A little knowledge goes a long way: knowledge-based derivations and correctness proofs for a family of protocols. *Journal of the ACM*, 39(3):449–478, 1992.

12. J. Hintikka. *Knowledge and Belief.* Cornell University Press: Ithaca, NY, 1962.

13. G. Holzmann. *Design and Validation of Computer Protocols.* Prentice Hall International: Hemel Hempstead, England, 1991.

14. G. Holzmann. The Spin model checker. *IEEE Transaction on Software Engineering*, 23(5):279–295, May 1997.

15. Z. Manna and A. Pnueli. *The Temporal Logic of Reactive and Concurrent Systems.* Springer-Verlag: Berlin, Germany, 1992.

16. Z. Manna and A. Pnueli. *Temporal Verification of Reactive Systems - Safety.* Springer-Verlag: Berlin, Germany, 1995.

17. K. L. McMillan. *Symbolic Model Checking.* Kluwer Academic Publishers: Boston, MA, 1993.

18. J.-J. Ch. Meyer and W. van der Hoek. *Epistemic Logic for AI and Computer Science.* Cambridge University Press: Cambridge, England, 1995.

19. A. S. Rao and M. P. Georgeff. A model-theoretic approach to the verification of situated reasoning systems. In *Proceedings of the Thirteenth International Joint Conference on Artificial Intelligence (IJCAI-93)*, pages 318–324, Chambéry, France, 1993.

20. R. van der Meyden. Finite state implementations of knowledge-based programs. In *Proceedings of the Conference on Foundations of Software Technology and Theoretical Computer Science (LNCS Volume 1180)*, pages 262–273, 1996.

21. R. van der Meyden. Knowledge based programs: On the complexity of perfect recall in finite environments. In Y. Shoham, editor, *Proceedings of the Sixth Conference on Theoretical Aspects of Rationality and Knowledge*, pages 31–50, De Zeeuwse Stromen, Renesse, Holland, March 1996.

22. R. van der Meyden and N. Shilov. Model checking knowledge and time in systems with perfect recall. In *Proceedings of the Conference on Foundations of Software Technology and Theoretical Computer Science (LNCS Volume 1738)*, pages 432–445. Springer-Verlag: Berlin, Germany, 1999.

23. M. Y. Vardi. Implementing knowledge-based programs. In *Proceedings of the Sixth Conference on Theoretical Aspects of Rationality and Knowledge (TARK 1996)*, pages 15–30, De Zeeuwse Stromen, Renesse, The Netherlands, March 1996.

24. M. Y. Vardi. Branching vs. linear time: Final showdown. In T. Margaria and W. Yi, editors, *Proceedings of the 2001 Conference on Tools and Algorithms for the Construction and Analysis of Systems, TACAS 2001 (LNCS Volume 2031)*, pages 1–22. Springer-Verlag: Berlin, Germany, April 2001.

25. M. Wooldridge, C. Dixon, and M. Fisher. A tableau-based proof method for temporal logics of knowledge and belief. *Journal of Applied Non-Classical Logics*, 8(3):225–258, 1998.

Partial Order Reduction
in Directed Model Checking

Alberto Lluch-Lafuente, Stefan Edelkamp, and Stefan Leue

Institut für Informatik, Albert-Ludwigs-Universität
Georges-Köhler-Allee, D-79110 Freiburg
{lafuente,edelkamp,leue}@informatik.uni-freiburg.de

Abstract. Partial order reduction is a very succesful technique for avoiding the state explosion problem that is inherent to explicit state model checking of asynchronous concurrent systems. It exploits the commutativity of concurrently executed transitions in interleaved system runs in order to reduce the size of the explored state space. Directed model checking on the other hand addresses the state explosion problem by using guided search techniques during state space exploration. As a consequence, shorter errors trails are found and less search effort is required than when using standard depth-first or breadth-first search. We analyze how to combine directed model checking with partial order reduction methods and give experimental results on how the combination of both techniques performs.

1 Introduction

Model checking [3] is a formal analysis technique for the verification of hardware and software systems. Given the model of the system as well as a property specification, typically formulated in some temporal logic formalism, the state space of the model is analyzed to check whether the property is valid or not. The main limitation of this method is the size of the resulting state space, known as the *state explosion problem*. It occurs due to non-determinism in the model introduced by data or concurrency.

Different approaches have been proposed to tackle this problem. One of the most successful techniques is partial order reduction [22]. This method explores a reduced state space by exploiting the independence of concurrently executed events. Partial order reduction is particularly efficient in asynchronous systems, where many interleavings of concurrent events are equivalent with respect to a given property specification. Considering only one or a few representatives of one class of equivalent interleavings leads to drastic reductions in the size of the state space to be explored.

Another technique that has been suggested in dealing with the state explosion problem is the use of heuristic search techniques. It applies state evaluation functions to rank the set of successor states in order to decide where to continue the search. Applying such methods often allows to find errors at optimal or sub-optimal depths and to find errors in models for which "blind" search

D. Bošnački and S. Leue (Eds.): SPIN 2002, LNCS 2318, pp. 112–127, 2002.
© Springer-Verlag Berlin Heidelberg 2002

strategies like depth-first and breadth-first search exceed the available time and space resources. Optimal or near-to optimal solutions are particularly important for designers to understand the sequence of steps that lead to an error, since shorter trails are likely to be more comprehensible than longer ones. In protocol verification, heuristic search model checking has been shown to accelerate the search for finding errors [7] and to shorten already existing long trails [6].

It is not a priori obvious to what extent partial order reduction and guided search can co-exist in model checking. In fact, as we show later, applying partial-order reduction to a state space does not preserve optimality of the shortest path to a target state. It is the goal of this paper to show that nevertheless, partial order reduction and directed model checking can co-exist, and that the mutual negative influence is only minimal.

In this paper, we will focus on safety error detection in model checking. We will establish a hierarchy of relaxation of the cycle condition for partial order reduction known as C3, and we will classify the relaxations with respect to their applicability to different classes of heuristic search algorithms. To the best of our knowledge, at the time of writing no publication addressing heuristic search in model checking [7,8,6,12,4,17,24] has analyzed how to combine guided search with partial order reduction.

The paper is structured as follows. Section 2 gives some background on directed model checking. Section 3 discusses partial order reduction and a hierarchy of conditions for its application to different search algorithms. This Section also addresses the problem of optimality in the length of the counterexamples. Section 4 presents experimental results showing how the combination of partial order reduction and directed model checking perform. Section 5 summarizes the results and concludes the paper.

2 Directed Model Checking

Analysts have different expectations regarding the capabilities of formal analysis tools at different stages of the software process [4]. In *exploratory* mode, usually applicable to earlier stages of the process, one wishes to find errors fast. In *fault-finding* mode, which usually follows later, one expects to obtain meaningful error trails while one is willing to tolerate somewhat longer execution times. Directed model checking has been identified as an improvement of standard model checking algorithms that help in achieving the objectives of both modes.

Early approaches to directed model checking [17,24] propose the use of best-first search algorithms in order to accelerate the search for error states. Further approaches [8,7,6,4] propose the full spectrum of classical heuristic search strategies for the verification process in order to accelerate error detection and to provide optimal or near-to-optimal trails. Most of these techniques can be applied to the detection of safety properties only or for shortening given error traces corresponding to liveness violations [6].

Contrary to blind search algorithms like depth- and breadth-first search, heuristic search exploits information of the specific problem being solved in or-

procedure search
  $Closed \leftarrow \emptyset$
  $Open \leftarrow \emptyset$
  $Open.insert(start\_state)$
  while $(Open \neq \emptyset)$ **do**
    $u \leftarrow Open.extract()$
    $Closed.insert(u)$
    if $error(u)$ **then**
      exit $ErrorFound$
    for each successor v of u **do**
      if not $v \in Closed \cup Open$ **then**
        $Open.insert(v)$

Fig. 1. A general state expanding search algorithm.

der to guide the search. Estimator functions approximate the distance from a given state to a set of goal states. The values provided by these functions decide in which direction the search will be continued. Two of the most frequently used heuristic search algorithms are A* [10] and IDA* [15]. In the following we describe a general state expanding search algorithm that can be either instantiated as a depth or breadth first search algorithm or as one of the above heuristic search algorithms. We briefly the basic principles of heuristic search algorithms, and consider different heuristic estimates to be applied in the context of directed model checking for error detection. In our setting we interpret error states as goal nodes in an underlying graph representation of the state space with error trails corresponding to solution paths.

2.1 General State Expanding Search Algorithm

The general state expanding search algorithm of Figure 1 divides the state space S into three sets: the set $Open$ of visited but not yet expanded states, the set $Closed$ of visited and expanded states and the set $S \setminus (Closed \cup Open)$ of not yet visited states. The algorithm performs the search by extracting states from $Open$ and moving them into $Closed$. States extracted from $Open$ are expanded, i.e. their successor states are generated. If a successor of an expanded state is neither in $Open$ nor in $Closed$ it is added to $Open$.

Breadth-first search and depth-first search can be defined as concrete cases of the general algorithm presented above, where the former implements $Open$ as a FIFO queue and the latter as a stack.

2.2 Algorithm A*

Algorithm A* treats $Open$ as a priority queue in which the priority of a state v is given by function $f(v)$ that is computed as the sum of the length of the path from the start state $g(v)$ and the estimated distance to a goal state $h(v)$. In addition to the general algorithm, A* can move states from *Closed* to *Open* when they are reached along a shorter path. This step is called reopening and is necessary to guarantee that the algorithm will find the shortest path to the goal state when non-monotone heuristics are used. For the sake of simplicity, throughout the paper we only consider monotone heuristics which do not require reopening [20]. Monotone heuristics satisfy that for each state u and each successor v of u the difference between $h(u)$ and $h(v)$ is less or equal to the cost of the transition that goes from u to v. Assuming monotone estimates is not a severe restriction, since it turns out that in practical examples most proposed heuristics are indeed monotone. If h is a lower bound of the distance to a goal state, then A* is admissible, which means that it will always return the shortest path to a goal state [19]. Best-first search is a common variant of A* that takes only h into account.

2.3   Iterative-Deepening A*

Iterative-deepening A*, IDA* for short, is a refinement of the brute-force depth-first iterative deepening search (DFID) that combines the space efficiency of depth-first search and the admissibility of A*. While DFID performs successive depth-first search iterations with increasing depth bound, in IDA* increasing cost bounds are used to limit search iterations. The cost bound f of a state is the same as in A*. Similar to A*, IDA* guarantees optimal solution paths if the estimator is a lower bound.

2.4   Heuristic Estimates

The above presented search algorithms require suitable estimator functions. In model checking, such functions approximate the number of transitions for the system to reach an error state from a given state. During the model checking process, however, an explicit error state is not always available. In fact, in many cases we do not know if there is an error in the model at all. We distinguish the cases when errors are unknown and when error states are explicit.

If an explicit error state is given, estimates that exploit the information of this state can be devised. Examples are estimates based on the Hamming distance of the state vectors for the current and the targe state, and the FSM distance that uses the minimum local distances in the state transition graph of the different processes to derive an estimat [6].

Estimating the distance to *unknown* error states is more difficult. The formula-based heuristic [7] constructs a function that characterizes error states. Given an error formula f and starting from state s, a heuristic function $h_f(s)$ is constructed for estimating the number of transitions needed until a state s' is reached, where $f(s')$ holds. Constructing an error formula for deadlocks is not trivial. In [7] we discuss various alternatives, including formula based approaches, an estimate based on the number of non-blocked processes, and an estimate derived from user-provided characterizations of local control states as deadlock-prone.

3   Partial Order Reduction

Partial order reduction methods exploit the commutativity of asynchronous systems in order to reduce the size of the state space. The resulting state space is constructed in such a manner that it is equivalent to the original one with respect to the specification. Several partial order approaches have been proposed, namely those based on "stubborn" sets [23], "persistent" sets [9] and "ample" sets [21]. Although they differ in detail, they are based on similar ideas. Due to its popularity, in this paper we mainly follow the ample set approach. Nonetheless, most of the reasoning presented in this paper can be adjusted to any of the other approaches.

3.1   Stuttering Equivalence of Labeled Transition Systems

Our approach is mainly focused to the verification of asynchronous systems where the global system is constructed as the asynchronous product of a set of local component processes following the interleaving model of execution. Such systems can be modeled by labeled transitions systems.

A labeled finite transition system is a tuple $\langle S, S_0, T, AP, L \rangle$ where S is a finite set of states, S_0 is the set of initial states, T is a finite set of transitions such that each transition $\alpha \in T$ is a partial function $\alpha : S \to S$, AP is a finite set of propositions and L is a labeling function $S \to 2^{AP}$. The execution of a transition system is defined as a sequence of states interleaved by transitions, i.e. a sequence $s_0 \alpha_0 s_1 \ldots$, such that s_0 is in S_0 and for each $i \geq 0$, $s_{i+1} = \alpha_i(s_i)$.

The algorithm for generating a reduced state space explores only some of the successors of a state. A transition α is *enabled* in a state s if $\alpha(s)$ is defined. The set of enabled transitions from a state s is usually called the *enabled set* and denoted as *enabled(s)*. The algorithm selects and follows only a subset of this set called the *ample set* and denoted as *ample(s)*. A state s is said to be *fully expanded* when $ample(s) = enabled(s)$.

Partial order reduction techniques are based on the observation that the order in which some transitions are executed is not relevant. This leads to the concept of independence between transitions. Two transitions $\alpha, \beta \in T$ are independent if for each state $s \in S$ in which both transitions are defined the following two properties hold:

1. α and β do not disable each other: $\alpha \in enabled(\beta(s))$ and $\beta \in enabled(\alpha(s))$.
2. α and β are *conmutative*: $\alpha(\beta(s)) = \beta(\alpha(s))$.

Two transitions are dependent if they are not independent. A further fundamental concept is the fact that some transitions are *invisible* with respect to atomic propositions that occur in the property specification. A transition α is invisible with respect to a set of propositions P if for each state s and for each successor s' of s we have $L(s) \cap P = L(s') \cap P$.

We now present the concept of *stuttering equivalence* with respect to a property P. A *block* is defined as a finite execution containing invisible transitions

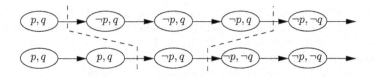

Fig. 2. Stuttering equivalent executions.

only. Intuitively, two executions are stuttering equivalent if they can be defined as a concatenation of blocks such that the atomic propositions of the i-th block of boths executions have the same intersection with P, for each $i > 0$. Figure 2 depicts two stuttering equivalent paths with respect to a property in which only propositions p and q occurr.

Two transition systems are stuttering equivalent if and only if they have the same set of initial states and for each execution in one of the systems starting from an initial state there exists a stuttering equivalent execution in the other system starting from the same initial state. It can be shown that LTL_{-X} formulae[1] cannot distinguish between stuttering equivalent transition systems [3]. In other words, if M and N are two stuttering equivalent transition systems, then M satisfies a given LTL_{-X} specification if and only if N also does.

3.2 Ample Set Construction for Safety LTL_{-X}

The main goal of the ample set construction is to select a subset of the successors of every state such that the reduced state space is stuttering equivalent to the full state space with respect to a property specification given by a set P of atomic propositions. The construction should offer significant reduction without requiring a high computational overhead. The following four conditions are necessary and sufficient for the proper construction of a partial order reduced state space for a given property specification P.

Condition C0: $ample(s)$ is empty exactly when $enabled(s)$ is empty.

Condition C1: Along every path in the full state space that starts at s, a transition that is dependent on a transition in $ample(s)$ does not occur without a transition in $ample(s)$ occurring first.

Condition C2: If a state s is not fully expanded, then each transition α in the ample set must be invisible with regard to P.

Condition C3: If for each state of a cycle in the reduced state space, a transition α is enabled, then α must be in the ample set of some of the states of the reduced state space.

Observe that the approximations used in **C0**, **C1** and **C2** can be implemented independently from the particular search algorithm used. It was shown in [3] that the complexity of checking **C0** and **C2** does not depend on the search

---

[1] LTL_{-X} is the linear time temporal logic without the next-time operator X.

algorithm. Checking Condition **C1** is more complicated. In fact, it has been shown to be at least as hard as checking reachability for the full state space. It is, however, usually over-approximated by checking a stronger condition [3] that can be checked independently of the search algorithm.

Condition **C3** has been implicitly proposed in [11]. In the following we focus on this condition. We will see that the complexity of checking it depends on the search algorithm used.

3.3   Dynamically Checking C3

Checking **C3** can be reduced to detecting cycles during the search. Cycles can easily be established in depth-first search: Every cycle contains a *backward edge*, i.e. an edge that links back to a state that is stored on the search stack [3]. Consequently, avoiding ample sets containing only backward edges except when the state is fully expanded ensures satisfaction of **C3** when using depth-first search or IDA*, since both methods perform a depth-first traversal. The resulting stack-based characterization $C3_{stack}$ can be stated as follows[11]:

Condition $C3_{stack}$: If a state s is not fully expanded, then at least one transition in $ample(s)$ does not lead to a state on the search stack.

The implementation of $C3_{stack}$ for depth-first search strategies marks each expanded state on the stack with an additional flag, so that stack containment can be checked in constant time. Depth-first strategies that record visited states will not consider every cycle in the state space on the search stack, since there might exist exponentially many of them. However, $C3_{stack}$ is still a sufficient condition for **C3** since every cycle contains at least a backward edge.

Detecting cycles with general state expanding search algorithms that do not perform a depth-first traversal of the state space is more complex. For a cycle to exist, it is necessary to reach an already visited state. If during the search a state is found to be already visited, checking that this state is part of a cycle requires to check if this state is reachable from itself which increases the time complexity of the algorithm from linear to quadratic in the size of the state space. Therefore the commonly adopted approach assumes that a cycle exists whenever an already visited state is found. Using this idea leads to weaker reductions, since it is known that the state spaces of concurrent systems usually have a high density of duplicate states. The resulting condition [2,1] is defined as:

Condition $C3_{duplicate}$: If a state s is not fully expanded, then at least one transition in $ample(s)$ does not lead to an already visited state.

A proof of sufficiency of condition $C3_{stack}$ for depth-first search is given in [11]. The proof of sufficiency of condition $C3_{duplicate}$ when combined with a depth-first search is given by the fact that $C3_{duplicate}$ implies $C3_{stack}$; if at least one transition in $ample(s)$ has a non-visited successor this transition certainly does not lead to a successor on the stack.

In order to prove the correctness of partial order reduction with condition **C3**$_{duplicate}$ for general state expanding algorithms in the following lemma, we will use induction on the state expansion ordering, starting from a completed exploration and moving backwards with respect to the traversal algorithm. As a by-product the more general setting in the lemma also proves the correctness of partial order reduction according to condition **C3**$_{duplicate}$ for depth-first, breadth-first, best-first, and A* like search schemes. The lemma fixes a state $s \in S$ after termination of the search and ensures that each enabled transition is executed either in the ample set or in a state that appears later on in the expansion process. Therefore, no transition is omitted. Applying the lemma to all states s in S implies **C3**, which, in turn, ensures a correct reduction.

Lemma 1. *For each state $s \in S$ the following is true: when the search of a general search algorithm terminates, each transition $\alpha \in enabled(s)$ has been selected either in $ample(s)$ or in a state s' such that s' has been expanded after s.*

Proof. Let s be the last expanded state. Every transition $\alpha \in enabled(s)$ leads to an already expanded state, otherwise the search would have been continued. Condition **C3**$_{duplicate}$ enforces therefore that state s is fully expanded and the lemma trivially holds for s.

Now suppose that the lemma is valid for those states whose expansion order is greater than n. Let s be the n-th expanded state. If s is fully expanded, the lemma trivially holds for s. Otherwise we have that $ample(s) \subset enabled(s)$. Transitions in $ample(s)$ are selected in s. Since $ample(s)$ is accepted by condition **C3**$_{duplicate}$ there is a transition $\alpha \in ample(s)$ such that $\alpha(s)$ leads to a state that has not been previously visited nor expanded. Evidently the expansion order of $\alpha(s)$ is higher than n. Condition **C1** implies that the transitions in $ample(s)$ are all independent from those in $enabled(s) \setminus ample(s)$ [3]. A transition $\gamma \in enabled(s) \setminus ample(s)$ cannot be dependent from a transition in $ample(s)$, since otherwise in the full graph there would be a path starting with γ and a transition depending on some transition in $ample(s)$ would be executed before a transition in $ample(s)$. Hence, transitions in $enabled(s) \setminus ample(s)$ are still enabled in $\alpha(s)$ and contained in $enabled(\alpha(s))$. By the induction hypothesis the lemma holds for $\alpha(s)$ and, therefore, transitions in $enabled(s) \setminus ample(s)$ are selected in $\alpha(s)$ or in a state that is expanded after it. Hence the lemma also holds for s. $\qquad\square$

3.4   Statically Checking C3

In contrast to the previous approaches the method to be presented in this Section explicitly exploits the structure of the underlying interleaving system. Recall that the global system is constructed as the asynchronous composition of several components. The authors of [16] present what they call a *static* partial order reduction method based on the following observation. Any cycle in the global state space is composed of a local cycle, which may be of length zero, in the state transition graph of each component process. Breaking every local cycle breaks every global cycle. The structure of the processes of the system is analyzed before the global state space generation begins. The method is independent from the search algorithm to be used during the verification.

Some transitions are marked are with a special flag, called *sticky*. Sticky transitions enforce full expansion of a state. Marking at least one transition in each local cycle as *sticky* guarantees that at least one state in each global cycle is fully expanded, which satisfies condition **C3**. The resulting **C3**$_{static}$ condition is defined as follows:

Condition C3$_{static}$**:** If a state s is not fully expanded then no transition in *ample*(s) is sticky.

Selecting one sticky transition for each local cycle is a naive approach that can be made more effective. The impact of local cycles on the set of variables of the system can be analyzed in order to establish certain dependencies between local cycles. For example, if a local cycle C_1 has an overall incrementing effect on a variable v, for a global cycle to exist, it is necessary (but not sufficient) to execute C_1 in combination with a local cycle C_2 that has an overall decrementing effect on v. In this case one can select only a sticky transition for this pair of local cycles.

3.5   Hierarchy of C3 Conditions

Figure 3 depicts a diagram with all the presented **C3** conditions. Arrows indicate which condition enforeces which other. In the rest of the paper we will say that a condition A is stronger than a condition B if A enforces B. The dashed arrow arrow from $C3_{duplicate}$ to **C3**$_{stack}$ denotes that when search is done with a depth-first search based algorithm **C3**$_{stack}$ enforces $C3_{duplicate}$ but not viceversa. The dashed regions contain the conditions that can be correctly used with general state expanding algorithms, and those that work only for depth-first search like algorithms. For a given algorithm, the arrows also denote that a condition will produce better or equal reduction.

3.6   Solution Quality and Partial Order

One of the goals of directed model checking is to find shortest paths to errors. Although from a practical point of view near-to optimal solutions may be sufficient to help designers during the debugging phase, finding optimal counterexamples still remains an important theoretical question. Heuristic search algorithms require lower bound estimates for guaranteeing optimal solution lengths.

Partial order reduction, however, does not preserve optimality of the solution length for the full state space. In fact, the shortest path to an error in the reduced state space may be longer than the shortest path to an error state in the full state space. Intuitively, the reason is that the concept of stuttering equivalence does not make assumptions about the length of the equivalent blocks. Suppose that the transitions α and β of the state space depicted in Figure 4 are independent

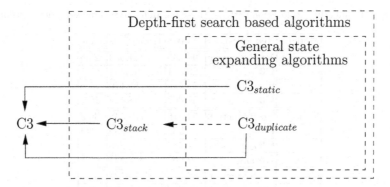

Fig. 3. C3 conditions.

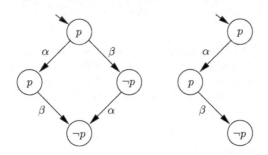

Fig. 4. Example of a full state space (left) and a reduction (right).

and that α is invisible with respect to the set of propositions p. Suppose further that p is the only atomic proposition occurring in the safety property we want to check. With these assumptions the reduced state space for the example is stuttering equivalent to the full one. The shortest path that violates the invariant in the reduced state space is $\alpha\beta$, which has a length of 2. In the full one the path β is the shortest path to an error state and the error trail has a length of 1. Section 4 presents experimental evidence for a reduction in solution quality when applying partial order reduction.

4   Experiments

The experimental results that we report in this Section have been obtained using our experimental directed model checker HSF-SPIN[2] [7] for which we have implemented the described reduction methods. All results were produced on a SUN workstation, UltraSPARC-II CPU with 248 Mhz.

---

[2] Available at www.informatik.uni-freiburg.de/~lafuente/hsf-spin

Table 1. Exhaustive exploration with depth-first search and several reduction methods.

Model	Reduction	States	Transitions	Time
marriers	No Reduction	96,295	264,053	20.6
	$C3_{stack}$	29,501	37,341	5.5
	$C3_{duplicate}$	72,536	111,170	17.5
	$C3_{static}$	57,067	88,119	10.7
leader	No Reduction	54,216	210,548	36.3
	$C3_{stack}$	963	4,939	4.4
	$C3_{duplicate}$	1,417	6,899	5.0
	$C3_{static}$	2,985	7,527	4.8
giop	No Reduction	664,376	2,579,722	259.3
	$C3_{stack}$	65,964	90,870	23.1
	$C3_{duplicate}$	284,083	605,147	115.0
	$C3_{static}$	231,102	445,672	79.0

We use a set of Promela models as benchmarks including a model of a leader election protocol[3] [5] (leader), the CORBA GIOP protocol [13] (giop), a telephony model[4] [14] (pots), and a model of a concurrent program that solves the stable marriage problem [18] (marriers). The considered versions of these protocols violate certain safety properties.

4.1 Exhaustive Exploration

The objective of the first set of experiments is to show how the different variants of the **C3** condition perform. We expect that stronger **C3** conditions according to hierarchy in Figure 3 lead to weaker reductions in the number of stored and expanded states and transitions.

We use the marriers, leader and giop protocols in our experiments. The pots model is too large to be explored exhaustively. In this and all following experiments we have selected the biggest configuration of these protocols that can still be exhaustively analyzed. Exploration is performed by depth-first search.

Table 1 depicts the size of the state space as a result of the application of different **C3** conditions. The number of transitions performed and the running time in seconds are also included. For each model, the first row indicates the size of the explored state space when no reduction is used.

As expected stronger conditions offer weaker reductions. This loss of reduction is especially evident in the giop protocol, where the two conditions potentially applicable in A*, namely $C3_{duplicate}$ and $C3_{static}$, are worse by about a factor of 4 with respect to the condition that offers the best reduction, namely $C3_{stack}$.

For the marriers and giop protocols the static reduction yields a stronger reduction than condition $C3_{duplicate}$. Only for the leader election algorithm this

---

[3] Available at `netlib.bell-labs.com/netlib/spin`

[4] Available at `www.informatik.uni-freiburg.de/~lafuente/models/models.html`

Table 2. Finding a safety violation with A* and several reduction methods.

Model	Reduction	States	Transitions	Time	Length
marriers	no	5,077	12,455	0.93	50
	$C3_{duplicate}$	2,988	4,277	0.51	50
	$C3_{static}$	1,604	1,860	0.31	50
pots	no	2,668	6,519	1.57	67
	$C3_{duplicate}$	1,662	3,451	1.08	67
	$C3_{static}$	1,662	3,451	1.00	67
leader	no	7,172	22,876	6.87	58
	$C3_{duplicate}$	65	3,190	4.76	77
	$C3_{static}$	399	3,593	4.88	66
giop	no	31,066	108,971	26.50	58
	$C3_{duplicate}$	21,111	48,870	16.68	58
	$C3_{static}$	12,361	24,493	9.36	58

is not true. This is probably due to the relative high number of local cycles in the state transition graph of the processes in this model, and to the fact that there is no global cycle in the global state space. Since our implementation of the static reduction considers only the simplest approach where one transition in each cycle is marked as sticky, we assume that the results will be even better with refined methods for characterizing transitions as sticky.

In addition to the reduction in space consumption, partial order reduction also provides reduction in time. Even though the overhead introduced by the computation of the ample set and the static computation prior to the exploration when $C3_{static}$ is used, time reduction is still achieved in all cases.

4.2   Error Finding with A* and Partial Order Reduction

The next set of experiments is intended to highlight the impact of various reduction methods when detecting errors with A*. More precisely, we want to compare the two **C3** conditions $C3_{duplicate}$ and $C3_{static}$ that can be applied jointly with A*.

Table 2 shows the effect of applying $C3_{duplicate}$ and $C3_{static}$ in conjunction with A*. The table has the same format as the previous one, but this time the length of the error trail is included. Similar to SPIN[5], we count a sequence of atomic steps (respectively expansions) as one unique transition (expansion), but length of the error trail is given in steps in order to provide a better idea of what the user of the model checker gets.

As expected, both conditions achieve a reduction in the number of stored states and transitions performed. Solution quality is only lost in the case of leader. This occurs also in experiments done with IDA*. In the same test case $C3_{static}$ requires the storage of more states and the execution of more transitions

---

[5] Available at **netlib.bell-labs.com/netlib/spin/whatispin.html**

Table 3. Finding a safety violation with IDA* with and without reduction.

Model	Reduction	States	Transitions	Time	Length
marriers	no	4,724	84,594	19.29	50
	yes	1,298	4,924	8.40	50
pots	no	2,422	46,929	36.52	67
	yes	1,518	20,406	28.37	67
leader	no	6,989	141,668	210.67	56
	yes	55	50,403	73.90	77
giop	no	30,157	868,184	225.54	58
	yes	7,441	102,079	78.43	58

than $\mathbf{C3}_{duplicate}$. The reasons are the same as the ones mentioned in the previous set of experiments. On the other hand, $\mathbf{C3}_{duplicate}$ produces a longer error trail. A possible interpretation is that more reduction leads to higher probability that the anomaly that causes the loss of solution quality occurs. In other words, the bigger the reduction is, the longer the stuttering equivalent executions and, therefore, the longer the expected trail lengths become. Table 2 also shows that the overhead introduced by partial order reduction and heuristic search does not avoid time reduction.

4.3   Error Finding with IDA* and Partial Order Reduction

We also investigated the effect of partial order reduction when the state space exploration is performed with IDA*. The test cases are the same of the previous Section. Partial order reduction with IDA* uses the cycle condition $\mathbf{C3}_{stack}$.

Table 3 depicts the results on detecting a safety error with and without applying partial order reduction. The table shows the total number of transitions performed, the maximal peak of stored states and the length of the provided counterexamples. As in the previous set of experiments, solution quality is only lost when applying partial order reduction in the leader election algorithm. On the other hand, this is also the protocol for which the best reduction is obtained. We assume that the reason is the same as indicated in the previous set of experiments. In addition, the overhead introduced by partial order reduction and heuristic search does avoid time reduction as explained for previous experiments.

4.4   Combined Effect of Heuristic Search and Partial Order

In this Section we are interested in analyzing the combined state space reduction effect of partial order reduction and heuristic search. More precisely, we have measured the reduction ratio (size of full state space vs. size of reduced state space) provided by one of the techniques when the other technique is enabled or not, as well as the reduction ratio of using both techniques simultaneously.

The Table on the left of Figure 5 indicates the reduction factor achieved by partial order and heuristic search when A* is used as the search algorithm. The

marriers	N	C
H	2.3	6.5
PO	40.8	117.6
H+PO	267.0	

pots	N	C
H	5.9	8.4
PO	1.4	1.6
H+PO	9.5	

leader	N	C
H	1.9	2.6
PO	2.7	3.2
H+PO	5.9	

giop	N	C
H	1.3	1.3
PO	2.6	2.5
H+PO	3.3	

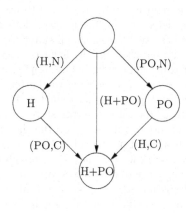

Fig. 5. Table with reduction factor due partial order and heuristic search (left) and an explanatory diagram (right).

Figure also includes a diagram that helps to understand the table. The reduction factor due to a given technique is computed as the number of stored states when the search is done without applying the respective technique divided by the number of stored states when the search is done applying the technique. Recall that when no heuristic is applied, A* performs breadth-first search. A search is represented in the diagram by a circle labeled with the applied technique(s), namely heuristic search (H), partial-order reduction (PO) or both (H+PO). The labels of the edges in the diagram refer to the cells of the table which contain the measured reduction factors. The leftmost column of the table indicates the technique(s) for which the reduction effect is measured. When testing the reduction ratios of the methods separately, we distinguish whether the other method is applied (C) or not (N).

In some cases the reduction factor provided by one of the techniques when working alone ((H,N) and (PO,N)) improves when the other technique is applied ((H,C) and (PO,C)). This is particularly evident in the case of the marriers model, where the reduction provided by heuristic search is improved from 2.3 to 6.5 and that of partial order reduction increases from 40.8 to 117.6. The expected gain of applying both independently would be $2.3 \times 40.8 = 93.8$ while the combined effect is a reduction of 267.0 which indicates a synergetic effect. However, as illustrated by the figures for the giop model, synergetic gains cannot always be expected.

5 Conclusions

When combining partial order reduction with directed search two main problems must be considered. First, common partial order reduction techniques require to check a condition which entails the detection of cycles during the construction of the reduced state space. Depth-first search based algorithms like IDA* can easily detect cycles during the exploration. On the other side, heuristic search algorithms like A* are not well-suited for cycle detection. Stronger cycle conditions or static reduction methods have to be used. We have established a hierarchy of approximation conditions for ample set condition **C3** and our experiments show that weaker the condition, the better the effect on the state space search.

Second, partial order reduction techniques do not preserve optimality of the length of the path to error states. In other words, when partial order is used there is no guarantee to find the shortest counterexample that lead to an error, which is one of the core objectives of the paradigm of directed model checking. In current work we are analyze the possibility of avoiding this problem by exploiting independence of events to shorten error trails.

Experimental results show that in some instances, partial order reduction has positive effects when used in combination with directed search strategies. Although solution quality is lost in some cases, significant reductions can be achieved even when using A* with weaker methods than classical cycle conditions. Static reduction, in particular, seems to be more promising than other methods applicable with A*. Partial order reduction provides drastic reductions when error detection is performed by IDA*. We have also analyzed the combined effect of heuristics and reduction, showing than in most cases the reduction effect of one technique is lightly accentuated by the other. Experimental results also show that both techniques reduce running time even though the overhead they introduce.

Acknowlegdements

The authors wish to thank the reviewers for their careful reviews and for their constructive criticism. The first two authors acknowledge support they received from the Deutsche Forschungsgemeinschaft through grants Ot 64/13-2 and Ed 74/2-1.

References

1. R. Alur, R. Brayton, T. Henzinger, S. Qaderer, and S. Rajamani. Partial-order reduction in symbolic state space exploration. In *Computer Aided Verification (CAV)*, Lecture Notes in Computer Science, pages 340–351. Springer, 1997.
2. C.-T. Chou and D. Peled. Formal verification of a partial-order reduction technique for model checking. In *Tools and Algorithms for Construction and Analysis of Systems*, pages 241–257, 1996.
3. E. M. Clarke, O. Grumberg, and D. A. Peled. *Model Checking*. MIT Press, 1999.
4. J. M. Cobleigh, L. A. Clarke, and L. J. Osterweil. The right algorithm at the right time: Comparing data flow analysis algorithms for finite state verification. In *Proceedings of the 23rd ICSE*, pages 37–46, 2001.
5. D. Dolev, M. Klawe, and M. Rodeh. An O(n log n) unidirectional distributed algorithm for extrema finding in a circle. *Journal of Algorithms*, 1982.

6. S. Edelkamp, A. L. Lafuente, and S. Leue. Trail-directed model checking. In S. D. Stoller and W. Visser, editors, *Electronic Notes in Theoretical Computer Science*, volume 55. Elsevier Science Publishers, 2001.

7. S. Edelkamp, A. Lluch-Lafuente, and S. Leue. Directed model-checking in HSF-SPIN. In *8th International SPIN Workshop on Model Checking Software*, Lecture Notes in Computer Science 2057, pages 57–79. Springer, 2001.

8. S. Edelkamp, A. Lluch-Lafuente, and S. Leue. Protocol verification with heuristic search. In *AAAI-Spring Symposium on Model-based Validation of Intelligence*, pages 75–83, 2001.

9. P. Godefroid. Using partial orders to improve automatic verification methods. In E. M. Clarke, editor, *Proceedings of the 2nd International Conference on Computer-Aided Verification (CAV '90), Rutgers, New Jersey, 1990*, number 531, pages 176–185, Berlin-Heidelberg-New York, 1991. Springer.

10. P. E. Hart, N. J. Nilsson, and B. Raphael. A formal basis for heuristic determination of minimum path cost. *IEEE Transactions on on Systems Science and Cybernetics*, 4:100–107, 1968.

11. G. Holzmann, P. Godefroid, and D. Pirottin. Coverage preserving reduction strategies for reachability analysis. In *Proc. 12th Int. Conf on Protocol Specification, Testing, and Verification, INWG/IFIP*, Orlando, Fl., June 1992.

12. G. J. Holzmann. Algorithms for automated protocol verification. *AT&T Technical Journal*, 69(2):32–44, Feb. 1990. Special Issue on Protocol Testing, Specification, and Verification.

13. M. Kamel and S. Leue. Formalization and validation of the General Inter-ORB Protocol (GIOP) using PROMELA and SPIN. *International Journal on Software Tools for Technology Transfer*, 2(4):394–409, 2000.

14. M. Kamel and S. Leue. VIP: A visual editor and compiler for v-Promela. In *Tools and Algorithms for the Construction and Analysis of Systems (TACAS)*, Lecture Notes in Computer Science, pages 471–486. Springer, 2000.

15. R. E. Korf. Depth-first iterative-deepening: An optimal admissible tree search. *Artificial Intelligence*, 27(1):97–109, 1985.

16. R. P. Kurshan, V. Levin, M. Minea, D. Peled, and H. Yenigun. Static partial order reduction. In *Tools and Algorithms for Construction and Analysis of Systems*, pages 345–357, 1998.

17. F. J. Lin, P. M. Chu, and M. Liu. Protocol verification using reachability analysis: the state space explosion problem and relief strategies. *ACM*, pages 126–135, 1988.

18. D. McVitie and L. Wilson. The stable marriage problem. *Communications of the ACM*, 14(7):486–492, 1971.

19. N. J. Nilsson. *Principles of Artificial Intelligence*. Tioga Publishing Co., Palo Alto, California, 1980.

20. J. Pearl. *Heuristics*. Addison-Wesley, 1985.

21. D. A. Peled. Combining partial order reductions with on-the-fly model-checking. *Formal Methods in Systems Design*, 8:39–64, 1996.

22. D. A. Peled. Ten years of partial order reduction. In *Computer Aided Verification*, number 1427 in Lecture Notes in Computer Science, pages 17–28. Springer, 1998.

23. A. Valmari. A stubborn attack on state explosion. *Lecture Notes in Computer Science*, 531:156–165, 1991.

24. C. H. Yang and D. L. Dill. Validation with guided search of the state space. In *Conference on Design Automation (DAC)*, pages 599–604, 1998.

Local Parallel Model Checking
for the Alternation-Free μ-Calculus

Benedikt Bollig[1], Martin Leucker[2], and Michael Weber[1]

[1] Lehrstuhl für Informatik II, RWTH Aachen, Germany
{bollig,michaelw}@informatik.rwth-aachen.de
[2] Dept. of Computer and Information Science, University of Pennsylvania, USA*
leucker@cis.upenn.edu

Abstract. We describe the design of (several variants of) a local parallel model-checking algorithm for the alternation-free fragment of the μ-calculus. It exploits a characterisation of the problem for this fragment in terms of two-player games. For the corresponding winner, our algorithm determines in parallel a winning strategy, which may be employed for debugging the underlying system interactively, and is designed to run on a network of workstations. Depending on the variant, its complexity is linear or quadratic. A prototype implementation within the verification tool TRUTH shows promising results in practice.

1 Introduction

Model checking [8] is a key tool for verifying complex hardware and software systems. However, the so-called *state-space explosion* still limits its application. While *partial-order reduction* or *symbolic model checking* reduce the state space by orders of magnitude, typical verification tasks still take modern sequential computers to their memory limits. On the other hand, cheap yet powerful parallel computers can be constructed of Networks Of Workstations (*NOW*s). From the outside, a NOW appears as one single parallel computer with high computing power and, more importantly, huge amount of memory. This enables parallel programs to use the accumulated resources of a NOW to solve large problems. Hence, it is important to find parallel model-checking algorithms, which then may be combined with well-known techniques to avoid the state-space explosion gaining even more speedup and further reduce memory requirements.

A well-known logic for expressing specifications is Kozen's μ-calculus [14], a temporal logic offering Boolean combination of formulae and, especially, labelled *next*-state, minimal fixed-point, and maximal fixed-point quantifiers. For practical applications, however, it suffices to restrict the μ-calculus to the alternation-free fragment, denoted by L^1_μ, in which nesting of minimal and maximal fixed-point operators is prohibited. It allows the formulation of many *safety* as well as *liveness* properties and subsumes the logic CTL [10], which is employed in many practical verification tools. It can be shown that the model-checking problem for this fragment is linear in the length of the formula as well as the size of the

---

* Most of the work was done during the author's employment at the RWTH Aachen.

D. Bošnački and S. Leue (Eds.): SPIN 2002, LNCS 2318, pp. 128–147, 2002.
© Springer-Verlag Berlin Heidelberg 2002

underlying transition system. Several sequential model-checking procedures are given in the literature (cf. [4] for an overview). The algorithms can be classified into *global* and *local* algorithms. The first require the underlying transition system to be completely constructed while local ones compute the necessary part of a transition system *on-the-fly*.

In complexity theory, it is a well-accepted view that P-complete problems are so-called *inherently sequential*. It was shown in [23,15,5] that model checking L_μ^1 is P-complete. Thus, all we can hope is to find a linear-time algorithm and no one in the parallel complexity class NC, unless NC equals P. We present a parallel local model-checking algorithm and several of its variations which have linear or quadratic time complexity, thus matching the perfect bounds. We implemented the algorithm within our verification tool TRUTH [17] and learned that it behaves well for practical problems.

Our algorithm uses a characterisation of the model-checking problem for this fragment in terms of two-player games [11,21]. Strictly speaking, we present a parallel algorithm for colouring a so-called game graph answering the underlying model-checking problem. We show that the game graph has a certain characteristic structure when considering the alternation-free μ-calculus. This is one of the crucial observations and guides us to define a sequential algorithm (without cycle detection) that can easily be parallelised, which we do to obtain our parallel model-checking algorithm. Furthermore, we explain how to extend our algorithm for computing winning strategies without further costs. A strategy may be employed by the user of a verification tool for debugging the underlying system interactively [21].

A different characterisation of the model-checking problem can be given in terms of so-called 1-letter-simple-weak alternating Büchi automata [15]. These are related to games in a straightforward manner [11,16]. Hence, our algorithm can also be understood as a parallel procedure for checking the emptiness of these automata, thus, also as an automata-theoretic model-checking algorithm, which are in general considered to be local algorithms. Indeed, our parallel algorithm is inspired by a solution of the model-checking problem described in [15]. However, the proposed algorithm employs a detection of cycles, which is unlikely to be parallelised in a simple way. Our key observation is that we can omit this step yielding a simple parallel algorithm. Note that the game graph is also a Boolean graph and that our algorithm has similarities with the ones of [1,18].

Until today, not much effort has been taken to consider parallel model-checking algorithms. In [20], a parallel reachability analysis is carried out. The distribution of the underlying structure is similar to the one presented here. But their algorithm is not suitable for model checking temporal-logic formulae. [13,22,2] present parallelised data structures which employ further computers within a network as a substitute for external storage. The algorithms described in [19,7] divide the underlying problem into several tasks. However, they are designed in the way that only a single computer can be employed to sequentially handle one task at a time. In [5], we presented a parallel algorithm for a fragment of L_μ^1. [12] introduced a symbolic parallel algorithm for the full μ-calculus.

However, both are global so that the transition system has to be constructed totally. [6] presents a model-checking algorithm for LTL using a costly parallel cycle detection. Confer [4] for further related work. Our main contribution is the first *local* parallel model-checking algorithm for L_μ^1 that supports interactive debugging and omits a cycle detection, which allows a powerful parallel realisation of it.

In Section 2, we fix some notions on graphs, recall the syntax and semantics of the μ-calculus as well as the definition of model checking. Furthermore, we describe model-checking games for the μ-calculus and provide an important characterisation of the game graph, which will be the basis for our sequential and parallel algorithms. To simplify our presentation, we start in Section 3 with the presentation of sequential model-checking algorithms that admit a simple parallel version. The corresponding parallel model-checking procedure is shown in Section 4. Before we draw the conclusion of our approach, we present our experimental results in Section 5. A full version of the paper including precise definitions, proofs, and further explanations is available in [4].

2   Graphs, μ-Calculus, and Games

Graphs. A tree order is a pair $(Q, \leq)$ such that $\leq$ is a partial ordering relation on Q and its covering relation is a tree. More specifically, assume $\leq$ is a reflexive, antisymmetric, and transitive relation and $\lessdot = \leq -(\leq \circ \leq)$ its *covering relation*. We call $\leq$ a *tree order* iff $\lessdot$ is a tree in the usual sense. Notions of *parents* and *children* for elements of Q wrt. $\leq$ correspond to the usual ones for elements of Q wrt. $\lessdot$.

A directed *graph* $\mathcal{G}$ is a pair $\mathcal{G} = (Q, \rightarrow)$ where Q is a set of *nodes* and $\rightarrow \subseteq Q \times Q$ is the set of (directed) *edges*. We use notions as *path*, *cycle*, (strongly connected) components, *(induced) subgraphs* as usual. Let $\mathcal{G}' = (Q', \rightarrow')$ and $\mathcal{G}'' = (Q'', \rightarrow'')$ be two components of $\mathcal{G}$ with $Q' \cap Q'' = \emptyset$. Assume that $\rightarrow \cap (Q'' \times Q') = \emptyset$. Then every edge from a node $q' \in Q'$ to a node $q'' \in Q''$ $(q' \rightarrow q'')$ is called a *bridge*.

In the next sections, we consider graphs that are labelled by formulae. We say that a cycle *contains* a formula φ iff the cycle contains a node labelled by φ.

$Q_1, \ldots, Q_m$ is a *tree decomposition* of a graph $(Q, \rightarrow)$ iff the Q_i form a partition of Q, i.e., $Q = \bigcup_{i \in \{1, \ldots, m\}} Q_i$ and for all $i, j \in \{1, \ldots, m\}$ with $i \neq j$, it holds $Q_i \cap Q_j = \emptyset$, and furthermore, there exists a tree order $\leq$ on the collection of the Q_i's such that we have $Q_i \lessdot Q_j$ iff there is a bridge from Q_i to Q_j. Without loss of generality, we may assume that $Q_i \leq Q_j$ implies $i \leq j$.

The μ-Calculus. Let *Var* be a set of fixed-point variables and $\mathcal{A}$ a set of actions. Formulae of the modal μ-calculus over *Var* and $\mathcal{A}$ in positive form as introduced by [14] are defined as follows:

$$\varphi ::= \mathtt{false} \mid \mathtt{true} \mid X \mid \varphi_1 \wedge \varphi_2 \mid \varphi_1 \vee \varphi_2 \mid [K]\varphi \mid \langle K \rangle \varphi \mid \nu X.\varphi \mid \mu X.\varphi$$

where $X \in Var$ and $K \subseteq \mathcal{A}$ [1]. For a formula φ of the μ-calculus, we introduce the notion of *subformulae* (denoted by $Sub(\varphi)$), *free* and *bound* variables, and

---

[1] $\langle - \rangle \varphi$ is an abbreviation for $\langle \mathcal{A} \rangle \varphi$.

sentences as usual. We call φ a μ-formula iff $\varphi = \mu X.\psi$ for appropriate X and ψ. ν-formulae are introduced analogously. From now on, we assume all formulae to be sentences.

A formula φ is *normal* iff every occurrence of a binder μX or νX in φ binds a distinct variable. For example, $(\mu X.X) \vee (\mu X.X)$ is not normal but $(\mu X.X) \vee (\mu Y.Y)$ is. By renaming, every formula can easily be converted into an equivalent normal formula. If a formula φ is normal, every (bound) variable X of φ *identifies* a unique subformula $\mu X.\psi$ or $\nu X.\psi$ of φ where X is a free variable of ψ. We call X a ν-variable iff it identifies a ν-formula, and μ-variable otherwise. From now on, we assume all formulae to be normal.

Throughout the paper, let us fix a *labelled transition system* $T = (S, T, \mathcal{A}, s_0)$ where S is a finite set of states, $\mathcal{A}$ a set of actions, and $T \subseteq S \times \mathcal{A} \times S$ denotes the transitions. As usual, we write $s \xrightarrow{a} t$ instead of $(s, a, t) \in T$. Furthermore, let $s_0 \in S$ be the *initial state* of the transition system. The satisfaction of φ wrt. T and a state $s \in S$ is denoted by $T, s \models \varphi$ and defined as usual [21,4]. We use identifiers like $\varphi, \psi, \ldots$ for formulae, $s, t, \ldots$ for states, and $a, b, \ldots$ for actions of the transition system under consideration. K denotes a set of actions. Whenever the sort of the fixed point does not matter, we use σ for either μ or ν.

Essential for our further development is a formula's graph representation. To simplify the definition, let us recall its tree (term) representation. Let φ be a formula. The *occurrence set* of φ, denoted by $Occ(\varphi)$, is inductively defined by $\epsilon \in Occ(\varphi)$, $i\pi \in Occ(\varphi)$ if $i \in \{1, 2\}$, $\varphi = \varphi_1 \star \varphi_2$, and $\pi \in Occ(\varphi_i)$, and $1\pi \in Occ(\varphi)$ if $\varphi = \#\varphi_1$ and $\pi \in Occ(\varphi_1)$, where $\star$ denotes a binary and $\#$ a unary operator. Let $\varphi|_\pi$ denote the subformula of φ at position π, that is $\varphi|_\epsilon = \varphi$ and $\varphi|_{i\pi} = \varphi_i|_\pi$ where $i \in \{1, 2\}$ and $\varphi = \varphi_1 \star \varphi_2$, or $i = 1$ and $\varphi = \#\varphi_1$.

We can now assign to every φ a $Sub(\varphi)$-labelled tree with nodes $Occ(\varphi)$ and edge set $\rightarrow$ defined by $\rightarrow = \{(\pi, i\pi) \mid \pi, i\pi \in Occ(\varphi), \pi \in \mathbb{N}^*, i \in \mathbb{N}\}$. The labels are assigned in the expected manner by $\lambda(\pi) = \varphi|_\pi$. Altogether, $T(\varphi) = (Occ(\varphi), \rightarrow, \lambda)$ is defined to be the *tree representation* of φ.

We are now ready to define the graph representation of a formula φ. Basically, a formula's graph is its canonical tree representation enriched by edges from fixed-point variables back to the fixed-point formula it identifies.

Definition 1. *Let φ be a formula of the μ-calculus and $T(\varphi) = (Occ(\varphi), \rightarrow, \lambda)$ its tree representation. The* graph *of φ, denoted by $\mathcal{G}(\varphi)$, is $(Occ(\varphi), \rightarrow', \lambda)$ where $\rightarrow' = \rightarrow \cup \{(\pi, \pi') \mid \lambda(\pi) = X$ and $\lambda(\pi') = \sigma X.\varphi'$ for $X \in Var$ and appropriate $\varphi'\}$.*

The graph of the formula $\mu X.((\nu Y.\langle b \rangle Y) \vee \langle a \rangle X) \vee \mu X'.((\nu Y'.\langle b \rangle Y') \wedge \langle a \rangle X')$ is shown in Figure 1(a).

The *alternation-free fragment* of the μ-calculus is the sublogic of the μ-calculus where no subformula ψ of a formula φ contains both a free variable X bound by a μX in φ as well as a free variable Y bound by a νY in φ. In terms of the graph representation, a formula φ is alternation free iff $\mathcal{G}(\varphi)$ contains no cycle with a ν-variable as well as a μ-variable. Figure 1(b) shows the graph of an alternating formula which has a cycle containing X as well as Y. Contrary, Fig-

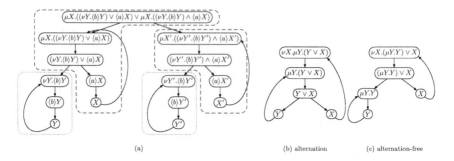

(a)   (b) alternation   (c) alternation-free

Fig. 1. Graphs of formulae

ure 1(c) shows the graph of an alternation-free formula which has two maximal strongly connected components, one on which X occurs, a second containing Y.

An essential observation is that the graph of an alternation-free formula can naturally be decomposed into so-called μ- and ν-components (cf. Figure 1(a)).

Theorem 1. *Let φ be an alternation-free formula that contains at least one fixed-point formula and let $\mathcal{G}(\varphi) = (Q, \rightarrow, \lambda)$ be its graph representation. Then there exists a tree decomposition $Q_1, \ldots, Q_m$ of $\mathcal{G}(\varphi)$ such that every subgraph induced by Q_i either contains only μ-cycles (called μ-component in the following) or only ν-cycles (ν-component).*

In our graphical representation, the previous components are enclosed by a (red) dashed line and the latter by a (green) dotted line. Note that the components are no-longer necessarily strongly connected. For formulae without any fixed-point formula, we will get a single component, which we call arbitrarily a μ-component.

Proof. Consider the nodes of maximal non-trivial strongly connected components. Alternation freeness guarantees that not both a ν-variable as well as a μ-variable is reached on a cycle in such a component. It is now easy to see that all remaining nodes form trees. Since a formula's graph is connected, the strongly connected components can be canonically ordered by bridges. Please note that maximality of the strongly connected components and trees guarantees the order defined to be a tree order. To obtain the required type of components, strongly connected components are united with their children (components) that are trees. If the root component is a tree, this is united with the first strongly connected component. See [4] for details.

Note that, for the previous decomposition, it is essential that we distinguish between syntactically identical subformulae, which is achieved by using occurrences of formulae instead of directly formulae. In Section 4, we will discuss an alternative definition of a formula's graph, which yields partially ordered but no longer tree ordered components and, as we will see, a slightly different parallel algorithm.

It is easy to see that the time complexity of computing the decomposition is linear wrt. the formula's length. Thus, we can label every subformula of a formula with its component number within linear time wrt. the length of the formula.

Model-checking games for the μ-calculus. Let us recall Stirling's characterisation of the model-checking problem in terms of games [21]. As we will see, deciding whether a given transition system satisfies a formula is reduced to the colouring of a structure called *game graph*. We will explain that the decomposition of a formula's graph induces a decomposition of the game graph. The latter will simplify our sequential as well as parallel colouring algorithm. The experienced reader will notice that our definition is a little different from Stirling's original approach. We do so to obtain a tree-like decomposition of the game graph instead of a more general dag-like decomposition (cf. Section 4).

Consider the transition system T and the formula φ. The *model-checking game* of T and φ has as the board the Cartesian product $S \times Q$ of the set of states and φ's positions. The game is played by two players, namely ∀belard (the pessimist), who wants to show that $T, s_0 \models \varphi$ does *not* hold, whereas ∃loise (the optimist) wants to show the opposite.

The model-checking game $G(s, \varphi)$ for a state s and a formula φ is given by all its *plays*, i.e. (possibly infinite) sequences $C_0 \Rightarrow_{P_0} C_1 \Rightarrow_{P_1} C_2 \Rightarrow_{P_2} \ldots$ of *configurations*, where for all i, $C_i \in S \times Q$, $C_0 = (s, \epsilon)$, and P_i is either ∃loise or ∀belard. We write $\Rightarrow$ instead of $\Rightarrow_{P_i}$ if we abstract from the players. Each next turn is determined by the current subformula of φ. Hence, the label of the second component of a configuration C_i determines the player P_i who has to choose the next move. ∀belard makes universal $\Rightarrow_\forall$-moves, ∃loise makes existential $\Rightarrow_\exists$-moves. More precisely, whenever $C_i = (s, \pi)$ and

1. $\lambda(\pi) = \texttt{false}$, then the play is finished.
2. $\lambda(\pi) = \psi_1 \wedge \psi_2$, then ∀belard chooses $j = 1$ or $j = 2$, and $C_{i+1} = (s, \pi j)$.
3. $\lambda(\pi) = [K]\psi$, then ∀belard chooses a transition $s \xrightarrow{a} t$ with $a \in K$ and $C_{i+1} = (t, \pi 1)$.
4. $\lambda(\pi) = \nu X.\psi$, then $C_{i+1} = (s, \pi 1)$.

If $\lambda(\pi) \in \{\texttt{true}, \psi_1 \vee \psi_2, \langle K \rangle \psi\}$ (moves 5–8), it is ∃loise's turn; her rules are dually defined to the ones for ∀belard. For $\lambda(\pi) = X$, let π' be the position of the μ-/ν-formula X identifies. Then $C_{i+1} = (s, \pi')$ (move 9). We will speak of ∀*belard-moves* in cases 1–4 and 9, and ∃*loise-moves* in all other cases. C_i is called ∀-configuration or ∃-configuration, respectively (cf. [4]).

A configuration is called *terminal* if no (further) move is possible. A play G is called *maximal* iff it is infinite or ends in a terminal configuration. The *winner* of a maximal play is defined in the following way: If the play is finite, thus ending in a configuration (s, π), then ∀belard wins G iff $\lambda(\pi) = \texttt{false}$ or $\lambda(\pi) = \langle K \rangle \psi$ [2]. Dually, ∃loise wins G iff $\lambda(\pi) = \texttt{true}$ or $\lambda(\pi) = [K]\psi$ [2]. An infinite play is won by ∀belard iff the outermost fixed point that is unwinded

---

[2] Note that, due to maximality, we have $\nexists t : s \xrightarrow{a} t$ for any $a \in K$.

infinitely often is a μ-fixed point. Otherwise, when the outermost fixed point that is unwinded infinitely often is a ν-fixed point, then $\exists$loise wins the game.

A *strategy* is a set of rules for a player P telling her or him how to move in the current configuration. It is called *history free* if the strategy only depends on the current configuration without considering the previous moves. A *winning strategy* guarantees that the play that P plays according to the rules will be won by P. [21] shows that model checking for the μ-calculus is equivalent to finding a history-free winning strategy for one of the players: Let T be a transition system with state s and φ a μ-calculus formula. $T, s \models \varphi$ implies that $\exists$loise has a history-free winning strategy starting in (s, φ), and $T, s \not\models \varphi$ implies that $\forall$belard has a history-free winning strategy starting in (s, φ).

All possible plays for a transition system T and a formula φ are captured in the *game graph* whose nodes are the elements of the game board (the possible configurations) and whose edges are the players' possible moves. The game graph can be understood as an *and-/or-*graph where the *or*-nodes (denoted by $\bigvee$) are $\exists$-configurations and the *and*-nodes (denoted by $\bigwedge$) are $\forall$-configurations.

The following characterisation of the game graph for this fragment is essential for formulating our sequential and parallel algorithms, but only holds for the alternation-free μ-calculus.

Theorem 2. *Let T be a labelled transition system and let φ be a formula of the alternation-free μ-calculus. Furthermore, let $\mathcal{G} = (Q, E)$ be their game graph. Then there exists a tree decomposition $Q_1, \ldots, Q_m$ of $\mathcal{G}$ such that in every subgraph induced by Q_i, either μ-formulae and no ν-formulae are unwinded or ν-formulae and no μ-formulae. We call Q_i μ-component or ν-component, resp.*

Proof. By Theorem 1, φ's graph admits a decomposition into either μ- or ν-components $Q'_1, \ldots, Q'_m$. Let Q_i be the set of configurations whose formulae are in Q'_i. It is a simple task to show that the Q_i have the desired properties.

Figure 2 shows a game graph for a transition system that has two states s_1 and s_2, an a-loop from s_1 to itself, and a b-edge from s_1 to s_2, and the formula $\Phi = \mu X.((\nu Y.\langle b \rangle Y) \vee \langle a \rangle X) \vee \mu X'.((\nu Y'.\langle b \rangle Y') \wedge \langle a \rangle X')$. $\forall$belard-configurations are marked by rectangular boxes while $\exists$loise-configurations are drawn as oval nodes. The dashed and dotted lines identify μ-components and respectively ν-components.

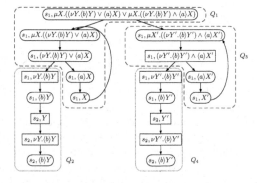

Fig. 2. A partitioned game graph.

Let us fix the decomposition of the game graph shown in the previous proof and further helpful notions in the following definition:

Definition 2. *Let $\mathcal{T}$ be a labelled transition system and let φ be a formula of the alternation-free μ-calculus. Furthermore, let $\mathcal{G} = (Q, E)$ be their game graph.*

- *The canonical decomposition of $\mathcal{G}$ is the decomposition according to Theorem 2 into $Q_1, \ldots, Q_m$, which are tree-like ordered by $\leq$.*
- *The escape configurations of a component Q_i (denoted by $\lfloor Q_i \rfloor$) are the configurations which are in a child component and are successor configurations of a configuration in Q_i. That is:*

$$\lfloor Q_i \rfloor = \{q \in Q_j \mid Q_j \text{ is a child of } Q_i \text{ and } \exists q' \in Q_i \text{ such that } (q', q) \in E\}$$

- *The component number of a configuration of the game graph is the (unique) index i of a component that contains the configuration.*

It is obvious that every infinite play gets trapped within one Q_i. If the component is a ν-component, then ∀belard has lost the game. So he tries to leave a ν-component by reaching an escape configuration. Note that the second component of an escape configuration is labelled by a fixed-point formula and that $\lfloor Q_i \rfloor = \emptyset$ iff it is a leaf wrt. $\leq$.

The number of a component of a game graph's canonical decomposition is identical to the number of the component of the formula's graph according to Theorem 1. Even more, the component number of a configuration is identical to the number of the component of its formula label (which is defined in the obvious manner). Thus, once computed the component number of a (sub)formula as described in Section 2, it is a constant operation to check the component number of a configuration.

3 Sequential Model Checking

In the following, we restrict to the alternation-free μ-calculus. In this section, we present two sequential approaches for determining winning strategies, hereby solving the model-checking problem. The algorithms are designed in the way that they can easily be parallelised, which is carried out in the next section.

The basic idea of both algorithms is labelling a configuration q by *green* or *red*, depending on whether ∃loise or ∀belard has a winning strategy for the game starting in this configuration q. Furthermore, they both employ the canonical decomposition of the game graph (cf. Section 2). They differ in the order in which the several components are processed. The first algorithm proceeds bottom-up, the second top-down.

Colouring bottom-up. First, let us discuss how to colour a single component. Let Q_i be a component of the canonical decomposition. To simplify the presentation, assume that Q_i is a μ-component. The forthcoming explanation can be dualised for ν-components. Let $\lfloor Q_i \rfloor$ denote its set of escape configurations and assume that every configuration in $\lfloor Q_i \rfloor$ is either labelled with *green* or *red* expressing that either ∃loise or ∀belard has a winning strategy from this configuration, resp. It is now obvious, that every play starting in a configuration of Q_i will either

1. eventually reach an escape configuration and never touch a configuration of Q_i again,
2. will end in a terminal configuration within Q_i, or
3. will go on infinitely within Q_i.

In the first situation, the winner is determined by the colour of the escape configuration. In the second case, the terminal configuration signalises whether ∃loise or ∀belard has won. The last case goes to ∀belard since a μ-formula is unwinded infinitely often.

The second case justifies colouring every terminal configuration within Q_i in the following way: If the formula component of the configuration is **true** or a box formula, then the configuration is coloured with *green*. Otherwise, when the formula component is **false** or a diamond formula, then the configuration is coloured with *red*.

Once a configuration $q \in Q_i \cup \lfloor Q_i \rfloor$ is labelled with *red* or *green*, its predecessors are labelled if possible: An $\bigwedge$-node q' is labelled with *red* if q is *red*, but labelled *green*, if all successors, i.e., q and all its neighbours, are *green*. An $\bigvee$-node is treated dually. If the predecessor has obtained a new colour, the labelling is propagated further. It is easy to see that, once a configuration obtained a colour, the colour is never changed.

Lemma 1. *The colouring process is terminating.*

However, the labelling process may leave some configurations of Q_i uncoloured. Let us understand that all remaining uncoloured configurations can be labelled with *red*.

Theorem 3. *For any game starting in a configuration without a colour, ∀belard has a winning strategy for a game starting in this configuration.*

Proof. First, check that every uncoloured configuration has at least one uncoloured successor configuration. ∀belard's strategy will be any choosing one uncoloured successor in this situation. Then he will win every play. Every uncoloured ∃loise-configuration has *red* or uncoloured successors, so ∃loise has the choice to move to configurations which are winning for ∀belard or to move to an uncoloured configuration. ∀belard will choose in an uncoloured configuration an uncoloured successor, or, if ∃loise has moved to a *red* configuration, he will choose a *red* successor. Summing up, every play will either end in a *red* terminal configuration, lead to a *red* escape configuration in which ∀belard has a winning strategy, or will go on infinitely often within Q_i and ∀belard wins.

The previous theorem is the crucial observation allowing a powerful parallel version of this algorithm. Unlike in many existing works on model checking this fragment, we do not use any cycle detection algorithm in the labelling process. We know that the described backward colour propagation process leaves only configurations uncoloured that are on or lead to a cycle which furthermore can be controlled by ∀belard.

The first sequential algorithm now processes the components in a bottom-up fashion. First, leaf components which have no escape configurations are considered and coloured. Now, for any parent component, the escape configurations are labelled and, again, our procedure will colour the component.

Let us turn back to our example shown in Figure 2. We have four components, $Q_1, \ldots Q_4$. One leaf component is Q_2. The single terminal configuration $(s_2, \langle b \rangle Y)$ requires ∃loise to present a b-successor of s_2. However, in the underlying transition system, there is no successor. Thus, the configuration will be labelled with red. Propagating the colours to the predecessor configurations will colour every configuration of Q_2 with red.

The other leaf component Q_4 will be treated in the same manner as Q_2.

The next component to handle wrt. our tree order is Q_3. It has the single escape configuration $(s_1, \nu Y'.\langle b \rangle Y')$ which is already coloured with red. This colour is propagated to $(s_1, \nu Y'.\langle b \rangle Y' \wedge \langle a \rangle X')$ which now is coloured red. Further propagation will colour the whole component Q_3 with red.

We have to proceed with Q_1. $(s_1, \nu Y.\langle b \rangle Y)$ propagates red to $(s_1, \nu Y.\langle b \rangle Y \vee \langle a \rangle X)$. Since the latter is an ∃loise-configuration, it remains uncoloured. A similar situation occurs for the propagation due to $(s_1, \mu X'.((\nu Y'.\langle b \rangle Y') \wedge \langle a \rangle X'))$. Thus, all colour information is propagated within Q_1. The current situation is depicted in Figure 3, in which red configurations are filled with ■ . Now, the second

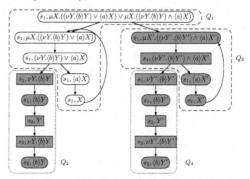

Fig. 3. Before the second phase

phase of colouring a component comes into play. All remaining configurations will be labelled with red since Q_1 is a μ-component. Thus, ∀belard has a winning strategy for the presented game and we know that the underlying formula is not valid in the initial state of the transition system.

Complexity. It is a simple matter to see that the previous labelling algorithm has a linear running time (in the worst case) wrt. the size of the game graph. The latter is bounded by the size of the underlying transition system (denoted by s) times the length of the formula (denoted by l). Hence, it is bounded by $s \times l$. However, only the part of the transition system *related* to the underlying formula has to be considered. For example, checking $\langle a \rangle \varphi$ in a state s requires only to look for a successor reachable by an action a that satisfies φ. All successors reachable by different actions need not be considered. While in the worst case, the whole transition system has to be considered checking a formula, only a part of the system has to be generated in typical examples. Thus, we can call our algorithm to be *local* or *on-the-fly*.

Colouring top-down. For the second algorithm, assume that the game graph is again partitioned into components Q_i which form a tree. To consider as few components as possible, the algorithm will process the components in a top-down manner.

Again, let us first discuss how to colour a single component. Let Q_i be a component of the canonical decomposition. Again, we assume that Q_i is a μ-component recalling that the forthcoming explanation can be dualised for ν-components. Let $\lfloor Q_i \rfloor$ denote its escape configurations. However, we will *not* assume that every configuration in $\lfloor Q_i \rfloor$ is already coloured. Still, every play will either

1. eventually reach an escape configuration and never touch a configuration of Q_i again,
2. will end in a terminal configuration within Q_i, or
3. will go on infinitely within Q_i.

Again, the winner of a play is clear in Case 2. Furthermore, if ∃loise has neither a way to reach a winning terminal configuration, nor to leave the component she will loose. So, if she has no chance to reach a winning terminal configuration, the best we can hope for her, is that she indeed has a chance to leave the component successfully. The crucial point of our algorithm is that we initially colour all escape configurations of the component under consideration with *lightgreen* denoting that this configuration is probably a winning configuration for ∃loise.

As before, the colour information (full as well as light colours) is propagated to predecessor configurations and used for colouring it. That means, an $\bigwedge$-node is labelled with *red* if one successor is *red*, labelled with *lightred*, if no successor is *red* but at least one is *lightred*, labelled *lightgreen*, if all successors are *lightgreen* or *green*, and labelled with *green*, if all successors are *green*. In all other cases, the configuration remains unlabelled. An $\bigvee$-node is treated dually. Note that *lightred* comes only into play for ν-components. If the predecessor has got a new colour, the labelling is propagated further. A simple case analysis shows that once a configuration obtained a full colour, the colour is never changed. A light colour is only changed to the corresponding full colour.

Lemma 2. *The colouring process is terminating.*

Again, the labelling process may leave some configurations of Q_i uncoloured. Let us now understand, that all remaining uncoloured configurations can be labelled with *red*.

Theorem 4. *For any game starting in a configuration without a colour, ∀belard has a winning strategy for a game starting in this configuration.*

Proof. First, check that every uncoloured configuration has at least one uncoloured successor configuration. ∀belard's strategy will be any choosing one uncoloured successor. Then he will win every play. Every uncoloured ∃loise-configuration has *red*, or uncoloured successors, so ∃loise has the choice to move to a configuration which is winning for ∀belard or to move to an uncoloured configuration. $\forall$belard will choose in an uncoloured configuration an uncoloured successor, or, if $\exists$loise has moved to a non-terminal *red* configuration, he will choose a *red* successor. Summing up, every play will either end in a *red* terminal configuration, move to a *red* escape configuration, in which $\forall$belard has a winning strategy, or will stay infinitely often within Q_i and $\forall$belard wins.

Still, the previous theorem is crucial for getting a powerful parallel algorithm.

Our component now may contain configurations which are coloured with *lightgreen*. However, we cannot guarantee that $\exists$loise has indeed a winning strategy for games starting in such a configuration. Thus, we remove the colour of such a configuration. If the initial configurations of the component are coloured, we are done. If not, we have to consider a child component to get further evidence.

Let us turn back to our example shown in Figure 2. We introduce the colour *white* to identify uncoloured configurations, assuming that initially every configuration has a *white* colour. We start with the root component Q_1. Both escape configurations are initially labelled with *lightgreen* (Figure 4(a)[3]).

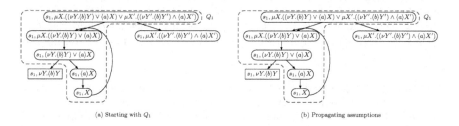

(a) Starting with Q_1 (b) Propagating assumptions

Fig. 4. Two steps in the algorithm.

As shown in Figure 4(b), propagating the colour information will colour every configuration of Q_1 with *lightgreen*.

The subsequent phase of colouring *white*-configurations *red* and *lightgreen*-configurations *white* will turn the whole component to a complete *white* one so that the corresponding system looks similar to the one in the beginning. Thus, the assumptions did not help to find a winner. Therefore, we have to check a child component of Q_1. Let us proceed with Q_2. Since there are no escape configurations, the whole component is coloured as before. We learn that the *lightgreen* assumption for the initial configuration of Q_2 was too optimistic. Redoing the colouring of Q_1, now with more but still not full information, will colour some configurations of Q_1 *red* but will still leave the initial configuration uncoloured. Figure 5(b) shows the coloured game graph right before recolouring the assumed coloured *lightgreen* back to *white*.

We turn our attention to Q_3. We assume that $\exists$loise has a chance to leave the component via $(s_1, \nu Y'.\langle b \rangle Y')$. Thus, we colour this configuration *lightgreen*.

___

[3] *lightgreen* configurations are identified by writing their label in the following style: xxx

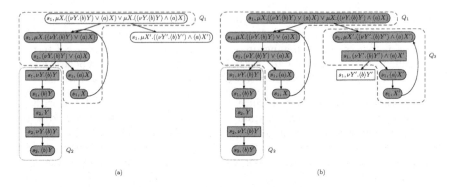

Fig. 5. Subsequent steps in the algorithm.

However, the propagation does not influence the preceding $\bigwedge$-node. So all remaining configurations are coloured *red*. Now, all escape configurations of Q_1 are coloured and a further colouring process will colour the complete component Q_1 *red*. Note that we saved the time and especially space for considering Q_4. Figure 5(b) shows the coloured game graph, again right before recolouring the assumed coloured *lightgreen* back to *white*.

Complexity. It is a simple matter to see that the previous labelling algorithm has a running time bounded by $n \times m$ where n is the number of configurations and m is the size of the maximum length of a path from the root component to a leaf component. The latter number is bounded by the nesting of fixed-point formulae, which is at most the length of the formula. Thus, we get as an upper bound $s \times l^2$ where s is the size of the underlying transition system and l is the length of the formula. While in the worst case, this complexity is worse than in the bottom-up approach, we found out that the algorithm often detects the truth-value of a formula in a given state much faster. Note, that this algorithm behaves *even more on-the-fly* than the previous one.

4   Parallel Model Checking

Given a transition system and an L_μ^1-formula, our approach is both to construct the game graph as well as to determine the colour of its nodes in parallel. The idea of our parallel algorithm is that all processors are working in parallel on one component, whereas the components are treated one-by-one.

Distributing the game graph. We employ a somehow standard approach distributing and constructing a (component of the) game graph in parallel [20,4,5]. As a data structure, we employ adjacency lists. We need also links to the predecessor as well as to the successor of a node for the labelling algorithm. A component is constructed in parallel by a typical breadth-first strategy. Given

a node q, determine its successors $q_1, \ldots, q_n$. To obtain a deterministic distribution of the configurations over the workstation cluster, one takes a function
in the spirit of a hash function assigning to every configuration an integer and
subsequently its value modulo the number of processors. This function f determines the location of every node within the network uniquely and without
global knowledge. Thus, we can send each $q \in \{q_1, \ldots, q_n\}$ to its processors $f(q)$.
If q is already in the local store of $f(q)$, then q is reached a second time, hence
the procedure stops. If predecessors of q were sent together with q, the list of
predecessors is augmented accordingly. If q is not in the local memory of $f(q)$, it
is stored there together with the given predecessors as well as all its successors.
These are sent in the same manner to their (wrt. f) processors, together with the
information that q is a predecessor. The corresponding processes update their
local memory similarly.

Please consult [4] for a thoroughly discussion of this and other possible approaches storing distributed transition systems.

Labelling the game graph. As many of the existing model-checking algorithms
that we are aware of, use cycle detection algorithms, which are unlikely to be
parallelised in a simple way, we extend our sequential algorithms described in
Section 3 towards a parallel implementation. As explained in the previous paragraph, it is easy to construct (a component of) the game graph in parallel employing a breadth-first search. When a terminal configuration is reached, a backwards colouring process can be initiated as described in Section 3. This can be
carried out in parallel in the obvious manner. If all colour information is propagated, the sequential algorithm performs a colouring of uncoloured nodes and an
erasing of light colours (cf. Section 3). It is no problem to do this recolouring on
the distributed game graph in parallel. Thanks to Theorem 3 or Theorem 4, no
cycle detection is necessary but every workstation can do this recolouring step
on its local part of the game graph.

However, to check that all colour information has been propagated, a distributed termination-check algorithm is employed. We use a token termination
algorithm due to [9]. It has the advantage that it scales well wrt. the number
of workstations and that its complexity is independent of the size of the game
graph. The components may be labelled in a bottom-up or top-down manner as
described in Section 3. Thus, we get a set of algorithms differing in the order
the components are processed.

The algorithm. To describe our approach in more detail, we show several fragments of our algorithm in *pseudo code*. Especially, we note that the two steps
of constructing the game graph and labelling the nodes can be carried out in
an integrated way. The most important function is shown in Figure 6(a). Given
a component number, it expands all nodes of the component. It can be applied
either for a parallel bottom-up or top-down labelling algorithm. Since the colour
information of a terminal node is always a correct (full) colour, a colouring process is initiated, if a terminal configuration is reached.

```
1     Function processSuccs(node) // compute and expand succs
2       succs ← computeSuccs(node.conf)
3       for s ∈ succs do
4         sendMessageTo (Expand s node.conf) f(s)
5       succss ← [ ( suc.conf ← s, suc.colour ← white) | s in succs ]
6       node.succs ← succss
7     end
8
9     Function expandComp(comp)
10      for node in graph[comp].initialNodes // start with initial nodes
11        processSuccs(node)
12      until hasTerminated do
13        msg ← readMessage;
14        case msg of
15          Expand conf pred:
16            if lookupGraph(conf, node) ≠ fail then // node already visited
17              if node.colour ≠ white and pred ∉ node.preds then
18                sendMessageTo (Colour pred node.conf colour) f(pred)
19                addPreds(node.preds, pred)
20            else
21              node ← newNode, node.conf ← conf, node.pred ← pred
22              if isTerminal(node) then
23                node.colour ← InitialColor (node.conf)
24                sendMessageTo (Colour pred node.conf colour) f(pred)
25              else  // new node
26                node.colour ← white
27              if not (isTerminal(node) or (IsEscapeConf(comp,s))) then
28                processSuccs(node)
29          Colour conf child colour:
30            lookupGraph(conf, node)
31            updateSucc(node.succs, child, colour)
32            newcolour ← computeColour(node)
33            if newcolour ≠ oldcolour then
34              node.color ← newcolour
35              for p ∈ preds do sendMessageTo (Colour p conf newcolour) f(p)
36      end
```

(a) Expanding a component

```
1   Function recolourComp(comp)
2     case type(comp) of
3       μ : colour := red
4       ν : colour := green
5     for node in graph[comp]
6       if node.color = white then
7         node.color := colour
8       if node.color in
9         {lightred, lightgreen} then
10        node.color := white
11  end
```

(b) Recolouring

```
1   Function computeColour(node,succs)
2   begin
3     case
4       node is ⋁−node:
5         case
6           all (= Red) succs: Red
7           any (= Green) succs: Green
8           else: White
9       node is ⋀−node:
10        case
11          all (= Green) succs: Green
12          any (= Red) succs: Red
13          else: White
14  end
```

(c) Computing the colour

Fig. 6. The algorithms

We assume that the game graph is represented as a list of nodes where each node is a record containing the label of the current configuration, its colour, and a list of predecessors and successors. Furthermore, we assume that initial configurations are already stored in the graph when calling the function expandComp. The latter are first expanded (lines 10–11). Then, the function enters a message loop awaiting either expand or colour requests. If a configuration should be expanded, it is checked whether the configuration has already been processed (16). If so, a possible new predecessor of this configuration is stored. Furthermore, the predecessor is informed about the colour of the current node, if it has been coloured already. Otherwise, the node is added to the graph, and the configuration and the predecessor are stored (21). A colouring process is initiated, if the current node is a terminal one (22–26). Furthermore, if the node is neither terminal or an escape configuration, its successors are considered (28). Thus, its successors are computed and expanded (2–4). Furthermore, the successors together with an initially white-colour are stored in the current node (5–6). Colour informations are processed in the expected manner (29–35).

The function expandComp is the main ingredient for building a complete algorithm. If one is interested in a bottom-up algorithm, one can call expandComp in a depth-first manner for the components of the game-graph. Then, starting from the leafs, the function recolourComp (Figure 6(b), *light* colours are only present in the top-down version) can be called in a bottom-up manner. Of course, after processing a component, a colour propagation process for the initial nodes of the component has to be initiated before recolouring the next component.

For the bottom-up algorithm, the colour can be computed as described in Figure 6(c).

For the top-down colouring version of our algorithm, the expandComp function is called first. Then, a colouring process with light colours is initiated starting from the escape configurations of the component. Now, a recolour process (Figure 6(b)) is started.

There are several possibilities to process the components. In the examples shown in Section 3, we suggested a depth-first strategy. However, one could also use a breadth-first, bounded depth-first, or parallel breadth-first strategy. Depending on the employed strategy, the run-time of our algorithm is linear or quadratic. Note that the space required by our algorithm is linear in the size of the game graph. The employment of light colours might save considering a significant part of the game graph but may also augment the runtime, if the whole game graph has to be considered.

Theorem 5. *The algorithms described before label a node (s, ψ) of the game graph with green if $\mathcal{T}, s \models \psi$. Otherwise, the node is labelled with red.*

Variations of the algorithm. We already mentioned that there are several possibilities to process the components. Note that only the colour of the escape configuration is needed when colouring a component. Thus, all other nodes of a child component can be deleted for colouring the current component. In general, it is possible to formulate the algorithm in the way that only a *single* component plus some control information is stored in the workstation cluster at the same time certainly lifting the limits for systems to be model checked in practice. For lack of space, we do not provide the details.

Another variant of our algorithm can be obtained by taking subformulae instead of the occurrence set of the subformulae for defining the graph of the formula (Definition 1). The resulting effect will be that the components of the game graph no longer constitute a natural tree order but form a directed acyclic graph which is no longer necessarily a tree. Although the resulting game graph can be expected to be smaller, the tree order simplifies the decision when a component can be removed, as described in the previous paragraph.

Winning strategies. As pointed out already when motivating the use of games, the winning strategy does not only provide an answer to the model-checking question but can also be applied for interactively debugging the underlying system. It is easy to extend our algorithm towards providing a winning strategy. Note that the colour of a terminal node in the game graph indicates a winning position for one of the players. If the colour information is propagated to a predecessor without a colour (*white*) and this leads to a colour of the predecessor, it is clear how the corresponding winner has to chose. In other words, when a node gets a colour because of a (`Colour conf succ colour`) message, the strategy is choosing `succ` in configuration `conf`. If a node is coloured in the function recolourComp, we pointed out in the proof of Theorem 3 and Theorem 4 that the right strategy is choosing a previously *white* successor.

5   Experimental Results

We have tested our approach within our verification tool TRUTH [17] implemented in Haskell as well as with a stand-alone version written in C++.

The Haskell version. We implemented the distribution routine on its own as well as the combined iterative labelling routine described in the previous section. As implementation language we have chosen the purely functional programming language Haskell allowing us to embed this algorithm in the verification tool TRUTH and to prototype a *concise* reference implementation. The actual Haskell source code of the algorithm has less than 280 lines of code. As the distribution routine is the same as in [5], we refer to this paper for the positive results we obtained using this distribution mechanism. Figure 7 shows the measured runtime results of the state distribution integrated with the parallel labelling algorithm for a single component on a NOW consisting of up to 52 processors and a total of 13GB main memory, which are connected with a usual 100MBit Fast-Ethernet network.

Our approach also scales very well with regard to the overall runtime (Figure 7). Note that, because of the size of the game graphs we inspected, we did not get results when running the algorithm on less than five workstations due to memory restrictions. Therefore, the shown speedups are calculated relative to 5 processors instead of one. We found that we gain a linear speedup for reasonably large game graphs (in fact, for graphs with more than 500.000 states, we even got *superlinear* speedups, which we will discuss later). The results are especially satisfying, if one considers that – for reasons of simplicity – we did not try to employ well-known optimisation means, for example reducing the communication overhead by packing several states into one message.

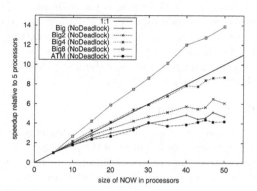

Fig. 7. runtime results

Also, due to our choice of Haskell as implementation language and its inherent inefficiency, we did not focus on optimising the internal data structures either. We use purely functional data structures like balanced trees and lists rather than destructively updateable arrays or hash tables. This is also the reason for the superlinear speedups we mentioned before. We found that the overhead for insertions and lookups on our internal data structures dramatically increases with the number of stored states. We verified this by running all processes on a *single processor* in parallel and replacing the network message passing with inter-process communication. The expected result would have been to find similar runtimes as one process would achieve in this situation, or even slightly worse due to operating-system context switches between the processes running in parallel. However, we found that there is a significant speedup, because the internal data structures are less crowded and therefore lookups and insertions are considerably cheaper.

The C++ version. We have implemented a simple prototype tailored for transition systems computed by the μCRL tool set [3]. We have tried the version on a transition system with 13 million states. We were able to check a mutual exclusion property within 9 minutes on the NOW. Note that existing model checkers for μCRL failed to show the property due to memory restrictions. However, we have to learn that the algorithm does not scale as good as the Haskell version. As soon as the transition system fits into the accumulated memory of the computers, further computers provide no significant speed-up. The reason is that, in contrast to the Haskell version where the transition system is computed on-the-fly from a given system of CCS process equations, the system is already computed in the C++ version, a fact which is not used by our algorithm. Thus, every computer is mainly concerned with labelling the game graph and sending colour information to the other computers, and communication is a costly operation within a NOW. It is therefore important to interleave the computation of the transition system together with the computation of the model-checking algorithm. Note that it took 3 hours to produce the mentioned transition system with the μCRL tool set before we were able to check the system within 9 minutes with our tool.

Since our C++ version is just a simple prototype and provides a lot of optimisation possibilities, we currently work on a sophisticated version of our parallel model checker, which can be applied for getting further insights to the run-time behaviour of our approach. This will be integrated with the routines of μCRL for generating a transition system, so that we will get a parallel on-the-fly model checker for μCRL [4].

6   Conclusion

In this paper, we have presented a *parallel* game-based model-checking algorithm for an important fragment of the μ-calculus. The demand for parallel algorithms becomes visible by considering the memory and run-time consumptions of sequential algorithms. Since the employed fragment of the μ-calculus subsumes the well-known logic CTL, it is of high practical interest. We have implemented a prototype of our approach within the verification platform TRUTH. We found out that the algorithm scales very well wrt. run-time and memory consumption when enlarging the NOW.

With our parallel algorithm, answers are computed more quickly, and, more importantly, there are numerous cases in which the sequential algorithm fails because of memory restrictions and the parallel version is able to check a formula. From the practical point of view, it is a central feature of a verification tool to give an answer in as many cases as possible. Thus, a decent implementation of this algorithm will be carried out to get further practical results.

References

1. H. R. Andersen. Model checking and Boolean graphs. *Theoretical Computer Science*, 126(1):3–30, 11 Apr. 1994.
2. S. Basonov. Parallel implementation of BDD on DSM systems. Master's thesis, Computer Science Department, Technion, 1998.
3. S. Blom, W. Fokkink, J. F. Groote, I. van Langevelde, B. Lisser, and J. van de Pol. μCRL: a toolset for analysing algebraic specifications. In G. Berry, H. Comon, and A. Finkel, editors, *Proc. of the 13th Conference on Computer-Aided Verification (CAV'01)*, LNCS 2102, p. 250–254. Springer, July 2001.
4. B. Bollig, M. Leucker, and M. Weber. Local parallel model checking for the alternation free μ–calculus. Technical Report AIB-04-2001, RWTH Aachen, 03/2001.
5. B. Bollig, M. Leucker, and M. Weber. Parallel model checking for the alternation free μ-calculus. In T. Margaria and W. Yi, editors, *Proc. of the 7th International Conference on Tools and Algorithms for the Construction and Analysis of Systems (TACAS'01)*, LNCS 2031, p. 543–558. Springer, Apr. 2001.
6. L. Brim, I. Černá, P. Krčál, and R. Pelánek. Distributed LTL model-checking based on negative cycle detection. In *Proc. of 21st Conference on Foundations of Software Technology and Theoretical Computer Science (FSTTCS'01)*, LNCS. Springer, Dec. 2001.

---

[4] This is also the reason why we did not optimise our algorithm wrt. an a-priori-known transition systems.

7. G. Cabodi, P. Camurati, and S. Que. Improved reachability analysis of large FSM. In *Proc. of the IEEE International Conference on Computer-Aided Design*, p. 354–360. IEEE Computer Society Press, June 1996.

8. E. M. Clarke, O. Grumberg, and D. A. Peled. *Model Checking*. The MIT Press, Cambridge, Massachusetts, 1999.

9. E. W. Dijkstra, W. H. J. Feijen, and A. J. M. van Gasteren. Derivation of a termination detection algorithm for distributed computations. *Information Processing Letters*, 16(5):217–219, June 1983.

10. E. A. Emerson and E. M. Clarke. Using branching time temporal logic to synthesize synchronization skeletons. *Science of Computer Programming*, 2(3):241–266, 1982.

11. E. A. Emerson, C. S. Jutla, and A. P. Sistla. On model-checking for fragments of mu-calculus. In C. Courcoubetis, editor, *Proc. 5th International Computer-Aided Verification Conference*, *LNCS* 697, p. 385–396. Springer, 1993.

12. O. Grumberg, T. Heyman, and A. Schuster. Distributed symbolic model checking for μ-calculus. In G. Berry, H. Comon, and A. Finkel, editors, *Proc. of the 13th Conference on Computer-Aided Verification (CAV'01)*, of *LNCS* 2102, p. 350–362. Springer, July 2001.

13. H. Hiraishi, K. Hamaguchi, H. Ochi, and S. Yajima. Vectorized symbolic model checking of computation tree logic for sequential machine verification. In K. G. Larsen and A. Skou, editors, *Proc. of Computer Aided Verification (CAV '91)*, *LNCS* 575, p. 214–224, Berlin, Germany, July 1992. Springer.

14. D. Kozen. Results on the propositional mu-calculus. *Theoretical Computer Science*, 27:333–354, Dec. 1983.

15. O. Kupferman, M. Y. Vardi, and P. Wolper. An automata-theoretic approach to branching-time model checking. *Journal of the ACM*, 47(2):312–360, Mar. 2000.

16. M. Leucker. Model checking games for the alternation free mu-calculus and alternating automata. In H. Ganzinger, D. McAllester, and A. Voronkov, editors, *Proc. of the 6th International Conference on Logic for Programming and Automated Reasoning "(LPAR'99)"*, *LNAI* 1705, p. 77–91. Springer, 1999.

17. M. Leucker and T. Noll. Truth/SLC - A parallel verification platform for concurrent systems. In G. Berry, H. Comon, and A. Finkel, editors, *Proc. of the 13th Conference on Computer-Aided Verification (CAV'01)*, *LNCS* 2102, p. 255–259. Springer, July 2001.

18. A. Mader. *Verification of Modal Properties Using Boolean Equation Systems*. PhD thesis, Technische Universität München, 1996.

19. A. A. Narayan, J. J. J. Isles, R. K. Brayton, and A. L. Sangiovanni-Vincentelli. Reachability analysis using partitioned–roBBDs. In *Proc. of the IEEE International Conference on Computer-Aided Design*, p. 388–393. IEEE Computer Society Press, June 1997.

20. U. Stern and D. L. Dill. Parallelizing the Murφ verifier. In O. Grumberg, editor, *Computer-Aided Verification, 9th International Conference*, *LNCS* 1254, p. 256–267. Springer, June 1997. Haifa, Israel, June 22-25.

21. C. Stirling. Games for bisimulation and model checking, July 1996. Notes for Mathfit Workshop on finite model theory, University of Wales, Swansea,.

22. A. L. Stornetta. Implementation of an efficient parallel BDD package. Master's thesis, University of California, Santa Barbara, 1995.

23. S. Zhang, O. Sokolsky, and S. A. Smolka. On the parallel complexity of model checking in the modal mu-calculus. In *Proc. of the 9th Annual IEEE Symposium on Logic in Computer Science*, p. 154–163, Paris, France, 4–7 July 1994. IEEE Computer Society Press.

The Agreement Problem Protocol Verification Environment

J.S. Pascoe[1], R.J. Loader[1], and V.S. Sunderam[2]

[1] Department of Computer Science
The University of Reading
United Kingdom,
RG6 6AY
{J.S.Pascoe,Roger.Loader}@reading.ac.uk
[2] Math & Computer Science
Emory University
Atlanta, Georgia
30322
vss@mathcs.emory.edu

Abstract. The *Agreement Problem Protocol Verification Environment* (APPROVE) for the automated formal verification of solutions to agreement problems is presented. Agreement problems are characterized by the need for a group of processes to agree on a proposed value and are exemplified by group membership, consensus and leader election schemes. Generally it is accepted by practitioners in both academia and industry that the development of reliable and robust solutions to agreement problems is essential to the usability of group communication infrastructures. Thus, it is important that the correctness of new agreement algorithms be verified formally. In the past, the application of manual proof methods has been met with varying degrees of success, suggesting that a less error prone automated tool approach is required. Furthermore, an observation made during a review of such proofs is that a significant amount of effort is invested into repeatedly modeling re-usable themes. The APPROVE project addresses these issues by introducing a usable **Spin** based framework that exploits the potential for model re-use wherever possible[1].

1 Introduction

The field of group communications has become a well established discipline within distributed systems research. Traditionally, group communications has been employed in a variety of settings often characterized by some degree of *replication*. The recent development of related technologies means that group communications is now becoming increasingly important in areas such as: Collaborative applications and Metacomputing infrastructures. In developing new group communication systems, researchers are often required to design novel solutions to a set of well known questions that are termed *agreement problems* [2]. Agreement problems are characterized by the need for a group of processes to agree on a value after one or more other processes has proposed what that value

---

[1] APPROVE v1.0 is available from: http://www.james-pascoe.com.

D. Bošnački and S. Leue (Eds.): SPIN 2002, LNCS 2318, pp. 148–169, 2002.
© Springer-Verlag Berlin Heidelberg 2002

should be [7]. Thus, typical examples include group membership, consensus and election based fault-tolerance algorithms [5].

As the error free operation of agreement algorithms is generally fundamental to a systems usability, it is important that the correctness of proposed solutions be determined rigorously. Several formalisms have been applied to accomplish this task. Birman adopted temporal logic to reason about the correctness of the virtually synchronous group membership model which was first introduced as part of the seminal ISIS system [4]. Lamport employed numerous techniques in the study of consensus [10] as did Hadzilacos, Chandra and Toueg in their research on failure detectors [6]. Current group communication project's suggest that one method is emerging as a possible *de facto* standard. This method is termed *rigorous argument* and it is based around the notion that the correctness of an algorithm can be determined by arguing that four widely adopted invariants always hold, namely: *termination, uniform agreement, validity* and *irrecoverability*. There are numerous applications of rigorous argument with two of the more notable successes being in the Totem [12, 1] and InterGroup [3] projects. Indeed rigorous argument was used to establish the correctness of the authors recent work on the design and implementation of the *Collaborative Group Membership* (CGM) algorithm (see section 7) [16, 13, 11].

The application of the manual proof methods discussed above have met with varying degrees of success. The temporal logic proof of the ISIS group membership service was later found to contain fundamental flaws (a caveat that is discussed in Birman's comprehensive text [5]). In the application to CGM, rigorous argument failed to identify a number of design errors despite months of effort invested in applying the technique. These problems were only discovered during the projects implementation phase and were later attributed to its design. Although in this instance, rigorous argument failed to identify a number of design issues, we do not consider the method to be invalid. However, we postulate that it can be prohibitively difficult to achieve the level of rigor required to instill confidence in the correctness of a proof by rigorous argument.

Following the completion of the proof, it was pertinent to study the effect of employing CGM with a wireless model of failure. In terms of failure, wireless networks differ fundamentally from wired systems because they exhibit an element of *intermittent connectivity*, that is, hosts may become unpredictably disconnected for arbitrary periods of time. Thus, in a wireless network, hosts that are disconnected are indistinguishable from hosts that have failed. Although manually specifying a wireless model of failure is not complex, it became clear that integrating and reasoning about it in the original proof was so difficult that it effectively meant restarting the process.

This experience motivated an investigation into the feasibility of developing a configurable *automated verification* environment that could quickly and exhaustively verify the correctness of a proposed solution to an agreement problem. Through the comparison of previous proofs, it was observed that there exist central themes which are modeled repeatedly, albeit in different formalisms. Thus, additional motivation for the project was to exploit this potential for *re-use*. Furthermore, as the formalism adopted varied between different applications, the possibility of exploiting direct re-use of existing model components was limited. Thus, we propose the **APPROVE** framework, its design philosophy being to provide a configurable, extensible, automated verification environment through which a catalog of previously verified re-usable components can be quickly composed to suit an application. In doing so, the researcher need only model the algorithm or protocol under test and invoke the automated verifier to establish its correctness. The aim is to not only drastically reduce the amount of effort and error associated with developing such proofs, but to also instill a much higher degree of confidence in the process and demonstrate the effectiveness of formal tools to more practical communities.

2   Background

A number of other formal techniques to facilitate reasoning about the development of group communication systems exist. For example, one of the more notable projects is the application of the *NuPrl* theorem prover (pronounced 'new' program refinement logic) [24] to the *Ensemble* group communication system. Ensemble [18] develops network protocol support for secure fault-tolerant applications and is the successor to the Horus [23] and ISIS [4] toolkits. An Ensemble developer *composes* the required system from a catalog of *micro protocols*. Each micro protocol is coded in OCaml (ML) and thus has formal semantics which can be translated into *type theory*, that is, the input language to NuPrl. Through NuPrl, the developer can prove correctness theorems or partially evaluate the type theory and so automatically perform some optimizations for common occurrences. This result is then translated back into ML and reflected in the original implementation.

2.1   Why Spin?

Although in this case, the NuPrl / Ensemble combination is a powerful mechanism for reasoning about micro protocols, NuPrl was not deemed to be a suitable basis for the realization of APPROVE. This was mainly due to the level of user interaction NuPrl (and indeed most theorem provers) require. Since one of the primary project goals was to encourage a greater utilization of formal tools in more practical communities, it was beneficial that APPROVE should offer a 'press-on-the-button' approach. Due to previous experience, we initially considered the FDR [19] model checker. However, concerns from more practical researchers over its terse interface meant that Spin [8] was selected instead.

As Spin is stable, well documented and uses a C like syntax, we postulate that it is ideal for group communications researchers. Indeed papers presenting the development phases of APPROVE have been well received in other communities [15, 13]. Furthermore, as the XSpin interface is also very usable, Spin was ultimately deemed the most suitable platform on which to base APPROVE.

2.2   Spin in Relation to Group Communications

Further motivation for using Spin stemmed from the prior work of Ruys [21, 20]. In his thesis ([21] section 4.11), Ruys provides a pragmatic insight into the modeling of *weak* multicast and broadcast protocols using Spin. The distinction between weak and *strong* models of group communication, is that all strong peers are furnished with a *view*, that is, a formalized notion of membership[2]. Thus, APPROVE has leveraged this work and aims to take it one stage further by investigating a model of group communication that is strong.

2.3 Literate Verification Using noweb

Possibly one of the most central issues to the usability of formal tools, is the provision for high quality documentation. In an imperative language such as C, programs can often effectively be documented through comments. However, the inherent power of formal notations such as Promela, often leads to a scenario where the verbosity and number of comments necessary to convey sufficient intuition compromises the readability of the code. Thus, APPROVE was developed using the *literate programming* tool noweb [17].

Literate programming was first proposed by Knuth [9] as a new programming paradigm that primarily promoted two philosophies. Firstly, literate programming combines documentation and source into a fashion suitable for reading by humans, the underlying premise being that the experts insight is more likely to be conveyed if it is stored alongside the code to which it corresponds. Literate programming also aims to free the developer from ordering programs in a compiler specified manner, that is, when writing a program, the developer need not initially concern themselves with distracting side issues but instead focus on the problem in hand. In order to facilitate literate programming, Knuth provided a tool termed WEB [9] which produced both TeX documentation and PASCAL code from a file written in the WEB notation. One of WEBs drawbacks, was that it was PASCAL specific. This was addressed by Ramsey who produced noweb, a literate programming tool that embodies the same philosophies, but can be applied to any language.

In terms of applying noweb to Promela, Ruys has contributed significant insight in [22, 21]. Thus, through the use of noweb, the researcher is able to read the APPROVE source code and the corresponding LaTeX documentation at all levels of combination.

3 The APPROVE Architecture

At the highest level, the architecture of APPROVE consists of essentially three major components (see fig. 1). Each of these is discussed below with the exception of the *test protocol*, that is, a Promela model of the proposed algorithm. Although inherently this component can not be provided, APPROVE offers a template and guidance for its construction. As one of the primary benefits of APPROVE lies in its re-configurability, extensive investigation of a test protocol becomes simple. For example, the researcher may wish to examine the verification consequences of employing a different failure detector in the overall model. Using APPROVE, this is a matter of modifying the environment's configuration, whereas traditional manual methods would require extensive alterations.

---

[2] On page 132 of [21], Ruys alludes to a destination set which could be considered an implicit form of membership. However, as there is no notion of a view, we conclude that the membership model is weak.

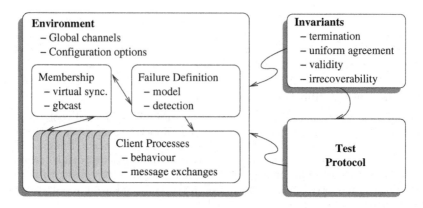

Fig. 1. The high level **APPROVE** architecture. It later became clear that the environment, invariants and test protocol could not be modeled as distinct entities. Although this has relatively little consequence (other than to mildly complicate the template for the test protocol), a more realistic illustration would possibly resemble a Venn diagram. Nevertheless, at a high level, it is considered somewhat more succinct to diagrammatically express the architecture in the manner shown here.

3.1   The Environment

The environment is the collective *term* for the entities required to support the simulation and verification of the test protocol. At this level, global channels which facilitate message passing amongst the various sub-entities are declared as are a suite of options which can be used to configure **APPROVE** for a specific scenario. Possibly the most complex environmental component is the *Group Membership Service* (or GMS). There are several definitions for a GMS, but it is generally accepted that it has at least the following responsibilities [7]:

1. *Providing an interface for group membership changes* – The GMS furnishes processes with a means to create or remove process groups and to join or leave process groups.
2. *Notifying members of group membership changes* – All members of a process group are notified when a *membership change* occurs, that is, all processes are informed when hosts join and leave the group or are evicted because they have failed.

In addition, the model of group membership offered in **APPROVE** is *virtually synchronous*. Virtual synchrony was proposed by Birman [5] in the ISIS toolkit [4] and through the success of ISIS, has become widely adopted in the field. Virtual synchrony can be effectively summarized by the simplifying abstraction it presents to the developer, namely, that a group of processes all see the same events in the same *logical* order. This reduces the design complexity of agreement protocol's since the same algorithms can be executed by all processes.

As with the GMS, client processes exhibit a specific behavior in relation to their operation. Before being admitted to the group, a client must send a *join request* message to the GMS. In a virtually synchronous system, membership

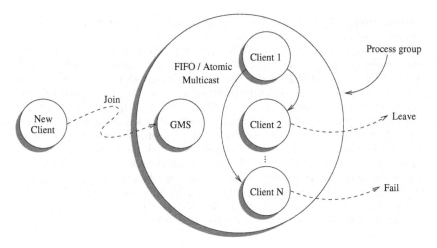

Fig. 2. The APPROVE concept of a group. To manage the size of the state space, the number of client processes is dynamic and is specified by the NUM_CLIENTS flag.

change messages are called *view change operations* and are dealt with differently than in weak group communication systems. In order to guarantee virtual synchrony, messages transmitted in one view must be delivered in the same view, so a virtually synchronous GMS responds to a view change operation by broadcasting a *flush*[3] message. On reception of a flush message, each client entity delivers any outstanding messages before signaling the GMS of the flush protocols completion. On receiving an acknowledgment from all of the group members, the GMS adds the joining process to the membership and the new view is broadcast. Once part of the group, an APPROVE client is free to transmit an arbitrary number of messages to other clients using two group communication primitives, namely, reliable FIFO multicast (or *fbcast*) and atomic multicast (or *abcast*). Reliable FIFO multicast states that if a process p transmits a message m_1 before a message m_2, then m_1 is delivered before m_2 at any common destinations, and p is notified of any message that can not be delivered. The atomic primitive behaves in the same manner as fbcast, but offers the additional guarantee that either *all* of the destination processes deliver a given message, or none do. The motivation for specifically selecting this pair of primitives is that FIFO multicast often forms the basis of quiescent failure detection and atomic ordering is frequently used to transmit the results of agreement algorithms. It is noteworthy to add, that at a time which is non-deterministic, a client can either request to

---

[3] In group communications literature, 'flush' messages are sometimes referred to in relation to the totally ordered message passing primitive *gbcast*. For more information on delivery ordered message passing primitives, see Birman [5] (page 266). Note that the 'b' is a legacy label that implies broadcast communication. Possibly a more suitable label would be 'm' (suggesting multicast communication), but this has not been adopted since all of the literature uses the original terminology.

leave the group (in which case the GMS performs a protocol symmetric to the join) or it can fail.

In some systems, a further responsibility of the GMS is to provide a failure detector and implicitly, a model of failure. In traditional group communications, often a *fail-stop* model of failure is adopted and processes fail by either halting prematurely or being irrecoverably partitioned away. Currently, only the fail-stop model of failure is supported by APPROVE, but investigation into a wireless model and its effect on traditional group infrastructures is planned for the near future. In APPROVE, three failure detection mechanisms are modeled, two in an independent *heartbeat* process and the third as part of the client. This not only reduces the complexity of the GMS, but also provides what is possibly now a more realistic model. The heartbeat or *keepalive* mechanisms are protocols that *periodically* transmit messages to announce their continued presence. The third failure detector is a quiescent algorithm that monitors the session's liveness each time the reliable fbcast primitive is used to transmit a message.

4   Modeling APPROVE: **Phase 1 (An Ideal System)**

The initial phase of the APPROVE realization process developed an *ideal* model of group communication; ideal in the sense that nothing was permitted to fail. The first phase developed models for the global aspects, the GMS and the client entities. This section describes each of these presenting select fragments of Promela code in the form of the following noweb chunks:

154   ⟨*Phase 1 list of selected chunks* 154⟩≡
        ⟨*Global channel definitions* 155⟩
        ⟨*Message types – the mtype definition* 156a⟩
        ⟨*Modeling the view* 156b⟩
        ⟨*Join protocol* 157a⟩
        ⟨*Flush protocol* 157b⟩

4.1   Global Considerations: Channel and Message Definitions

Based on the conclusions of Ruys [21], APPROVE uses a *matrix* of nine channels to model communication between the various entities. Each client process indexes into the channel matrix by using an identification number assigned to it at instantiation by the `init` process. Individually, each of the APPROVE channels can be classified into one of the following three categories:

1. *General channels* – To facilitate communication amongst the group entities.
2. *Message guarantees* – Channels that model delivery ordering semantics.
3. *Failure channels* – For co-ordinating failure resolution.

Channels of the first group conform to the labeling convention entity '2' entity, where an entity can be one of: `cli` = client, `gms` = group membership service, `hfd` = heartbeat failure detector, `eh` = error handler and `em` = error master. An *error handler* is a process that embodies an instance of the protocol under test. The *error master* is an explicit term used to address the co-ordinator

⟨*Global channel definitions* 155⟩≡   (154)

```
chan cli2gms[NUM_CLIENTS] = [BUFFER_SIZE] of { byte }
chan gms2cli[NUM_CLIENTS] = [BUFFER_SIZE] of { byte, int }
/* Channels for communicating primarily outside of the group */

chan cli2hfd[NUM_CLIENTS] = [BUFFER_SIZE] of { byte }
chan hfd2cli[NUM_CLIENTS] = [BUFFER_SIZE] of { byte, int }
/* Channels for querying the heartbeat failure detector */

chan fbcast[NUM_CLIENTS] = [BUFFER_SIZE] of { byte, byte, byte }
chan abcast[NUM_CLIENTS] = [BUFFER_SIZE] of { byte, byte, byte }
chan gbcast[NUM_CLIENTS] = [0] of { byte }
/* Delivery ordering channels */

chan fail = [BUFFER_SIZE] of { byte, int }
chan eh2eh[NUM_CLIENTS] = [NUM_CLIENTS] of { byte, int, int }
chan em2gms = [BUFFER_SIZE] of { byte, int }
/* Failure channels */
```

of a protocol, viz. the process which collates and determines the algorithm's result. Typically, this is then sent to the GMS (using the **em2gms** channel) which evicts any failures and distributes the new view.

The second group of channels form the basis of the delivery ordering guarantees. Note that the **gbcast** channel is synchronous and only carries a single byte. In practice, often the only messages to be sent using the totally ordered message passing primitive is the instruction to flush and symmetrically, the acknowledgment from a client that it has completed the protocol. Thus, in **APPROVE**, the **gbcast** channel is only permitted to carry the **FLUSH** and **FLUSH_ACK** messages. Conversely, the *failure channels* provide facilities for announcing failures and serve as a modeling interface to the researcher. Other channels in this category deal with communication between the error handlers and provide the error master with a means of informing the GMS of those processes deemed to have failed. All of the **APPROVE** channels are defined with a maximum of three fields where the first is the message type (e.g. JOIN) and the others are values. Thus, the message exchange cli2gms[2]!JOIN would correspond to a request from client 2 to join the group.

The APPROVE Message Types. In conjunction with the CGM example, APPROVE defines sixteen messages (see chunk 156a) which are again split into several sub-groups:

1. *Membership messages* – For standard membership changes.
2. *Data messages* – For quiescent reliable failure detection.
3. *Failure messages* – For querying heartbeat failure detectors and announcing failures to the error handler.
4. *CGM messages* – For co-ordinating the CGM membership algorithm.

As the denotation of each message can be inferred from its name, we do not discuss the topic further. Additional details can be found in the **APPROVE** documentation [14].

156a   ⟨*Message types – the mtype definition* 156a⟩≡   (154)

```
mtype = {
JOIN, LEAVE, LEAVE_ACK, FLUSH, FLUSH_ACK, VIEW,
/* Membership messages */
DATA, ACK,
/* Arbitrary data transfer messages */
QUERY, SUSPECTS, FAIL,
/* Failure detector messages */
EL_START, EL_CALL, EL_PROBE, EL_RETURN, EL_RESULT
/* CGM Specific messages */
}
```

4.2   The Group Membership Service

Apart from the roles discussed above, the GMS is also implicitly responsible for managing the view. As Spin opts to convert bit arrays into arrays of bytes, APPROVE models the view using the more efficient *bitvector* representation. Through the **unsigned** keyword, the size of each value can be set to the number of clients and so a minimal amount of memory is consumed. Manipulation is performed using bit-wise operators wrapped in macros.

156b   ⟨*Modeling the view* 156b⟩≡   (154)

```
unsigned view:NUM_CLIENTS=0;
```

The GMS executes continuously and is instantiated by the **init** process. In its idle state, the GMS waits for a message to arrive on one of its input channels. Regardless of whether a client wishes to join, leave, or the error master is reporting evictions, the GMS behaves in essentially the same manner. On reception of a message, the GMS initially updates its internal view. Then, the FLUSH message is sent to all operational clients instructing them to perform the flush protocol (see chunk 157b). Each client processes all of the outstanding messages in its channels before returning a FLUSH_ACK to the GMS. Once all of the clients have completed the flush, the GMS distributes the new view and the operation is complete. Note that priority is given to dealing with membership changes originating from the error master, that is, the GMS explicitly checks for messages on the em2gms channel before dealing with standard membership operations.

The length of the Promela GMS specification prevents its inclusion as a literate programming chunk here. Instead, a pseudo-code outline of the algorithm is given in fig. 3.

4.3   The Client Process

The APPROVE client process is intended to model a typical group participant. Each client process executes a join protocol and once admitted to the group, is free to exchange an arbitrary number of messages with the other group members or leave the session and terminate its execution. The simplistic join protocol executed by all of the clients is shown in chunk 157a below:

Algorithm 1: *Pseudo-code Outline for the Group Membership Service*

Initially view = 0, i = 0;

1. if
2. :: nempty(em2gms) → em2gms?*message* → atomic { *update view* }; i = 0;
3.   do
4.   :: ((i < NUM_CLIENTS) && (view & (1<<i))) → gms2cli[i]!FLUSH; i++
5.   :: (i == NUM_CLIENTS) → i = 0; break
6.   :: else → i++
7.   od;
8.   *Collect the* FLUSH_ACK *messages* → atomic { *broadcast the new view* }
9. :: else → skip
10. fi;

11. do
12. :: (i < NUM_CLIENTS) → *repeat lines 1–10, but substitute* cli2gms[i] *for* em2gms
13. :: (i == NUM_CLIENTS) → i = 0; *goto line 1*
14. od

Fig. 3. Pseudo-code Outline for the Group Membership Service

157a   ⟨*Join protocol* 157a⟩≡   (154)

```
cli2gms[id]!JOIN -> gms2cli[id]?eval(VIEW),view ->
printf("APPROVE (client %d): view received %d.\n",id,view);
```

Recall that after requesting admission to the group, the GMS broadcasts the instruction to FLUSH. If the session is empty, a singleton view is immediately returned to the client. Otherwise, each client executes the flush protocol:

157b   ⟨*Flush protocol* 157b⟩≡   (154)

```
if
:: gbcast[id]?eval(FLUSH) ->
do
:: fbcast[id]?receiver_set,from,msg ->
 if
  :: (msg != ACK) -> fbcast[from]!from,id,ACK
  :: else -> skip
 fi /* do the same for the abcast channel */
:: gbcast[id]?_
:: gms2cli[id]?_,_
:: (empty(fbcast[id]) && empty(abcast[id]) && empty(gbcast[id]) &&
 empty(gms2cli[id])) -> gbcast[id]!FLUSH_ACK; gms2cli[id]?eval(VIEW),view;
 break
od;
printf("APPROVE (client %d): flush completed.\n",id)
:: empty(gbcast[id]) -> skip
fi;
```

Once part of the group, each client is free to either leave the session or exchange an arbitrary number of f/abcast messages with other processes. As it

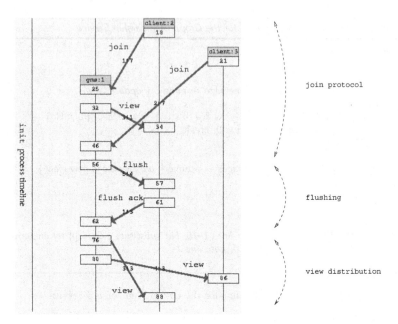

Fig. 4. A message sequence chart depicting a typical simulation of the initial model using XSpin. The first line is the `init` process which after invoking the GMS and two clients, does not interact further. The first client (process 2) joins the empty session and so immediately receives its view at time step 34. The second client (process 3) joins the group, but has to wait for the first client to flush before the new view is distributed.

is not meaningful to model message delivery ordering semantics in a failure free environment, the topic was addressed in the second modeling stage. Thus, at this point, APPROVE was tested and debugged before the second phase commenced.

5   Modeling APPROVE: **Phase 2 (Introducing Failure)**

In traditional group communications, the notion of failure is twofold. In the first instance, APPROVE must incorporate at least one *failure model*, viz. a description of exactly how a process behaves when it fails. The second aspect is the concept of *detection*, that is, by what means are process failures discovered. As before, select Promela fragments will be presented in the following literate programming chunks:

158   ⟨*Phase 2 list of selected chunks* 158⟩≡
         ⟨*Fail-stop model of failure* 159a⟩
         ⟨*Selecting a random receiver set* 159b⟩
         ⟨*FIFO delivery and quiescent failure detection* 160a⟩
         ⟨*Atomic delivery and quiescent failure detection* 160b⟩

5.1   The Fail-Stop Model of Failure

Traditional group communications software models failure as a *primary partition* fail-stop event, that is, when a process fails it either prematurely halts or is irrecoverably partitioned away from the group. Modeling this in APPROVE essentially means adding a further non-deterministic clause to the main do loop in the client process. Note that clients are only permitted to fail when no other operation is in progress. For example, a client may send a message and *then* fail, but not fail *during* a message exchange. The reason for this abstraction is to eliminate failure events that would not be handled by the protocol under test e.g. a failure during group admission would be dealt with by the join protocol and not by the error handler.

Intuitively, one would expect to model a fail-stop failure as a simple termination event. However, as Promela abstracts away from the low-level details of a processes execution status, some form of external 'announcement' is required as a testable interface to the failure detectors. This was incorporated as a global bitvector mask (termed the *failed_members_mask*) which operates in the same manner as the view, but denotes failure rather than membership. Thus, we have:

159a   ⟨*Failure model* 159a⟩≡   (158)
```
/* main client do loop (other non-deterministic clauses) */
:: (FAIL_MODEL == FAIL_STOP) ->
atomic { failed_members_mask = failed_members_mask | (1<<id); }
printf("APPROVE (client: %d): failed.\n",id); break
```

5.2   Delivery Ordering Primitives and Quiescent Failure Detection

The pertinent question of how to model the delivery ordering primitives and quiescent reliable failure detection is now addressed. A quiescent reliable failure detector treats reliable communications as probes of the sessions liveness. The main advantage of a quiescent mechanism over a periodic heartbeat algorithm is that a quiescent strategy will not incur any processing overhead in a failure free environment. Conversely, the main drawback (and indeed a fundamental distinction) is that quiescent failure detection is arbitrary and offers no timely properties.

In order to model an arbitrary message exchange, each client must be furnished with the ability to select a receiver set at random. In APPROVE, this is achieved using a rationalized random number generated by the inline **random** definition suggested by Ruys [21].

159b   ⟨*Selecting a random receiver set* 159b⟩≡   (158)
```
random(receiver_set,(2^NUM_CLIENTS)-1);
receiver_set = receiver_set & view;
if
:: (receiver_set & (1<<id)) ->
 receiver_set = receiver_set ^ (1<<id)
:: else -> skip
fi
/* rationalize the value into a valid destination set */
```

Modeling the reliable FIFO primitive is a case of selecting a random receiver set and iteratively inspecting each of its members. If a host is a member of both the receiver set and the failed members mask, then a new failure has been detected and is announced through the `fail` channel. Note that duplicate failure reports are ignored by the error master. If a recipient has not failed, then a `DATA` message is exchanged for an acknowledgment.

160a   ⟨*FIFO delivery and quiescent failure detection* 160a⟩≡   (158)

```
   i = 0 ->
   do
   :: ((i < NUM_CLIENTS) && (receiver_set & (1<<i)) ->
    if
    :: (failed_members_mask & (1<<i)) ->
      fail!FAIL,i; i++ /* announce the failure */
    :: else ->
      fbcast[i]!DATA,id,receiver_set; fbcast[i]?eval(ACK),_,_; i++
    fi
   :: (i == NUM_CLIENTS) -> break
   :: else -> i++
   od
```

The difference between the model for the reliable FIFO primitive and the atomic algorithm is that the latter will initially check that none of the recipients have failed. If this is the case, then an atomic message exchange is executed. Conversely, the operation is aborted, and the failures are reported.

160b   ⟨*Atomic delivery and quiescent failure detection* 160b⟩≡   (158)

```
   i = 0 -> atomic { if
   :: (receiver_set & failed_members_mask) ->
    do
    :: ((i < NUM_CLIENTS) && (receiver_set & (1<<i)) &&
      (failed_members_mask & (1<<i))) -> fail!FAIL,i; i++
    :: (i == NUM_CLIENTS) -> break
    :: else -> i++
    od
   :: else -> i = 0 ->
    do
    :: ((i < NUM_CLIENTS) && (receiver_set (1<<i))) ->
     abcast[i]!DATA,id,receiver_set; abcast[i]?eval(ACK),_,_; i++
    :: (i == NUM_CLIENTS) -> break
    :: else -> i++
    od
   fi }
```

5.3   Heartbeat Failure Detection

Heartbeat failure detectors (HFDs) are used in many systems (though not in CGM) and so were deemed essential to the APPROVE catalog. Heartbeat failure detection differs from quiescent mechanisms in one important aspect, namely, HFDs are triggered *periodically*. In Spin, the notion of time is implicit, that is,

---

Algorithm 2: *Pseudo-code Outline for the Heartbeat Failure Detector (Pending)*

Initially old_failed_members_mask = failed_members_mask, i = 0;

```
1.  if
2.  :: (old_failed_members_mask != failed_members_mask) →
3.     i = 0;
4.     do
5.     :: (failed_members_mask & (1<<i)) && (!(old_failed_members_mask & (1<<i)))
6.          → fail!FAIL,i; i++
7.     :: else → i++
8.     od;
9.     old_failed_members_mask = failed_members_mask; goto line 1
10. fi
```

Fig. 5. Pseudo-code Outline for a Pending Heartbeat Failure Detector

it is not possible to reason about specific durations and so the **Promela** model of an HFD has to abstract away from its traditional implementation. Note that the key distinction preserved by **APPROVE** is that heartbeat failure detection is *independent* from the pattern of communication, that is, an HFD detects failures on the basis of a loop, whereas quiescent mechanisms detect failures arbitrarily.

In a similar vein, the mechanism by which HFDs detect failure is also modeled differently from a traditional implementation. It is generally accepted, that HFDs can be categorized into two groups: *ping* (or *explicit acknowledgment*) and *'I am alive'*. When using a ping HFD, each group member will periodically broadcast a message to all others before awaiting a series of acknowledgments. If after waiting δ_t units of time an acknowledgment has not been received, then the host it refers to is suspected of failure. Similarly, a process using an 'I am alive' HFD will periodically broadcast a message announcing its continued presence to the group. If such a message is not received in δ_t units of time, then again the corresponding host becomes a failure suspect. In terms of triggering the HFD, it is not possible to effectively reason about a specific timeout duration (δ_t). In **APPROVE**, two heartbeat failure detectors are modeled. The first is a general model which *polls* the value of the **failed_members_mask** for changes, whereas, the latter *pends* on the failure event (see fig. 5). This triggering abstraction results in a significant decrease in interleaving and so reduces complexity.

6   Verifying APPROVE

The development of the heartbeat failure detectors concluded the initial **AP-PROVE** modeling phases. Subsequently, the question of instrumenting the model for the purposes of verification was considered. One of the beneficial aspects of the project was that the termination, uniform agreement, validity and irrecoverability invariants were known from its inception. As with group membership, there are numerous definitions for the invariants listed here and so, the most generally accepted were adopted [2, 7]:

1. *Termination* – In every admissible execution of the test protocol, a result is eventually assigned for every process that has not failed.
2. *Uniform Agreement* – Agreement as defined by [2] states that in every execution, if a result is set by all live processes, then that result is an agreed common value. However, it is feasible for a failing and a live process to settle on differing values immediately before the failing process crashes. Uniform agreement states that this can not be the case, i.e. even for processes that fail, if they have received a value, then that value must be the same as the other results.
3. *Validity* – If N processes have the same input, then any value decided upon must be the same.
4. *Irrecoverability* – When a result is set, then that value can not be changed.

Termination is tested through the introduction of a series of end state labels in combination with an explicit idle state in the error handler. Thus, if a verification terminates and any of the error handlers are not idling, then Spin detects and reports the violation. Conversely, the other invariants are somewhat interrelated; thus, we discuss these issues in combination. Note, that the noweb chunks referred to throughout the next section are listed below:

162a   ⟨*List of selected verification chunks* 162a⟩≡
        ⟨*Assigning a new result* 162b⟩
        ⟨*Checking validity* 163⟩

6.1   Irrecoverability, Validity and Agreement

The main distinction between termination and the other invariants is that irrecoverability, validity and agreement are only in question when a new result is assigned, that is, when the error handler master receives a result from a client and wishes to store it. In this case, testing for irrecoverability is the same as verifying that a result has not been previously received (and so set) for a particular client. This is achieved using an assert statement in conjunction with a bitvector of flags. Thus, the assignment of a new result implies verifying that a result has not been set previously, before storing the clients input and resultant views in global arrays. This is encapsulated in the following inline definition which comprises part of the APPROVE user template model:

162b   ⟨*Inline: result assignment* 162b⟩≡   (162a)

```
inline ASSIGN_RESULT(input_view,result,id) {
  atomic {
  assert(!(verification_result_set & (1<<id)));
  verification_input_view[id] = input_view;
  verification_output_view[id] = result;
  verification_result_set = verification_result_set | (1<<id);
  CHECK_VALIDITY()
  CHECK_AGREEMENT() /* use inlines for validity and agreement */
  }
  }
```

Inlines vs. Never Claims to Guarantee Validity and Agreement. Note the use of the inline statements CHECK_VALIDITY and CHECK_AGREEMENT in chunk 162b above. Intuitively, the validity and agreement invariants lend themselves to expression by a Spin *never* claim; indeed a significant amount of effort was invested in pursuing this idea. Spin never claims generally apply invariants to the *global* space of the model whereas in this case, the validity and agreement invariants only apply to the client processes. It is possible for never claims to inspect variables local to processes suggesting the idea of using a bounded do loop to cycle through each client process checking the invariants in turn. However, due to the assignment of the counting index, Spin objects warning that the never claim contains side effects. Although in this case, the side effect in question is known to be safe, it is arguable that the approach contravenes the philosophy of the never claim and so the alternative method of using inline definitions was adopted.

The mechanics of actually checking the invariants are again based around a bounded do loop and are similar in both cases. For brevity, only the chunk which checks for validity is presented:

163   ⟨*Checking validity* 163⟩≡   (162a)
```
  inline CHECK_VALIDITY() {
  i = 0 ->
   do
   :: ((i < NUM_CLIENTS) && (verification_result_set & (1<<i))) ->
    j = 0 ->
    do
    :: ((j < NUM_CLIENTS) && (verification_result_set & (1<<j)) && (i!=j)
    && (verification_input_view[i] == verification_input_view[j])) ->
     assert(verification_output_view[i] == verification_output_view[j]);
     j++;
    :: (j == NUM_CLIENTS) -> i++; break
    :: else -> j++
    od
   :: (i == NUM_CLIENTS) -> break
   od;
  }
```

7   Applying APPROVE: Collaborative Group Membership

Next consider the application of **APPROVE** to an actual agreement problem. The example adopted is that of the *Collaborative Group Membership* (CGM) algorithm i.e. the protocol to which rigorous argument was applied in our recent work. The distinguishing feature of collaborative technologies over other group systems is their multi-channel architecture, that is, collaborative applications exhibit a *further group abstraction* which permits messages to be simultaneously transferred using different delivery semantics. As traditional group membership algorithms were unsuitable, this prompted the development of CGM.

CGM is based on two complementary entities that are executed by all clients to perform the actions necessary to participate in two elections [16, 13, 11]. The *error monitor* is an arbitration entity that primarily maintains a log of error reports from the failure detector. It also mediates the invocation of an agent which performs two consensual elections. The first of these is termed the *membership removal election* and is designed to deal with fail-stop failures. Conversely, the *session* election is used to detect and resolve the more subtle *partial failures*. In multi-channel collaborative systems, it has been observed that *part* of the software can fail i.e. the system has not crashed out-right, but is malfunctioning. In APPROVE terminology, this agent corresponds to the error handler, that is, the component under test. A further distinction, is that the most senior error handler has the additional role of calculating and distributing the results of the two elections and thus is the error master. In the event that the error master fails, the next most senior group member assumes the role and if necessary restarts the election.

The development of the initial CGM model abstracted away from the error monitor and session election, focusing primarily on the membership removal election. When triggered, the error handler broadcasts an EL_START message followed by an EL_CALL. This informs the other group members that an election is about to take place and that they should *refresh* their view. Using the quiescent failure detector, each client reliably broadcasts an EL_PROBE message to its peers. The underlying reasoning being that this will generate new fault reports for failures that were previously undetected. Client views based on heartbeat failure detectors can be refreshed by consulting the failure detector directly. This returns a list of suspects in the form of a bitvector. Based on its refreshed view, each client votes for the removal of members it deems to have failed and sends a digest of the result to the error master via a point-to-point EL_RETURN message. Having received all of the votes, the error master determines the outcome and instructs the GMS to evict any agreed failures.

8   Results

8.1   Qualitative Analysis

Initial experiments using APPROVE quickly identified two termination violations in the model of CGM. Essentially, APPROVE demonstrated that if a failure detector based on reliable communication was used, and a failure occurred after the EL_PROBE, the error master would infinitely wait for an EL_RETURN (since at this point, the protocol does not transmit any reliable messages and the failure remains undetected). Several strategies exist to solve this problem using a quiescent reliable failure detector, but it was decided that for now the remainder of the analysis would be conducted using a heartbeat failure detector. Reconfiguring the model highlighted a second termination flaw. Although new failures were now being detected and acted upon, the occurrence of a client *leave* during the election would also invalidate the termination property. Heartbeat failure detectors do not announce valid departures and the GMS is unable to circulate a new view whilst the current view is in question (i.e. an election is in progress). Thus, the protocol design was modified to include a timeout entity which circumvents these issues and allows the error master to restart the election if necessary. Note

Table 1. APPROVE verification results showing the quantitative effect of toggling the CGM probe. Note the following key: **SV** is the state vector measured in bytes, **DR** is the depth reached, **SS** is the number of states stored (the decimals are e+08) and **T** is the averaged elapsed time (hours:minutes:seconds). All of the experiments used 219.02 Mb of memory and no errors were reported at any stage.

	Probe enabled / NUM_CLIENTS							
	3	4	5	6	7	8	9	10
SV	572	820	1108	1440	1808	2216	2708	3200
DR	935864	1288425	1388202	1227178	1819674	1639334	1244615	1454759
SS	2.11743	2.10856	2.26861	2.22499	2.12071	3.16569	2.70916	2.23208
T	1:25:54	1:40:50	2:32:17	2:36:55	2:56:02	6:28:39	5:56:39	4:50:41

	Probe disabled / NUM_CLIENTS							
	3	4	5	6	7	8	9	10
SV	524	724	928	1152	1388	1640	1952	2240
DR	1158358	1288748	1464371	1933316	1895244	1312446	1415283	1356739
SS	1.02681	1.89953	2.07028	2.12812	2.18374	2.25818	2.85684	2.46325
T	0:37:35	1:22:52	1:40:50	1:58:37	2:19:03	2:39:49	4:23:59	3:42:05

that this strategy also solves the first termination problem and so permits the use of the failure detector based on reliable communication.

8.2   Using APPROVE to Empirically Investigate Extraneous Code

During the initial CGM design phases [16], the cost of the algorithm was approximated in terms of its *message complexity*. Message complexity (MC) is defined by Attiya and Welch [2] as the maximum, over all admissible executions of the total messages sent for both synchronous and asynchronous message passing systems. In terms of a CGM session with N_s participants and n_f failures, MC can be approximated to the following:

$$MC \approx (N_s^2 + n_f(N_s - n_f)) + c_m + ac_m$$

where N_s^2 is the message complexity of the probe mechanism, $n_f(N_s - n_f)$ is due to the resulting failure reports, c_m represents a fixed number of control messages and a indicates $N_s - n_f$ acknowledgments. From this it is evident that the approached message complexity is quadratic, indeed it is noteworthy to highlight that the majority of current group membership algorithms exhibit the same property (certainly [3] supports this view). As the CGM probing mechanism is responsible for the quadratic overhead, this raised the question of whether the EL_PROBE message could safely be removed without introducing semantic violations. Using APPROVE, it was now possible to formally determine whether or not this was the case.

In addition, it was decided that these experiments would investigate APPROVEs performance in relation to larger groups (i.e. between 3 and 10 clients). The expected result, indeed the characteristic under test, is that there exists a small linear increase in overhead for each additional client process. Note that a session consisting of two client processes is an exception to this hypothesis since the system is effectively point-to-point and so has a significantly simpler

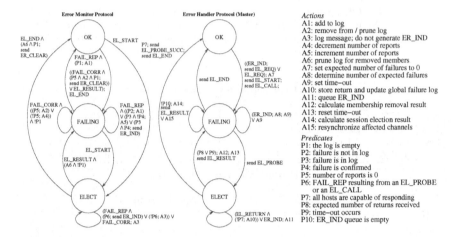

Fig. 6. The amended (final) state transition diagrams for CGM. For fuller explanations see [16, 13]. The Journal of Supercomputing article is the canonical CGM paper but is in press (pre-prints available on request). The COMPSAC paper [13] gives an overview of the original protocol theory and includes references to our proof by rigorous argument.

interaction. The experimental environment consists of one Pentium III desktop machine using a 600 MHz processor and 768 Mb of RAM. In terms of software, the PC is running Linux Mandrake 6.5 and Spin version 3.4.10. Each experiment was conducted using the same compiler and run-time options, thus, in order to repeat these experiments, define -D_POSIX_SOURCE -DBITSTATE -DSAFETY -DNOCLAIM -DXUSAFE -DNOFAIR -DVECTORSZ=4000 on the compilation line and -X -m3000000 -w29 -c1 as the arguments to pan. Note the use of the partial search. Normally, an APPROVE verification is performed exhaustively using a smaller number of clients (e.g. 3 or 4), however, studying APPROVE in the context of larger groups necessitates the use of the partial search.

When the model was re-configured to not probe, Spin did not detect any invariant violations, suggesting that the probe could indeed be removed. In addition, a significant decrease in the overhead required to complete the verification (particularly for the larger groups) was observed. The cause for the sudden increase in verification time (at 8 clients) is currently being investigated. However, this anomaly appears to pose only performance implications, as no semantic violations were detected. During Spin guided simulations, it was noted that if further failures occurred during an election, the CGM algorithm would simply iterate up-to n_f times. Based on these results, it was decided that the probe would not be removed completely, but its use would be restricted to environments where failures occur in rapid succession. Under normal circumstances, the algorithm operates without the probe yielding a linear message complexity and less overhead in the Promela model, but, in the rare cases where failures occur in rapid succession, the probe can be employed to avoid multiple CGM iterations.

9   Conclusion

Following the completion of APPROVE and its application to CGM, the insight gained from the process was reflected back into the original design (see fig. 6). In terms of critique and future work, there are a number of developments which are to be pursued:

- *A Wireless model of failure* – Through the maturation of related technologies, wireless group communications is being touted as the next paradigm in the field. Currently, APPROVE supports only a fail-stop model of failure. In the projects next phase, it is planned that APPROVE will be used to formally investigate the effect of failure in the wireless domain. The distinction between the two environments is that wireless hosts often experience a level of *intermittent connectivity*. Thus, traditional group communications systems are unequipped to distinguish between temporarily dis-connected live hosts and outright failures. In practice, this phenomenon manifests itself through the erroneous triggering of membership algorithms suggesting that APPROVE be employed to investigate solutions.
- *Scoped never claims* – During the verification process, it was noted that the Spin never claim operated on the global state space and so was not suitable to apply the APPROVE invariants. In future work, it may be pertinent to investigate the notion of a *scoped* never claim which can apply an invariant to a subset of processes.
- *Service based strong group communications* – Based on the suggestions in the online Spin help, APPROVE models communication at the client level, that is, each client is responsible for the execution of the f/abcast protocols. In the next phase of APPROVE, a *service* based model of group communication will be added. This will not only provide a platform for studying transport layer issues in the context of group communications (e.g. message loss) but will also form the basis of a 'low-fat' analysis (see Ruys' recipes [20]).

One of the most encouraging aspects of APPROVE has been the positive reaction by the more practical protocol communities. Tools such as Spin have repeatedly demonstrated how they can be employed to tangibly improve projects. It is hoped that through frameworks such as APPROVE, the technology transfer gap between these communities will lessen and so, this stands as one of the APPROVE projects long term goals.

Acknowledgments

The authors would like to thank Gerard J. Holzmann for his numerous patient and prompt answers to questions that have undoubtedly been asked before. We would also like to thank Theo C. Ruys for sending a copy of his thesis and G M. Megson for his proof reading and critique.

References

1. D. A. Agarwal. *Totem: A Reliable Ordered Delivery Protocol for Interconnected Local-Area Networks*. PhD thesis, University of California, Santa Barbara, 1994.
2. H. Attiya and J. Welch. *Distributed Computing: Fundamentals, Simulations and Advanced Topics*. McGraw-Hill, 1998.
3. K. Berket. *The InterGroup Protocols: Scalable Group Communication for the Internet*. PhD thesis, University of California, Santa Barbara, December 2000.
4. K. P. Birman. The Process Group Approach to Reliable Distributed Computing. *Communications of The ACM*, pages 37–53, December 1993.
5. K. P. Birman. *Building Secure and Reliable Network Applications*. Prentice Hall, 1997. Available at: `http://www.cs.cornell.edu/ken/`.
6. T. D. Chandra and S. Toueg. Unreliable Failure Detectors for Reliable Distributed Systems. *Journal of the Association for Computing Machinery*, 43(2), 1996.
7. G. Coulouris, J. Dollimore, and T. Kindberg. *Distributed Systems Concepts and Design*. Addison-Wesley, third edition, 2001. See chapter 11 for Coordination and Agreement problems.
8. G. J. Holzmann. *Design and Validation of Computer Protocols*. Prentice Hall, 1991. An online version is available at:
   `http://cm.bell-labs.com/cm/cs/what/spin/Doc/Book91.html`.
9. D. E. Knuth. *Literate Programming*. Center for the Study of Language and Information, 1992.
10. L. Lamport, R. Shostak, and M. Pease. Byzantine Generals Problem. *ACM Transactions Programming Languages and Systems*, 4(3):382–401, 1982.
11. R. J. Loader, J. S. Pascoe, and V. S. Sunderam. A Novel Approach To Group Membership In Collaborative Computing Environments. In *Proc. of The 2001 International Conference on Parallel and Distributed Processing Techniques and Applications (PDPTA'2001)*. CSREA Press, June 2001.
12. L. E. Moser, P. M. Melliar-Smith, D. A. Agarwal, R. K. Budhia, and C. A. Lingley-Papadopoulos. Totem: A Fault-Tolerant Multicast Group Communication System. In *Communications of the ACM*, April 1996.
13. J. S. Pascoe, R. J. Loader, and V. S. Sunderam. An Election Based Approach to Fault-Tolerant Group Membership in Collaborative Environments. In *Proc. of The 25th Anniversary Annual International Computer Software and Applications Conference (COMPSAC)*. IEEE Press, October 2001.
14. J. S. Pascoe, R. J. Loader, and V. S. Sunderam. APPROVE Technical Documentation. Technical report, Department of Computer Science, The University of Reading, November 2001. Available from: `http://www.james-pascoe.com`.
15. J. S. Pascoe, R. J. Loader, and V. S. Sunderam. Working Towards the Agreement Problem Protocol Verification Environment. In Alan Chalmers, Majid Mirmehdi and Henk Muller, editor, *Communicating Process Architectures 2001*, Concurrent Systems Engineering, pages 213–229, Bristol, September 2001. IOS Press.
16. J. S. Pascoe, R. J. Loader, and V. S. Sunderam. Collaborative Group Membership. *The Journal of Supercomputing*, 22(1):55–68, 2002. Accepted: 30th November 2001, In press.
17. N. Ramsey. Literate programming simplified. *IEEE Software*, 11:95–105, 1994.
18. O. Rodeh, K. P. Birman, and D. Dolev. The Architecture and Performance of Security Protocols in the Ensemble Group Communication System. Technical Report TR2000-1791, Cornell University, March 2000.
19. A. W. Roscoe. *The Theory and Practice of Concurrency*. Prentice Hall, 1997.
20. Theo C. Ruys. Low-Fat Recipes for SPIN. In *Proc. of The 7th International SPIN Workshop*, volume 1885 of *Lecture Notes in Computer Science*. Springer, 2000.

21. Theo C. Ruys. *Toward Effective Model Checking*. PhD thesis, University of Twente, March 2001. ISBN: 90-365-1564-5.
22. Theo C. Ruys and Ed Brinksma. Experience with Literate Programming in the Modeling and Validation of Systems. In Bernhard Steffen, editor, *Proceedings of the Fourth International Conference on Tools and Algorithms for the Construction and Analysis of Systems (TACAS'98)*, number 1384 in Lecture Notes in Computer Science (LNCS), pages 393–408, Lisbon, Portugal, April 1998. Springer-Verlag.
23. R. van Renesse, K. P. Birman, and S. Maffeis. Horus, A Flexible Group Communication System. In *Communications of the ACM*, April 1996.
24. Liu Xiaoming, Christoph Kreitz, Robbert van Renesse, Jason Hickey, Mark Hayden, Ken Birman, and Robert Constable. Building reliable, high-performance systems from components. In *Proc. 17th ACM Symposium on Operating System Principles (SOSP'99) – Operating Systems Review*, volume 34(5), pages 80–92, 1999.

Bottleneck Analysis of a Gigabit Network Interface Card: Formal Verification Approach*

Hyun-Wook Jin[1], Ki-Seok Bang[1], Chuck Yoo[1],
Jin-Young Choi[1], and Ho-jung Cha[2]

[1] Department of Computer Science and Engineering,
Korea University
Seoul, 136-701 Korea
{hwjin,hxy}@os.korea.ac.kr
{kbang,choi}@formal.korea.ac.kr
[2] Department of Conputer Science, Yonsei University,
Seoul, 120-749 Korea
hjcha@cs.yonsei.ac.kr

Abstract. This paper addresses how formal verification can be applied to find a bottleneck in a gigabit network interface card that prevents the card from achieving the best possible performance. Finding a bottleneck in a gigabit network interface card is not an easy task because it is equipped with sophisticated hardware components, such as multiple DMA engines and separate CPU and memory. Therefore, the interactions between a network interface card and the host are very complex so that the firmware to manage the interactions is also complicated, which makes the bottleneck analysis very difficult. As an alternative approach of the bottleneck analysis, we specify the firmware in a gigabit network interface card and analyze the behavior of the specification with SPIN. As an example of gigabit network interface cards, Myrinet is used in this paper. We show that SPIN can easily verify whether the Myrinet firmware has a bottleneck once the state transitions inside the firmware are modeled properly.

1 Introduction

Gigabit network interface cards (NIC) are getting popular. A notable example is Myrinet [3]. In order to achieve the best possible performance out of Myrinet, several user-level communication primitives have been proposed [4,6,12], and Berkeley-VIA [4] is a well-known implementation of Virtual Interface Architecture (VIA) [5] that is an industrial standard for user-level communication primitives. VIA allows user processes to directly access NIC bypassing the kernel that has multiple communication layers. Therefore, it is generally expected that VIA can achieve near physical bandwidth of gigabit networks.

* This research was supported in part by the University Software Research Center Supporting Project of the Korea Ministry Information & Communication and by the Korea Science & Engineering Foundation under grant No. R01-2000-00287.

D. Bošnački and S. Leue (Eds.): SPIN 2002, LNCS 2318, pp. 170–186, 2002.

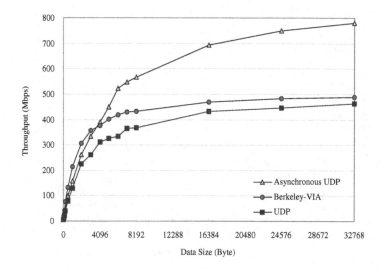

Fig. 1. Throughput comparison of Asynchronous UDP, Berkeley-VIA, and UDP

However, our research shows that Berkeley-VIA is able to achieve a slightly higher throughput than UDP on Myrinet as shown in Figure 1 (only 6% improvement at 32KB data size). Furthermore, Berkeley-VIA has much less throughput than an improved UDP named Asynchronous UDP [13]. It turns out that Berkeley-VIA utilizes only about 1/2 of bandwidth of Myrinet. On the other hand, we find that Berkeley-VIA has the shortest one-way latency as shown in Figure 2, which indicates that Berkeley-VIA has less communication overhead than UDP and Asynchronous UDP. So a question is why Berkeley-VIA has a very low overhead but is not able to achieve the best possible throughput. Our goal is to find the performance bottleneck.

The firmware of Myrinet NIC needs to be analyzed to see where the bottleneck is. Because Myrinet NIC has three DMA engines and separate memory and CPU, the firmware itself is very complicated. Therefore, the analysis of the firmware is not an easy task. Also the interaction between the firmware and the host is very complex so that the firmware analysis becomes even more complicated.

This paper attempts an alternative approach. In order to analyze the firmware of Myrinet NIC, we first build state transition diagrams to model the firmware. Second, we translate the state transition diagrams into specifications written in PROMELA (PROcess MEta LAnguage) [7]. Third, we derive verification formulas. Then the formulas are verified with SPIN [8].

Specifically, we analyze Lanai Control Program (LCP) and Myrinet Control Program (MCP), where LCP is the firmware for Berkeley-VIA and MCP is the firmware for traditional protocols, such as UDP and TCP. Since our goal is to find a performance bottleneck, we focus on how well DMA engines of Myrinet NIC are utilized because the utilization of DMA engines determines the throughput.

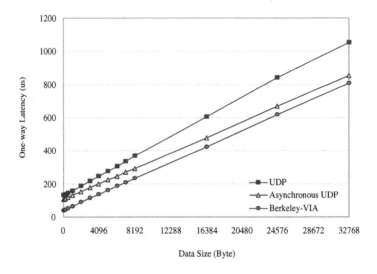

Fig. 2. One-way latency comparison of Asynchronous UDP, Berkeley-VIA, and UDP

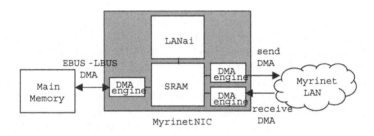

Fig. 3. Hardware feature of Myrinet NIC

This paper is organized as follows. Section 2 describes the hardware components in Myrinet NIC. Section 3 models LCP and MCP. We construct state transition diagrams and specify them with PROMELA. LCP and MCP are analyzed in Section 4 with SPIN. Finally, Section 5 concludes the paper.

2   Myrinet Network Interface Card

Myrinet is a gigabit Local Area Network (LAN). Many researches apply Myrinet to clustering systems or storage area networks [1,2]. In this section, we describe the hardware components of Myrinet NIC based on LANai-4 [10].

Myrinet NIC consists of a RISC processor named LANai, Static Random Access Memory (SRAM), and three DMA engines (i.e. EBUS-LBUS, send-DMA, and receive-DMA engines) as shown in Figure 3. LANai executes the firmware, and SRAM stores the data for sending or receiving. Each DMA engine works as follows.

The EBUS-LBUS DMA engine is responsible for the data movement between the main memory and the SRAM. The firmware initializes the EBUS-LBUS DMA by setting the DMA direction register (DMA_DIR), main memory address register (EAR), SRAM address register (LAR), and DMA counter register (DMA_CTR). The DMA_DIR register indicates that the DMA operation moves data whether from main memory to SRAM or vice versa. The EAR and LAR registers point the start of main memory buffer and SRAM buffer, respectively. The DMA_CTR register contains the number of bytes for DMA. In the case of sending, the data in the area indicated by the EAR register is moved to the buffer indicated by the LAR register as many as the value of DMA_CTR register, which is the same in the case of receiving excepting the data moving direction.

The send-DMA engine moves the data in SRAM to the Myrinet physical network. The firmware sets the sending memory pointer register (SMP) and sending memory limit register (SML). The SMP register specifies the beginning of the SRAM buffer to send-DMA, and the SML register indicates the end of the buffer.

The receive-DMA engine receives a data from Myrinet LAN into the SRAM. The registers of receive-DMA engine are receiving memory pointer register (RMP) and receiving memory limit register (RML). The registers have the same role as the registers of send-DMA engine excepting the registers specify the receiving buffer.

The firmware initiates the DMA operations by setting the proper registers of each DMA engine and notices the completion of corresponding DMA operation via the 32-bit Interrupt Status Register (ISR) on LANai processor. Each bit of ISR indicates a specific hardware event. The bit number 4 (dma_int bit) is set when an EBUS-LBUS DMA operation is completed. The bit number 3 (send_int bit) and 1 (recv_int bit) are set when a send-DMA and receive-DMA are completed, respectively. We refer the details of Myrinet NIC to [2].

3   Modeling of Firmware

This Section performs the modeling of LCP and MCP based on their source codes. We construct the state transition diagrams for concerned modules and specify them with PROMELA.

3.1   Lanai Control Program

LCP is the firmware for Berkeley-VIA. LCP consists of four modules: hostDma, lcpTx, lcpRx, and main. Figures 4, 5, and 6 show the state transition diagrams of former three modules.

The hostDma module is responsible for EBUS-LBUS DMA. The initial sate of the hostDma module is HostDmaIdle. The lcpTx and lcpRx modules invoke the method of the hostDma module. Then, the hostDma module initializes the

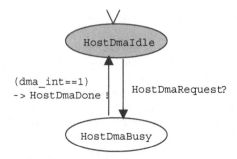

Fig. 4. State transition diagram of the hostDma module

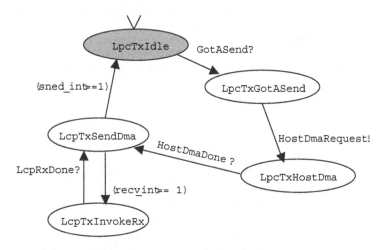

Fig. 5. State transition diagram of the lcpTx module

EBUS-LBUS DMA operation, and its state moves to HostDmaBusy. When the EBUS-LBUS DMA operation is done (i.e. dma_int bit of ISR is set), the state of the hostDma module moves from HostDmaBusy to HostDmaIdle, and the method returns to its invoker.

The lcpTx module sends a data. The initial state is LcpTxIdle and moves to the LpcTxGotASend state when there is a data to send. Then, the lcpTx module invokes the method of the hostDma module moving to LcpTxHostDma. After the return of the invoked method, the state of the lcpTx module moves to LcpTxSendDma. In this state, the lcpTx module initializes the send-DMA operation and is waiting the completion of send-DMA. If a data is received from the network during the send-DMA operation, the lcpTx module invokes the method of the lcpRx module and moves to the LcpTxInvokeRx state. When the lcpRx module has received a data completely, its method returns to the lcpTx module, and the state of the lcpTx module moves to LcpTxSendDma again. The

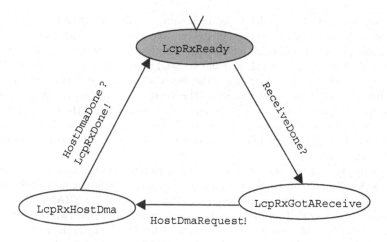

Fig. 6. State transition diagram of the lcpRx module

LcpTxSendDma state can be changed to LcpTxIdle when the send-DMA is done
(i.e. send_int bit of ISR is set).

The lcpRx module is responsible for receiving a data. The initial state is
LcpRxReady that initializes a receive-DMA operation beforehand because it is
hard to know when a data gets in. When a data is received from the network to
Myrinet NIC (i.e. recv_int bit of ISR is set), the state moves to LcpRxGotARe-
ceive, and the lcpRx module invokes the method of the hostDma module moving
its state to LcpRxHostDma. After the method of the hostDma module returns,
the lcpRx module changes its sate from LcpRxHostDma to LcpRxReady and
reinitializes the receive-DMA operation.

The main module invokes the methods of the lcpTx and lcpRx modules when
there is a data to send or receive, respectively. Note that the entry point (gray
ellipses of Figures 4, 5, and 6) of the hostDma, lcpTx, and lcpRx modules is
the initial state of each module. We will discuss more about the entry point in
Section 3.2.

We specify the modules as processes in PROMELA. All invocations between
modules are performed in a synchronous manner. Therefore, we implement the
invocation by using two rendezvous communication channel for each process.
One is the channel to pass an argument, and the other returns a return value.
An event is passed as an argument or return value via the rendezvous channels.
In addition, we specify ISR bits that notify the completion of DMA operations.
Appendix A shows the part of the specification written in PROMELA.

3.2   Myrinet Control Program

MCP is included in Myrinet Software package [11] that contains a device driver
and firmware (i.e. MCP). While Berkeley-VIA supports only VIA protocol,

Myrinet Software does TCP/IP protocol suite. MCP consists of five modules: hostSend, netSend, hostReceive, netReceive, and main. The hostSend and net-Send modules are responsible for sending. The hostSend module moves a data from main memory to SRAM, and the netSend module sends a data in SRAM to the network. On the other hand, the receiving of data is performed by the hostReceive and netReceive modules. The netReceive module receives a data from the network to SRAM. The hostReceive module moves the received data to the main memory. The state transition diagrams of four modules are shown in Figures 7, 8, 9, and 10. The main module invokes the methods of the former four modules according to the event occurred.

The initial state of the hostSend module is HostSendIdle. The state is moves to HostSendGotASend when there is a data to send. Then, the hostSend module checks some conditions. If there is no buffer available in SRAM, the state becomes HostSendFull and returns to the main module. Otherwise, the host-Send module examines whether the EBUS-LBUS DMA engine is occupied by the hostReceive module. If the EBUS-LBUS DMA engine is idle, then the state moves to HostSendDma initializing an EBUS-LBUS DMA operation and re-turns to the main module without a waiting for the completion of the DMA. If the EBUS-LBUS DMA engine is occupied by the hostReceive module, the state moves to HostSendDmaBusy and returns to the main module. In the case of reaching the HostSendFull state, the state transition is performed when the netSend module consumes a data in SRAM. The state transition from HostSend-

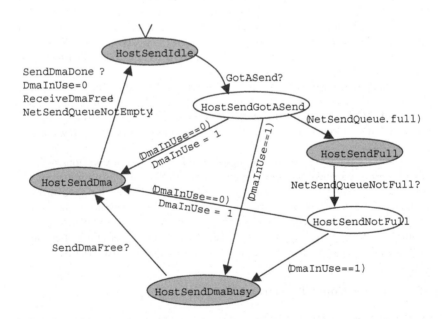

Fig. 7. State transition diagram of the hostSend module

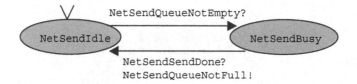

Fig. 8. State transition diagram of the netSend module

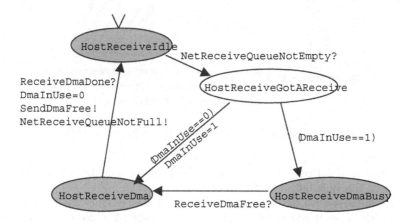

Fig. 9. State transition diagram of the hostReceive module

DmaBusy is occurred after the completion of EBUS-LBUS DMA performed by the hostReceive module. When the state is HostSendDma, the hostSend module moves its state to the initial state after the completion of EBUS-LBUS DMA (i.e. dma_int bit of ISR is set).

The initial state of the netSend module is NetSendIdle. If there is a data moved from main memory to SRAM by the hostSend module, the method of the netSend module is invoked moving its state to NetSendBusy. The netSend module in NetSendBusy initializes the send-DMA operation, then the method returns. When the send-DMA operation is completed (i.e. send_int bit of ISR is set), the state is changed to NetSendIdle.

The hostReceive module starts from HostReceiveIdle. If there is a data received from the network to SRAM by the netReceive module, the state moves to HostReceiveGotAReceive. Then, like the hostSend module, the hostReceive module checks whether the other party uses the EBUS-LBUS DMA engine or not. If the EBUS-LBUS DMA engine is occupied by the hostSend module, the state moves to HostSendDmaBusy. Otherwise, the state is changed to HostReceiveDma, and the module initializes EBUS-LBUS DMA. In both case, after the state transition, the method returns to the main module. The state transition is performed from HostReceiveDmaBusy to HostReceiveDma when the hostSend module releases the EBUS-LBUS DMA engine. The state moves from HostRe-

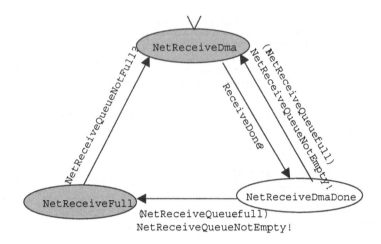

Fig. 10. State transition diagram of the netReceive module

ceiveDma to HostReceiveIdle, after the completion of the EBUS-LBUS DMA operation (i.e. dma_int bit of ISR is set).

The initial state of the netReceive module is NetReceiveDma that is the same state with LcpRxReady of LCP. When the receive-DMA is done (i.e. recv_int bit of ISR is set), the state moves to NetReceiveDmaDone that checks whether the receiving buffer in SRAM is available for the next receiving. If it is available, the state is returns to the initial state; else, the state is changed to NetReceive-Full. The netReceive module can escape from the NetReceiveFull state when the hostReceive module consumes a data in SRAM.

Comparing with modules of LCP, the notable difference is that each module of MCP has plural entry points. This means that the method of each module is invoked from an entry point and returns when it reaches to another entry point without waiting for the next event. Therefore, the method invoked in the next time starts from the state in which the method returns right before. On the other hand, in the case of LCP, a method is invoked when the module is in the initial sate and returns only when it backs to the initial state.

Like LCP, we implement an invocation by using two rendezvous communication channel of PROMELA. The events are stored in the channel named Events. The main module gets an events from the Events channel and invokes the correspond method. Appendix B shows the part of the specification written in PROMELA.

4   Comparison of Firmware

This section analyzes the behaviors of LCP and MCP from the viewpoint of throughput. The key factor that determines the throughput of NIC is how well the DMA engines are utilized. The maximum throughput can be achieved when the EBUS-LBUS DMA engine performs in parallel with the send-DMA and receive-DMA engine.

For example, let $DMA_{EBUS-LBUS}$ be the throughput of the EBUS-LBUS DMA and DMA_{send} be the throughput of the send-DMA. $DMA_{EBUS-LBUS}$ is determined by the bandwidth of the I/O bus (e.g. PCI) that connects the main memory and SRAM of NIC. On the other hand, DMA_{send} is determined by the network physical media. When DMA engines perform in parallel, the throughput is evaluated as follows:

$$Throughput = MIN(DMA_{EBUS-LBUS}, DMA_{send})$$

However, if DMA engines perform sequentially, the throughput is limited as follows:

$$Throughput = DMA_{EBUS-LBUS}/(1 + DMA_{EBUS-LBUS}/DMA_{send})$$

If $DMA_{EBUS-LBUS}$ and DMA_{send} are the same, the throughput achieved is reduced to 1/2 of $DMA_{EBUS-LBUS}$. The next step of the analysis is to derive verification formulas. Because the verification formulas need to reflect the utilization of DMA engines, we use the following formulas written in LTL [9]:

1. LCP
    A. ◇ (LTIR && HDB && ! LTHD)

       Can the lcpTx module initiate send-DMA while the hostDma module is using EBUS-LBUS DMA that moves data from main memory to SRAM?
    B. ◇ (LRR && HDB && ! LRHD)

       Can the lcpRx module initiate receive-DMA while the hostDma module is using EBUS-LBUS DMA that moves data from SRAM to main memory?
       - LTIR : The state of lcpTx is LcpTxInvokeRx.
       - LTHD : The state of lcpTx is LcpTxHostDma.
       - LRR : The state of lcpRx is LcpRxReady.
       - LRHD : The state of lcpRx is LcpRxHostDma.
       - HDB : The state of hostDma is HostDmaBusy.
2. MCP
    A. ◇ (HSD && NSB)

       Can the netSend module initiate send-DMA while the hostSend module occupies the EBUS-LBUS DMA engine?
    B. ◇ (HRD && NRD)

       Can the netReceive module initiate receive-DMA while the hostReceive module occupies EBUS-LBUS DMA engine?
       - HSD : The state of hostSend is HostSendDma.
       - NSB : The state of netSend is NetSendBusy.
       - HRD : The state of hostReceive is HostReceiveDma.
       - NRD : The state of netReceive is NetReceiveDma.

If DMA engines perform in parallel, each verification formulas should result in "True". When we run SPIN with the above formulas, the verification formulas of MCP are "True". However, the formulas for LCP result in "False". That is, LCP

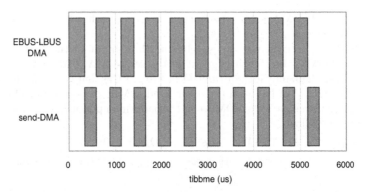

Fig. 11. DMA overheads of LCP

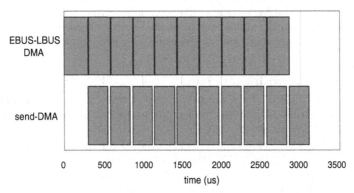

Fig. 12. DMA overheads of MCP

cannot perform the send-DMA during the EBUS-LBUS DMA that moves data from main memory to SRAM (formula 1-A). In order to quantify the parallelism of each firmware, we measure the DMA overheads of sender on M2F-PCI32C Myrinet NIC when 10 UDP packets of 32KB are sent. Figures 11 and 12 are the time charts. The x-axis indicates the time. The y-axis represents the DMA engine that each packet goes through in order to be processed. A rectangle in a DMA engine is the time spent in the DMA engine to process a packet. A rectangle starts at the time when the corresponding rectangle in upper DMA finishes. Figure 12 shows that the DMA overheads of MCP are fully overlapped, while the overheads of LCP cannot be pipelined at all as shown in Figure 11.

Also LCP cannot perform the receive-DMA as well during the EBUS-LBUS DMA that moves data from SRAM to main memory (formula 1-B). This result explains why the performance of Berkeley-VIA is limited. The simulation results also show that LCP performs DMA sequentially but MCP performs DMA in parallel. We have run random and interactive simulations and confirmed the same results.

In addition, we verify the correctness that only one module should occupy the EBUS-LBUS DMA engine at a time. The EBUS-LBUS DMA engine moves data not only from main memory to SRAM for sending, but also from SRAM to main memory for receiving. Therefore, a module should wait until the DMA engine becomes idle, if the other module already occupies the DMA engine. The formulas used are as follows:

1. LCP
   [] ! (LTHD && LRHD)
   The lcpTx module cannot use the EBUS-LBUS DMA engine during the lcpRx module occupies it.
2. MCP
   [] ! (HSD && HRD)
   The hostSend module cannot use the EBUS-LBUS DMA engine during the hostReceive module occupies it.

The verification results show that both LCP and MCP satisfy the above correctness property.

5   Conclusions

This paper investigates the bottleneck of the Myrinet firmware. Specifically, we model LCP and MCP with state transition daigrams and translate them into specifications written in PROMELA. Then the verification formulas are derived, and they are verified with SPIN. The verification result shows that LCP serializes the operations of DMA engines, which leads to the low throughput of Berkeley-VIA. On the other hand, MCP fully utilizes three DMA engines. It means that the internal structure of MCP is more elaborative than that of LCP. In other words, the modules of MCP have multiple entry points, while each module of LCP has only one entry point. The multiple entry points make MCP perform DMA engines in parallel.

In addition, we verify the correctness of the firmware that a module does not initialize the EBUS-LBUS DMA while another module occupies the EBUS-LBUS DMA engine. The verification results show that both LCP and MCP satisfy the correctness property.

In summary, this paper demonstrates that the bottleneck analysis of a gigabit network interface card can be done effectively with the formal verification approach. It also shows that SPIN is an excellent tool for modeling and analysis of the firmware running on a gigabit NIC. The firmware of gigabit NIC consists of many event handlers that perform independently with other handlers, and SPIN is suitable for the model checking of the dynamic firmware.

References

1. D. Anderson, J. Chase, S. Gadde, A. Gallatin, K. Yocum, and M. Feeley, "Cheating the I/O Bottleneck: Network Storage with Trapeze/Myrinet," *Proceedings of the 1998 USENIX Technical Conference*, June 1998.

2. T. E. Anderson, D. E. Culler, D. A. Patterson, and the NOW Team, "A Case for Networks of Workstations: NOW," *IEEE Micro*, February 1995.
3. N. J. Boden, D. Cohen, R. E. Felderman, A. E. Kulawik, C. L. Seitz, J. N. Seizovic, and W. -K. Su, "Myrinet – A Gigabit-per-Second Local-Area Network," *IEEE-Micro*, Vol. 15, No. 1, pp. 29-36, February 1995.
4. P. Buonadonna, A. Geweke, and D. Culler, "An Implementation and Analysis of the Virtual Interface Architecture," *Proceedings of SC'98*, November 1998.
5. D. Dunning, G. Regnier, G. McAlpine, D. Cameron, B. Shubert, A. M. Berry, E. Gronke, and C. Dodd, "The Virtual Interface Architecture," *IEEE Micro*, Vol. 8, pp. 66-76, March-April 1998.
6. T. V. Eicken, A. Basu, V. Buch, and W. Vogels, "U-Net: A User-Level Network Interface for Parallel and Distributed Computing," *Proceedings of 15th ACM SOSP*, pp. 40-53, December 1995.
7. G. J. Holzmann, *Design and Validation of Computer Protocols*, Prentice Hall, 1991.
8. G. J. Holzmann, "The Model Checker SPIN," *IEEE Transactions on Software Engineering*, May 1997.
9. Z. Manna, A. Pnueli, *The Temporal Logic of Reactive and Concurrent Systems*, Springer-Verlag, 1992.
10. Myricom Inc., *LANai 4*, http://www.myri.com, February 1999.
11. Myricom Inc., *Myrinet User's Guide*, http://www.myri.com, 1996.
12. L. Prylli and B. Tourancheau, "BIP: a new protocol designed for high performance networking on myrinet," *Proceedings of IPPS/SPDP98*, 1998.
13. C. Yoo, H. -W. Jin, and S. -C. Kwon, "Asynchronous UDP," *IEICE Transactions on Communications*, Vol.E84-B, No.12, December 2001.

A   Promela Specification of LCP

```
/* Promela Specification of LCP - hostDma */
active proctype hostDma()
{
  int event;

  do
  :: (hd_state == HostDmaIdle) ->
        Tohd?event;
        if
        :: (event == HostDmaRequest) ->
                hd_state = HostDmaBusy
        :: else -> skip
        fi;
        do
        :: (dma_int == 1) ->
                hd_state = HostDmaIdle;
                dma_int = 0;
                goto endofhd
        od;
  endofhd:
        ret2txrx!HostDmaDone
  od
}
```

```
/* Promela Specification of LCP - lcpTx */
active proctype lcpTx()
{
  int event;

  do
  :: (lt_state == LcpTxIdle) ->
        Tolt?event;
        if
        :: (event == GotASend) ->
                lt_state = LcpTxGotASend;
                Tohd!HostDmaRequest;
                lt_state = LcpTxHostDma;
                ret2txrx?event;
                if
                :: (event == HostDmaDone) ->
                        lt_state = LcpTxSendDma;
                        do
                        :: if
                           :: (send_int == 1) ->
                               lt_state = LcpTxIdle;
                               send_int = 0;
                               goto endoflt
                           :: (recv_int == 1) ->
                               lt_state = LcpTxInvokeRx;
                               Tolr!ReceiveDone;
                               ret2tx?event;
                               if
                               :: (event == LcpRxDone) ->
                                       lt_state = LcpTxSendDma
                               :: else -> skip
                               fi
                           :: else -> skip
                           fi
                        od
                :: else -> skip
                fi
        :: else -> skip
        fi;
  endoflt:
        ret2lcp!0
  od
}
```

B   Promela Specification of MCP

```
/* Promela Specification of MCP - hostSend */
active proctype hostSend()
{
  int event;
  do
  :: (hs_state == HostSendIdle) ->
       Tohs?event;
       if
       :: (event == GotASend) ->
               if
               :: (nempty(hs_buffer)) ->
                       hs_buffer?hs_data;
                       hs_state = HostSendGotASend;
                       if
                       :: (full(ns_buffer)) ->
                               hs_state = HostSendFull
                       :: (nfull(ns_buffer)) ->
                               if
                               :: (DmaInUse==1) ->
                                       hs_state = HostSendDmaBusy
                               :: else ->
                                       DmaInUse = 1;
                                       hs_state = HostSendDma
                               fi
                       fi
               :: (empty(hs_buffer)) -> skip
               fi
       :: else -> skip
       fi;
       Return!0
  :: (hs_state == HostSendFull) ->
       Tohs?event;
       if
       :: (event == NetSendQueueNotFull) ->
               hs_state = HostSendNotFull;
               if
               :: (DmaInUse == 1) ->
                       hs_state = HostSendDmaBusy
               :: else ->
                       DmaInUse = 1;
                       hs_state = HostSendDma
               fi
       :: else -> skip
       fi;
       Return!0
```

```
:: (hs_state == HostSendDmaBusy) ->
      Tohs?event;
      if
      :: (event == SendDmaFree) ->
            hs_state = HostSendDma
      :: else -> skip
      fi;
      Return!0

:: (hs_state == HostSendDma) ->
      Tohs?event;
      if
      :: (event == SendDmaDone) ->
            DmaInUse = 0;
            if
            :: (hr_state == HostReceiveDmaBusy) ->
                  Return!ReceiveDmaFree;
                  DmaInUse = 1
            :: else -> skip
            fi;
            ns_buffer!hs_data;
            Return!NetSendQueueNotEmpty;
            if
            :: (nempty(hs_buffer)) ->
                  Return!GotASend
            :: (empty(hs_buffer)) -> skip
            fi;
            hs_state = HostSendIdle;
            dma_int = 0
      :: else -> skip
      fi;
      Return!0
  od
}
```

```
/* Promela Specification of MCP - netSend */
active proctype netSend()
{
  int event;

  do
  :: (ns_state == NetSendIdle) ->
       Tons?event;
       if
       :: (event == NetSendQueueNotEmpty) ->
               if
               :: (nempty(ns_buffer)) ->
                       ns_buffer?ns_data;
                       ns_state = NetSendBusy
               :: (empty(ns_buffer)) -> skip
               fi
       :: else -> skip
       fi;
       Return!0

  :: (ns_state == NetSendBusy) ->
       Tons?event;
       if
       :: (event == NetSendSendDone) ->
               Return!NetSendQueueNotFull;
               if
               :: (nempty(ns_buffer)) ->
                       Return!NetSendQueueNotEmpty
               :: (empty(ns_buffer)) -> skip
               fi;
               ns_state = NetSendIdle;
               send_int = 0
       :: else -> skip
       fi;
       Return!0
  od
}
```

Using SPIN to Verify Security Properties of Cryptographic Protocols

Paolo Maggi and Riccardo Sisto

Dip. di Automatica e Informatica – Politecnico di Torino
Corso Duca degli Abruzzi 24, I-10129 Torino, Italy
maggi@athena.polito.it, sisto@polito.it

Abstract. This paper explores the use of Spin for the verification of cryptographic protocol security properties. A general method is proposed to build a Promela model of the protocol and of the intruder capabilities. The method is illustrated showing the modeling of a classical case study, i.e. the Needham-Schroeder Public Key Authentication Protocol. Using the model so built, Spin can find a known attack on the protocol, and it correctly validates the fixed version of the protocol.

1 Introduction

All the solutions adopted to ensure security properties in distributed systems are based on some kind of cryptographic protocol which, in turn, uses basic cryptographic operations such as encryption and digital signatures. Despite their apparent simplicity, such protocols have revealed themselves to be very error prone, especially because of the difficulty generally found in foreseeing all the possible attacks. For this reason, researchers have been working on the use of formal verification techniques to analyze the vulnerability of such protocols.

Both the theorem proving and the model checking approaches have been investigated. Some of the researchers who have investigated the model checking approach have developed specific model checkers for cryptographic protocols (e.g. [1]), whereas others have shown how general purpose tools such as FDR [2] and Murphi [3] can be used for the same purpose. In this paper, we follow the latter kind of approach, and we explore the possibility of using Spin, which is one of the most powerful general purpose model checkers, to verify cryptographic protocols. Instead of simply porting the approaches developed by other researchers to the Spin environment, we develop a new approach which makes use of static analysis techniques in order to get simpler models. The main idea is that the protocol configuration to be checked (i.e. the protocol sessions included in the model) can be statically analyzed in order to collect data-flow information, which can be used to simplify the intruder knowledge representation. For example, such a preliminary analysis can identify which data can potentially be learned by the intruder and which cannot, thus avoiding the representation of knowledge elements that will never occur. Similarly, it is possible to foresee which of the messages that the intruder could build will never be accepted as valid by any protocol agent, and so avoid their generation.

D. Bošnački and S. Leue (Eds.): SPIN 2002, LNCS 2318, pp. 187–204, 2002.
© Springer-Verlag Berlin Heidelberg 2002

The use of Spin for cryptographic protocol verification has already been proposed and discussed in [4], where, however, the author does not give a concrete proposal, but just some general ideas and evaluations of the complexity of the verification task.

This paper is organized as follows. In section 2, we briefly introduce the Needham-Schroeder Public Key Authentication Protocol, which will be used throughout the article to illustrate our modeling approach. In section 3, we present the basic choices and the main underlying principles of our modeling approach, whereas, in section 4, we give a detailed description of the procedure to build a Promela model of an instance of a cryptographic protocol, using the sample protocol as an example. In section 5, we present verification results related to the sample protocol. Section 6 concludes.

2   The Needham-Schroeder Public Key Protocol

The Needham-Schroeder Public Key Protocol [5] is a well known authentication protocol that dates back to 1978. It aims to establish mutual authentication between an *initiator* A and a *responder* B, after which some session involving the exchange of messages between A and B can take place.

As its name clearly suggests, the protocol uses public key cryptography [6,7]. Each agent H possesses a *public key*, denoted $PK(H)$, and a *secret key* $SK(H)$, which can be used to decrypt the messages encrypted with $PK(H)$. While $SK(H)$ should be known only by H, any other agent can obtain $PK(H)$ from a key server. Any agent can encrypt a message x using H's public key to produce the encrypted message $\{x\}PK(H)$. Only the agents that know H's secret key can decrypt this message in order to obtain x. This property should ensure x secrecy. At the same time, any agent H can sign a message x by encrypting it with its own secret key, $\{x\}SK(H)$, in order to ensure its integrity. Any agent can decrypt $\{x\}SK(H)$, using H's public key.

The complete Needham-Schroeder Public Key Protocol [5] involves seven steps and it is described in figure 1, where A is an *initiator* agent who requests to establish a session with a *responder* agent B and S is a trusted key server.

Any run of the protocol opens with A requesting B's public key to the trusted key server S (step 1). S responds sending the message 2. This message, signed by S to ensure its integrity, contains B's public key, $PK(B)$, and B's identity. If S is trusted, this should assure A that $PK(B)$ is really B's public key. It is worth noting that the protocol assumes that A can obtain $PK(A)$, needed to decrypt message 2, in a reliable way. If this assumption is not true, an intruder could try to replace S providing an arbitrary value that A thinks to be $PK(A)$. Note also, that, as pointed out in [8], there is no guarantee that $PK(B)$ is really the current B's public key, rather that a replay of an old and compromised key (however this attack can be easily prevented using timestamps [8]).

Once obtained B's public key, A selects a *nonce*[1] Na and sends message 3 to B. This message can only be understood by B, beeing encrypted with its

---

[1] A *nonce* is a random number generated with the purpose to be used in a sinlge run of the protocol.

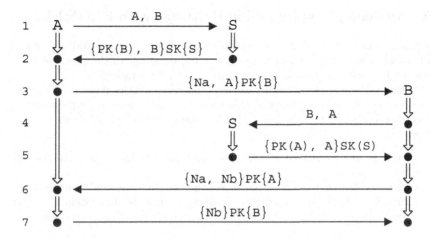

Fig. 1. The complete Needham-Schroeder Public Key Protocol.

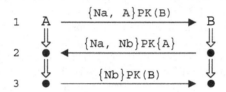

Fig. 2. The reduced Needham-Schroeder Public Key Protocol.

public key, and indicates that someone, supposed to be A, whishes to autheticate himself to B.

After having received message 3, B decrypts it using its secret key to obtain the nonce Na and then requests A's public key to S (steps 4 and 5).

At this point, B sends the nonce Na to A, along with a new nonce Nb, encrypted with A'a public key (message 6). With this message, B authenticates itself to A, since, receiving it, A is sure that it is communicating with B, being B the only agent that should be able to obtain Na decrypting message 3.

To finish the protocol run, A returns the nonce Nb to B in order to authenticate itself to B (message 7).

Looking at the protocol, it is easy to observe as four of the seven steps can be removed if we assume that A and B already know each other's public keys. Indeed, messages 1, 2, 4 and 5 make up a protocol that aims to obtain A's and B's public keys from a trusted key server S, whereas messages 3, 6 and 7 make up the real authentication protocol.

In the following of this paper, we will assume that all the agents already know each other's public keys and so we focus our attention on the reduced protocol obtained removing messages 1, 2, 4 and 5 and described in figure 2.

3   Modeling Cryptographic Protocols with PROMELA

Formal models of cryptographic protocols are typically composed of a set of principals which send messages to each other according to the protocol rules, and an intruder, representing the activity of possible attackers.

Since such models are meant to reveal possible security flaws in the protocols and not flaws in the cryptosystems used by the protocols, cryptography is modeled in a very abstract way and it is assumed to be "perfect". This means that:

- the only way to decrypt an encrypted message is to know the corresponding key;
- an encrypted message does not reveal the key that was used to encrypt it;
- there is sufficient redundancy in messages so that the decryption algorithm can detect whether a ciphertext was encrypted with the expected key.

Although such assumptions are obviously not completely true for real cryptosystems, they represent the properties of an ideal cryptosystem, so they are useful to isolate the flaws of the protocol itself. In other words, any flaw found with this model is a real protocol flaw, but it is possible that the model does not reveal other weaknesses due to the used cryptosystems.

Both the principals and the intruder are represented in our models by means of Promela processes that communicate with each other through shared channels. More precisely, we have a different process definition for each protocol role, and a process definition for the intruder. Principals do not communicate with each other directly, but all the messages they send are intercepted by the intruder which eventually will forward them to the right addressee. This approach has been followed by other researchers too (e.g. [1]) and avoids redundant execution paths.

The intruder can interact with the protocol in any way we would expect a real-word attacker to be able to do, but at the same time it is also able to behave like a normal user of the computer network. For this reason other principals may initiate protocol runs with it. It is even possible that the intruder behaves as a set of different cooperating malicious users.

At any instant, the behavior of the intruder depends on the knowledge it has acquired. Before a protocol run starts, it is assumed that the intruder knows only a given set of data. For example, such data normally include the intruder identity(ies), its public and private keys, the identity of the other principals, their public keys, and, possibly, any secret keys the intruder shares with other principals.

Every time the intruder intercepts a message, it can increase its knowledge. Indeed, if the intercepted message or part of it is encrypted and the intruder knows the decryption key, it can decrypt it and learn its contents. Otherwise, if the intruder is not able to decrypt the intercepted message or parts of it, it can remember the encrypted components even if it cannot understand them. Since we are interested in modeling the most powerful intruder, we assume it always learns as much as possible from the intercepted messages.

Of course, besides intercepting messages the intruder can also forge and send new ones into the system. These ones are created using all the items it currently knows. Since it is normally assumed that the intruder can also create new data items from scratch (e.g. nonces), and use them to forge new messages, this capability can be represented including one or more generic distinguished data items in the initial intruder knowledge. Such data items represent the ones the intruder will generate from scratch during the protocol runs.

Note that, even if a message can be forged by the intruder, it could be that it cannot be accepted by the receiving principal. This fact can be exploited to safely restrict the messages the intruder can generate, excluding the ones that will not be accepted by the receiving processes.

In order to have finite models, we follow the common practice of putting some restrictions on the modeled behaviors. First of all, the model can represent only a finite number of parallel protocol sessions. Each principal can be engaged in a finite number of runs of the protocol, each run being modeled by a different instance of the corresponding process definition. Nonces created during a protocol run are represented as process parameters, and are assigned different actual values at each process instantiation.

Another possible source of infinite behaviors is the intruder. In fact, it can in principle forge and send infinite different messages. A typical solution to this problem is to restrict the way the intruder can generate messages, e.g. by restricting the maximum complexity of the generated messages [1,2] and by limiting the number of different data items it can generate by scratch. More recent works [9] have shown that such restrictions can be avoided by representing the messages that can be generated by the intruder symbolically, and by specializing them as soon as the receiving process performs some checks on them. In this paper we follow a simplified symbolic approach inspired by the one reported in [9], which consists of symbolically representing all the data items the intruder can generate from scratch as well as all the other complex data items it can generate from its knowledge by means of a single distinguished symbolic identifier. Such an identifier is always part of the intruder knowledge. However, instead of saying that the intruder always sends a generic message which is then specialized, we statically determine all the possible specializations it can take, which are finite, and we use the symbolic identifier only for the leaves of the possible message structures.

4   Building the Promela Model

In this section we describe a procedure to build a Promela model of a cryptographic protocol instance, to be used for security property verification. Such a procedure is illustrated using the reduced Needham-Schroeder Public Key Authentication Protocol as an example. The Promela model we build can be divided into two parts:

- the description of the protocol rules and of the protocol instance
- the description of the intruder behavior

The first part is quite simple and should be written manually, whereas the second part can be generated automatically.

The instance of the sample protocol we deal with is fairly small. It includes three principals: A, B and I. A plays the role of the *initiator*, whereas principal B plays the role of the *responder*. I is one of the possible identities of the intruder, so principal I can play any role.

4.1   The Protocol Instance Model

The first step in the construction of the model is the definition of the finite set of *names*. With the term name we mean any distinguished identifier, key, nonce or data used in the protocol. As already explained, we also use a special name which symbolically represents nonces and other generic data items generated by the intruder. For our specific sample case, we need a name for each identity and a name for each nonce. The resulting set of names we will use is then defined as follows:

```
mtype = {A, B, I, Na, Nb, gD, R};
```

where A, B and I are the identities we consider, Na is the nonce generated by principal A, Nb the nonce generated by B and gD the symbolic representation of a generic data item used by the intruder. R is a service costant we will use in the intruder process definition, as explained later on.

The second step in the construction of the model is the definition of the channels used by the principals to communicate with each other. A different global channel is defined for each different message structure used by the protocol. Of course, each protocol uses a finite number of different message structures, which can be easily identified by a simple inspection of the protocol messages. For example, the reduced version of the Needham-Schroeder Public Key Authentication Protocol uses only two message structures, i.e $\{x_1, x_2\}PK(x_3)$ (a pair of elements encoded with a public key) and $\{x_1\}PK(x_2)$ (a single element encoded with a public key). Since we want to enforce the fact that messages are always exchanged between the intruder and one of the other principals, we always specify the identity of the principal involved in the communication with the intruder as the first data exchanged on the channel, while we do not specify the identifier of the other party, because it is always the intruder. The subsequent data exchanged on the channel are the data components of the message in order of occurrence in the message. So for example, the two global channels for the sample protocol are defined as follows:

```
chan ca = [0] of {mtype, mtype, mtype, mtype};
chan cb = [0] of {mtype, mtype, mtype};
```

Channel ca is used to transfer messages of type $\{x_1, x_2\}PK(x_3)$, whereas channel cb is used to transfer messages of type $\{x_1\}PK(x_2)$.

If, for example, the process representing principal A has to send the message $\{Na, A\}PK(B)$, the following statement has to be used:

```
ca ! A, Na, A, B
```

where the first A represents the sender of the message, and the other three items represent the message components (in this case, B is considered as a component as well, since it uniquely identifies $PK(B)$). The reception of a message by a principal is expressed similarly. Here it is possible to express any requirements on the received message as well. For example, to express the fact that A must receive a message of type $\{x_1, x_2\}PK(x_3)$, and that it will accept as valid only messages with $x_1 = Na$ and $x_3 = A$, we can use the following statement:

```
ca ? eval(A), eval(Na), x2, eval(A);
```

where x2 is a local variable. In general, since all the messages sent by the intruder have the indentity of the receiver as their left most item, when a *normal* host has to receive a message, it must also require that the first data item is its name, which means checking that the message is really addressed to it.

The next step in the model construction is the definition of the processes representing the various roles of the protocol. Such processes must be parameterized with the data that may change from session to session and from instance to instance. Their definition is the Promela representation of the sequence of message exchanges prescribed by the protocol. The definition must include also the recording of particular conditions that are useful in the expression of the security properties to be checked. For our sample protocol, we define proctype PIni which describes the behavior of the *initiator* as follows:

```
proctype PIni (mtype self; mtype party; mtype nonce)
{
  mtype g1;

      atomic {
      IniRunning(self,party);
      ca ! self, nonce, self, party;
    }

    atomic {
      ca ? eval (self), eval (nonce), g1, eval (self);
      IniCommit(self,party);

      cb ! self, g1, party;
    }
}
```

Parameter self represents the identity of the host where the initiator process is running, whereas party is the identity of the host with which the self host wants to run a protocol session. Finally, nonce is the nonce that the initiator process will use during the protocol run.

The atomic sequences have been used to reduce the amount of allowed interleavings and so to reduce the complexity of the model from the verification point of view.

IniRunning and IniCommit are two macros used to update the values of the variables recording the atomic predicates that are used to express the authentication properties. In order to explain this part, we have to explain the technique used for property specifications, which is similar to the one presented in [2]. We say that a protocol agent X takes part in a protocol run with agent Y if X has initiated a protocol session with Y. Similarly, we say that a protocol agent X commits to a session with agent Y if X has correctly concluded a protocol session with Y. The fact that a responder with identity B correctly authenticates to an initiator with identity A can be expressed by the following proposition: A commits to a session with B only if B has indeed taken part in a run of the protocol with A. A similar proposition expresses the reciprocal property, i.e. the fact that an initiator with identity A correctly authenticates to a responder with identity B.

Each one of the basic propositions involved in the above properties can be represented in Promela by means of a global boolean variable which becomes true at a particular stage of a protocol run. In the protocol configuration we want to analyze, we have to express that initiator A and responder B correctly authenticate each other, so we need 4 variables, that we define as follows:

```
bit IniRunningAB = 0;
bit IniCommitAB  = 0;
bit ResRunningAB = 0;
bit ResCommitAB  = 0;
```

IniRunningAB is true iff initiator A takes part in a session of the protocol with B. ResRunningAB is true iff responder B takes part in a session of the protocol with A. IniCommitAB is true iff initiator A commits to a session with B. ResCommitAB is true iff responder B commits to a session with A.

Authentication of B to A can thus be expressed saying that ResRunningAB must become true before IniCommitAB, whereas the converse authentication property corresponds to saying that IniRunningAB becomes true before ResCommitAB. In the LTL formalism, such precedence properties can be expressed as:

- [] (([] !IniCommitAB) || (!IniCommitAB U ResRunningAB))
- [] (([] !ResCommitAB) || (!ResCommitAB U IniRunningAB))

So, the macros IniRunning and IniCommit used in the protocol definition update the values of the global variables IniRunningAB and IniCommitAB and are defined in Promela as follows:

```
#define IniRunning(x,y) if                                \
                :: ((x==A)&&(y==B))-> IniRunningAB=1 \
                :: else skip                         \
                fi
```

```
#define IniCommit(x,y)   if                                          \
                         :: ((x==A)&&(y==B))-> IniCommitAB=1  \
                         :: else skip                                \
                         fi
```

The proctype PRes of the *responder* processes is defined according to the same principles as follows:

```
proctype PRes (mtype self; mtype nonce)
{
        mtype g2, g3;

        atomic {
          ca ? eval (self), g2, g3, eval (self);
          ResRunning(g3,self);

          ca ! self, g2, nonce, g3;
        }

        atomic {
          cb ? eval (self), eval (nonce), eval (self);
          ResCommit(g3,self);
        }
}
```

where parameter self represents the identity of the host where the responder process is running and nonce is the nonce it will use during the protocol run.

ResRunning and ResCommit are macros used to update the values of the global variables ResRunningAB and ResCommitAB and are defined as follows:

```
#define ResRunning(x,y) if                                          \
                        :: ((x==A)&&(y==B))-> ResRunningAB=1 \
                        :: else skip                                \
                        fi

#define ResCommit(x,y)  if                                          \
                        :: ((x==A)&&(y==B))-> ResCommitAB=1   \
                        :: else skip                                \
                        fi
```

At this stage it is also possible to define the protocol instance to be modeled. It is simply specified introducing a process instantiation statement in the init process for each instance of the initiator and for each instance of the responder. The init process must include also the instantiation of a process PI representing the intruder activity. PI is a process definition without parameters. Its construction is illustrated in the following section.

For our sample instance, we have the following init definition:

```
init
{
    atomic {
        if
        :: run PIni (A, I, Na)
        :: run PIni (A, B, Na)
        fi;

        run PRes (B, Nb);

        run PI ();
    }
}
```

The if statement specifies that principal A may initiate a protocol run with any other principal, i.e. either with B or with I. A similar statement is not needed for the responder, because it cannot decide the party with which it must communicate.

4.2   The Intruder Model

The automatic construction of the intruder process definition requires a preliminary static analysis in order to collect all the needed information.

First of all, we need to determine the sets of possible values taken by the free variables occurring in each protocol process. For our sample protocol, such variables are g1, g2 and g3. This operation can be performed using a simple data-flow analysis. For example, since initiator processes never check the value of g1, but they simply pass it on, such an analysis will yield that in principle g1 can assume any possible value, i.e. Na, Nb, gD, A, B and I. The same argument is valid for variable g2, while, since g3 is used as an host identifier, the analysis will yield that it can assume only the values A, B and I.

A second static analysis is then needed to restrict the potential intruder knowledge representation to the minimum actually needed. First of all we have to define the intruder's initial knowledge, which, in our sample, is made up of the identities and the public keys of all the principals of the system, i.e. A, B and I, the intruder own private key, and the generic data gD. Such a knowledge can increase when the intruder intercepts messages. If we compute all the possible messages the intruder can intercept during the protocol run we can deduce also which are the possible messages the intruder can add to its knowledge. For example, if the intruder intercepts the message $\{Na, A\}PK(I)$ it can learn the nonce Na. In order to avoid the representation of redundant knowledge elements, we assume that the intruder always records the learned items in their most elementary forms. For example, if message $\{Na, A\}PK(I)$ is intercepted, we assume that the intruder records only Na, and not the whole message $\{Na, A\}PK(I)$, since this message can be built from Na and from A, which is always known to the intruder. In other words, the intruder records a complex message in its knowledge only if it cannot decrypt it. For example, if the intruder intercepts the message $\{Na, A\}PK(B)$, it can only remember the message as a whole.

Table 1. Knowledge elements that the intruder can eventually acquire.

Received message	Learned item
$\{Na, A\}PK(I)$	Na
$\{Na, A\}PK(B)$	$\{Na, A\}PK(B)$
$\{Na\}PK(I)$	Na
$\{Nb\}PK(I)$	Nb
$\{gD\}PK(I)$	-
$\{A\}PK(I)$	-
$\{B\}PK(I)$	-
$\{I\}PK(I)$	-
$\{Na\}PK(B)$	$\{Na\}PK(B)$
$\{Nb\}PK(B)$	$\{Nb\}PK(B)$
$\{gD\}PK(B)$	$\{gD\}PK(B)$
$\{A\}PK(B)$	$\{A\}PK(B)$
$\{B\}PK(B)$	$\{B\}PK(B)$
$\{I\}PK(B)$	$\{I\}PK(B)$
$\{Na, Nb\}PK(I)$	Na, Nb
$\{Nb, Nb\}PK(I)$	Nb
$\{gD, Nb\}PK(I)$	Nb
$\{Na, Nb\}PK(A)$	$\{Na, Nb\}PK(A)$
$\{Nb, Nb\}PK(A)$	$\{Nb, Nb\}PK(A)$
$\{gD, Nb\}PK(A)$	$\{gD, Nb\}PK(A)$
$\{A, Nb\}PK(I)$	Nb
$\{B, Nb\}PK(I)$	Nb
$\{I, Nb\}PK(I)$	Nb
$\{A, Nb\}PK(A)$	$\{A, Nb\}PK(A)$
$\{B, Nb\}PK(A)$	$\{B, Nb\}PK(A)$
$\{I, Nb\}PK(A)$	$\{I, Nb\}PK(A)$

Knowledge items are represented in the intruder process `PI` by means of local boolean variables. For atomic data items (names) such variables have the same name of the data item itself, with the 'k' prefix. For example, variable `kNa` represents the knowledge of Na. Similarly, the knowledge of structured data items can be represented by means of bit variables whose names have the 'k' prefix and include the various data fields in order of occurrence. For example, variable `k_Na_A_B` will represent the knowledge of message $\{Na, A\}PK(B)$.

Since the messages the intruder can intercept are finite, we will also have a finite number of corresponding possible knowledge elements. Table 1 lists all the possible messages that the intruder can intercept in our sample protocol instance and, for each of them, the data items the intruder can learn from it.

A further restriction of the intruder knowledge items to be recorded is possible if we exclude the ones which can never be used by the intruder to generate valid messages. For example, if the intruder knows message $\{Na\}PK(B)$ as a

Table 2. Knowledge elements potentially needed by the intruder.

Message	Needed knowledge (besides initial knowledge)
$\{Na, A\}PK(B)$	Na or $\{Na, A\}PK(B)$
$\{Na, B\}PK(B)$	Na or $\{Na, B\}PK(B)$
$\{Na, I\}PK(B)$	Na or $\{Na, I\}PK(B)$
$\{Nb, A\}PK(B)$	Nb or $\{Nb, A\}PK(B)$
$\{Nb, B\}PK(B)$	Nb or $\{Nb, B\}PK(B)$
$\{Nb, I\}PK(B)$	Nb or $\{Nb, I\}PK(B)$
$\{gD, A\}PK(B)$	-
$\{gD, B\}PK(B)$	-
$\{gD, I\}PK(B)$	-
$\{Na, A\}PK(A)$	Na or $\{Na, A\}PK(A)$
$\{Na, B\}PK(A)$	Na or $\{Na, B\}PK(A)$
$\{Na, I\}PK(A)$	Na or $\{Na, I\}PK(A)$
$\{A, A\}PK(B)$	-
$\{A, B\}PK(B)$	-
$\{A, I\}PK(B)$	-
$\{B, A\}PK(B)$	-
$\{B, B\}PK(B)$	-
$\{B, I\}PK(B)$	-
$\{I, A\}PK(B)$	-
$\{I, B\}PK(B)$	-
$\{I, I\}PK(B)$	-
$\{Nb\}PK(B)$	Nb or $\{Nb\}PK(B)$
$\{Na, Na\}PK(A)$	Na or $\{Na, Na\}PK(A)$
$\{Na, Nb\}PK(A)$	(Na and Nb) or $\{Na, Nb\}PK(A)$
$\{Na, gD\}PK(A)$	Na or $\{Na, gD\}PK(A)$

whole, it can potentially send it to B, but this one will not accept it, so it is not useful for the intruder to know that message. The set of data items potentially useful to the intruder can be computed listing all the valid messages that the intruder could eventually send to the other principals and determining, for each of them, which data items the intruder could use to build it. The result of this analysis is showed in Table 2 for our sample protocol instance.

The actual set of knowledge elements to be stored in the intruder is the intersection of the two sets just computed (the right columns of Tables 1 and 2):

- Nonces: Na and Nb;
- Messages as a whole: $\{Na, Nb\}PK(A)$, $\{Na, A\}PK(B)$ and $\{Nb\}PK(B)$.

Preformed these preliminary analyses, the PI proctype definition can be written as follows:

```
proctype PI ()
{
        /* The intruder always knows
           A, B, I, PK(A), PK(B), PK(I), SK(I) and gD
        */
```

```
bit kNa = 0;          /* Intruder knows Na */
bit kNb = 0;          /* Intruder knows Nb */
bit k_Na_Nb__A = 0; /*     "       "   {Na, Nb}{PK(A)} */
bit k_Na_A__B = 0;  /*     "       "   {Na, A}{PK(B)}  */
bit k_Nb__B = 0;    /*     "       "   {Nb}{PK(B)}     */

mtype x1 = 0, x2 = 0, x3 = 0;

do
::    ca ! B, gD, A, B
::    ca ! B, gD, B, B
::    ca ! B, gD, I, B
::    ca ! B, A, A, B
::    ca ! B, A, B, B
::    ca ! B, A, I, B
::    ca ! B, B, A, B
::    ca ! B, B, B, B
::    ca ! B, B, I, B
::    ca ! B, I, A, B
::    ca ! B, I, B, B
::    ca ! B, I, I, B
::    ca ! (kNa -> A : R), Na, Na, A
::    ca ! (((kNa && kNb) || k_Na_Nb__A) -> A : R),
          Na, Nb, A
::    ca ! (kNa -> A : R), Na, gD, A
::    ca ! (kNa -> A : R), Na, A, A
::    ca ! (kNa -> A : R), Na, B, A
::    ca ! (kNa -> A : R), Na, I, A
::    ca ! ((kNa || kNa_A__B) -> B : R), Na, A, B
::    ca ! (kNa -> B : R), Na, B, B
::    ca ! (kNa -> B : R), Na, I, B
::    ca ! (kNb -> B : R), Nb, A, B
::    ca ! (kNb -> B : R), Nb, B, B
::    ca ! (kNb -> B : R), Nb, I, B
::    cb ! ((k_Nb__B || k_Nb) -> B : R), Nb, B

:: d_step {
    ca ? _, x1, x2, x3;          if
                                 :: (x3 == I)-> k(x1);
                                             k(x2)
                                 :: else k3(x1,x2,x3)
                                 fi;
                                 x1 = 0;
                                 x2 = 0;
                                 x3 = 0;

    }
```

```
:: d_step {
        cb ? _, x1, x2;              if
                                     :: (x2 == I)-> k(x1)
                                     :: else k2(x1,x2)
                                     fi;
                                     x1 = 0;
                                     x2 = 0;

        }
    od
}
```

Let us first comment the variable declaration part. We have a bit variable for each knowledge item to be represented in the intruder. These variables are initially set to 0, because initially the corresponding data items are not known to the intruder. They will be set to 1 as soon as the intruder learns the corresponding item. Besides the variables used to represent the knowledge of the intruder (the ones whose name begins with k), three services variables x1, x2 and x3 are declared. The use of these ones will be explained later on.

Let us now consider the behavior description. The intruder behaves as a never ending process that spends all its time sending messages to and receiving messages from the protocol channels (ca and cb). Since each operation is atomic, the state of the intruder is determined only by the current contents of its knowledge variables (service variables are always reset to 0 after each use).

Each branch of the main repetition construct represents an input or output operation on the global channels (ca and cb).

There is one output branch for each possible message sent by the intruder. Some output branches have a pre-condition which enables them, while other output branches are not conditioned by the intruder knowledge, because the intruder always knows how to build the corresponding messages. For example, the branch:

```
:: ca ! B, gD, A, B
```

representing the intruder sending the message $\{gD, A\}PK(B)$ to B, is always executable if a process, in this case the process associated to the principal B, is ready to synchronize with the intruder process. In contrast, the branch:

```
:: ca ! (kNa-> A : R), Na, Na, A
```

representing the intruder sending the message $\{Na, Na\}PK(A)$ to A, requires also that the intruder knows Na, i.e. that the value of the local variable kNa is 1. The conditional expression in the first position evaluates to A only if the intruder knows Na, and evaluates to a the non-existing identity R otherwise. This correctly means that the intruder can send message $\{Na, Na\}PK(A)$ to A iff it knows Na.

For what concerns input branches, there is one of them for each channel. Each input branch includes the input operation, which records the message components in the service variables, and a series of subsequent decoding operations, which depends directly on the message structure. The setting of knowledge variables is technically obtained by the following macros, which automatically ignore useless knowledge elements:

```
#define k(x1)          if                                        \
                       :: (x1 == Na)-> kNa = 1                   \
                       :: (x1 == Nb)-> kNb = 1                   \
                       :: else skip                              \
                       fi;


#define k2(x1,x2)      if                                        \
                       :: (x1 == Nb && x2 == B)-> k_Nb__B = 1 \
                       :: else skip                              \
                       fi


#define k3(x1,x2,x3)   if                                        \
                       :: (x1 == Na && x2 == A   && x3 == B)    \
                          -> k_Na_A__B = 1                       \
                       :: (x1 == Na && x2 == Nb && x3 == A)     \
                          -> k_Na_Nb__A = 1                      \
                       :: else skip                              \
                       fi
```

So, for example, if the intruder receives the message $\{Na, A\}PK(I)$ from the channel ca, the variable kNa is set to 1, and, if it receives the message $\{Nb\}PK$ (B) from channel cb, the variable k_Nb__B is set to 1.

Note that input operations are included in d_step sequences and that variables x1, x2 and x3 are always set to 0 before the end of the d_step sequences. This has been done to reduce the amount of possible states of the intruder process.

The model built according to the technique presented here can represent all kinds of attack, including those based on type confusion (e.g. using the name of a principal as a nonce). If we are not interested in the latter, e.g. because the protocol imposes strict type checks, we can build a simplified model. Such a model can be obtained from the one we have just presented: it is enough to eliminate the output branches where type rules are violated in the intruder definition.

Of course, it is also possible to build models with more than one session, i.e. more than one initiator and/or more than one responder. This can be achieved extending the set of names (we need a different nonce for each initiator and each responder) and, consequently, adding new input and output branches in the intruder definition.

5   Verification Results

Analyzing the previously described model with Spin (we used version 3.4.12), we were able to discover the attack described in [2] by Lowe. The verification

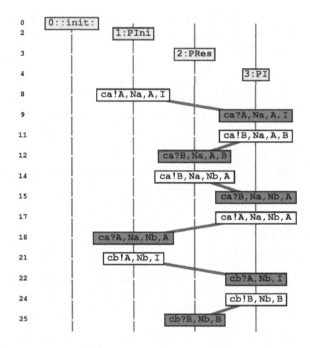

Fig. 3. The Lowe's attack on the Needham-Schroeder Public Key Authentication Protocol found by Spin.

of each property took a fraction of second on a Pentium III 800MHz PC with 512Mb of RAM. The first error trail generated by Spin is reported in figure 3. As expected, verifying the model of the fixed version of the protocol proposed in [2], we did not find any additional attack on the protocol. The number of reachable states and transitions of the two models (original and fixed protocol) for the verification of the first property (A correctly authenticates to B) are reported in table 3. The models are referred to two different configurations. The first one includes one initiator, one responder and an intruder with one identity. The second one is similar to the first one, but includes two initiators, thus making two parallel protocol sessions possible. Both configurations have been checked with two different kinds of model: a full model that takes type confusion attacks into account and a simplified model where such attacks are not considered.

To evaluate the efficiency of our modeling approach, we have compared our results with the ones obtained analyzing the same instance of the Needham-Schroeder protocol using the CSP base tools Casper [10] and FDR [11] as described in [12] and the model checker Murhi [3]. The comparison results related to Casper and FDR have been obtained running the programs with the model provided by the author (using FDR 2.77 and Casper 1.2.3) and are reported in table 4 for the original protocol using the simplified model (not taking type flaws

Table 3. Verification results using our approach.

Model Configuration			With type flaws		No type flaws	
Initiators	Responders	Protocol	States	Trans.	States	Trans.
1	1	Original version	381	1195	99	265
1	1	Fixed version	378	1275	97	262
2	1	Original version	8245	35613	1213	4489
2	1	Fixed version	7179	32090	955	3582

Table 4. Comparison between our approach and the Casper/FDR approach.

Model Configuration		SPIN		FDR	
Initiators	Responders	States	Trans.	States	Trans.
1	1	99	265	120	344
2	1	1213	4489	2888	11568

Table 5. Comparison between our approach and the Murphi approach.

Model Configuration		SPIN	Murphi
Initiators	Responders	States	States
1	1	381	1706
2	1	8245	17277

into account). The comparison results related to Murphi instead are taken by [3] and regard the original protocol with a model which apparently takes type confusion attacks into account. They are reported in table 5 and include only the number of states, because the number of transitions is not present in [3]. All the approaches are able to discover the Lowe's attack but there are some differences in the complexity of the obtained models. The number of reachable states of our model is always lower than the ones obtained using the other tools. The larger difference with respect to Murphi can be probably due to the fact that it models the network as a one slot buffer instead of considering synchronous message exchanges.

6   Conclusions

We have presented a way to model cryptographic protocols using Promela. The modeling approach we propose consists of specifying the protocol rules and the configuration to be checked directly in Promela. Instead, the model of the intruder, which is the most difficult part, can be constructed automatically. We described a procedure for the automatic generation of the intruder definition. Such a procedure uses complexity reduction techniques based on a preliminary data-flow analysis to build a simplified model. Following this approach we succeeded in finding the well-known attack on the Needham-Shroeder Public Key Authentication Protocol. The complexity of the resulting model is lower than the one obtained with other modeling techniques based on the general purpose model checkers FDR and Murphi.

In this paper we have informally illustrated the procedure to construct the intruder model, using a case study. Future work includes a formal definition of the intruder construction procedure and its implementation in an automatic intruder model generator. Another possible future development is the construction of a user-friendly specification interface which makes it possible to describe the protocol rules and configuration more directly and generate the whole Promela model automatically.

Acknowledgments

This work has been (partially) funded by the Center of Excellence on Multimedia Radiocommunications (CERCOM) of Politecnico di Torino and by the Italian National Research Council (grant number CNRC00FE45_002).

References

1. Clarke, E.M., Jha, S., Marrero, W.: Verifying security protocols with Brutus. ACM Transactions on Software Engineering and Methodology **9** (2000) 443–487
2. Lowe, G.: Breaking and fixing the Needham-Shroeder public-key protocol using FDR. In: Proceeding of TACAS96, LNCS 1055, Springer-Verlag (1996) 147–166
3. Mitchell, J.C., Mitchell, M., Stern, U.: Automated analysis of cryptographic protocols using murphi. In: Proceedings of the 1997 Conference on Security and Privacy (S&P-97), Los Alamitos, IEEE Press (1997) 141–153
4. Josang, A.: Security protocol verification using SPIN. SPIN'95 Workshop (1995)
5. Needham, R.M., Schroeder, M.D.: Using encryption for authentication in large networks of computers. Communications of the ACM **21** (1978) 993–999
6. Diffie, W., Hellman, M.: New directions in cryptography. IEEE Transactions on Information Theory **IT-22** (1976) 644–654
7. Rivest, R.L., Shamir, A., Adleman, L.M.: A method for obtaining digital signatures and public-key cryptosystems. Communications of the ACM **21** (1978) 120–126
8. Denning, D.E., Sacco, G.M.: Timestamps in key distribution protocols. Communications of the ACM **24** (1981) 533–536
9. Durante, L., Sisto, R., Valenzano, A.: A state exploration technique for spi-calculus testing equivalence verification. In: Proceedings of FORTE/PSTV 2000, Pisa, Italy, Kluver (2000) 155–170
10. Lowe, G.: Casper: A compiler for the analysis of security protocols. In: PCSFW: Proceedings of The 10th Computer Security Foundations Workshop, IEEE Computer Society Press (1997)
11. Ltd., F.S.E.: Failures-Divergence Refinement. FDR2 User Manual. Available at http://www.formal.demon.co.uk/fdr2manual/index.html (3 May 2000)
12. Lowe, G.: Casper: A compiler for the analysis of security protocols - user manual and tutorial. Available at
http://www.mcs.le.ac.uk/ ˜glowe/Security/Casper/manual.ps (1999)

Modeling and Verification of Interactive Flexible Multimedia Presentations Using PROMELA/SPIN*

Ramazan Savaş Aygün and Aidong Zhang

Department of Computer Science and Engineering,
State University of New York at Buffalo,
Buffalo NY 14260-2000, USA
{aygun,azhang}@cse.buffalo.edu

Abstract. The modeling and verification of flexible and interactive multimedia presentations are important for consistent presentations over networks. There has been querying tools proposed whether the specification of a multimedia presentation satisfy inter-stream relationships. Since these tools are based on the interval-based relationships, they cannot guarantee the verification in real-life presentations. Moreover, the *irregular* user interactions which change the course of the presentation like backward and skip are not considered in the specification. Using PROMELA/SPIN, it is possible to verify the temporal relationships between streams using our model allowing irregular user interactions. Since the model considers the delay of data, the author is assured that the requirements are really satisfied.

1 Introduction

There have been models proposed for the management of multimedia presentations. The synchronization specification languages like SMIL [10] have been introduced to properly specify the synchronization requirements. Multimedia query languages have been developed to check the relationships defined in the specification [5]. These tools check the correctness of the specification. However, the synchronization tools do not satisfy all the requirements in the specification or put further limitations. Moreover, the specification does not include user interactions. The previous query-based verification techniques cannot verify whether the system remains in a consistent state after a user interaction.

There are also verification tools to check the integrity of multimedia presentations [7]. The user interactions are limited and interactions like backward and skip are ignored. This kind of interactions is hard to model. The Petri-Nets are also used to verify the specification of multimedia presentations [9]. But Petri-Net modeling requires complex Petri-Net modeling for each interaction possible. Authors usually do not have much information about Petri-Nets.

---

* This research is supported by NSF grant IIS-9733730 and NSF grant IIS-9905603.

D. Bošnački and S. Leue (Eds.): SPIN 2002, LNCS 2318, pp. 205–212, 2002.

PROMELA/SPIN is a powerful tool for modeling and verification of software systems [6]. Since PROMELA/SPIN traces all possible executions among parallel running processes, it provides a way of managing delay in the presentation of streams. In this paper, we discuss the properties that should be satisfied for a multimedia presentation. We report on the complexity introduced by user interactions. The experiments are conducted for parallel, sequential, and synchronized presentations.

This paper is organized as follows. The synchronization model and PROMELA are discussed in Section 2. Section 3 explains the properties that should be satisfied for a multimedia presentation. Section 4 reports the experiments. The last section concludes our paper.

2   Modeling of a Multimedia Presentation

The synchronization model is based on synchronization rules [2]. Synchronization rules form the basis of the management of relationships among the multimedia streams. Each synchronization rule is based on the Event-Condition-Action (ECA) paradigm. Our synchronization model has receivers, controllers and actors to handle events, condition expression and actor expression, respectively. Timelines are kept for receivers, controllers, actors and actions to keep track when events are signaled, when conditions are satisfied, and when actions start and end. This synchronization model is favored over the others since it allows interactions that change the course of the presentation.

2.1   Presentation

The presentation can be in *idle, initial, play, forward, backward, paused,* and *end* states (Figure 1 (a)). The presentation is initially in the *idle* state. The user interface is based on the model presented at [3]. When the user clicks START button, the presentation enters *play* state. The presentation enters *end* state when the presentation ends in the forward presentation. The presentation enters the *initial* state when it reaches its beginning in the backward presentation. The user may quit the presentation at any state. Skip can be performed in *play, forward, backward, initial,* and *end* states. If the skip is clicked in *play, forward,* and *backward* states, it will return to the same state unless skip to *initial* or *end* state is not performed. If the presentation state is in *end* or *initial* states, skip interaction will put into the previous state before reaching these states.

2.2   Containers and Streams

A container or a stream may enter 4 states. A container is in *IdlePoint* state initially. Once started, a container is at *InitPoint* state in which it starts the containers and streams that it contains. After the *InitPoint* state, a container enters its *RunPoint* state. In *RunPoint* state, a container has some streams that are being played. When all the streams it contains reach their end or when the container is notified to end, it stops execution of the streams and signals its end and then enter *idle* state again. In the backward presentation, the reverse path is followed (Figure 1 (b)). If a stream has to signal an event, a new state is added

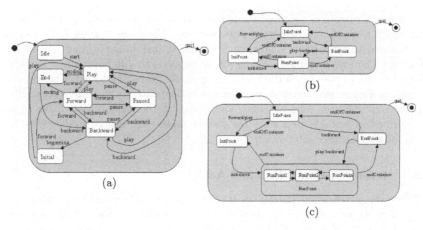

Fig. 1. (a) Presentation states (b) container states (c) stream states

to *RunPoint* state per event. So after the stream signals its event, it will be still in *RunPoint* state (Figure 1 (c)). The following is a portion of a PROMELA code for playing a stream:

```
1    proctype playStream (byte stream) {
2    #if (FC==3 || FC==4 || FC==5 || FC==6)
3    progressIdleStreams:
4    #endif
5    do
6    #if FC!=4
7       :: atomic{ (eventHandled && getState() == RUN) &&
8             (getStream(stream) == INIT_POINT) ->
9             setStream(stream, RUN_POINT);
10            if
11            :: (stream==A1)->timeIndex=1;
12            :: else -> skip;
13            fi; }
14       :: atomic{ (eventHandled && getState() == RUN) &&
15            (getStream(stream) == RUN_POINT) ->
16            setStream(stream, END_POINT);}
17       :: atomic{ (eventHandled && getState() == RUN) &&
18            (getStream(stream) == END_POINT) ->
19            to_end: setStream(IDLE_POINT);
20                     signalEvent(stream,END_POINT) }
21   #endif
:
45       :: atomic{ (eventHandled && getState() == QUIT) ->
46            to_playStream_quit: goto playStream_quit;}
47       :: else -> skip;
48       od;
49       playStream_quit: skip;}
```

The #if directives are used for hard-coded fairness constraints. There are 3 states for forward and backward presentations. The cases at lines 7, 14 and 17 correspond to forward presentation. The case at line 45 is required to quit the process. The else statement at line 49 corresponds to *IdlePoint* state. Streams signal events as they reach the beginning and end (lines 23 and 30). The variable *eventHandled* is used to check whether the system enters a consistent state after an user interaction. The checking and updating the stream state have to be performed in a single step since the stream state may also be updated by the system after an user interaction.

2.3 Receivers, Controllers and Actors

A receiver is set when it receives its event. When a controller is satisfied, it activates its actors. And to disable the reactivation of the actors, the controller is reset. An actor is either in idle or running state to start its action after sleeping. Once it wakes up, it starts its action and enters the idle state. The following is a code for receiver definition (lines 51-52), controller satisfaction (lines 54-59) and actor activation (lines 61-64). The expression "receivedReceiver(receiver_Main_INIT)" (line 52) corresponds to the receipt of the event when the main container starts. The expression "setActorState(...,RUN_POINT)" activates the actors (line 58-59). The expression "activateActor(actor_Main_START)" (line 63) elapses the time and the action follows (line 64).

```
51  #define Controller_Main_START_Condition
52      (receivedReceiver(receiver_Main_INIT) && (direction==FORWARD))
53
54  :: atomic{(eventHandled
55      && !(satisfiedController(controller_Main_START))
56      && Controller_Main_START_Condition) ->
57          setController(controller_Main_START);
58          setActorState(actor_A1_START,RUN_POINT);
59          setActorState(actor_A2_START,RUN_POINT)}
60
61  :: atomic{(eventHandled
62      && getActorState(actor_Main_START) == RUN_POINT) ->
63          activateActor(actor_Main_START);
64          setContainerState(Main,INIT_POINT);}
```

3 Specification

Two basic properties that should be checked are *safety properties* and *liveness properties*. *Safety properties* assert that the system may not enter undesired state or "something bad will not happen". *Liveness properties* on the other hand assure that system executes as expected or "something good will eventually happen". Fairness constraints are necessary to prove some properties of the system. For example, to prove that "stream A is played before stream B", no

Table 1. Properties and LTL formulas

	Properties	LTL Formulas
1	Clicking button for START enables buttons for PAUSE, FORWARD, and BACKWARD, and it changes the simulations state to RUN.	$\Box\,(actionStartClicked \rightarrow \Diamond\,actionToRun)$
2	Clicking button for PAUSE enables buttons for PLAY, FORWARD, and BACKWARD and it changes the presentation's state to PAUSED.	$\Box\,(actionPauseClicked \rightarrow \Diamond\,actionToPaused)$
3	The presentation will eventually end.	$\Box\,(stateRun \rightarrow !\,\Diamond\,stateEnd)$
4	A stream may start if it is active.	$\Diamond\,(streamRunPoint\ \mathbf{U}\ streamInitPoint)$
5	A stream may terminate if it is idle.	$\Diamond\,(streamIdlePoint\ \mathbf{U}\ streamEndPoint)$
6	Stream A is before stream B.	$(Q\ \mathbf{U}\ ((R \wedge M)\ \mathbf{U}\ K))$
7	Stream A starts with stream B.	$\Diamond(P \wedge K)$
8	Stream A ends with stream B.	$\Diamond(Q \wedge L)$
9	Stream A is equal to stream B.	$\Diamond(P \wedge K \wedge \Diamond\,(Q \wedge L))$
10	Stream B is not during stream A.	$!(\Diamond(P \wedge \Diamond K) \vee \Diamond\,(Q \wedge \Diamond L))$
11	Stream B does not overlap stream A.	$!(\Diamond(Q \wedge \Diamond K) \vee \Diamond\,(L \wedge \Diamond Q))$
12	Stream A is played.	$\Diamond(P \wedge \Diamond\,Q)$
13	(a) The *state* is reachable in forward presentation. (b) It is possible to reach the *state* in the backward presentation.	(a) $!\Diamond state$ (b) $\Box!state$
14	(a) The *state* is reachable in forward presentation. (b) It is possible to reach the *state* after user interactions.	(a) $!\Diamond state$ (b) $\Box!state$

skip operation should be allowed. Skip operation may skip to any segment of the presentation and thus violating the above expression. To prove the properties of the system, we should have at least the following fairness constraint: "Eventually the user clicks START button and no user interaction is allowed after that $(\Diamond\,(userStart \rightarrow \Box noInteraction))$". If a property is stated as undesirable, the system should not allow it. The properties and their corresponding LTL formulas are given in Table 1. Properties 1 and 2 are sample properties about state transitions that are allowed by buttons. For LTL formulas 1 and 2, *actionButtonClicked* corresponds to successful clicking *Button* when the button is enabled. *actionToState* corresponds to state transition to *State* after the *action*. Some of the specification patterns are presented in [4,8]. These specification patterns can be used in the verification. The number of properties about the user interface and state transitions can be increased. Property 3 corresponds to a liveness property that should be checked whether the presentation reaches to its end once it starts. Properties 4 and 5 are undesirable properties that allow streams to restart and terminate when they are in *RunPoint* (active) and *InitPoint* states, respectively.

In [7], some properties between two consecutive user interactions based on time are verified. In a distributed system, these constraints cannot be satisfied due to delay of data. In our case, time is associated with actors. Since there is no delay in passing of time, the actor elapses its time right away once it is activated.

Table 2. No interaction.

Type	No of streams	Depth	States	Transitions	Memory
single	1	67	177	306	1.5
seq	2	99	432	865	1.5
seq	3	143	1021	2321	1.6
seq	4	209	2347	5868	2.0
par	2	101	488	1021	1.5
par	3	139	1699	4642	1.8
sync	2	73	185	334	1.5
sync	3	78	201	398	1.5
sync	4	83	233	542	1.5

Table 3. All interactions allowed

Depth	States	Transitions	Memory
745	24586	46364	4.8
1954	103197	200756	18.5
5717	424039	846276	85
18676	2.21 K	4.50 K	500
1509	184092	351747	31
3571	1.75 K	3.42 K	318
823	30299	57461	6.1
869	38179	74420	8.3
871	53939	109319	12

Properties 6 to 11 are related with verification of Allen's [1] temporal relationships. Properties 10 and 11 are undesirable. For LTL formulas 6 to 11, $P = streamA\_InitState$, $Q = streamA\_EndState$, $R = streamA\_IdleState$, $K = streamB\_InitState$, $L = streamB\_EndState$, and $M = streamB\_IdleState$.

Property 12 checks whether stream A is eventually played. For a multimedia presentation, the states of streams that are possible to visit in the backward presentation should also be reachable in the forward presentation. So, Property 13 is stated as two fold. Part (a) is an undesirable property. If the part (a) is wrong, then Part (b) is verified. The number of states that need to be checked is $\lfloor m^n \rfloor$ where m is the number of states that a stream may enter and n is the number of streams. Eventually, we need to convert Property 13 to Property 14.

4   Experiments

We firstly developed a complex model to handle the user interactions. Since this user interface increases the number of initial states significantly, we removed the user interface during verification. Only buttons change their states as part of the user interface. We considered the number of streams and their organization. The streams are presented in a sequential order or in parallel. If the streams are presented in parallel, they may also be presented in a synchronized fashion. A tool is developed for automatic generation of PROMELA code for this kind of presentations. For each interaction, there is a fairness constraint and these are hard-coded in the model (e.g. FC==3 in line 2 of PROMELA code in Section 2.2).

We conducted tests for each type of interaction using only buttons. The complexity of verification in terms of states and depth are given for no interaction and all interactions in Table 3. The elapsed time of verification of properties is given in Figure 3.

5   Evaluation

The previous work on checking the integrity of multimedia presentations deal with presentations that are presented in nominal conditions (i.e., no delay). Since

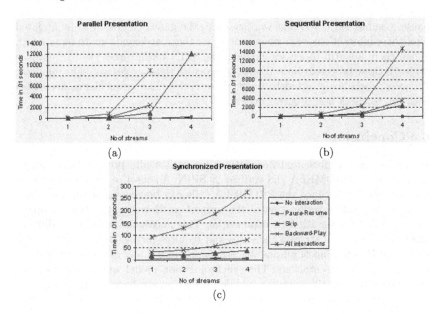

Fig. 2. Elapsed time for verification of properties on (a) parallel (b) sequential (c)synchronized presentations.

the processes may iterate at different states as long as they are enabled, this introduces processes proceeding at different speeds. From the perspective of a multimedia presentation, this may correspond to delay of data in the network. The detection of non-progress cycles when all the user interactions are allowed yields a general status of the presentation model. During the initial modeling phases of our model, SPIN verifier detected a case which naturally is less likely to occur. In this case, the user starts the presentation and then clicks the BACKWARD button just before the presentation proceeds. This leads to an unexpected state where the presentation enters an infinite loop. After the user starts a presentation and just before the presentation proceeds if the user attempts to backward the presentation, the presentation then enters an unexpected state and stays in this state forever.

Multimedia presentations which provide interactions that change the course of the presentation like skip and backward restricts using PROMELA structures like message channels. If processes are blocked and an interaction (interrupt) requires these processes to abort, significant coding is required to cope with the blocked processes. The PROMELA language does not provide time in the modeling. Thus it is not possible to incorporate time directly in the model. RT-SPIN [11] enables the declaration of time constraints and checks acceptance cycles, non-progress cycles and some liveness properties. The first problem is some guards may be skipped due to lazy behavior of RT-SPIN. In our case, most of the time constraints are equality constraints. Also the interactions like pause, resume, skip, and backward requires the guard condition to be updated after these interactions even when waiting for the guard condition to be satisfied. When there are still processes enabled, the SPIN verifier may yield acceptance cycles. If those processes were allowed to proceed, those cycles would be removed. Progress labels are inserted to break these cycles. The never claims are added with np_- to check non progress cycles.

6   Conclusion

In this paper, we presented how interactive multimedia presentations can be modeled using PROMELA and verified by SPIN. A subset of these properties is given in Section 3. Since the PROMELA code can be generated automatically, it allows automatic verification of the properties. However, the time complexity of parallel presentations is exponential. This makes the verification difficult when the number of streams increases and requires further optimization in the model. SPIN's tracing of all possible states provides a way of modeling of delay for multimedia presentations. The synchronization model will be incorporated into the NetMedia [12] system, a middleware design strategy for streaming multimedia presentations in distributed environments. It is necessary to assure that the system will present a consistent presentation after user interactions.

References

1. J. Allen. Maintaining Knowledge about Temporal Intervals. *Communications of ACM*, 26(11):823–843, November 1983.
2. R. S. Aygun and A. Zhang. Middle-tier for multimedia synchronization. In *2001 ACM Multimedia Conference*, pages 471,474, Ottawa, Canada, October 2001.
3. CMIS. http://www.cis.ksu.edu/ robby/classes/spring1999/842/index.html.
4. M. B. Dwyer, G. S. Avrunin, and J. C. Corbett. Patterns in property specifications for finite-state verification. In *Proceedings of 21st International Conference on Software Engineering*, May 1999.
5. S. Hibino and E. A. Rundensteiner. User interface evaluation of a direct manipulation temporal visual query language. In *ACM Multimedia'97 Conference Proceedings*, pages 99–107, Seattle, USA, November 1997.
6. G. J. Holzmann. The model checker spin. *IEEE Transactions on Software Engineering*, 23(5):279–295, May 1997.
7. I. Mirbel, B. Pernici, T. Sellis, S. Tserkezoglou, and M. Vazirgiannis. Checking temporal integrity of interactive multimedia documents. *VLDB Journal*, 9(2):111–130, 2000.
8. D. O. Paun and M. Chechik. Events in linear-time properties. In *Proceedings of 4th International symposium on Requirements Engineering*, June 1999.
9. B. Prabhakaran and S. Raghavan. Synchronization Models for Multimedia Presentation with User Participation. *Multimedia Systems*, 2(2), 1994.
10. SMIL. http://www.w3.org/AudioVideo.
11. S. Tripakis and C. Courcoubetis. Extending promela and spin for real time. In *Proceedings of TACAS, LNCS 1055*, 1996.
12. A. Zhang, Y. Song, and M. Mielke. *NetMedia*: Streaming Multimedia Presentations in Distributed Environments. *IEEE Multimedia*, 9(1):56–73, 2002.

SPINning Parallel Systems Software[*]

Olga Shumsky Matlin, Ewing Lusk, and William McCune

Mathematics and Computer Science Division
Argonne National Laboratory
Argonne, IL 60439, USA
{matlin,lusk,mccune}@mcs.anl.gov

Abstract. We describe our experiences in using SPIN to verify parts of the Multi-Purpose Daemon (MPD) parallel process management system. MPD is a distributed collection of processes connected by Unix network sockets. Its dynamic nature is easily expressible in the SPIN/PROMELA framework but poses performance and scalability challenges. We present here the results of expressing some of the parallel algorithms of MPD and executing verification runs with SPIN.

1 Introduction

Reasoning about parallel programs is surprisingly difficult. Even small parallel programs are difficult to write correctly, and an incorrect parallel program is equally difficult to debug, as we experienced while writing the Multi-Purpose Daemon (MPD), a process manager for parallel programs [1,2]. Despite MPD's small size and apparent simplicity, errors have impeded progress toward code in which we have complete confidence. Such a situation motivates us to explore program verification techniques. In our first attempt [9], based on the ACL2 [7] theorem prover, formulating desired properties of and reasoning about models of MPD algorithms proved difficult. Our second approach employs the model checker SPIN [6].

MPD is itself a parallel program. Its function is to start the processes of a parallel job in a scalable way, manage input and output, handle faults, provide services to the application, and terminate jobs cleanly. MPD is the sort of process manager needed to run applications that use the standard MPI [10,11] library for parallelism, although it is not MPI specific. MPD is distributed as part of the portable and publicly available MPICH [4,5] implementation of MPI.

The remainder of the paper is structured as follows. In Section 2 we describe MPD in more detail and outline our method for modeling a distributed, dynamic set of Unix processes in PROMELA. In Section 3 we present the concrete results of specific verification experiments. We conclude in Section 4 with a summary of the current project status and our future plans.

---

[*] This work was supported by the Mathematical, Information, and Computational Sciences Division subprogram of the Office of Advanced Scientific Computing Research, U.S. Department of Energy, under Contract W-31-109-Eng-38.

D. Bošnački and S. Leue (Eds.): SPIN 2002, LNCS 2318, pp. 213–220, 2002.

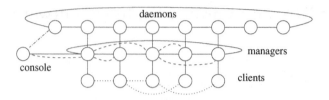

Fig. 1. Daemons with console process, managers, and clients

2   Approach

The MPD system comprises several types of processes. The *daemons* are persistent (may run for weeks or months at a time, starting many jobs) and are connected in a ring. *Manager* processes, started by the daemons to control the application processes (*clients*) of a single parallel job, provide most of the MPD features and are also connected in a ring. A separate set of managers supports an individual process environment for each user process. A *console* process is an interface between a user and the daemon ring. A representative topology of the MPD system is shown in Figure 1. The vertical solid lines represent connections based on pipes; the remaining solid lines all represent connections based on Unix sockets. The remainder are potential or special-purpose connections.

Each of the daemon, manager, and console process types has essentially the same pattern of behavior, which is important for our purpose. After initialization, the process enters an infinite, mostly idle, loop, implemented by a Unix socket function **select**. When a message arrives on one of its sockets, the process calls the appropriate message handler routine and reenters the idle **select** state. The handler does a small amount of processing, creating new sockets or sending messages on existing ones. The logic of the distributed algorithms executed by the system as a whole is contained primarily in the handlers, and this is where the difficult bugs appear.

2.1   Modeling Components of the Multi-purpose Daemon

Components of the MPD system map naturally to PROMELA entities: a `proctype` is defined for each MPD process type, and sockets are represented by channels. The structure of the MPD process types allows us to treat them as comprising three tiers. The top tier corresponds to the upper-level sequential logic of the process (initialization, **select** loop, calling the handlers). Handlers form the second tier. The bottom tier corresponds to well-understood Unix socket operations.

An MPD programmer uses, but does not implement, predefined libraries of the socket functions. However, having to model the socket operations explicitly, we created a PROMELA library of the primitives, which allows us to (1) hide the details of the socket model from both the verification and the future mapping of the model to the executable code, (2) interchange, if need be, different models of sockets without changing the remainder of the model, and (3) reuse the socket model in verifying independent MPD algorithms.

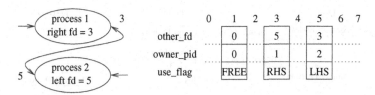

Fig. 2. Connected MPD processes and corresponding socket records array

2.2 Modeling Unix Sockets

A Unix socket, an endpoint of a bidirectional communication path, is manipulated when a connection between two processes is established or destroyed. A socket is referenced by a file descriptor (fd) and represents a buffer for reading and writing messages. Our PROMELA model of a socket consists of a channel and a three-part record. The first record field references the fd at the other endpoint of the connection. The second field identifies a process that has an exclusive control over the socket. The third field indicates whether the socket is free and, if not, how it can be used by the owner process. Figure 2 shows two connected processes and the corresponding state of an array of the socket descriptors.

Five Unix socket primitives have been modeled according to [13]: connect, accept, close, read, and write. As select appears only in the top tier of the MPD process, its implementation is specific to an MPD algorithm. Below is an excerpt of the socket library.

```
typedef conn_info_type {              /* socket descriptor */
   unsigned other_fd   : FD_BITS;
   unsigned owner_pid  : PROC_BITS;
   unsigned use_flag   : FLAG_BITS;
   };
conn_info_type conn_info[CONN_MAX];
chan connection[CONN_MAX] = [QSZ] of {msg_type};

inline read(file_desc, message)  {
  connection[file_desc]?message; }

inline write(file_desc, message)                     {
  connection[conn_info[file_desc].other_fd]!message;
  fd_select_check(conn_info[file_desc].other_fd)  }

inline close(file_desc)             {
   IF  /* other side has not been closed yet */
   :: (conn_info[file_desc].other_fd != INVALID_FD) ->
     set_other_side(conn_info[file_desc].other_fd,INVALID_FD);
     fd_select_check(conn_info[file_desc].other_fd)
   FI;
   deallocate_connection(file_desc) }
```

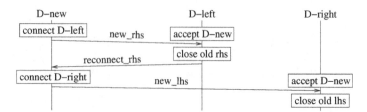

Fig. 3. Parallel ring insertion algorithm

```
inline connect(file_desc, lp) {
   allocate_connection(j);            /* server's connection */
   set_owner(j, lp);                  /* finalized by accept */
   set_handler(j, AWAIT_ACCEPT);
   allocate_connection(file_desc);    /* client's connection */
   set_owner(file_desc, _pid);
   set_other_side(j, file_desc);      /* relate connections */
   set_other_side(file_desc, j);      /* to each other        */
   lp_select_check(lp)         }

inline accept(file_desc)  {
   file_desc = 0;
   do            /* next line is a simplification of real accept */
   :: (file_desc >= CONN_MAX) -> assert(0) /* error, no connect */
   :: (readable_lp(file_desc,_pid)) ->
      set_handler(file_desc, NEW); break
   :: else -> file_desc = file_desc + 1
   od                          }
```

3   Verification of MPD Algorithms

Most interesting MPD algorithms reside in the daemons and the managers. We modeled and verified algorithms for daemon ring creation and recovery and a manager-level barrier algorithm. The models conform to the three-tiered view of the algorithms and rely on the socket library. We used bit-arrays and followed recommendations from [12] and employed ideas from [3].

3.1   Ring Establishment Algorithm

To create a daemon ring, the initial daemon establishes a listening port to which subsequent connections are made. A ring of one daemon is created. The other daemons enter the ring by connecting to the first daemon. Figure 3 shows an MSC representation of an algorithm that allows several daemons to enter the ring simultaneously. To establish the ring and to recover from a failure, each daemon maintains identities of the two right-hand side neighbors (**rsh** and **rhs2**). Upon receipt of **new_rhs**, *D-left* sends a message of type **rhs2info** (not shown in the figure), counterclockwise along the ring, to notify its left-hand side neighbor that **D-new** is its new **rhs2**. Upon receipt of **new_lhs**, *D-right* sends **rhs2info**, also counterclockwise, to notify *D-new* that its **rhs2** is the **rhs** of *D-right*.

We verify that, upon algorithm completion, the resulting system topology implicit in the socket descriptor structures array is a ring of the correct size. We also check that in each daemon the identities of **rhs** and **rhs2** agree with the information in the array. These two conditions are collectively referred to as the *state* property. MPD designers and users test the ring by invoking **mpitrace**, which reports the identities and positions of all daemons. To convince our "customers" (i.e., MPD designers) of the correctness of our model, we model the trace algorithm and prove its termination. Because the algorithm involves sending additional messages, verification of the trace completion is more expensive, in time and memory, than verification of the state property.

3.2   Recovery from a Single Nondeterministic Failure

Upon daemon crash, the operating system will close all associated sockets, which will be visible to its neighbors. When the right-hand side socket of the daemon to the left of the crash is closed unexpectedly, the daemon reinstates the ring by connecting to its **rhs2** neighbor. In our model a random daemon in the initial hard-coded ring is directed to fail, and the recovery procedure is initiated. The model was verified against the state and trace termination correctness properties.

3.3   Manager-Level Barrier Algorithm

Parallel jobs (programs running on the clients) rely on the managers to implement a synchronization mechanism, called *barrier*. In our model of the algorithm some messages are abstracted, and the clients are not modeled explicitly. When a leader manager receives a barrier request from its client (represented by setting the **client_barrier_in** bit), it sends the message **barrier_in** along the ring. A non-leader manager holds the message (setting the bit **holding_barrier_in**) until its client requests the service. Once the **barrier_in** is received by the leader, the message is converted to **barrier_out** and sent along the ring. Upon receipt of **barrier_out**, managers notify the clients, setting the **client_barrier_in** bit, that the synchronization has occurred. A special constant **ALL_BITS** corresponds to a bit-vector with all bits set.

We verified two correctness conditions. First, all clients pass the barrier.

```
timeout -> assert(client_barrier_out==ALL_BITS)
```

Second, an invariant holds: a client is allowed to proceed only when all clients have reached the barrier and all managers have released the **barrier_in** message.

```
assert((client_barrier_out==0) ||
       ((client_barrier_in==ALL_BITS) && (holding_barrier_in==0)))
```

Table 1. Verification statistics summary

Algorithm	Property	Model Size	Time (s)	Memory (MB)	Vector Size (byte)	States Stored/Matched	Search Depth
Insert	State	4	105.35	768	224	3.83e+06/7.97e+06	115
Insert	Trace	3	0.80	3.3	136	5743/6718	58
		4*	159.33	173	224	4.57e+06/9.28e+06	115
Recover	State	9	69.70	376.0	520	734040/3.26e+06	158
		12*	5340.19	772.6	876	2.75e+07/1.76e+08	209
Recover	Trace	8	163.39	814.1	464	1.93e+06/7.83e+06	199
		9*	1919.94	502.5	520	1.62e+07/7.85e+07	232
Barrier		12	127.97	549.2	288	1.95e+06/1.18e+07	101
		14*	3050.96	571.3	332	1.75e+07/1.25e+08	117

3.4   Verification Statistics

Table 1 summarizes verification statistics for the three algorithms. All verification runs were conducted on a 933 MHz Pentium III processor with 970 MB of usable RAM, with default XSPIN settings, except the memory limit. Compression (-DCOLLAPSE compile-time directive) was used in cases identified by an asterisk. We show statistics for the largest models on which verification succeeded with and without compression.

We were unable to exhaustively verify the ring insertion algorithm on models with five or more daemons, even with compression. Applying predicate abstraction techniques enabled verification of models of eight daemons, but a desirable correlation of the model to the C code was lost, as was the ability to perform meaningful simulations. For other algorithms, verification succeeded for larger models, although, admittedly, the algorithms are rather simple.

Let us put in perspective the size of models on which verification succeeds. While a running MPD may consist of tens or hundreds of processes, prior experience with debugging MPD code suggests that even the most difficult errors manifest themselves in systems of four to ten processes. Therefore, the models of some MPD algorithms at the current level of abstraction allow us to verify some algorithms on models of satisfactory size. For other algorithms, such as the ring establishment algorithm, a slightly more abstract model or a more efficient socket library will enable meaningful verification.

4   Summary and Future Plans

We described here our initial experiences in applying the SPIN-based approach to verifying a parallel process management system called MPD. Our models relied on a reusable model of Unix socket operations. For the ring establishment algorithm, we were able to complete exhaustive verification only on models with up to four daemons. We were, however, able to exhaustively verify larger models of other algorithms.

```
p.1  :: (msg.cmd == barrier_in) ->
p.2     if
p.3     :: (IS_1(client_barrier_in,_pid)) ->
p.4        if
p.5        :: (_pid == 0) ->
p.6           make_barrier_out_msg;
p.7           find_right(fd,_pid);
p.8           write(fd,msg)
p.9        :: else ->
p.10          make_barrier_in_msg;
p.11          find_right(fd,_pid);
p.12          write(fd,msg)
p.13       fi
p.14    :: else ->
p.15       SET_1(holding_barrier_in,_pid)
p.16    fi
```

```
c.1  if ( strcmp( cmdval, "barrier_in" ) == 0 ) {
c.2    if ( client_barrier_in ) {
c.3      if ( rank == 0 ) {
c.4        sprintf( buf, "cmd=barrier_out dest=anyone src=%s\n", myid );
c.5        write_line( buf, rhs_idx );
c.6      }
c.7      else {
c.8        sprintf( buf, "cmd=barrier_in dest=anyone src=%s\n", origin );
c.9        write_line( buf, rhs_idx );
c.10     }
c.11   }
c.12   else {
c.13     holding_barrier_in = 1;
c.14   }
c.15 }
```

Fig. 4. Portion of the PROMELA model and C implementation of the barrier algorithm

Based on our experiences, we believe that design and development of algorithms for MPD and similar systems can benefit greatly from application of the
SPIN-based software verification methods. SPIN's simulation capability enables
rapid prototyping of new algorithms. Since even the most difficult errors can be
discovered on models comprising only a few processes, the verification engine of
SPIN enables us to verify the algorithms on models that are sufficiently large for
our purposes.

A long-term goal of this project is to model and verify MPD algorithms and
then translate them into C or another programming language, while preserving
the verified properties. Ideally, translation should be automated. To allow this
to happen, the PROMELA model must not be overly abstract. Figure 4 shows
a PROMELA model and a C implementation of a portion of the barrier algorithm. Given the one-to-one correspondence between the control structures, and

a mapping between the rest of the code, automated translation certainly appears feasible for this level of abstraction. In general, verifiable models of the MPD algorithms should fall into just a few different classes with respect to the level of abstraction, and a separate mapping can be defined for each class to enable the PROMELA-to-C translation. Only the handlers in the middle tier of the process model need to be translated.

Many algorithms execute in parallel in a running MPD system, and their interaction is important. We hope to be able eventually to reason formally about MPD models that consist of several related and interdependent algorithms.

More information on the project, including the discussed PROMELA models, can be found in [8] and at `http://www.mcs.anl.gov/~matlin/spin-mpd`.

References

1. R. Butler, W. Gropp, and E. Lusk. A scalable process-management environment for parallel programs. In J. Dongarra, P. Kacsuk, and N. Podhorszki, editors, *Recent Advances in Parallel Virutal Machine and Message Passing Interface*, LNCS 1908, pages 168–175. Springer Verlag, September 2000.
2. R. Butler, W. Gropp, and E. Lusk. Components and interfaces of a process management system for parallel programs. *Parallel Computing*, 27:1417–1429, 2001.
3. E. Fersman and B. Jonsson. Abstraction of communication channels in Promela: A case study. In K. Havelund, J. Penix, and W. Visser, editors, *Proceedings of the 7th International SPIN Workshop*, LNCS 1885, pages 187–204. Springer Verlag, 2000.
4. W. Gropp and E. Lusk. MPICH. `ftp://info.mcs.anl.gov/pub/mpi`.
5. W. Gropp, E. Lusk, N. Doss, and A. Skjellum. A high-performance, portable implementation of the MPI Message-Passing Interface standard. *Parallel Computing*, 22(6):789–828, 1996.
6. G. J. Holzmann. The model checker SPIN. *IEEE Transactions on Software Engineering*, 22(5):279–295, May 1997.
7. M. Kaufmann, P. Manolios, and J S. Moore. *Computer-Aided Reasoning: An Approach*. Kluwer Academic Publishers, 2000.
8. O. S. Matlin, E. Lusk, and W. McCune. SPINning parallel systems software. Preprint ANL/MCS-P921-1201, Argonne National Laboratory, 2001.
9. W. McCune and E. Lusk. ACL2 for parallel systems software. In M. Kaufmann and J S. Moore, editors, *Proceedings of the 2nd ACL2 Workshop*. University of Texas, 2000. `http://www.cs.utexas.edu/users/moore/acl2/workshop-2000`.
10. Message Passing Interface Forum. MPI: A Message-Passing Interface standard. *International Journal of Supercomputer Applications*, 8(3/4):165–414, 1994.
11. Message Passing Interface Forum. MPI2: A message passing interface standard. *International Journal of High Performance Computing Applications*, 12(1–2):1–299, 1998.
12. T. C. Ruys. Low-fat recipes for SPIN. In K. Havelund, J. Penix, and W. Visser, editors, *Proceedings of the 7th International SPIN Workshop*, LNCS 1885, pages 287–321. Springer Verlag, 2000.
13. W. R. Stevens. *Unix Network Programming*, volume 1. Prentice Hall PTR, second edition, 1998.

Dynamic Bounds and Transition Merging
for Local First Search

D. Lugiez, P. Niebert, and S. Zennou

Laboratoire d'Informatique Fondamentale (LIF) de Marseille
Université de Provence – CMI
39, rue Joliot-Curie / F-13453 Marseille Cedex 13
[lugiez,niebert,zennou]@cmi.univ-mrs.fr

Abstract. Local First Search (LFS) was recently introduced as a new partial order reduction approach. It is based on the observation that local properties can be found searching on paths with a low degree (LFS-number) of concurrent progress. It has shown its potential to find sequences to local states fast. In this paper, we explore several improvements of LFS: On the one hand, we propose a replacement of the static bound on LFS-numbers by a dynamic criterion to detect exhaustion of reachable local properties faster. On the other hand, we explore the possibilities of combining LFS with other partial order reduction methods. It turns out that the combination with *transition merging* is possible and rewarding, while the sleep-set method is incompatible with LFS.

1   Introduction

Local First Search (LFS) was recently introduced by the authors as a heuristic method to reduce the state explosion problem in the search (verification) of *local properties* of distributed systems. It is based on the (theoretically founded) observation that in systems with local (binary, ternary, ...) communication the number of components progressing in true parallelism (called *LFS-number*) can be bounded to a logarithmic fraction of the number of processes when searching for path leading to local goals (local states of one or two processes independent of the states of the other processes). This is not the case if an arbitrary number of processes may synchronize in a single transition. As a heuristic search strategy, *local first* means to explore paths with a low LFS-number first.

The potential interest of LFS to the Spin community results from the fact that the method is based on state exploration while providing reductions related to the Unfolding approach [ERV96]. Like the sleep-set method [GW93], LFS relies solely on properties of an independence relation and does not require static analysis of the source code. It is thus relatively easy to integrate LFS with a tool for state exploration as is SPIN.

However, the basic method presented in [NHZL01] still needs refinement to become a practical tool. The present work establishes important steps in this direction.

D. Bošnački and S. Leue (Eds.): SPIN 2002, LNCS 2318, pp. 221–229, 2002.
© Springer-Verlag Berlin Heidelberg 2002

In [NHZL01], we observed that LFS does indeed expose paths to local properties rapidly if they exist, and the LFS-numbers found for these cases stayed far below the theoretically predicted bound. However, exploration up to this bound was needed to show the absence of such a path, and this turned out to yield state spaces exceeding those without reduction. The reason is that the LFS procedure presented requires some overhead information and that this overhead need not always be compensated by the reductions. In [BMNZ02], we combined LFS with ideas from unfoldings (adequate orders) in order to eliminate the double exploration of states due to the overhead information. With this refinement, one is guaranteed to obtain a state spaces inferior to the state space without reduction. On the other hand, *unfolding LFS* does not (as yet) seem to allow an efficient incremental exploration with growing LFS number: Its use would require either to unfold up to the theoretical bound or to recalculate unfoldings for some or all of the lower bounds.

At least for the non-unfolding version of LFS, we propose a solution for dynamically detecting that the exploration of local properties *has already been* exhaustive at some LFS-level. For the case of binary communication, the *dynamic LFS-bound* can be stated as follows: If for some LFS-number $n+1$ no local states were detected that were not already detected at LFS-number n then no new local states will be found at any higher level. In practice, this means that we can stop exploration at *just one level above* the actually highest LFS-number of local properties of the system.

As a second contribution of this paper, we have studied the potential of combining LFS with other partial order reduction methods.

On the positive side, we show the strong compatibility of LFS with a technique known as *transition merging* (see e.g. [DR99]): Transition merging preserves the parameters of a system essential to LFS and in particular excludes the possibility of an increased LFS-number of a local property. Moreover, it seems that the reductions achieved by LFS and transition merging are complementary. The experimental results indicate that this combination has a great potential. On the negative side, we found that LFS and sleep-set reductions interact and are incompatible.

Finally, we did some experimentation with a prototype implementation written in Caml. The rapid prototyping approach that we currently follow has allowed us to explore a number of combinations of methods in a short time, but of course it does not scale up as would an efficient implementation in an imperative language. Indeed, LFS only starts to unfold its potential (reductions for systems with *many* processes) where our implementation already suffers resource problems. We believe that nevertheless the potential of the method is visible through these results.

The organization of the paper is as follows: In Section 2, we develop the formal Framework of transition systems with an independence relation. In Section 3, we restate the formal particularities of LFS and the theorem on the static LFS-bound taken from [NHZL01]. In Section 4, we indicate the functioning of the LFS-methods of [NHZL01]. Section 5 contains the main technical contributions of the present article: The dynamic bound for LFS and the combination of LFS with transition merging. In Section 6, we give some experimental results for illustration. Due to lack of space, we omit all proofs and reduce the formal development to a strict minimum. For a more thorough treatment of LFS we refer the reader to [NHZL01,BMNZ02].

2   Formal Framework

Our formal setting relies on the theory of Mazurkiewicz traces (for a thorough treatment, see [DR95]; for verification applications, see also [GW93,Pel93]).

Independence and asynchronous transition systems. Let Σ be a finite alphabet, and let $\| \subseteq \Sigma \times \Sigma$ denote an (irreflexive and symmetric) *independence relation*. Intuitively, this relation represents concurrency between actions occurring on distinct processes in a distributed system.

Definition 1. *We say that $(\Sigma, \|)$ has parallel degree m if m is the maximal number of pairwise independent actions in Σ,*
(i.e. $m = max\{|A| \mid A \subseteq \Sigma$ and $a, b \in A, a \neq b \implies a \| b\}$)

Next, we look at the interleaving semantics of parallel systems: A transition system is a triple $T = (S, \rightarrow, s_0)$ with S a finite set of states, $s_0 \in S$ the initial state, and $\rightarrow \subseteq S \times \Sigma \times S$ a transition relation. As usual in partial order reduction literature, we assume T to be deterministic. By the *language* $L(T) \subseteq \Sigma^*$ we denote the set of all sequences corresponding to paths in T in the usual sense.

On the level of transition systems, the independence relation results in the following structural properties for independent actions a, b:

ID: $s \xrightarrow{a} s_1 \xrightarrow{b} s_2$ implies $s \xrightarrow{b} s'_1 \xrightarrow{a} s_2$ for some state s'_1 *[Independent Diamond]*

FD: $s \xrightarrow{a} s_1$ and $s \xrightarrow{b} s'_1$ implies $s_1 \xrightarrow{b} s_2$ for some state s_2 *[Forward Diamond]*

A transition system respecting the axioms **ID** and **FD** is called an *asynchronous transition system*.

From now on, we consider only an asynchronous transition system $T = (S, \rightarrow, s_0)$ w.r.t. an independence alphabet $(\Sigma, \|)$.

Mazurkiewicz traces and partial orders. The axiom **FD** states that it is possible to exchange consecutive occurrences of independent transitions on paths in an asynchronous transition system. The axiom **ID** in exchange says that independent transitions cannot be in conflict (taking one will not disable the other). This gives rise to the idea of equivalence classes of executions, where the equivalence is *generated* by (iteratively) exchanging independent transitions.

Formally, the *Mazurkiewicz trace equivalence* associated to the independence alphabet $(\Sigma, \|)$ is the least congruence $\sim$ over Σ^* such that $ab \sim ba$ for any pair of independent actions $a \| b$. A *trace* $[u]$ is the equivalence class of a word $u \in \Sigma^\star$.

Since all paths corresponding to one trace lead to the same state, it is natural to consider *traces as abstractions of executions*.

In particular for cyclic systems, it is useful to consider an *unfolding* representing the paths and the prefix relation. For a transition system without independence relation, this unfolding will typically be a tree with paths as vertices.

For asynchronous transition systems however, we prefer not to make a distinction between paths of the same equivalence class. This gives rise to a natural generalization of tree unfoldings called *trace systems*. These are acyclic asynchronous transition system with all paths leading to the same state belonging to the same equivalence class.

Definition 2. *Let $T = (S, \rightarrow, s_0)$ be an asynchronous transition system w.r.t. $(\Sigma, \|)$. Then the* trace system *of T is the transition system $\mathcal{TS}(T)$ whose states are the traces associated to an execution sequence, with the empty trace $[\varepsilon]$ as initial state and $\rightarrow = \{([w], a, [w.a]) \mid w.a \in L(T)\}$ as transition relation.*

Given a sequence $u = a_1 a_2 \ldots a_n$, there is a unique $s = \sigma(u) \in S$ such that $s_0 \xrightarrow{a_1} \ldots \xrightarrow{a_n} s$. Similarly, we define $\sigma([u]) = \sigma(u)$ for any trace $[u]$ (for any trace $[v]$ equivalent to $[u]$ we have $\sigma([v]) = \sigma([u])$).

Traces are partially ordered according to the *prefix relation* defined as follows: We put $[u] \preceq [v]$ whenever there exists a word $w \in \Sigma^*$ such that $u.w \sim v$.

A crucial notion for our development concerns the "last" letters in a trace, again as a generalization of the last letter in a word.

Definition 3. *For a trace $[w]$ let $last([w]) = \{a \mid [w] = [va]\}$ denote the set of last letters of representatives of $[w]$, and let $\#_{last}([w]) = |last([w])|$ denote their number. A trace $[w]$ with $\#_{last}([w]) = 1$ is a* prime trace.

In other words, a trace $[u]$ is prime if, and only if, it has a unique last letter, or equivalently a unique predecessor in the trace system.

3   Paths Leading to Local Properties

Local properties are the basis of several partial order reduction methods such as the ample set method [Pel93]. The latter article formalizes locality via the visibility of a transition: A transition is visible iff it has an effect on the property. A property then is local iff no two transitions visible for it are independent.

LFS is designed for the reachability problem of local properties. As such, it profits from the fact that a local property is reachable iff *it is reachable via a prime trace*. Hence, a method exploring all prime traces is complete with respect to the local reachability problem.

Communication degree and character. The fundamental reason for the reductions achieved by LFS is that communication in parallel systems is typically rather local. More precisely, LFS will give good reductions for systems where the number of components/variables affected by transitions is very small compared to the parallelism in the system.

We formalize these important parameters for LFS as follows:

Definition 4. *The* communication degree *of* $(\Sigma, \|)$ *is the maximal number* n *of pairwise independent actions which all depend on a common action, i.e.* $n = max\{|B| \mid B \subseteq \Sigma$ *and* $\forall b, b' \in B, b \neq b' \implies b \| b'$ *and* $\exists c \in \Sigma$ *s.t.* $\forall b \in B, c \nparallel b\}$. *The* character *of* $(\Sigma, \|)$ *is* (m, n) *where* m *is the parallel degree (Def. 1) and* n *the communication degree.*

LFS-numbers of traces. The crucial ordering criterion for the "complexity" of a trace concerning LFS is called "LFS-number".

Definition 5. *The* LFS-number *of a trace* $[w]$, *denoted by* $LFS([w])$, *is the least number* l *such that there exists a representative* $v = a_1 \ldots a_k \in [w]$ *such that for each* $1 \leq j \leq k$ *we have* $\#_{last}([a_1 \ldots a_j]) \leq l$.

The LFS approach relies on the following theorem stated in [NHZL01]:

Theorem 1. *For all* prime *traces* $[w]$, *the LFS-number of* $[w]$ *is at most* $\lfloor (n - 1)log_n(m) \rfloor + 1$, *where* (m, n) *is the character of* $(\Sigma, \|)$.

The bound $\lfloor (n - 1)log_n(m) \rfloor + 1$ is referred to as the *static LFS-bound* of $(\Sigma, \|)$. To illustrate the meaning of this theorem let us consider the case of a system of 1000 components with binary communication. While the trace system of this system may contain traces with up to 1000 last elements (otherwise stated: States with up to 1000 predecessors), its static LFS-bound states that all local properties are reachable on paths with intermediate traces with no more than 10 last elements (states with no more than 10 predecessors).

In [NHZL01], we also show that the static LFS-bound given in Theorem 1 cannot essentially be improved, i.e. for any character it is possible to construct systems with local properties with LFS-number equal to the static LFS-bound (or in some cases equal to the static LFS-bound minus one).

4   Search Procedures

Theorem 1 assures the existence of a path with a bound on the number of last elements of the traces on the path, but there will still be an infinite number of such traces. We have found two ways to exploit this property of traces on finite structures.

Local First Search. The first method [NHZL01] is based on the following observation: $last([ua]) = \{a\} \cup \{b \in last([u]) \mid b \| a\}$. In particular, if $last([u]) \subseteq last([v])$ then $last([ua]) \subseteq last([va])$. This leads to the definition of the *last label tracking transition system*: Given the transition system $(S, \rightarrow, s_0)$, the last label tracking transition system $LLTTS(T, \Sigma)$ is defined by $LLTTS(T, \Sigma) = (S', \rightarrow, s'_0)$, where $s'_0 = (s_0, \emptyset), S' = \{(s, M) \mid s \in S, M \subseteq 2^\Sigma\}$, $(s, M) \xrightarrow{a} (s', M')$ iff $s \xrightarrow{a} s'$ and $M' = M \backslash \{b \in M \mid b \nparallel a\}$. In [NHZL01], we proved that a local property is reachable in the original transition system T iff it is reachable in $LLTTS(T, \Sigma)$.

The basic algorithm for model-checking local properties is described by the scheme at right (see [NHZL01] for details). It obviously terminates for finite state systems, but the necessity to keep the set of last labels may add a significant overhead to the construction, notably it can necessitate to explore a same state s with several incomparable sets M. *Local First Search* as a refinement of the above algorithm

$B := \lfloor (n-1) \log_n m + 1 \rfloor$;
$Explore := \{(s_0, \emptyset)\}$; $Visited := \emptyset$;
while $Explore \neq \emptyset$
    choose (s, M) from $Explore$;
    for each transition $s \xrightarrow{a} s'$ **do**
        if $s' \models P$ **then** return(s')
        else $M' := \cup\{a\} \cup \{b \in M \mid a \parallel b\}$;
            if $|M'| \leq B$ and for all (s'', M'')
                $\in Explore \cup Visited$: $M'' \not\subseteq M$
            then add (s', M') to $Explore$
    remove (s, M) from $Explore$,
    add (s, M) to $Visited$;

chooses (s, M) *in Explore such that* $|M|$ *is minimal.* Our first experiments [NHZL01] showed that this heuristic could be quite effective in finding states, whereas the exploration up to the theoretical bound for showing the absense of a state usually fails. A crucial remark is that usually the set of states corresponding to prime traces generated by the method quickly stabilizes which suggests that we could use a dynamic bound instead of the static theoretical bound. In this paper, we give such a dynamic bound (see Section 5), which will help make LFS usable also for showing the non reachability of local properties.

Unfolding. In order to avoid the overhead caused by exploring certain states more than once, in [BMNZ02] ideas were taken from McMillan prefixes (notably the notion of an *adequate order* [ERV96]) and adapted to LFS. As a result, it is possible to construct a *locally complete finite prefix* of the trace system that uses the static LFS-bound as a cutting criterion and avoids double exploration of states. While it is a very promising approach, it does not currently allow the incremental computation with growing LFS-numbers. Therefore, the dynamic bound elaborated in Theorem 2 is not immediately applicable, but we will nevertheless evaluate this bound on the unfolding approach to illustrate its potential.

5   LFS Optimizations

This section contains the two main technical innovations of this paper: A dynamic LFS-bound that allows to stop much earlier in an exhaustive LFS-search with the result "unreachable" than with the static worst case bound; and a combination of LFS with a wide spread partial order reduction technique called "transition merging". Negatively, we show that at least a straight forward combination of LFS with the "sleep set method" is not possible.

LFS with dynamic bound. The static LFS-bound of Theorem 1 is a bound for the worst case. This has motivated us to look for tighter criteria for discovering bounds on the LFS-numbers of a concrete system.

Let $\mathcal{TS}(T)$ be the trace system associated to a transition system $T = (S, \rightarrow, s_0)$ w.r.t. $(\Sigma, \|)$ where $(\Sigma, \|)$ has character (m, n) with $n \geq 2$. Let L_p denote the set $\{[u] | [u]$ *is prime and LFS* $([u]) \leq p\}$. Theorem 1 can be rephrased in saying that L_B, where B is the static LFS-bound, already contains all prime configurations, and thus $L_B = L_{B+1} = L_{B+2} = \ldots$. In short, the sequence $L_1, L_2, \ldots$ converges latest at L_B. The following theorem gives a criterion to *detect* convergence:

Theorem 2. $L_p = L_{p+1} = \ldots = L_{p+n-1} \Rightarrow \forall k \geq 0 \; L_{p+k} = L_p$.

The proof follows the structure of the proof of Theorem 1 given in [NHZL01]. A immediate consequence of this theorem is the following improvement for the LFS basic algorithm: In the search algorithm, which iterates over the LFS-number p, we check for *new* states (in $L_{p+1} \setminus L_p$) where $L_p = \{(s, M) \mid |M| = 1\}$ and we stop the search as soon as we have $L_{p+1} \setminus L_p = \ldots = L_{p+n-1} \setminus L_{p+n-2} = \emptyset$. In practice, there is no need to compare sets, it suffices to use boolean variables to memorize the detection of new prime traces at the last n levels.

In the examples treated in Section 6, always the actual LFS-bound turns out to be 2, i.e. exhaustive search stops at 3 rather than at the logarithmic bound predicted by Theorem 1.

Transition merging. A simple and yet very effective reduction method in the partial order family is called *transition merging* (see e.g. [DR99]). The basic observation is that often system descriptions contain sequences of local transitions (of one process of a system) that do not interfere with the behavior of the rest of the system and the local property to verify. Merging such an *invisible transition* that does not take part in a choice to a predecessor thus preserves local properties. It turns out that transition merging is compatible with LFS and that the reductions achieved by the two methods are nearly orthogonal.

In our formalization, we assume a fixed local property and correspondingly a fixed set of visible transitions. Our formalization is a semantic one, defined on trace systems. In practice, sufficient syntactic criteria to be detected by the static analysis component of the verification system must be used.

We say that a transition $[u] \longrightarrow [ua]$ is *local* iff there exists a decomposition $[u] = [u_1 b u_2]$ such that $a \not\| b$ but $a \| u_2$ and $[u_1 b]$ is a prime trace. We say that a transition $[u] \longrightarrow [ua]$ is *in conflict* iff there exists a decomposition $[u] = [u_1 u_2]$ such that $b \| u_2$ for some b and furthermore there exists in the trace system a trace $[u_1 v b]$ such that $a \| v$ but $a \neq b$ and $a \not\| b$. Otherwise, we call $[u] \longrightarrow [ua]$ conflict free.

For a transition $[u] \rightarrow [ub]$, we say that the sequence $v = a_1 \ldots a_n$ is mergeable to b (yielding the merged transition $[u] \rightarrow [uba_1 \ldots a_n]$ iff for all i with $1 \leq i \leq n$ we have $a_i \not\| ba_1 \ldots a_{n-1}$, and furthermore $[uba_1 \ldots a_{i-1}] \rightarrow [uba_1 \ldots a_i]$ is a local invisible conflict free transition. For simplicity, we call the latter transitions "attachable".

Let a *merged trace system* be the trace system where each transition $[u] \rightarrow$ $[ub]$ is replaced by an arbitrary set of mergeable transitions[1] $[u] \rightarrow [uba_1 \ldots a_n]$.

With these definitions, we observe the following properties for the merged trace system.

Proposition 1. *(1) The communication degree of transitions in the merged trace system is bounded by the communication degree of simple transitions. (2) The static and dynamic LFS-bounds determined for the simple trace system hold for the merged trace system. (3) A local property reachable in the merged trace system is reachable in the simple trace system. (4) A local property is reachable in the trace system with LFS-number l is reachable in the merged trace system with LFS-number $\leq l$.*

Sleep sets and LFS are incompatible. A well known partial order reduction technique is the sleep set method [GW93]. While sleep sets combine well with a certain number of partial order reduction methods, in the full paper we explain by a counter example, why sleep sets and LFS are incompatible. In fact, both methods cut paths rather than states (and while LFS thus indirectly removes states, sleep sets preserve all states), and their interaction in pruning can lead to the elimination of prime traces, thus not preserving local properties.

6   Experiments

We have tested our Objective CAML prototype implementation on a number of parametric examples. Here we give tables for the experimental results for dining philosophers and a network broadcast protocol, each time varying the number of components as well as the reduction method: LLTTS approach with dynamic bound and with or without transition merging; transition merging in isolation; unfolding LFS with the static bound; unfolding LFS using the dynamic bound (oracle) obtained via the LLTTS approach; unfolding LFS with transition merging.

For each experiment, we measured the number of states explored on the LFS level (states in the hash table). (e.g. on two process systems, it will give no reduction at all) For all examples, the stabilization according to Theorem 2 occurs at LFS-number 2, which is detected after exploring the LLTTS up to LFS-number 3. Unfortunately, the first occurrence of a difference between the dynamic bound and the static bound occurs at $m = 8$ and lacking an efficient implementation we cannot go much further than $m = 10$.

The two series of examples differ in that the state copying problem is rather light for the philosophers and nearly disappears in presence of transition merging, whereas this is not the case for the instances of the echo protocol: Indeed, the LLTTS approach does not give any reduction compared to merging in that

---

[1] In practice, we will use a merging strategy in order to reduce the number of states visited. Intuitively, we want to join a maximal number of attachable transitions to b, thus obtaining a single replacement for b. Care has to be taken concerning cycles.

case. As a consequence, the combination LLTTS with dynamic bound and merging gives the best reduction for the philosophers, whereas unfolding LFS with merging gives the best results for the echo protocol.

philosophers (m)	1	2	3	4	5	6	7	8	9	10	20
dynamic bound, merging	2	4	9	16	25	36	49	64	81	100	400
dynamic bound (no merging)	2	8	37	202	1006	4195	13981	38759	–	–	–
merging (no LFS)	2	5	16	45	116	283	666	1529	3448	7611	–
no reduction	2	8	26	80	242	728	2186	6560	19682	59048	–
unfolding LFS	2	8	25	79	226	598	1450	5347	13372	31286	–
unfolding LFS, oracle bound	2	8	25	79	226	598	1450	3229	6655	12806	–
unfolding LFS, merging	2	4	8	15	26	42	64	163	256	386	–

echo processes (m)	2	4	6	8	10	12
dynamic bound, merging	8	47	208	885	3631	14395
dynamic bound (no merging)	16	190	1763	10844	–	–
merging (no LFS)	8	51	216	843	3120	11139
no reduction	18	827	–	–	–	–
unfolding LFS	13	278	5646	–	–	–
unfolding LFS, oracle bound	13	278	5646	–	–	–
unfolding LFS, merging	6	18	54	162	482	1452

It must be noted that LFS is a reduction method tailored to systems with a lot of parallelism – beyond our current experimental possibilities. As a rule, the higher the degree of parallelism in the system, the better LFS performs compared to other reduction methods (whereas it will give no reduction at all for small systems, e.g. just two parallel processes). While the results are encouraging already on our small examples, the potential on large examples is likely to be much stronger.

Acknowledgements

Thanks go to Rémi Morin for valuable discussions.

References

BMNZ02. S. Bornot, R. Morin, P. Niebert, and S. Zennou, *Blackbox unfolding with local first search*, TACAS, Springer, 2002, accepted for publication.

DR95. V. Diekert and G. Rozenberg (eds.), *The book of traces*, World Scientific, 1995.

DR99. Y. Dong and C. Ramakrishnan, *An optimizing compiler for efficient model checking*, FORTE/PSTV, 1999.

ERV96. J. Esparza, S. Römer, and W. Vogler, *An improvement of McMillan's unfolding algorithm*, TACAS, LNCS, vol. 1055, 1996, pp. 87–106.

GW93. P. Godefroid and P. Wolper, *Using partial orders for the efficient verification of deadlock freedom and safety properties*, Formal Methods in System Design **2** (1993), 149–164.

NHZL01. P. Niebert, M. Huhn, S. Zennou, and D. Lugiez, *Local first search – a new paradigm in partial order reductions*, CONCUR, LNCS, no. 2154, 2001, pp. 396–410.

Pel93. D. Peled, *All from one, one for all: On model checking using representatives*, CAV, LNCS, vol. 697, 1993, pp. 409–423.

Comparing Symbolic and Explicit Model Checking of a Software System

Cindy Eisner[1] and Doron Peled[2]

[1] IBM Haifa Research Laboratory
Haifa, Israel
[2] Dept. of Elec. and Comp. Eng.
The University of Texas at Austin
Austin, TX 78712

Abstract. There are two main paradigms for model checking: symbolic model checking, as is performed by the tool RULEBASE, and explicit state model checking, as is performed by SPIN. It is often accepted that the former is better for verifying hardware systems, while the latter has advantages for verifying software. We examine this piece of common wisdom in light of experience in verifying the software of a disk controller using both symbolic and explicit state model checking.

1 Introduction

Hardware and software model checkers are often distinct. The former are usually based on a symbolic search strategy [14] that examines sets of states in each step, while the latter are often based on explicit state search, where progress is made one state at a time. More importantly, hardware model checkers usually use a synchronous model of execution, in which all the enabled processes progress simultaneously, while the execution model of software model checkers is usually asynchronous (not to be confused with asynchronous message passing), where the execution of independent transitions can be interleaved in all possible orders.

In this paper we report on a verification project performed at the IBM Haifa Research Laboratory. In this project, we verified the software for a disk controller using both symbolic as well as explicit model checking. This verification project stands on the cutting edge of verification technology for the following reasons:

- The size of the project. We deal with actual software, over 2,500 lines of code, with minimal number of abstractions. The attempt is to avoid manual modeling, and verify the software *almost as is*. We used abstraction only when absolutely necessary, in particular, when pointer manipulation is involved. The checked software involves several concurrent processes with shared variables, each consisting of tens of recursive procedures.
- The state space involved. The system has a parametric number of processes. Even a single process of this system involves a huge number of states due to its interaction with the environment.

D. Bošnački and S. Leue (Eds.): SPIN 2002, LNCS 2318, pp. 230–239, 2002.

- The modeling technique, which involved direct compilation of the C code into the target languages used by the two model checkers. Since several different efficiency issues were involved, we constructed a parametric automatic translator and compared the efficiency of the different translation modes. For this reason, the usual methodology of repeatedly refining the model using the counterexample found during verification was augmented by repeatedly refining the translator. We believe that the translation techniques and the tool generated for this project can be useful for similar projects, especially taking into account the popularity of the C language.

The symbolic part of the work was performed using RULEBASE [4,3]. RULE-BASE was originally based on a version of SMV [14]. After eight years of development, the original SMV code is a small part of the whole. Alternative model checking algorithms [17,16,1,6] have been added, the original engine has been optimized [15,10], the temporal logic has been enhanced [2], and features [5] supporting debugging of formulas (as opposed to debugging of the model) have been developed. The explicit model checker used in the work described in this paper was SPIN [11].

2   The Verified Software

The software verified is a distributed storage subsystem software application. In other words, it is the software that runs on hardware that connects one or more computers with one or more magnetic disks. It is a distributed application that runs on several nodes, providing full data availability after the failure of a single node, and at least partial service in the event of simultaneous failures. Like most storage subsystems, it contains a cache to speed up read and write operations. The algorithms used to implement the software cache are the subject of the work described in this report.

A software cache, like a hardware cache, holds a copy of the data stored elsewhere (on disk in the case of a software cache, in main memory in the case of a hardware cache). The copy can be either *clean*, which means that the data is identical to that on disk, or *dirty*, which means that the cached copy is different from (and newer than) that on disk. If the cached copy is dirty, then the cache algorithms must ensure that any read of the dirty address gets the newer (cached) copy, and that the new data is written back to disk before the address is discarded from the cache. Because the system is distributed, the cache algorithms must also provide the coordination between multiple nodes. In the case of multiple cached copies, all are identical. Because the system must ensure high availability, there is an additional functionality, which is to ensure that there are always at least two copies of dirty data; a second copy is used in the case of a failure of the node holding the first copy.

The software consists of approximately 20,000 lines of C code; the part that was verified in this project is approximately 2,500 lines. The code is structured as a large number (slightly more than 100) small functions and procedures, which pass pointers to *work buffers*, each of which contains information regarding a single request being processed. The procedures are (non-tail) recursive, although a bound on the depth of the stack is known. A set of procedures operating on one request communicate using shared variables.

3   Issues in Model Translation

Issues in Representing C Programs for RULEBASE

The input language of hardware model checkers is usually very simple, reflecting the simple semantics of hardware description languages. EDL, the input language of the RULEBASE model checker, is no exception. An EDL model basically consists of a set of next state functions, describing a synchronous model in which the next state of each variable is calculated in parallel with all the others. The basic idea behind translating software into EDL follows directly from [13,8], and was described in [9]. A simple example will suffice to explain the main idea. Consider first the C function getmax() shown below.

```
getmax (){
    int max, a;
0   a = max = 0;
1   do {
2     if (a > max)
3       max = a;
4     a = input();
5   } while(a);
6   return(max);
7 }
```

We start by annotating the code with the value of the program counter (pc). We then restrict the integers a and max to a finite range, say 0 through 3. If we interpret the call to $a = input()$ on line 4 as a non-deterministic assignment to the variable a, it is a simple process to rewrite getmax() in terms of next-state functions of the variables, as shown below.

```
next(a) = if pc=0 then 0
                    else if pc=4 then {0,1,2,3}
                    else a
next(max) = if pc=0 then 0
                      else if pc=3 then a
                      else max
next(pc) = if pc=0 then 1
                    else if pc=1 then 2
                    else if pc=2 then if a>max then 3 else 4
                    else if pc=3 then 4
                    else if pc=4 then 5
                    else if pc=5 then if a then 1 else 6
                    else if pc=6 then 7
                    else if pc=7 then 7
```

With minor syntactic changes and the addition of state variable declarations, this is a complete EDL program, and can be model checked using RULEBASE.

The code verified in this project contains many constructs not covered by the basic solution described in [9] and presented above. Among these are: use of complex data types, such as structures and pointers, overloading of memory location names through the use of unions, and support for local variables and parameters. Structures, pointers, and unions were solved manually, by modifying the C code before the automatic translation into EDL: structures were flattened into sets of individual variables; pointers were converted into integer indices into an array of variables of the types pointed to; unions were resolved so that only one name was used for each data location. Support for local variables and paramters were solved automatically, by modifying the tool, with one caveat: one of the characteristics of local variables is that a recursive function call gets its own copy (unless the variables are declared as static). Because the software verified in this project contains no local variables which need this behavior to function correctly, this feature of local variables was ignored.

Issues in Representing C Programs in SPIN

The input language of software model checkers is usually much richer than that of hardware model checkers. However, even software model checkers usually allow a restricted syntax for representing the model of the checked system. The design of such a syntax is influenced by several objectives:

Expressiveness. The class of systems that may be verified is quite large. It can include hardware designs, as well as sequential or concurrent programs.

Simplicity. Modeling is perhaps the most difficult task of the verification. Thus, it should be made as easy as possible for the user.

Efficiency. The translation from the syntactic representation of the model into the internal representation, used by the tool, should be as fast and as space efficient as possible.

SPIN's modeling language PROMELA has a rich syntax. It includes C expressions, Dijkstra's *guarded command* sequential constructs and Hoare's CSP communication operators, representing synchronous and asynchronous communication. It also allows a mode of lossy communication channels, and the use of shared variables. Thus, PROMELA allows modeling a wide range of software systems. Still, translation is often required, since the verified system can be represented using any programming language. Because of the wealth of programming languages, automatic translation is usually not available.

The easiest part of the translation is changing the C syntax into PROMELA. Another straightforward problem is the representation of procedures. PROMELA does not have a special construct for representing procedures. However, as shown in the SPIN manual [12], we can simulate procedures with processes. Consider for example the following C code:

```
int firstproc (int num)
{
   int local;
   ...
   sv=secondproc(d);
   ...
   return local;
   ...
}
```

We simulate procedure firstproc with a process of the same name. In order not to allow concurrency between the process representing the calling procedure (firstproc) and the process representing the called procedure (secondproc), the calling procedure waits until it receives the returned value from the called procedure. If no value is returned in the original code, we return a dummy value. Thus, the PROMELA code for firstproc is as follows:

```
proctype firstproc(int num; chan ret)
{
   int local;
   chan mychan = [1] of {int};
   ...
   run secondproc(d, mychan);
   mychan?sv;
   ...
   ret!local;
   goto end_firstproc;
   ...
   end_firstproc:skip}
```

We use the same channel name in all processes that simulate a procedure. According to our translation, the channel is called mychan by the calling procedure, while the called procedure recognizes the channel by the name ret (since the channels it uses to communicate with the procedures it calls are called mychan). We also include the directives xs ret and xr mychan at the beginning of each process in order to report that the process exclusively sends messages on ret and exclusively receives messages on mychan. These directives allow the partial order reduction algorithm used in SPIN to better reduce the number of states and transitions explored. However, when a procedure calls more than one other procedure, then it can receive messages from the multiple corresponding processes on the same channel. In this case, sending to the channel mychan (recognized as ret in the called procedures) is not exclusive. It can be shown that because of the sequentiality in the execution of these procedures, the partial order reduction could be executed correctly albeit the non exclusiveness. However, SPIN is not programmed to deal with such a special case. One solution is to manually remove such directives when they do not truly reflect exclusivity. Experiments we have performed in doing that show that the reduction obtained by adding such directives in our code was negligible anyhow, and thus eliminating the need for a complicated solution.

A trickier problem involves the spawning of multiple copies of a process. The checked system is designed to work with a parameterized number of processes. Each copy starts with one main procedure, `main`, which calls other procedures recursively. Each `main` needs to communicate with the processes it has spawned using a set of shared variables. We model these shared variables in PROMELA as a set of global variables, one per main process. Say, for instance, that we want to declare the integer variable `glb` for 3 processes. We declare it as an array variable using `int glb[3]`. Access to these global variables now depends on the process number, which we pass as a parameter from the main process to its called processes. Thus, we execute `run main(1)`, `run main(2)`, `run main(3)`, and convert a process `firstproc(parm)` that calls `secondproc(moreparm)` into `firstproc(id,parm)` calling `secondproc(id,moreparm)`.

Tradeoffs in the Translation Process

Instead of the solution presented above for spawning multiple copies of a process, we can choose to define the fixed processes `main_1`, `main_2`, ..., and similarly, `firstproc_1`, `firstproc_2`, etc. We then declare copies of the global variables, e.g., `glb_1`, `glb_2`, ... This generates, for n processes, n times more code, and more entries in the process table. This can be a disadvantage, since SPIN keeps several internal enumerating mechanisms limited to one byte.

For non-recursive procedures, we also have an alternative to the representation of procedures as processes as described above. For procedures which are not recursive, we can replace the call for that procedure with its code, as in macro expansion. There is an obvious tradeoff in doing so. When a procedure is represented as a process, extra memory is allocated in each state for the program counter and its local variables. These include in particular the channels through which the process communicate with the processes representing the procedures calling it or called by it. This is avoided when a macro expansion is performed. The macro expansion usually involves only an increase in the address space of the program counter of the process that includes this procedure. In this case, the trace of the counterexample loses the information about the original chain of procedure calls. For this matter, some additional assignments can be performed in order to annotate the counterexamples with the necessary information.

State Size vs. State Space Size

There are two separate measures of the size of the model under model checking. One is the number of bits needed to represent a single state (state size), while the other is the number of states in reachable state space (state space size). While related, these two measures are not tightly coupled. In particular, if we model a digital circuit with n bits, there can be no more than 2^n reachable states. In practice, there are many dependencies, thus the number of reachable states is usually much less than 2^n.

In symbolic model checking, the number of bits needed to represent a single state is limited by the internal data structures. However, because BDDs give a

CPU time to compile the EDL model	3.5 minutes
memory use to compile the EDL model	625M
CPU time to perform the model checking	28 hours
memory to perform the model checking	249M
lines of pseudo-code in C model	2478
number of state variables in EDL model	362
number of reachable states	10^{150}

Fig. 1. Run time, memory usage, and model size for a 2-process system under RULE-BASE

compact way to represent sets of states, the number of reachable states is not a problem: the size of a BDD is not proportional to the number of states it represents. In explicit model checking, both state size and the state space size are important.

4 Experimental Results

4.1 Results with Symbolic Model Checking under RULEBASE

Using the translation process described in Section 3, the RULEBASE model was built. Due to size problems, only a 2-process system could be model checked. In that configuration, problems were found. Of those, nine were modeling errors, one was deemed a possible bug, one a real bug, and one a problem in a portion of the code not yet relevant to the current release.

All other rules passed for the 2-process configuration. Run time [1], memory usage, and model size is summarized in Figure 1. There are two surprises in Figure 1. First of all, the fact that the memory requirements of the compilation phase of RULEBASE were 625M, while the memory requirements of the model checking itself were only 249M. Model checking is usually much more expensive in terms of memory requirements than any pre-processing phase. A reduction algorithm dedicated to software could probably do a better job at reduction while reducing the memory requirements considerably. The second surprise is that despite the long run time (28 CPU hours), the memory requirements of the model checking itself were quite small - there was no state space explosion. This was not true of early runs of the model, which exploded quickly. Additions of hand-coded hints [16] achieved this impressive result. The hints controlled the interleaving of the concurrent runs of the two work buffers, so that a fixed-point was first reached with control belonging only to the first work buffer, then only to the second, and so on. Only after a number of iterations were the hints released so that more complicated interleavings could be examined.

---

[1] All run times in this paper are for an IBM RS/6000 workstation model 270

CPU time to compile the Promela model	negligible
memory use to compile the Promela model	negligible
CPU time to perform the model checking	1 cpu sec. per 20K st.
memory to perform the model checking	spaced out at 2G
lines of pseudo-code in C model	2478
number of state variables in Promela model	419
number of states seen	10^8

Fig. 2. Run time, memory usage, and model size for a 3-process system under SPIN

4.2   Results with Explicit Model Checking under SPIN

The SPIN model was built using the translation process described in Section 3, The hope was to be able to verify a larger system than the 2-process configuration which was the limit for RULEBASE. Obviously, with the number of states reported in the table in Figure 1, we did not expect to be able to cover even a small fraction of the states. Despite this, it was decided to attempt model checking of a 3-process system using SPIN in the hopes of encountering new behavior which might uncover problems not seen in the 2-process system. Several runs were done, each restricting the environment (inputs to the system) in a different way. All of these runs spaced out at 10^8 states without finding any new problems. Run time, memory usage, and model size for a 3-process configuration under SPIN is summarized in the table in Figure 2.

5   Discussion

The size of the state space for a 2-process model as shown in Figure 1 was 10^{150}. Why then did we expect to be able to veirfy something even larger by explicit state model checking? The answer is that things are not as straightforward as they seem, even in a simple matter like counting the number of states.

In explicit state model checking, we perform a search (usually depth first search) through the states of the checked system. The search proceeds state by state (although some reduction techniques allow us to skip some states or to step through representatives of equivalence classes of states). The search is performed in the *forward* direction, from a state to its successors, unless the search strategy requires backtracking. Thus, it is straightforward to assess the number of states encountered during the verification. Moreover, all the states participating in the search are reachable from the initial state(s).

In symbolic model checking, we keep a compressed representation of the state space (usually, using a binary decision diagram, or BDD [7]). At each stage, the representation holds a collection of states. We can apply a transformation to that set of states, finding the set of states reachable from them with one transition (forward search) or the set of states from that can transform to the given set within one transition (backward search). Then we can append the given set of states or restrict it depending on the search strategy and the property checked.

Symbolic model checking can be performed using the classic algorithm [14] in which state traversal is performed backward from the set of states violating the property checked. In backwards traversal, we either hit an initial state, in which case we have found a violation of the property being checked, or we have reached a fixed-point, in which case we know that there is no violation. In backwards traversal, we do not calculate the set of reachable states, hence we do not report the number of reachable states.

The application of symbolic model checking described in this paper was done using *on-the-fly* symbolic model checking [6], in which we use forward traversal, just like explicit state model checking. Since we know how to count the number of states seen in each symbolic step, it is straightforward, as with explicit state space traversal, to assess the number of states encountered during the verification. Moreover, as with explicit state space traversal, all the states participating in the search are reachable from the initial state(s). The 10^{150} states report in Figure 1 are states reachable from the initial state in the constructed RULEBASE model.

However, because of its particular way of compressing the state space, it is often the case that the BDD representation requires less memory when *more* states are added. In fact, it may be beneficial to 'pad' the state space with extra states in order to reduce the size of the BDD. This is done, in fact, in our EDL representation of the checked system. One example of this is that since the recursive stack is represented on the state space, its unused slots are padded with all possible values. Thus, the number of reachable states in an EDL model does not mean that an equivalent model in PROMELA necessarily reaches the same number of states. Thus, our initial optimism even in the face of the huge number of reachable states reported by RULEBASE.

As expected, when applying SPIN, we encountered an explosion in the number of states. The state space problem was more severe with the explicit state model checking with SPIN. We could only check 10^8 states before spacing out at 2G memory, and our gut feeling was that this was a small part of the real state space of the model. In order to check our intuition, we ran RULEBASE on a 2-process model, after modifying the code in order to cancel out the states that were 'padded' for RULEBASE performance reasons as described above. This analysis showed that the SPIN model could be expected to contain at least 10^{65} reachable states. Even with advanced hashing modes, which allow representing each state as a small number of bits (even as one bit), we cannot expect to cover this number of states with the explicit search strategy. On the other hand, because of the limit on state size, RULEBASE could not represent a state large enough to include the information needed for more than a 2-process configuration. In that respect, RULEBASE gave us a better assurance about the verified system for a low number of processes, while SPIN allowed us to simulate executions with more processes.

References

1. J. Baumgartner, T. Heyman, V. Singhal, and A. Aziz. Model checking the IBM Gigahertz Processor: An abstraction algorithm for high-performance netlists. In *Proc.* 11th *International Conference on Computer Aided Verification (CAV)*, LNCS 1633, pages 72–83. Springer-Verlag, 1999.
2. I. Beer, S. Ben-David, C. Eisner, D. Fisman, A. Gringauze, and Y. Rodeh. The temporal logic Sugar. In G. Berry, H. Comon, and A. Finkel, editors, *Proc.* 13th *International Conference on Computer Aided Verification (CAV)*, LNCS 2102. Springer-Verlag, 2001.
3. I. Beer, S. Ben-David, C. Eisner, D. Geist, L. Gluhovsky, T. Heyman, A. Landver, P. Paanah, Y. Rodeh, G. Ronin, and Y. Wolfsthal. RuleBase: Model checking at IBM. In *Proc.* 9th *International Conference on Computer Aided Verification (CAV)*, LNCS 1254. Springer-Verlag, 1997.
4. I. Beer, S. Ben-David, C. Eisner, and A. Landver. RuleBase: an industry-oriented formal verification tool. In *Proc.* 33rd *Design Automation Conference (DAC)*, pages 655–660. Association for Computing Machinery, Inc., June 1996.
5. I. Beer, S. Ben-David, C. Eisner, and Y. Rodeh. Efficient detection of vacuity in temporal model checking. *Formal Methods in System Design*, 18(2), 2001.
6. I. Beer, S. Ben-David, and A. Landver. On-the-fly model checking of RCTL formulas. In *Proc.* 10th *International Conference on Computer Aided Verification (CAV)*, LNCS 1427, pages 184–194. Springer-Verlag, 1998.
7. R. Bryant. Graph-based algorithms for boolean function manipulation. *IEEE Transactions on Computers*, C-35(8), 1986.
8. E. Clarke, O. Grumberg, and D. Peled. *Model Checking*. MIT Press, 1999.
9. C. Eisner. Model checking the garbage collection mechanism of SMV. In S. D. Stoller and W. Visser, editors, *Electronic Notes in Theoretical Computer Science*, volume 55. Elsevier Science Publishers, 2001.
10. D. Geist and I. Beer. Efficient model checking by automated ordering of transition relation partitions. In *Proc.* 6th *International Conference on Computer Aided Verification (CAV)*, LNCS 818, pages 299–310. Springer-Verlag, 1994.
11. G. Holzmann. On the fly, ltl model checking with spin: Simple spin manual. In *http://cm.bell-labs.com/cm/cs/what/spin/Man/Manual.html*.
12. G. Holzmann. *Design and Validation of Computer Protocols*. Prentice Hall, 1991.
13. Z. Manna and A. Pnueli. *Temporal Verification of Reactive Systems: Safety*. Springer-Verlag, New York, 1995.
14. K. McMillan. *Symbolic Model Checking*. Kluwer Academic Publishers, 1993.
15. K. Ravi, K. McMillan, T. Shiple, and F. Somenzi. Approximation and decomposition of binary decision diagrams. In *Proc.* 35th *Design Automation Conference (DAC)*. Association for Computing Machinery, Inc., June 1998.
16. K. Ravi and F. Somenzi. Hints to accelerate symbolic traversal. In *Proceedings 10th IFIP WG 10.5 Advanced Research Working Conference on Correct Hardware Design and Verification Methods (CHARME)*, LNCS 1703, Bad Herrenalb, Germany, September 1999. Springer-Verlag.
17. O. Shtrichman. Pruning techniques for the SAT-based bounded model checking problem. In T. Margaria and T. F. Melham, editors, *CHARME*, volume 2144 of *Lecture Notes in Computer Science*. Springer, 2001.

Industrial Model Checking
Based on Satisfiability Solvers

Per Bjesse

Prover Technology
917 SW Oak
Portland, OR 97227
bjesse@prover.com

Abstract. Until recently, symbolic model checking was synonymous with fix-point calculations using Binary Decision Diagrams (BDDs). However, today there are a number of approaches to symbolic model checking that avoid the use of BDDs altogether.

One of the most successful of these new approaches is model checking using satisfiability solvers (SAT-solvers). Although the body of literature on SAT-based model checking is small, it is already clear that this approach makes it possible to achieve order of magnitude performance improvements compared to BDD-based model checking, even when relatively unsophisticated algorithms are used.

In this talk, I will present three different approaches to SAT-based model checking, and discuss the experiences we have had at Prover Technology when applying them to industrial problems.

The first of the approaches I will present, Bounded Model Checking (BMC), attempts to reduce the search for counterexamples and witnesses to satisfiability checking. BMC has proved to be a strong technique for finding bugs. The second approach, induction, is a method that extends the BMC analysis in such a way that safety properties also can be proved. The third approach, SAT-based reachability analysis, is a method in which the BDD package used in the standard reachability algorithms is replaced by a SAT-solver and an algorithm for translating quantified boolean formulas.

In addition to giving an introduction to the SAT-based verification algorithms, I will discuss some of the strengths and weaknesses of SAT-solvers compared to BDDs, and the relative performance of the three SAT-based approaches compared to traditional BDD-based model checking.

One of the aims of this talk is to present a "from the trenches" perspective on the use of SAT-based model checking. Industrial problems are rarely as clean and structured as the problems that are encountered in academia, and the demands that are put on a model checker by industrial users are very different from the demands of researchers. I will discuss some of the experiences we have had at Prover Technology when dealing with designs from our customers, and the challenges that we have had to overcome. I will also present two industrial case studies from the domains of safety critical software verification, and industrial hardware verification.

D. Bošnački and S. Leue (Eds.): SPIN 2002, LNCS 2318, p. 240, 2002.
© Springer-Verlag Berlin Heidelberg 2002

A Typical Testing Problem:
Validating WML Cellphones

Yves-Marie Quemener

France Telecom R&D, 2 av. Pierre Marzin, 22300 Lannion Cedex
yvesmarie.quemener@rd.francetelecom.com

Abstract. I will present in my talk a problem typical for the activity of
telecommunications operators where formal methods should bring some
help: validating equipment (for example, cellphones) which is supposed
to act as an interpreter for an XML-like language (in that case, WML,
a script language for the WAP protocol). Testing interpreters suppose
that test scripts have to be separated in two parts: a data part which
is a program in the interpreted language, and a script part which describes what the interpreted program is supposed to do if it is correctly
interpreted. The data part is very often reduced to very simple programs
exercising only one feature of the language, and the script part is then
informal, in general a description in natural language. This does not enable to exercise combinations of features of the interpreted language. To
change this situation, it would be necessary to encode in some way the
semantics of the interpreted language. From that encoding, and from
a significant program in the interpreted language, automatic test generation tools derived from model-checking technology will provide test
suites of hopefully better quality.

D. Bošnački and S. Leue (Eds.): SPIN 2002, LNCS 2318, p. 241, 2002.
© Springer-Verlag Berlin Heidelberg 2002

Heuristic Model Checking for Java Programs

Alex Groce[1] and Willem Visser[2]

[1] School of Computer Science, Carnegie Mellon University
agroce+@cs.cmu.edu
[2] RIACS/NASA Ames Research Center
wvisser@riacs.edu

1   Introduction

Two recent areas of interest in software model checking are checking programs written in standard programming languages [1,5] and using heuristics to guide the exploration of an explicit-state model checker [3]. Model checking real programs has the drawback that programs often contain a larger degree of detail than designs and hence are more difficult to check (due to the more acute state-explosion problem); however the large amount of detail in a program allows more precise heuristics for narrowing down the search space when using a model checker for error-detection. This paper describes the addition of support for heuristic (or directed) search strategies to Java PathFinder (JPF), an explicit state model checker for Java bytecode that uses a custom-made Java Virtual Machine (JVM) [5].

The primary benefits of heuristic search are: discovery of errors that a depth-first search fails to find, and shorter (and thus easier to understand and correct) counterexample paths. In JPF a number of pre-defined heuristics are provided, but a user can also write their own by using an interface to the JVM. The rest of the paper is structured as follows: in section 2 we illustrate JPFs heuristic capabilities by showing two novel predefined heuristics as well as a simple user-defined heuristic, in section 3 we give results of using JPF with heuristics and in section 4 be briefly sketch some future work.

2   Search Capabilities

The heuristic search options in JPF are primarily aimed at checking for deadlocks and assertion violations. Using heuristics for more general LTL properties is possible, but complicates the search strategy (heuristic searches are not very effective for cycle detection[4]). We have found that two kinds of heuristics work well for a variety of programs in searching for assertion violations and deadlocks.

Branch Exploration: Traditional branch coverage metrics measure the percent of branches in a program covered by test cases. Although using a heuristic that greedily searches for high branch coverage over paths (or globally) performs poorly, something more complex works well: (1) States covering a previously untaken branch receive the best heuristic value. (2) States that are not reached

D. Bošnački and S. Leue (Eds.): SPIN 2002, LNCS 2318, pp. 242–245, 2002.
© Springer-Verlag Berlin Heidelberg 2002

by taking a branch receive the next best heuristic value. (3) States that cover a branch already taken are ranked according to how many times that branch has been taken.

Thread Interleaving: Another useful heuristic is to maximize the interleaving of threads along each path in order to find deadlocks or race conditions that cause null pointer exceptions or assertion violations. Many JVMs and JIT compilers only switch between threads at explicit yields inserted in the code or after multiple bytecodes have been executed (for obvious efficiency reasons). This scheduling can leave errors based on subtle interleavings undetected until the code is used in a different setting. By context switching as much as possible, the interleaving heuristic uncovers some of these subtle errors.

What makes these two heuristics particularly interesting is that they focus on the structure of the program being analyzed: the interleaving heuristic will only work well if a program is concurrent whereas the branch-exploration heuristic is best suited to programs where nondeterministic actions are explored (nondeterminism is most often encoded in a branching control structure, such as an if or case statement). These observations are supported by the results shown in the next section. JPF also includes other heuristics: maximizing the number of blocked threads out of running threads (for deadlock detection), randomized exploration, and counting executions of every bytecode rather than branches. Other options include using the sum of two heuristics, limiting the size of the search queue[1] (sacrificing completeness for focused exploration), and using an A^* search rather than the default best-first search. Users may also change the code in the file UserHeuristic.java to create their own heuristics. Consider a program with a class Main with a static field buffer, itself an object of a class with integer fields current and capacity. Following is the code for a heuristic returning either (capacity − current) or a default value (defined in the UserHeuristic class) if the Main.buffer field hasn't been initialized:

```
public int heuristicValue() {
  Reference m = getSystemState().getClass("Main");
  if (m != null) {
    Reference b = m.getObjectField("buffer");
    if (b != null) {
      int current = b.getIntField("current");
      int capacity = b.getIntField("capacity");
      if (current > capacity)
        return 0;
      return (capacity-current);
  } }
  return defaultValue;
}
```

Note that lower heuristic values are better, with zero (0) being the top priority, and negative values indicating that a state should not be queued for explo-

---

[1] Heuristic search in JPF is implemented by generating all successor states from the current state and then adding them to a priority queue depending on the heuristic(s) being used.

ration (for trimming the state space when a runtime computation can show that no successors of a state can give rise to a counterexample). Options allow states with the same heuristic value to be explored in the order they were generated (for BFS-like behavior when all states have the same value), in the reverse of the order in which they were generated (for DFS-like behavior), or in the order of their hash values. The code above would be useful if errors were suspected to occur when the buffer was at or near its capacity.

3   Experimental Results

DEOS					
Search/Heuristic	Time	Memory	States Explored	Length	Max Depth
branch	60	91	2,701	136	139
branch(A^*)	59	92	2,712	136	139
statement	62	88	2,195	136	137
statement(A^*)	63	94	2,383	136	137
BFS	FAILS	-	18,054	-	135
DFS	FAILS	-	14,678	-	14,678
DFS (depth 500)	6,782	383	392,479	455	500
DFS (depth 1000)	2,222	196	146,949	987	1,000
DFS (depth 4000)	171	270	8,481	3,997	4,000

Dining Philosophers						
Search/Heuristic	Size	Time	Memory	States Explored	Length	Max Depth
branch	8	FAILS	-	374,991	-	41
BFS	8	FAILS	-	436,068	-	13
DFS	8	FAILS	-	398,906	-	384,286
DFS (depth 100)	8	FAILS	-	1,357,596	-	100
DFS (depth 500)	8	FAILS	-	1,354,747	-	500
DFS (depth 1000)	8	FAILS	-	1,345,289	-	1,000
DFS (depth 4000)	8	FAILS	-	1,348,398	-	4,000
interleaving	8	FAILS	-	487,942	-	16
interleaving (queue 5)	8	2	1	1,719	66	66
interleaving (queue 40)	8	5	5	16,569	66	66
interleaving (queue 160)	8	12	27	62,616	66	66
interleaving (queue 1000)	8	60	137	354,552	67	67
interleaving (queue 5)	16	4	5	6,703	129	129
interleaving (queue 40)	16	16	45	69,987	131	131
interleaving (queue 160)	16	60	207	290,637	131	132
interleaving (queue 1000)	16	FAILS	-	858,818	-	41
interleaving (queue 5)	32	11	32	25,344	257	257
interleaving (queue 40)	32	FAILS	-	472,022	-	775
interleaving (queue 160)	32	FAILS	-	494,043	-	86
interleaving (queue 5)	64	59	206	101,196	514	514

The first results[2] are from the DEOS real-time operating system case study [5], where a very subtle error exists that can lead to an assertion violation. Because the error results from a particular choice of action at a particular point in time on the part of threads, the branch coverage based heuristics (and statement coverage heuristics) find the bug quickly by exercising different options as quickly as possible. The thread interleaving heuristics were not used as the real-time constraints prevent any thread interleaving choices in DEOS. Note how the limited depth DFS searches find much longer counterexamples in each case.

---

[2]   All results obtained on a 1.4 GHz Athlon with JPF limited to 512Mb. Times are in seconds and memory is in megabytes. FAILS indicates failure due to running out of memory.

The second table shows the results of applying heuristics to the classic dining philosophers problem. Here, branch based heuristics are not very successful (since there are almost no branches in the program), but the interleaving-based heuristic plus queue size limitation (analogous to the depth limitations for DFS) produces counterexamples even for quite large numbers of philosophers (threads).

4 Conclusions and Future Work

Explicit-state model checkers such as JPF and SPIN will always be faced with the state-explosion problem – it can be pushed further away but it will never go away – therefore it seems inevitable that unless we employ clever abstractions [1] we will need to focus on error-detection, in which case the development of clever heuristics to guide the model checker towards likely errors will be a fruitful area of research.

It is our view that when doing a heuristic search not only should one gear the heuristics towards the property to be checked, but also one should focus the selection of the heuristics to be used on the structure of the program being analyzed. We showed two such structure-dependent heuristics here: namely, one geared towards finding interleaving related problems, and one for analyzing highly nondeterministic programs. Furthermore, one should allow the capability for the user to specify heuristics, since the user's domain knowledge will be invaluable during model checking.

Many areas for future research exists within heuristic-based model checking, most notably how to select the best heuristic and heuristic parameters for a specific problem. This area has seen much attention in the AI community and we hope to leverage their results. We also believe a closer link between the property specific language and heuristics should exist: we envisage a property including certain heuristic guidelines, e.g. we might like to specify "DFS until full(queue) then show no-deadlock using branch-exploration". The next phase of the heuristic-based JPF development will therefore focus on learning when to use which heuristic as well as the development of a language for guiding the model checker during property checking.

References

1. Thomas Ball, Sriram K. Rajamani. Automatically Validating Temporal Safety Properties of Interfaces. In *SPIN 2001*, pages 103–122, 2001. LNCS 2057.
2. Gerard Holzmann and Doron Peled. The State of SPIN. In *CAV '96*, LNCS, 1996.
3. Stefan Edelkamp, Alberto Lluch Lafuente, and Stefan Leue. Directed explicit model checking with HSF-Spin. In *SPIN 2001*, pages 57–79, 2001. LNCS 2057.
4. Stefan Edelkamp, Alberto Lluch Lafuente, and Stefan Leue. Trail-Directed Model Checking. In *Proceedings of the Workshop of Software Model Checking*, Electrical Notes in Theoretical Computer Science, Elsevier, July 2001.
5. W. Visser, K. Havelund, G. Brat and S. Park. Model Checking Programs. In *IEEE International Conference on Automated Software Engineering (ASE)*, September 2000.

System Specification and Verification Using High Level Concepts – A Tool Demonstration

Christian Stehno

Carl von Ossietzky Universität Oldenburg
FB Informatik, Parallel systems group
D-26111 Oldenburg
Christian.Stehno@informatik.uni-oldenburg.de

Abstract. This paper describes a sample modelling and verification session using SDL and SPIN modelchecker via the PEP tool[1]. We will focus on the tight integration of all involved tools allowing the user to stay within his known environment of SDL specifications. Thus the user need not know about the underlying Petri net or the Promela language even while formulating the properties to be checked.

1 Introduction and Motivation

The PEP tool [1] provides an integrated development and verification environment for a selection of formal modelling techniques, including the Specification and Description Language (SDL, [10]). SDL is widely used in industry. It provides synchronous and asynchronous channels for communication of different processes, that run in parallel. In addition to the usual parts of most languages, like variables and control flow with choice and sequence, SDL also offers a procedure concept and dynamic process creation during runtime. This facilitates the system development and allows compact and readable models.

To support the user during the development process and further while verifying the model, it does not suffice to group different tools in one user interface. Instead, all tools have to be tightly connected making use of all features from a single point of view. It is usually best to stay at the top level of system description for ease of use and understanding, i.e. to allow a user to stay within his known environment even for verification purposes. Thus all of the involved steps have to relay their results to upper levels, providing simulation, verification and debugging in terms of the specification language.

This paper presents features offered by the PEP tool, that support all topics mentioned above, with an emphasis on temporal logics. It is structured as follows: Section 2 describes the modelling and simulation of SDL specifications. The verification of such specifications are presented in Sec. 3, while Sec. 4 concludes the paper and shows possible further developments.

---

[1] http://parsys.informatik.uni-oldenburg.de/~pep

D. Bošnački and S. Leue (Eds.): SPIN 2002, LNCS 2318, pp. 246–249, 2002.

2   High Level Modelling

An SDL system may be directly modelled within the PEP interface by entering SDL code in PEP's text editor, but may also be read from external specifications. The editor allows the selection of most SDL language blocks with the mouse and offers online syntax checking.

Before further action can take place, the SDL specification is translated into an M-net [2] representing its formal semantics. In conjunction with this and following transformations, a set of references is created [7], providing feedback from lower levels to the original specification and facilitating the methods described in this paper.

The first step to occur after the specification is usually simulation. Simple design flaws and unwanted behaviour may be detected this way. Due to the references, it is not only possible to simulate the net and gain the SDL behaviour from annotations, but also to simulate the SDL program directly. Simulation cannot guarantee properties though, it only helps in understanding the system. To verify properties for all possible states of the system, model checking provides an effective and widely used method. The next section will present some algorithms and PEP support of them.

3   Verification of the Specification

Various verification tools are integrated into the PEP tool to offer the user a large base of formal concepts to check properties of the system, e.g. partial order representation [4] and BDD based [11] algorithms. The SPIN tool [9] is used to verify LTL formulae over Petri net state properties.

To transform the high level M-net into Promela code, the net is first unfolded into a semantically equivalent low level net and subsequently compiled into Promela code according to [8]. This yields a SPIN compatible process version of the Petri net which emulates the net behaviour.

Properties that may be checked have to be defined over Petri nets. Depending on the model checker used, the temporal logic is determined. The SPIN tool provides LTL checking, while other tools may be used for branching time logics. The formula may be entered in the formula editor shown in Fig. 1. This editor not only offers a simple text entry to enter and save terms, but also allows the creation of formulae using the mouse. As shown in Fig. 1, all syntactical components of the logic are choosable.

While simple properties may be formulated directly in terms of net entities, e.g. $[](P1)$, stating "the place P1 is always marked", this method is tedious and error prone for more complex ones. Instead, a high-level syntax allows to state explicitly model properties within the formulae, which are automatically transformed into net formulae, using the mentioned references. A sample formula using this concept is shown in (1), stating the property "The send state in client process 1 is always reachable again" (liveness).

$$[] <> (\text{client}[1].\text{state} = \text{send}) \tag{1}$$

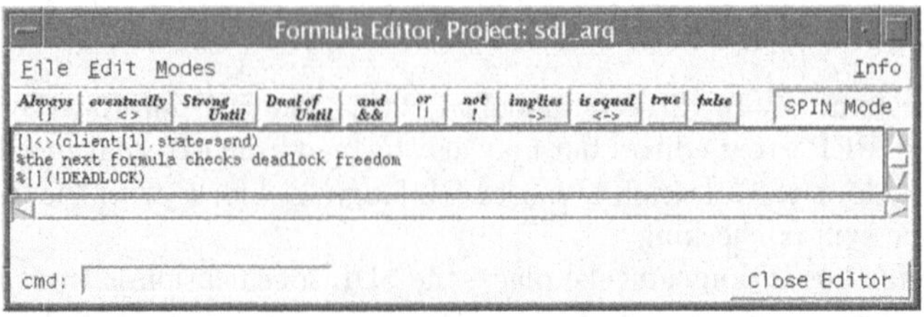

Fig. 1. Formula editor in PEP

To use these types of formulae, PEP provides two different mechanisms. The first is a reference mode of the SDL editor. The user may select states or components of the SDL specification and send their corresponding places into the formula editor. The second approach allows the high level terms to be entered into the formula and thus making it invariant to changes of the underlying Petri net, as the corresponding places are regenerated each time. Both techniques are available at the same time, so the user may choose depending on his needs.

Continuing the verification process, the formula is expanded into the corresponding net formula if some high level terms were used. Then it is translated into a "never claim" and included in the promela code. The model checking interface is started via the SPIN button and creates a window (cf. Fig. 2) offering a result display and buttons to change SPIN options and start checking. When the SPIN tool is invoked, the promela code is compiled into a binary which is automatically executed. The result is displayed in the model checker window. Additionally to the complete SPIN output, a transition sequence of the Petri net is calculated where applicable as shown in Fig. 2. Using the references ranging from the low level Petri net back to the SDL specification, the user may simulate the counterexample (if one is found) not only in the Petri net, but also in the original specification as defined at the beginning of the session. This allows a debugging technique solely based on high level terms of the chosen modelling language, reducing the efforts of users to a minimum.

4   Conclusion and Future Work

We have briefly presented the features of the PEP tool supporting the entire modelling process of SDL specifications, including simulation and verification, at the abstract SDL level. The user does not have to cope with different formal models but gets all results in terms of the specification. The development process will be completed by a graphical editor, that is currently being implemented, and an extension of the SDL fragment used towards SDL-2000.

While the PEP tool supports the transformation of low level Petri nets to Promela code only, [8] describes also possible transformation of high level nets and code of $B(PN)^2$ [3]. A further, very promising direction is the translation of time Petri nets into Promela code. Due to the variable concept in Promela it should be fairly easy to add this functionality.

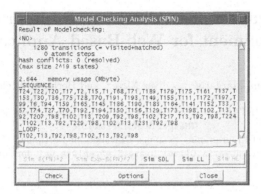

Fig. 2. Result of SPIN and counterexample

The PEP tool is currently extended by some additional LTL model checkers from [5] and [12]. This will give an opportunity to compare the different approaches and choose the algorithms best suiting the particular problem.

Acknowledgements

The author would like to thank Eike Best and an anonymous referee for their comments on this paper.

References

1. Best, E.: Partial Order Verification with PEP. In Proc. of POMIV'96. Am. Math. Soc. (1996) 305–328
2. Best, E., Fleischhack, H., Frączak, W., Hopkins, R.P., Klaudel, H., Pelz, E.: A Class of Composable High Level Petri Nets. In Proc. of ATPN'95. Volume 935 of LNCS. Springer-Verlag (1995) 103–118
3. Best, E., Hopkins, R.P.: B(PN)^2– a Basic Petri Net Programming Notation. Proc. of PARLE'93. Volume 694 of LNCS. Springer-Verlag (1993) 379–390
4. Esparza, J.: Model Checking Using Net Unfoldings. Science of Computer Programming **23**. Elsevier (1994) 151–195
5. Esparza, J., and Heljanko, K.: A new unfolding approach to LTL model checking. In Proc. ICALP 2000. Volume 1853 of LNCS. Springer-Verlag (2000) 475–486
6. Fleischhack, H., Grahlmann, B.: A Compositional Petri Net Semantics for SDL. In Proc. of ATPN'98. Volume 1420 of LNCS. Springer-Verlag (1998)
7. Grahlmann, B.: The Reference Component of PEP. In Proc. of TACAS'97. Volume 1254 of LNCS. Springer-Verlag (1997) 65–80
8. Grahlmann, B., Pohl, C.: Profiting from SPIN in PEP. In Proc. of SPIN'98. (1998)
9. Holzmann, G.J.: Design and Validation of Computer Protocols. Prentice Hall (1991)
10. CCITT: Functional Specification and Description Language (SDL). CCITT Z.100. Geneva (1992)
11. McMillan, K.: Symbolic model checking: An approach to the state explosion problem. Kluwer Academic Publishers (1993)
12. Wallner, F.: Model checking LTL using net unfoldings. In Proc. of CAV'98. Volume 1427 of LNCS. Springer-Verlag (1998) 207–218

Demonstration of an Automated Integrated Test Environment for Web-Based Applications

Tiziana Margaria[1,2], Oliver Niese[2], and Bernhard Steffen[2]

[1] METAFrame Technologies GmbH, Dortmund, Germany
TMargaria@METAFrame.de
[2] Chair of Programming Systems, University of Dortmund, Germany
{Tiziana.Margaria,Oliver.Niese,Steffen}@cs.uni-dortmund.de

1   Introduction

The state of the art of test tools for *web-based applications* is still dominated by static approaches, focussing on *a posteriori* link-structure reconstruction and interpretation [2,6], e.g. to determine unreachable pages, rather than on functional aspects directly related to the application's behaviour. As it has happened in the areas of telecommunications, evolution in this direction is however necessary in order to test applications also for their intention, rather than just for environmental accidents.

We demonstrate a methodology for functional testing of *web-based applications*. It bases on the experience we gained in system level test of Computer Telephony Integrated applications, where our coordination-based coarse grain approach has been successfully applied ([4]). Central properties of the test environment are:

- the capability of handling (distributed) testing of *web-based applications*
- the capability of proving properties about the test cases via model checking ensuring executability conditions and test purpose coverage.

We show in the demonstration how the approach works in practice, by testing complex role-based functional features of the Online Conference Service [1], a cooperative-work management system that supports the web-based organization of scientific conferences.

2   Dealing with Web-Based Applications

Modern *web-based applications* are complex multitiered, distributed applications that typically run on heterogeneous platforms. Their correct operation increasingly depends on the interoperability of single software modules, rather than just on their intrinsic algorithmic correctness. This has a huge impact on the test and validation requirements: it is increasingly unrealistic to restrict the consideration to single units, e.g. the client side only, since complex subsystems affect each other. Instead, scalable, integrated test methodologies are needed that can handle the application as a whole.

D. Bošnački and S. Leue (Eds.): SPIN 2002, LNCS 2318, pp. 250–253, 2002.

To our knowledge, our integrated test environment, which focusses on global functional aspects (informal described in [5]), is unique in addressing distributed web application in a whole. It is a modular and open environment, allowing the diverse units under test and their corresponding test tools to be added at need. The heart of our test environment is the *Test Coordinator*, built on top of METAFrame's *Agent Building Center (ABC)* [7], a generic and flexible development environment providing, in particular, support for the design, verification and execution of workflows. The *Test Coordinator* drives the generation, execution, evaluation, and management of the system-level tests in this highly heterogeneous landscape, as will be illustrated during the demonstration.

3 Case Study: Testing the Online Conference Service

We demonstrate the key features of the *test environment* on a real life example: the test of the Online Conference Service [1], a complex web-service that proactively helps authors, Program Committee chairs, and Program Committee members to cooperate efficiently during their collaborative handling of the composition of a conference program. The application provides a timely, transparent, and secure handling of the papers and of the related submission, review, report and decision management process. The online service includes in particular a role based access and rights management feature that is reconfigurable online, which accounts for a high flexibility and administration comfort. These features and their flexible administration, at the same time, also embody a potential for disruptive behavior in connection with sensitive information, which calls for intensive and well-guided testing in order to explore the full potential of the underlying complex workflows.

The test process supported by the *test environment* is organized in the following main steps: *identification* of generic test blocks, and *design, verification* and *execution* of test cases.

1. **Identification of Generic and Reusable Test Blocks.** The first task is to identify generic test actions which allow us to control the online service via a browser and also to validate certain properties of the service state (e.g. by checking the current state of the GUI or by checking the entries of an underlying database) according to the coarse grained design approach of services presented in [8]. For each action a test block is prepared: a name and a class characterizing the block are specified and a set of formal parameters is defined to enable a more general usage of the block. In this way, for the *Web-based application* to be tested a library of test blocks has been incrementally defined.

2. **Graphical Design of Test Cases.** The design of test cases consists of the behavior-oriented combination of test blocks. This combination is done graphically, i.e., icons representing test blocks are graphically stuck together to yield test graph structures that embody the test behavior in terms of control.

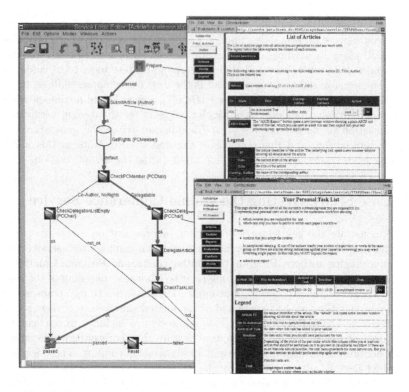

Fig. 1. Test Execution: A Successful Execution Path and the Users' Views

3. **Verification of the Test Cases.** In our environment, the design of test cases is constantly accompanied by online verification of the global correctness and consistency of the test cases' control flow logic [3]. During the test case design, vital properties concerning the usage of parameters (local properties) and the interplay between the stimuli and verification actions of a test case (global properties) can be verified. Test cases conflicting with the constraints and consistency conditions of the intended system are thus immediately detected.

4. **Execution of the Test Cases and Reporting.**   Test cases can be executed immediately in the *Test Coordinator*. Starting at the initial test block of a test graph the tracer proceeds in interpreter modus from test block to test block. Actions represented by a test block are treated in three steps as follows: stimuli and inspection requests are sent to the corresponding system's component, the responses are received and evaluated, and the evaluation results are used to select the relevant next test block.

Verification is crucial to support a reliable test case design, as tests for complex systems are complex themselves. The global properties, expressed in a user friendly specification language based on SLTL, the Semantic Linear-time Temporal Logic of [7], capture the essence of the expertise of test designers about do's and don'ts of test creation, e.g. which test blocks are incompatible, or which can or cannot occur before/after some other test blocks. Such properties are rarely straightforward, sometimes they are documented as exceptions in thick user manuals, but more often they are not documented at all, and have been discovered at a hard price as bugs of previously developed tests.

Systems developed with the Agent Building Center, like the Online Conference Service, enjoy in this respect a double bonus: the same functional constraints enforced at design time (as detailed for this particular service e.g. in [8,1]) can now be reused to validate the test cases, ensuring consistency of the test purposes with the original system specification.

Typical test-phase specific additional constraints for the test of *Web-based applications* refer e.g. to the resource management at test execution time: one can ensure that all used resources are correctly released after the execution of the test case, and this independently of the test's outcome. E.g. *every log-in for a user must be followed by a log-out for this user.* If the model checker detects an inconsistency, a plain text explanation of the violated constraint appears, together with the identification of a path responsible for this inconsistency. As will be illustrated during the demonstration, our test system also highlights local errors, like wrong parametrizations and incompatible branching in the test graph.

References

1. B. Lindner, T. Margaria, and B. Steffen. Ein personalisierter Internetdienst für wissenschaftliche Begutachtungsprozesse. In *GI-VOI-BITKOM-OCG-TeleTrusT Konferenz on "Elektronische Geschäftsprozesse"*(eBusiness Processes), Universität Klagenfurt, September 2001.
2. C.H. Liu, D.C. Kung, P. Hsia, and C.T. Hsu. Structural testing of web applications. In *Proc. of Int. Symposium on software reliability engineering (ISSRE 2000)*, pp. 84–96, 2000.
3. O. Niese, B. Steffen, T. Margaria, A. Hagerer, G. Brune, and H. Ide. Library-based design and consistency checks of system-level industrial test cases. *Proc. FASE 2001*, LNCS 2029, pp. 233–248. Springer Verlag, 2001.
4. O. Niese, T. Margaria, A. Hagerer, B. Steffen, G. Brune, and H. Ide. Automated regression testing of CTI-systems. In *Proc. of IEEE European Test Workshop (ETW 2001)*, 2001.
5. O. Niese, T. Margaria, B. Steffen. Automated functional testing of web-based applications. In *Proc. of 5th Intern. Quality Week Europe 2002*, Brussles, 2002.
6. F. Ricca and P. Tonella. Building a tool for the analysis and testing of web applications: Problems and solutions. *Proc. TACAS 2001*, LNCS 2031, pp. 372–388. Springer Verlag, 2001.
7. B. Steffen and T. Margaria. *METAFrame in Practice: Design of Intelligent Network Services*, LNCS 1710, pp. 390–415. Springer Verlag, 1999.
8. B. Steffen, T. Margaria, and V. Braun. Coarse-granular model checking in practice. Proc. 8th Intern. SPIN Workshop, LNCS 2057, pp. 304–312. Springer Verlag, 2001.

αSPIN: Extending SPIN with Abstraction

María del Mar Gallardo, Jesús Martínez, Pedro Merino, and Ernesto Pimentel

Dpto. de Lenguajes y Ciencias de la Computacion
University of Málaga, 29071 Málaga, Spain
{gallardo,jmcruz,pedro,ernesto}@lcc.uma.es

1 Introduction and Motivation

Model Checking is a powerful verification method to increase the quality of software systems. However, the application of this technique is only possible and fruitful if *useful models* of the software are available. A useful model is an abstract representation of a system, containing only the details necessary to ensure that satisfaction (non-satisfaction) of interesting properties in the model provides information about the behavior of the real system. Abstraction methods have become one of the hottest topics in the automatic verification of software systems because they can reduce the state space to be explored and allow the verification of more complex systems [1,3].

This paper presents an overview of αSPIN, a tool to introduce abstraction capabilities in the model checker SPIN[10]. αSPIN is oriented to the verification of universal temporal logic formulas using abstract models. Its theoretical basis were presented in [4] and [7]. The implementation has been carried out using XML[12], as presented in [6]. Advances in our project[1] will be found at [8].

2 Verification with αSPIN

The usual aim of SPIN users is to check a universal temporal formula F against a PROMELA model M. With αSPIN, we check an abstract formula F^α against an abstract version M^α of M, expecting verification results to provide information about the satisfaction of F against M (see Fig. 1). To do this, M and F are abstracted following the *data abstraction* approach (see [1,3]).

In the **syntactic transformation** module in Fig. 1, abstraction involves modifying the type of a given set of variables as well as the instructions that access these variables. These changes also affect the temporal formula. The transformation process is driven by an abstraction function α provided from a **library of abstraction functions**.

The "selection of α" depends on the predicates in the temporal formula, and may also depend on the relation among the variables in the model. An output like the one in Fig. 2 gives information about the model variables,

---

[1] This research is partially supported by the European Commission and CICYT under projects TIC99-1083-C02-01 and TAP-1FD97-1269-C02-02.

D. Bošnački and S. Leue (Eds.): SPIN 2002, LNCS 2318, pp. 254–257, 2002.

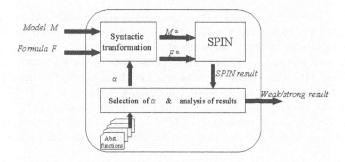

Fig. 1. αSPIN architecture

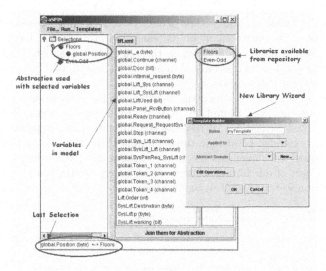

Fig. 2. User GUI

the abstraction functions available in the abstraction library and the assignment of functions to variables. The user can establish/delete relations between variables and abstraction functions. For example, the information in Fig. 2 corresponds to the model for an elevator controller. "Last selection" for the variable `Position` points to the function `Floors` that is useful to reduce any number of floors to the smaller set of abstract values: `Lower,Upper,Middle,` `NoLower,NoUpper,Unknown,Illegal` (see [8]). The user can apply abstraction to several variables in a single transformation step. Furthermore, it is possible to abstract a previously abstracted model.

To inform the user about the relation between SPIN output when verifying M^α and F^α and the expected output for checking F against M, the **analysis of results** relies on analyzing the correctness conditions to be held by α with regard to M (see [4,7]). This analysis is carried out at two complementary points:

- Off-line correctness.- Some correctness conditions should hold for any abstraction function α independently of the model, so they could be analyzed before putting the functions in the abstraction library.
- On-line correctness.- By inserting a special code in the PROMELA representation of M^α, it is possible to check whether the analysis of F^α implies some loss of information during model checking. Checking the way that predicates lose information, we can establish weak preservation ($M^\alpha \models F^\alpha \Rightarrow M \models F^\alpha$), or strong preservation ($M^\alpha \models F^\alpha \Rightarrow M \models F$) (see [7]). It is also possible to enforce the checking only for strong preservation purposes.

3 Implementation Notes

The syntactic transformation module of αSPIN has been implemented using XML-oriented tools. The PROMELA model is translated into an XML format, then a new XML document is produced using the selected abstraction function. The abstract PROMELA version is only obtained in the last step. Thus, most of the work is done with XML objects.

To employ existing tools for XML, we have defined a vocabulary of tags and a DTD (Document Type Definition). The DTD file helps to verify that an XML document is well formed, i.e., it respects the full PROMELA grammar. The same DTD may be extended to include the definition of the abstraction library, thus making it easier to implement the transformation tool. For example, the next code shows part of our library, containing an excerpt of the abstract version of the instruction v++ for the abstraction **Floors**:

```
<template name="Floors" concreteDomain="INT">
    <map><abstractValue name="LOWER" infoLevel="1">  ... </abstractValue>
        .......
        <abstractValue name="UNKNOWN" infoLevel="3" moreImpreciseThan="NOUPPER.NOLOWER" />
    </map>
    <operation id="INC">
        <option><test left="LOWER" /> <effect return="MIDDLE" /> </option>
        <option><test left="MIDDLE" /><effect return="NOLOWER" /></option>
        ....
```

Note that this is an internal representation and more friendly formats have been designed for users. The DTD for PROMELA can be downloaded from [8]. Implementation details of αSPIN can be found in [6] and [8].

4 Conclusions and Future Plans

There are other tools that add some kinds of abstraction to SPIN, like FeaVer [11], Bandera [2] or JPF [9], that have been applied to industrial problems. These tools follow the *model extraction* approach, which consists in producing a high level model (PROMELA) from the source code (C, Java). Although our work has been carried out independently, some problems and their solutions are similar. In particular, abstraction libraries and static analysis (like variable dependence) are also used in Bandera. However, even though some techniques are shared, we believe that αSPIN is complementary to other tools because it deals with different problems. In model extraction, the major aim seems to be how to "remove" great amounts of code to obtain the PROMELA model. In our case, we start with a relatively simple model, and our work is focused on incrementally applying abstraction to the initial and the new PROMELA models. Furthermore, it remains to be studied whether αSPIN could be employed to optimize the verification of the models extracted with other tools.

Specific future work to improve αSPIN consists of features like strategies to automatically analyze the correctness of complex abstraction functions (provably using a theorem prover), and more powerful methods to analyze the results (especially the counter-examples for non-deterministic executions). The use of XML as the intermediate language to support the abstraction process has been proven to be a good decision, so we plan to employ the same PROMELA DTD for other extensions to SPIN such as generating code skeletons or producing documentation. We are also considering the application of the same approach to extend other model checkers, as proposed in [5]. Advances will be found at [8].

References

1. E. Clarke, O. Grumberg, and D. Long. Model checking and abstraction. *ACM Trans. on Programming Languages and Systems*, 16(5):1512–1245, 1994.
2. M. Dwyer, J. Hatcliff, R. Joehanes, S. Laubach, C. Pasareau, W. Visser, H. Zheng. Tool-supported Program Abstraction for Finite-state Verification. *Proc. Int. Conf. on Software Engineering, ICSE 2001*, 2001.
3. D. Dams, R. Gerth, and O. Grumberg. Abstract interpretation of reactive systems. *ACM Transactions on Programming Languages and Systems*, 19(2):253–291, 1997.
4. M.M. Gallardo and P. Merino. A framework for automatic construction of abstract promela models. *Theoretical and Practical Aspects of* SPIN *Model Checking*, LNCS-1680:184–199, 1999.
5. M.M. Gallardo and P. Merino. A practical method to integrate abstractions into SDL and MSC based tools. In *Proc. of the 5th Int. ERCIM Workshop on Formal Methods for Industrial Critical Systems*, GMD Report 91, pages 84–89, 2000.
6. M.M. Gallardo, J. Martinez, P. Merino and E. Rosales, Using XML to implement Abstraction for Model Checking. In *Proc. of ACM Symposium on Applied Computing*, 2002.
7. M.M. Gallardo, P. Merino, and E. Pimentel. Abstract satisfiability of linear temporal logic. In *Proc. of I Jornadas sobre Programacion y Lenguajes*, pages 163–178, 2001.
8. M.M. Gallardo, J. Martinez, P. Merino and E. Pimentel. αSPIN project. University of Málaga. `http:\\www.lcc.uma.es\~gisum\fmse\tools`.
9. Havelund K., Pressburger T., Model Checking Java Programs using Java Path Finder. *Software Tools for Technology Transfer (STTT)* 2(4):366-381, 2000.
10. G. J. Holzmann. The model checker SPIN. *IEEE Trans. on Software Engineering*, 23(5):279–295, 1997.
11. G. J. Holzmann and M. H. Smith. A Practical Method for the Verification of Event Driven Systems. In *Proc. Int. Conf. on Software Engineering, ICSE99*, pages 597-608, 1999.
12. W3Consortium. Extensible Markup Language (XML) 1.0 (Second Edition), `http://www.w3.org/XML/`, 2000.

Author Index

Lecture Notes in Computer Science

For information about Vols. 1–2235
please contact your bookseller or Springer-Verlag

Vol. 2273: A.R. Coden, E.W. Brown, S. Srinivasan (Eds.), Information Retrieval Techniques for Speech Applications. XI, 109 pages. 2002.

Vol. 2274: D. Naccache, P. Paillier (Eds.), Public Key Cryptography. Proceedings, 2002. XI, 385 pages. 2002.

Vol. 2275: N.R. Pal, M. Sugeno (Eds.), Advances in Soft Computing – AFSS 2002. Proceedings, 2002. XVI, 536 pages. 2002. (Subseries LNAI).

Vol. 2276: A. Gelbukh (Ed.), Computational Linguistics and Intelligent Text Processing. Proceedings, 2002. XIII, 444 pages. 2002.

Vol. 2277: P. Callaghan, Z. Luo, J. McKinna, R. Pollack (Eds.), Types for Proofs and Programs. Proceedings, 2000. VIII, 243 pages. 2002.

Vol. 2278: J.A. Foster, E. Lutton, J. Miller, C. Ryan, A.G.B. Tettamanzi (Eds.), Genetic Programming. Proceedings, 2002. XI, 337 pages. 2002.

Vol. 2279: S. Cagnoni, J. Gottlieb, E. Hart, M. Middendorf, G.R. Raidl (Eds.), Applications of Evolutionary Computing. Proceedings, 2002. XIII, 344 pages. 2002.

Vol. 2280: J.P. Katoen, P. Stevens (Eds.), Tools and Algorithms for the Construction and Analysis of Systems. Proceedings, 2002. XIII, 482 pages. 2002.

Vol. 2281: S. Arikawa, A. Shinohara (Eds.), Progress in Discovery Science. XIV, 684 pages. 2002. (Subseries LNAI).

Vol. 2282: D. Ursino, Extraction and Exploitation of Intensional Knowledge from Heterogeneous Information Sources. XXVI, 289 pages. 2002.

Vol. 2283: T. Nipkow, L.C. Paulson, M. Wenzel, Isabelle/HOL. XIII, 218 pages. 2002.

Vol. 2284: T. Eiter, K.-D. Schewe (Eds.), Foundations of Information and Knowledge Systems. Proceedings, 2002. X, 289 pages. 2002.

Vol. 2285: H. Alt, A. Ferreira (Eds.), STACS 2002. Proceedings, 2002. XIV, 660 pages. 2002.

Vol. 2286: S. Rajsbaum (Ed.), LATIN 2002: Theoretical Informatics. Proceedings, 2002. XIII, 630 pages. 2002.

Vol. 2287: C.S. Jensen, K.G. Jeffery, J. Pokorny, Saltenis, E. Bertino, K. Böhm, M. Jarke (Eds.), Advances in Database Technology – EDBT 2002. Proceedings, 2002. XVI, 776 pages. 2002.

Vol. 2288: K. Kim (Ed.), Information Security and Cryptology – ICISC 2001. Proceedings, 2001. XIII, 457 pages. 2002.

Vol. 2289: C.J. Tomlin, M.R. Greenstreet (Eds.), Hybrid Systems: Computation and Control. Proceedings, 2002. XIII, 480 pages. 2002.

Vol. 2291: F. Crestani, M. Girolami, C.J. van Rijsbergen (Eds.), Advances in Information Retrieval. Proceedings, 2002. XIII, 363 pages. 2002.

Vol. 2292: G.B. Khosrovshahi, A. Shokoufandeh, A. Shokrollahi (Eds.), Theoretical Aspects of Computer Science. IX, 221 pages. 2002.

Vol. 2293: J. Renz, Qualitative Spatial Reasoning with Topological Information. XVI, 207 pages. 2002. (Subseries LNAI).

Vol. 2295: W. Kuich, G. Rozenberg, A. Salomaa (Eds.), Developments in Language Theory. Proceedings, 2001. IX, 389 pages. 2002.

Vol. 2296: B. Dunin-Kęplicz, E. Nawarecki (Eds.), From Theory to Practice in Multi-Agent Systems. Proceedings, 2001. IX, 341 pages. 2002. (Subseries LNAI).

Vol. 2299: H. Schmeck, T. Ungerer, L. Wolf (Eds.), Trends in Network and Pervasive Computing – ARCS 2002. Proceedings, 2002. XIV, 287 pages. 2002.

Vol. 2300: W. Brauer, H. Ehrig, J. Karhumäki, A. Salomaa (Eds.), Formal and Natural Computing. XXXVI, 431 pages. 2002.

Vol. 2301: A. Braquelaire, J.-O. Lachaud, A. Vialard (Eds.), Discrete Geometry for Computer Imagery. Proceedings, 2002. XI, 439 pages. 2002.

Vol. 2302: C. Schulte, Programming Constraint Services. XII, 176 pages. 2002. (Subseries LNAI).

Vol. 2303: M. Nielsen, U. Engberg (Eds.), Foundations of Software Science and Computation Structures. Proceedings, 2002. XIII, 435 pages. 2002.

Vol. 2304: R.N. Horspool (Ed.), Compiler Construction. Proceedings, 2002. XI, 343 pages. 2002.

Vol. 2305: D. Le Métayer (Ed.), Programming Languages and Systems. Proceedings, 2002. XII, 331 pages. 2002.

Vol. 2306: R.-D. Kutsche, H. Weber (Eds.), Fundamental Approaches to Software Engineering. Proceedings, 2002. XIII, 341 pages. 2002.

Vol. 2307: C. Zhang, S. Zhang, Association Rule Mining. XII, 238 pages. 2002. (Subseries LNAI).

Vol. 2308: I.P. Vlahavas, C.D. Spyropoulos (Eds.), Methods and Applications of Artificial Intelligence. Proceedings, 2002. XIV, 514 pages. 2002. (Subseries LNAI).

Vol. 2309: A. Armando (Ed.), Frontiers of Combining Systems. Proceedings, 2002. VIII, 255 pages. 2002. (Subseries LNAI).

Vol. 2310: P. Collet, C. Fonlupt, J.-K. Hao, E. Lutton, M. Schoenauer (Eds.), Artificial Evolution. Proceedings, 2001. XI, 375 pages. 2002.

Vol. 2311: D. Bustard, W. Liu, R. Sterritt (Eds.), Soft-Ware 2002: Computing in an Imperfect World. Proceedings, 2002. XI, 359 pages. 2002.

Vol. 2313: C.A. Coello Coello, A. de Albornoz, L.E. Sucar, O.Cairó Battistutti (Eds.), MICAI 2002: Advances in Artificial Intelligence. Proceedings, 2002. XIII, 548 pages. 2002. (Subseries LNAI).

Vol. 2314: S.-K. Chang, Z. Chen, S.-Y. Lee (Eds.), Recent Advances in Visual Information Systems. Proceedings, 2002. XI, 323 pages. 2002.

Vol. 2315: F. Arhab, C. Talcott (Eds.), Coordination Models and Languages. Proceedings, 2002. XI, 406 pages. 2002.

Vol. 2318: D. Bošnački, S. Leue (Eds.), Model Checking Software. Proceedings, 2002. X, 259 pages. 2002.

Vol. 2319: C. Gacek (Ed.), Software Reuse: Methods, Techniques, and Tools. Proceedings, 2002. XI, 353 pages. 2002.

Vol. 2322: V. Mařík, O. Stěpánková, H. Krautwurmová, M. Luck (Eds.), Multi-Agent Systems and Applications II. Proceedings, 2001. XII, 377 pages. 2002. (Subseries LNAI).